# EMERGING FRONTIERS IN POLYMER COMPOSITES

ADHESIVES, CATALYSTS, AND FUTURE TECHNOLOGIES

**Editors**

Dr. Prakash Chandra
M.Sc; D.Phil; NET-JRF, TARE Fellow
Department of Chemistry,
Bundelkhand University Jhansi-284128(U.P.) INDIA

Dr. Sarvesh Kumar Singh
M.Sc; NET-JRF
Department of Chemistry,
Bundelkhand University Jhansi-284128(U.P.) INDIA

**BLUEROSE PUBLISHERS**
India | U.K.

Copyright © Dr. Prakash Chandra, Sarvesh Kumar Singh 2025

All rights reserved by author. No part of this publication may be reproduced, stored in a retrieval system or transmitted in any form or by any means, electronic, mechanical, photocopying, recording or otherwise, without the prior permission of the author. Although every precaution has been taken to verify the accuracy of the information contained herein, the publisher assumes no responsibility for any errors or omissions. No liability is assumed for damages that may result from the use of information contained within.

BlueRose Publishers takes no responsibility for any damages, losses, or liabilities that may arise from the use or misuse of the information, products, or services provided in this publication.

For permissions requests or inquiries regarding this publication,
please contact:

BLUEROSE PUBLISHERS
www.BlueRoseONE.com
info@bluerosepublishers.com
+91 8882 898 898
+4407342408967

ISBN: 978-93-6452-632-6

Cover Design: Sadhna Kumari
Typesetting: Pooja Sharma

First Edition: January 2025

# Preface

Polymer composites have become a cornerstone in advancing material science, offering versatile applications across industries ranging from aerospace to medicine. As global challenges demand sustainable, high-performance materials, researchers and innovators continuously push the boundaries of polymer composite technologies. This edited book, Emerging Frontiers in Polymer Composites: Adhesives, Catalysts, and Future Technologies, provides a comprehensive exploration of recent advancements and future possibilities in this dynamic field.

The book is structured around three pivotal themes: adhesives, catalysts, and emerging technologies. Adhesives, an indispensable component in many engineering and industrial applications, are evolving with novel formulations that enhance performance while reducing environmental impact. Catalysts, essential for tailoring polymer synthesis and processing, are enabling groundbreaking developments in functionalized and recyclable materials. Finally, the book delves into futuristic technologies and approaches, including smart composites, self-healing materials, and bio-based polymers, which promise to reshape industries in the years to come. This compilation brings together contributions from leading experts and researchers worldwide. Each chapter delves into cutting-edge research, offering insights into theoretical principles, experimental methodologies, and real-world applications. The aim is to foster a deeper understanding of the intricate relationships between materials, processes, and properties while inspiring new ideas and innovation.

We hope this book serves as a valuable resource for students, researchers, and professionals keen on exploring the emerging frontiers of polymer composites. It is through collaboration and knowledge-sharing that we can collectively address the challenges and harness the opportunities presented by these fascinating materials.

We extend our heartfelt gratitude to the contributors for their exceptional work and to the readers for their curiosity and engagement. May this book spark new ideas and collaborations that propel the field of polymer composites into an even more promising future.

Editors

**Prakash Chandra**

**Sarvesh Kumar Singh**

**Emerging Frontiers in Polymer Composites: Adhesives, Catalysts, and Future Technologies**

# Acknowledgement

Dedicated to **Professor A. K. Saxena**, former Director and Outstanding Scientist, DMSRDE (DRDO) Kanpur, and General Secretary (Elected), Indian Science Congress Association, Kolkata, whose vision and dedication have been a source of constant inspiration for me to pursue research in the field of Inorganic Polymers and Adhesives.

# Contents

Chapter-1: Introduction of Polymer Composites ................................................................. 1

Chapter-2: Recent Developments in Adhesive Technologies for Polymer Composites: Techniques and Applications ................................................................. 15

Chapter-3: Catalytic Advances in Polymer Composites ................................................................. 35

Chapter-4: 3D Painting Innovations in Composite Materials ................................................................. 43

Chapter-5: Predicting the Next Decade in Polymer Composite Technologies: the Role of Islamic Endowment ................................................................. 57

Chapter-6: Development of Biodegradable and Bio-based Composite ................................................................. 71

Chapter-7: Polymer Composite in Energy Storage and Conversion ................................................................. 86

Chapter-8: Nanocomposites Based on Polyaniline: A Pathway to High-Performance Supercapacitors ................................................................. 103

Chapter-9: Rheological studies of Ecofriendly and Multifunctional materials ................................................................. 109

Chapter-10: The Impacts of Recycling of Polymers on Environment ................................................................. 132

Chapter-11: Recycling of Polymer Composites and its Environmental Aspects ................................................................. 159

Chapter-12: Emerging Materials: Biopolymers and Nanocomposites ................................................................. 170

Chapter-13: Advanced Uses of Sustainable Biobased Composites: Current Developments and Prospects ................................................................. 182

Chapter-14: A Brief Overview of Recent Advances in Polymer Composites ................................................................. 203

Chapter-15: BiopolymerBased Therapeutic Innovations in the Management of bacterial strain Klebsiella spp. Multidrug-Resistant Infections ................................................................. 213

Chapter-16: Plastic Polymers: Structure, Properties, and Recycling Technologies ................................................................. 220

Chapter-17: Biodegradable Polymers and their Applications ................................................................. 228

Chapter-18: Emerging Green Material: Biopolymer Composites ................................................................. 238

Chapter-19: Foxtail Millet-Based Churro Snack: Exploration of Compound Analysis Using GC-MS Technique ................................................................. 245

# Chapter-1

## Introduction of Polymer Composites

Pravin Chavan[1]

Dhanraj Kamble[2]

Dattatraya Pansare[3]

**Abstract-** Polymer composites are engineered materials that combine a polymer matrix with reinforcing agents to enhance mechanical, thermal, and electrical properties. This innovative combination allows for the optimization of material performance, resulting in a lightweight, strong, and versatile product suitable for a wide array of applications across industries such as aerospace, automotive, construction, and consumer goods. The choice of matrix thermoplastic or thermosetting and the type of reinforcement, including Fibers, fillers, and nanoparticles, significantly influence the composite's characteristics. Advances in processing techniques have expanded the potential for manufacturing these materials, while the development of bio-composites emphasizes sustainability by utilizing renewable resources. This abstract highlight the significance of polymer composites in modern engineering, their multifaceted applications, and the ongoing research aimed at improving their performance and environmental impact.

**Introduction**

Polymers are large, complex molecules composed of repeated structural units known as monomers, linked together through covalent bonds. These versatile materials can be found in both natural and synthetic forms, playing a critical role in various applications across multiple industries as follows- Packaging: Used in food and consumer goods due to their lightweight and barrier properties. Textiles: Employed in clothing and upholstery for comfort and durability. Automotive: Utilized in body panels, interiors, and components to enhance fuel efficiency and safety. Electronics: Found in circuit boards, casings, and insulation materials for their electrical properties. Healthcare: Used in medical devices, drug delivery systems, and prosthetics for their biocompatibility and versatility [1,2].

There are three main types of polymers such as- 1) Natural Polymers, for example, Proteins, cellulose, rubber. It is derived from biological processes and renewable resources. 2) Synthetic Polymers: for example, Polyethylene, nylon, and polystyrene. Source-Man-made through chemical processes, designed for specific properties. 3) Biopolymers: for example, Polylactic acid (PLA), polyhydroxyalkanoates (PHA). Source: Derived from renewable resources and often biodegradable, addressing environmental concerns [3, 4].

---

[1] *Department of Chemistry, Doshi Vakil Arts College and G.C.U.B. Science & Commerce College, Goregaon, Raigad 402103, MS, India.*
[2] *Department of Chemistry, S.B.E.S. College of Science, Chh. Sambhaji Nagar (Aurangabad), 431001, MS, India.*
[3] *Department of Chemistry, Deogiri College, Chh. Sambhaji Nagar (Aurangabad), 431005, MS, India.*
*Correspondences: chemistryp141286@gmail.com*

The polymer composite is one of the polymeric parts and it is used in various important applications.

composite of polymers typically refers to a material made by combining two or more different types of polymers to achieve improved properties compared to the individual components. These composites can enhance characteristics such as strength, durability, flexibility, thermal stability, and resistance to environmental factors [5].

Polymer composites are advanced materials that combine a polymer matrix with various reinforcing agents, such as fibers, fillers, or other materials, to enhance their overall properties. This combination allows for the creation of materials that exhibit superior mechanical, thermal, and electrical characteristics compared to their individual components. As a result, polymer composites are widely used in numerous industries, including aerospace, automotive, construction, and consumer products. Polymer composites can be categorized based on their matrix materials, reinforcement types, and functional properties [6, 7]. Here is an overview of the main types:

## 1. Reinforced Polymer Composites

Reinforced polymer composites enhance the mechanical properties of polymers by incorporating reinforcing materials, typically fibers. These composites combine the lightweight and corrosion-resistant characteristics of polymers with the strength and stiffness of the reinforcing materials, making them suitable for various demanding applications [8-9].

### *Types of Reinforced Polymer Composites*

**Fiber-Reinforced Composites-** *Glass Fiber Reinforced Polymer (GFRP):* it is used for various purposes Uses glass fibers as reinforcement. Known for good tensile strength, impact resistance, and corrosion resistance. and commonly used in automotive parts, construction, and marine applications.

*Carbon Fiber Reinforced Polymer (CFRP)*: Uses- Offering exceptional strength-to-weight ratios. High stiffness and fatigue resistance make it ideal for aerospace, sports equipment, and high-performance automotive applications.

*Aramid Fiber Reinforced Polymer (AFRP):* Uses- Utilizes aramid fibers (e.g., Kevlar) known for high impact resistance and toughness. And Commonly used in protective gear and ballistic applications[8-9].

### *Hybrid Fiber Reinforced Composites*

Combine two or more types of fibers (e.g., glass and carbon) to leverage the benefits of each. Designed to optimize properties like strength, weight, and cost.

**Advantages of Reinforced Polymer Composites:** several benefits of Reinforced Polymer Composites like-

- ❖ High Strength-to-Weight Ratio: Provides significant strength without the added weight, crucial for applications in aerospace and automotive sectors.
- ❖ Corrosion Resistance: Resistant to moisture, chemicals, and environmental degradation, enhancing longevity.
- ❖ Tailorable Properties: The ability to modify the type, orientation, and amount of reinforcement allows for customized performance.

- Energy Absorption: Excellent impact resistance makes them suitable for protective applications.

**Manufacturing Methods:** various manufacturing techniques for Reinforced Polymer Composites such as:

- Hand Lay-Up: A manual process where layers of fiber and resin are laid in a mold, often used for small-scale production.
- Resin Transfer Molding (RTM): A closed-mold process that injects resin into a mold filled with dry fibers, allowing for better control over resin distribution.
- Pultrusion: Continuous manufacturing process where fibers are pulled through a resin bath and then shaped and cured.
- Filament Winding: Fibers are wound around a mandrel, ideal for creating hollow structures like pipes and tanks [8-9].

**Applications:** The number of applications of Reinforced Polymer Composites is as follows:

- Aerospace: Used in aircraft components and spacecraft due to their lightweight and high strength.
- Automotive: Employed in body panels, chassis, and interior components for weight reduction and improved performance.
- Construction: Reinforcement for structures and infrastructure due to their durability and resistance to environmental factors.
- Sports Equipment: Found in high-performance items like bicycles, tennis rackets, and skis.

Reinforced polymer composites represent a crucial advancement in materials science, providing solutions that traditional materials cannot match in many applications [8-9].

## 2. Polymer Blends

Polymer blends are mixtures of two or more different polymers that combine to create a new material with improved or tailored properties. These blends can be miscible (fully compatible at the molecular level) or immiscible (not fully compatible, resulting in distinct phases). Here's a closer look at the types, properties, advantages, and applications of polymer blends [10].

**Types of Polymer Blends:** there are four types of polymer blends are as follows:

*Miscible Blends:* Miscible Blends are defined as two or more polymers that are compatible and form a single-phase material at certain compositions. For example, Polystyrene and poly(methyl methacrylate) (PS/PMMA) can blend to produce transparent, tough materials.

*Immiscible Blends:* Miscible Blends are defined as Polymers that do not mix completely, resulting in a multiphase system where distinct domains are present. For example, Polycarbonate and polystyrene may form a blend with different phases, affecting mechanical and thermal properties.

*Block Copolymers:* Block Copolymers are defined as Made from two or more different polymer blocks chemically linked together. These can exhibit unique phase separation properties. For example, Styrene-butadiene-styrene (SBS) is used in applications requiring rubbery flexibility and strength.

*Random Copolymers*: Random Copolymers are defined as Polymers made from two or more types of monomers randomly distributed along the chain. For example, Ethylene-vinyl acetate (EVA) combines properties of both ethylene and vinyl acetate [10, 11].

**Advantages of polymer blends:**

- Tailored Performance: Blends allow for the customization of material properties to meet specific application requirements.
- Cost-Effectiveness: Utilizing lower-cost polymers can reduce overall material costs while maintaining desired properties.
- Processability: Many polymer blends can be processed using standard techniques, making them versatile for manufacturing.

**Applications of polymer blends:**

- Packaging: Blends with improved barrier properties are widely used in food and pharmaceutical packaging.
- Automotive: Blended materials provide a balance of strength and flexibility for interior and exterior components.
- Consumer Goods: Items like toys, household products, and electronics often use polymer blends for enhanced durability and aesthetics.

Construction: Polymer blends are used in adhesives, coatings, and insulation materials for improved performance [10, 11].

## 3. Filled Polymers

Filled polymers are composite materials created by incorporating various fillers into a polymer matrix to enhance specific properties or reduce production costs. These fillers can be inorganic or organic materials and are used to improve the mechanical, thermal, electrical, and aesthetic characteristics of the base polymer [12].

**Types of Fillers polymers**

Various types of fillers polymers are as follows:

*Mineral Fillers:* Talc: Improves stiffness and thermal resistance, commonly used in polypropylene. Calcium Carbonate: Reduces cost and enhances mechanical properties; widely used in PVC and polyethylene. and Clay: Increases barrier properties and improves strength.

*Reinforcement Fillers:* Glass Fibers: Enhance strength and rigidity, used in composites for automotive and construction applications. Carbon Black: Used in rubber applications to improve strength and UV resistance.

*Organic Fillers:* Wood Flour: Used in wood-plastic composites to improve aesthetics and reduce weight. Natural Fibers: Such as hemp or flax, are used for sustainable composites.

*Conductive Fillers:* Metallic Particles: Such as silver or copper, used to make polymers electrically conductive for applications like antistatic materials. Carbon Nanotubes: Improve electrical conductivity and mechanical strength.

*Foaming Agents:* Added to create lightweight, low-density materials, commonly used in packaging and insulation [12, 13].

**Advantages of Filled Polymers:** various advantages of filled polymers are as follows:

- ❖ Cost Reduction: Fillers can lower material costs while maintaining desired properties.
- ❖ Improved Mechanical Properties: Fillers can enhance strength, stiffness, and impact resistance.
- ❖ Thermal Stability: Certain fillers improve heat resistance and thermal conductivity.
- ❖ Barrier Properties: Fillers like clay can enhance moisture and gas barrier performance.
- ❖ Weight Reduction: Fillers can reduce the weight of polymer materials without sacrificing strength.

**Applications of fillers polymers:**

- ❖ Construction: Used in adhesives, sealants, and coatings for improved durability and performance.
- ❖ Automotive: Common in interior and exterior parts, enhancing properties like impact resistance and aesthetics.
- ❖ Packaging: Fillers can improve barrier properties and reduce costs in plastic films and containers.
- ❖ Consumer Goods: Used in products such as toys, electronics housings, and kitchenware for better performance and cost efficiency [12, 13].

## 4. Nanocomposites (polymer)

Nanocomposites are advanced materials that incorporate nanoscale fillers (typically between 1 and 100 nanometers) into a polymer matrix. The unique properties of nanoscale materials can significantly enhance the performance of the composite, often resulting in superior mechanical, thermal, electrical, and barrier characteristics compared to conventional composites [14].

**Types of Nanocomposites**

There are four types of nanocomposite polymers. It has huge demands in the market due to their applications.

*Layered Silicate Nanocomposites:* Incorporate layered silicate materials (e.g., montmorillonite clay) into polymers. The layers can be intercalated or exfoliated, enhancing the material's properties. It is used in packaging films, automotive components, and coatings for improved barrier properties.

*Carbon Nanotube (CNT) Composites:* Incorporate carbon nanotubes to enhance mechanical strength, electrical conductivity, and thermal stability. It has been Utilized in electronics, sports equipment, and structural materials where high strength and conductivity are needed.

*Metal Nanoparticle Composites:* Embed metallic nanoparticles (e.g., silver, gold) within polymers to impart antibacterial properties or electrical conductivity. It is commonly used Common in medical devices, coatings, and sensors.

*Nanofiber Composites:* They utilize nanofibers (e.g., electrospun fibers) to enhance mechanical properties and create porous structures. Uses- Found in filtration, textiles, and biomedical applications [14, 15].

**Advantages of Nanocomposites**

- Enhanced Mechanical Properties: Nanoscale fillers can dramatically improve tensile strength, stiffness, and impact resistance.
- Improved Thermal Stability: Nanocomposites often exhibit better thermal stability and resistance to degradation at elevated temperatures.
- Electrical Conductivity: Incorporating conductive nanoparticles can create materials with tailored electrical properties for use in electronics.
- Barrier Performance: Nanocomposites can significantly enhance barrier properties against gases, moisture, and chemicals.
- Lightweight: Maintaining or reducing weight while improving performance is a significant advantage in applications like aerospace and automotive.

**Applications of nanocomposites**

- Aerospace: Lightweight, high-strength materials for aircraft components.
- Automotive: Improved performance in parts such as body panels, tires, and fuel systems.
- Packaging: Enhanced barrier properties for food and pharmaceutical packaging to extend shelf life.
- Electronics: Used in flexible electronics, conductive coatings, and thermal interface materials.
- Biomedical: Applications in drug delivery systems, scaffolds for tissue engineering, and antimicrobial coatings [15,16].

## 5. Thermosetting Composites

Thermosetting composites are materials made from thermosetting polymers that undergo a chemical change during curing, resulting in a rigid structure that cannot be remelted or reshaped. These composites combine the benefits of thermosetting resins with reinforcing materials, such as fibers, to enhance their mechanical and thermal properties [17].

**Types of Thermosetting Composites:** various types of Thermosetting Composites are as follows:

*Epoxy Composites:* Epoxy resins are widely used due to their strong adhesive properties and excellent mechanical performance. Uses- Common in aerospace, automotive, and marine industries, as well as in electronics and adhesives.

*Polyester Composites*: Unsaturated polyester resins are often reinforced with fiberglass. They are known for their relatively low cost and good performance. Used in automotive parts, boats, and consumer products.

*Vinyl Ester Composites*: Vinyl ester resins combine the properties of epoxy and polyester resins, offering better corrosion resistance and thermal stability. It is commonly used in chemical processing equipment and high-performance applications.

*Phenolic Composites*: Phenolic resins are known for their heat resistance and low smoke generation, making them ideal for high-temperature applications. It is used in aerospace, electrical insulations, and automotive components.

*Bismaleimide (BMI) Composites*: BMIs provide high thermal stability and mechanical performance, often used in aerospace applications. Uses- Ideal for high-performance aerospace and automotive components [17, 18].

**Advantages of Thermosetting Composites**

- Durability: Thermosetting composites are generally more durable and resistant to deformation over time compared to thermoplastics.
- High Performance: They provide excellent mechanical, thermal, and chemical properties, making them suitable for demanding applications.
- Design Flexibility: They can be molded into complex shapes during the curing process, offering versatility in design.

**Applications of Thermosetting Composites**

- Aerospace: Structural components in aircraft and spacecraft due to their strength-to-weight ratio and thermal stability.
- Automotive: Parts such as body panels, engine components, and interior features, contribute to weight reduction and safety.
- Construction: Used in beams, panels, and coatings for improved strength and resistance to environmental factors.
- Electronics: Encapsulation and insulation materials for electronic components, benefiting from their thermal and electrical properties [17-19].

## 6. Thermoplastic Composites

Thermoplastic composites are materials made by combining thermoplastic polymers with reinforcing agents, such as fibers or fillers. Unlike thermosetting composites, thermoplastic composites can be re-melted and reshaped upon heating, making them versatile for various applications. Their unique properties combine the advantages of both thermoplastics and reinforcing materials [20].

**Types of Thermoplastic Composites:** Various types of Thermoplastic Composites are as follows:

*Polypropylene (PP) Composites*: Often reinforced with glass fibers or natural fibers, these composites are lightweight and cost-effective. It is commonly used in automotive parts, consumer goods, and packaging.

*Polyamide (Nylon) Composites*: Polyamide (Nylon) Composites are known for high strength and heat resistance, nylon composites are often reinforced with glass or carbon fibers. Uses- Used in automotive components, industrial applications, and consumer products.

*Polycarbonate (PC) Composites*: PC composites offer high-impact strength and optical clarity, often reinforced with glass fibers. Uses- Found in safety glasses, electronic housings, and automotive parts.

*Polyethylene (PE) Composites*: These composites are flexible and resistant to moisture and chemicals, commonly reinforced with natural fibers or fillers. Uses- Used in packaging, geomembranes, and consumer products.

*Polyurethane (PU) Composites*: Known for their flexibility and toughness, polyurethane composites can be made with various reinforcing materials. Uses- Used in automotive applications, cushioning materials, and coatings.

*Thermoplastic Elastomer (TPE) Composites*: These composites combine the properties of rubber and thermoplastics, providing flexibility and processability. Uses- Found in seals, gaskets, and flexible automotive components [21].

**Advantages of Thermoplastic Composites**

- Lightweight: Thermoplastic composites are generally lighter than metals, contributing to energy efficiency in applications like automotive and aerospace.
- Versatility: Their ability to be reprocessed allows for more flexible manufacturing options and designs.
- Cost-Effectiveness: They can be less expensive to produce and process compared to thermosetting composites.
- Good Mechanical Properties: Many thermoplastic composites offer excellent strength, stiffness, and impact resistance [20].

**Applications of Thermoplastic Composites**

- Automotive: Used in various components, such as interior parts, bumpers, and structural elements, to reduce weight and improve fuel efficiency.
- Aerospace: Suitable for lightweight structural components and interiors, contributing to overall aircraft performance.
- Consumer Goods: Found in products like sports equipment, household items, and electronics due to their durability and design flexibility.
- Construction: Used in building materials, insulation, and piping systems for their resistance to moisture and chemicals [20, 21].

## 7. Multi-Phase Composites

Multi-phase composites are materials composed of two or more distinct phases, typically involving a combination of different polymers, fibers, or other materials. This design allows for the optimization of various properties by leveraging the strengths of each component. These composites can exhibit unique characteristics that are not achievable with single-phase materials [22].

**Types of Multi-Phase Composites:** Various types of Multi-Phase Composites are as follows:

*Polymer Blends*: Combinations of different polymers (miscible or immiscible) that create materials with combined characteristics. For example, A blend of polystyrene and polybutadiene offers good toughness and impact resistance.

*Fiber-Reinforced Composites*: Incorporate multiple types of fibers within a polymer matrix to optimize mechanical properties. For example, combining glass fibers with carbon fibers to achieve a balance of strength and weight.

*Nanocomposites*: Include nanoparticles along with traditional fillers or fibers to enhance properties at a molecular level. For example, adding carbon nanotubes to a polymer matrix improves strength and electrical conductivity.

*Rubber-Modified Composites*: Combine rigid polymers with rubber to improve toughness and flexibility, often used in applications requiring impact resistance. for example, adding rubber to polystyrene can improve its impact strength.

*Ceramic-Polymer Composites*: Incorporate ceramic materials into a polymer matrix to enhance thermal stability and wear resistance. for example, composites used in automotive brake systems or high-temperature applications [22, 23].

**Advantages of Multi-Phase Composites**

- ❖ Enhanced Performance: Multi-phase composites can outperform traditional materials in terms of strength, toughness, and other mechanical properties.
- ❖ Design Flexibility: The ability to customize the composition allows for a wide range of applications across industries.
- ❖ Improved Cost-Effectiveness: By using a combination of materials, it may be possible to reduce costs while maintaining or improving performance.

**Applications of Multi-Phase Composites**

- ❖ Automotive: Used in body panels, bumpers, and structural components to reduce weight and improve energy absorption during impacts.
- ❖ Aerospace: Ideal for lightweight structural elements and components that require high strength-to-weight ratios.
- ❖ Construction: Multi-phase composites can be used in building materials that need to withstand harsh environmental conditions.
- ❖ Consumer Products: Found in a variety of items, from sporting goods to household appliances, where a balance of durability and weight is essential [22, 23].

## 8. Bio-Composites

Bio-composites are materials that combine natural fibers or bio-based materials with polymers, which can be either synthetic or bio-based. These composites are designed to leverage renewable resources, offering an eco-friendly alternative to traditional materials while providing enhanced mechanical properties and reduced environmental impact [24].

**Characteristics of Bio-Composites**

- ❖ Sustainability: Made from renewable resources, bio-composites help reduce dependence on fossil fuels and lower carbon emissions.

- ❖ Biodegradability: Many bio-composites can break down naturally, minimizing waste and simplifying end-of-life disposal.
- ❖ Lightweight: Natural fibers are generally lighter than synthetic options, contributing to overall weight reduction in applications like automotive and construction.
- ❖ Mechanical Properties: Depending on the specific fibers and matrix used, bio-composites can exhibit favourable strength, stiffness, and impact resistance.

**Types of Bio-Composites:** various types Bio-Composites polymers are as follows:

*Natural Fiber-Reinforced Composites*: Incorporate natural fibers (e.g., hemp, flax, jute, bamboo) into a polymer matrix. uses- Used in automotive interiors, building materials, and various consumer products due to their lightweight and sustainable nature.

*Bio-Based Polymer Composites*: Utilize bio-based polymers (like polylactic acid [PLA] and polyhydroxyalkanoates [PHA]) as the matrix material. uses- Suitable for biodegradable packaging, disposable items, and other environmentally friendly products.

*Hybrid Bio-Composites*: Combine natural fibers with synthetic fibers or polymers to achieve a balance of properties. uses- Employed in applications requiring enhanced mechanical performance, such as automotive parts and structural components [24,25].

**Advantages of Bio-Composites**

- ❖ Environmental Benefits: Help reduce the carbon footprint and promote sustainability through the use of renewable resources.
- ❖ Cost-Effectiveness: Natural fibers can often be sourced at lower costs compared to synthetic fibers.
- ❖ Aesthetic Appeal: Natural fibers offer unique textures and appearances, making them desirable for consumer goods and design applications.
- ❖ Energy Efficiency: Generally requires less energy to produce compared to conventional composites.

**Applications Bio-Composites**

- ❖ Automotive: Used in interior panels, dashboards, and seat covers to reduce weight and improve sustainability.
- ❖ Construction: Applied in insulation, wall panels, and flooring materials, enhancing thermal performance and reducing environmental impact.
- ❖ Packaging: Ideal for biodegradable packaging solutions, contributing to waste reduction.
- ❖ Consumer Products: Found in furniture, kitchenware, and sporting goods, combining aesthetics with eco-friendliness [24, 25].

## 9. Conductive Composites

Conductive composites are materials that combine a polymer matrix with conductive fillers to enhance their electrical conductivity while maintaining the desirable properties of the base polymer. These composites are increasingly used in various applications due to their unique combination of flexibility, lightweight, and conductivity [26].

**Characteristics of Conductive Composites**

- Electrical Conductivity: Conductive composites can be engineered to exhibit varying levels of conductivity, from antistatic to highly conductive.
- Lightweight: These composites are generally lighter than traditional conductive materials like metals, making them suitable for applications where weight is a concern.
- Processability: The polymer matrix allows for versatile processing techniques, including injection molding, extrusion, and coating.
- Flexibility: Unlike rigid conductive materials, conductive composites can retain flexibility, making them suitable for applications that require bending or deformation [26,27].

**Types of Conductive composites:** Various types of conductive composites are as follows:

*Carbon-Based Fillers (Carbon-Based composites):*

Carbon Black: Commonly used in rubber and plastics, it provides good conductivity and is cost-effective.

Graphene: Offers high electrical conductivity and mechanical strength; used in advanced applications.

Carbon Nanotubes (CNTs): Provide excellent conductivity and strength, often used in high-performance applications.

*Metallic Fillers:*

Silver: Known for its high conductivity, used in applications requiring excellent electrical performance, though it can be expensive.

Copper: Provides good conductivity and is more affordable than silver; however, it can corrode.

Aluminum: Used for cost-effective conductive applications, especially where weight is a consideration.

*Metallic Coatings:* Conductive Coatings: Applying a thin layer of metal on a polymer substrate to enhance surface conductivity [26-28].

**Advantages of Carbon-Based composites**

- Tailored Conductivity: The level of conductivity can be adjusted by varying the type and amount of filler used.
- Versatility: Suitable for a wide range of applications, from antistatic packaging to sensors and electronic components.
- Lightweight and Flexible: Ideal for applications in electronics and automotive where weight and flexibility are important [27].

**Applications of Carbon-Based composites**

- ❖ Electronics: Used in flexible printed circuits, conductive adhesives, and coatings for electronic devices.

- ❖ Antistatic Materials: Employed in packaging and protective equipment to prevent static electricity buildup.

- ❖ Sensors: Used in various types of sensors, including pressure, temperature, and humidity sensors, where electrical properties are crucial.

- ❖ Automotive: Utilized in components that require electromagnetic shielding or static dissipation, such as dashboards and control panels.

- ❖ Biomedical: Used in medical devices and biosensors, where conductivity and biocompatibility are important 26-28].

**Conclusion**

Polymer composites represent a significant advancement in material science, offering a unique combination of properties that meet the demands of various industries. By integrating a polymer matrix with reinforcing agents: such as fibers, particles, or natural materials- these composites achieve enhanced mechanical strength, lightweight characteristics, corrosion resistance, and versatility in processing.

Their applications span a wide array of fields, including aerospace, automotive, construction, electronics, and consumer goods, making them essential for modern engineering solutions. The ongoing development of new materials, such as bio-composites and conductive polymers, highlights the potential for innovation in sustainability and functionality.

As the demand for high-performance, environmentally friendly materials continues to grow, polymer composites will play a pivotal role in shaping the future of manufacturing and design. Their ability to be tailored to specific needs ensures that they remain at the forefront of material technology, providing effective solutions for a rapidly evolving market.

**References**

1. Wypych, G. (2022). *Handbook of polymers*. Elsevier.
2. Aguilar, M. R., & San Román, J. (Eds.). (2019). *Smart polymers and their applications*. Woodhead publishing.
3. Mark, J. E., Allcock, H. R., & West, R. (2005). *Inorganic polymers*. Oxford University Press.
4. John, M. J., & Thomas, S. (Eds.). (2012). *Natural polymers: composites* (Vol. 16). Royal society of chemistry.
5. Baillie, C., & Jayasinghe, R. (Eds.). (2004). *Green composites: polymer composites and the environment*. Elsevier.
6. Seymour, R. B., & Deanin, R. D. (Eds.). (1987). *History of polymeric composites*. VSP.
7. Friedrich, K., Fakirov, S., & Zhang, Z. (Eds.). (2005). *Polymer composites: from nano-to macro-scale*. Springer Science & Business Media.
8. Nguong, C. W., Lee, S. N. B., & Sujan, D. (2013). A review on natural fibre reinforced polymer composites. *International Journal of Materials and Metallurgical Engineering*, *7*(1), 52-59.
9. Jariwala, H., & Jain, P. (2019). A review on mechanical behavior of natural fiber reinforced polymer composites and its applications. *Journal of Reinforced Plastics and Composites*, *38*(10), 441-453.
10. Mikitaev, A. K., Ligidov, M. K., & Zaikov, G. E. (2006). *Polymers, polymer blends, polymer composites and filled polymers: Synthesis, properties and applications*. Nova Publishers.
11. Mittal, V. (Ed.). (2012). *Functional polymer blends: synthesis, properties, and performance*. CRC Press.
12. Wang, X., Hall, J. E., Warren, S., Krom, J., Magistrelli, J. M., Rackaitis, M., & Bohm, G. G. (2007). Synthesis, characterization, and application of novel polymeric nanoparticles. *Macromolecules*, *40*(3), 499-508.
13. Guo, F., Aryana, S., Han, Y., & Jiao, Y. (2018). A review of the synthesis and applications of polymer–nanoclay composites. *Applied Sciences*, *8*(9), 1696.
14. Hassan, T., Salam, A., Khan, A., Khan, S. U., Khanzada, H., Wasim, M., ... & Kim, I. S. (2021). Functional nanocomposites and their potential applications: A review. *Journal of Polymer Research*, *28*(2), 36.
15. Camargo, P. H. C., Satyanarayana, K. G., & Wypych, F. (2009). Nanocomposites: synthesis, structure, properties and new application opportunities. *Materials Research*, *12*, 1-39.
16. Al-Mutairi, N. H., Mehdi, A. H., & Kadhim, B. J. (2022). Nanocomposites materials definitions, types and some of their applications: A review. *European Journal of Research Development and Sustainability*, *3*(2), 102-108.
17. Jin, F. L., & Park, S. J. (2015). Preparation and characterization of carbon fiber-reinforced thermosetting composites: a review. *Carbon letters*, *16*(2), 67-77.

18. Guo, Q. (Ed.). (2017). *Thermosets: structure, properties, and applications*. Woodhead Publishing.

19. Bhadra, J., Alkareem, A., & Al-Thani, N. (2020). A review of advances in the preparation and application of polyaniline based thermoset blends and composites. *Journal of Polymer Research*, *27*(5), 122.

20. Zaaba, N. F., Ismail, H., & Saeed, A. M. (2021). A review: metal filled thermoplastic composites. *Polymer-Plastics Technology and Materials*, *60*(10), 1033-1050.

21. Reis, J. P., de Moura, M., & Samborski, S. (2020). Thermoplastic composites and their promising applications in joining and repair composites structures: A review. *Materials*, *13*(24), 5832.

22. Šupová, M., Martynková, G. S., & Barabaszová, K. (2011). Effect of nanofillers dispersion in polymer matrices: a review. *Science of advanced materials*, *3*(1), 1-25.

23. Ma, S., Li, A., & Pan, L. (2024). Application Progress of Multi-Functional Polymer Composite Nanofibers Based on Electrospinning: A Brief Review. *Polymers*, *16*(17), 2459.

24. Roy, S. B., Shit, S. C., Sengupta, R. A., & Shukla, P. R. (2014). A review on bio-composites: fabrication, properties and applications. *Int. J. Innov. Res. Sci. Eng. Technol*, *3*(10), 16814-16824.

25. Khan, M. Z. R., & Srivastava, S. K. (2018, August). Development, characterization and application potential of bio-composites: a review. In *IOP Conference Series: Materials Science and Engineering* (Vol. 404, No. 1, p. 012028). IOP Publishing.

26. Poddar, A. K., Patel, S. S., & Patel, H. D. (2021). Synthesis, characterization and applications of conductive polymers: A brief review. *Polymers for Advanced Technologies*, *32*(12), 4616-4641.

27. Namsheer, K., & Rout, C. S. (2021). Conducting polymers: a comprehensive review on recent advances in synthesis, properties and applications. *RSC advances*, *11*(10), 5659-5697.

28. Naveen, M. H., Gurudatt, N. G., & Shim, Y. B. (2017). Applications of conducting polymer composites to electrochemical sensors: A review. *Applied materials today*, *9*, 419-433.

# Chapter-2

# Recent Developments in Adhesive Technologies for Polymer Composites: Techniques and Applications

Dr. Prakash Chandra[1*]

Dr. Sarvesh Kumar Singh[2]

Dr. Manvendra Sengar[3]

**Abstract:** This research focuses on the development and analysis of high-performance silicon polymer adhesives tailored for industrial applications. Silicon-based polymers, known for their exceptional thermal stability, flexibility, and chemical resistance, are synthesized and optimized to meet the stringent demands of modern industries. Through a combination of advanced synthesis techniques and strategic material functionalization, we have engineered adhesives with enhanced adhesion, durability, and resistance to environmental factors. The study provides a comprehensive characterization of the adhesives, including their mechanical properties, thermal stability, and adhesion performance on various substrates. The results demonstrate the potential of these high-performance silicon polymer adhesives to significantly improve the reliability and durability of industrial applications, making them ideal for use in sectors such as automotive, aerospace, and electronics. This work also highlights the future directions for further enhancing adhesive performance through molecular design and innovative processing techniques.

**Keywords:** Silicon Polymer Adhesives, Thermal Stability, Adhesion, Industrial Applications, Material Functionalization

## Introduction:

The recent development in the field of polymer composites has seen significant advancements, particularly in the novel development of adhesive technologies and their applications. The role of adhesive plays a crucial role in the reliability and durability of polymer composite materials, which are widely used across industries such as aerospace, automotive, packaging, dental, electronics, construction, and renewable energy. As the demand for high-performance composite materials increases, the need for innovative adhesive technologies that can provide strong, durable, and efficient bonding solutions has never been greater. Because of their exceptional blend of qualities, such as superior chemical resistance, thermal stability, flexibility, and long-term durability, silicon polymer-based adhesives have drawn a lot of interest among the different kinds of adhesives. Due to these properties, silicon polymers are especially well-suited for uses in harsh environments where traditional adhesives frequently prove to be ineffective.

---

[1,2] *Department of Chemistry, Institute of Basic Science, Bundelkhand University Jhansi-284128(U.P.) India*
*Corresponding Author Email: drprakashcy@gmail.com*
[3] *Department of Zoology, Bipin Bihari Degree College Jhansi(U.P.)*

To satisfy the changing needs of contemporary industries, silicon polymer adhesives must constantly improve their performance despite their inherent benefits. Enhancing their adhesive strength and endurance is just one aspect of this; other aspects include molding their characteristics to fit particular uses, like attaching various substrates or performing well under dynamic mechanical strains. High-performance silicon polymer adhesives created to meet these challenges are the main focus of this research's development and analysis. We hope to develop adhesives that are not only better at bonding but also hold up better over time, even in challenging conditions, by utilizing cutting-edge synthesis methods and creative material functionalization.

Recent advancements in adhesive technologies for polymer composites have opened up a wide array of new applications across various industries. The improvements in bonding strength, durability, and sustainability have made polymer composites even more versatile, driving innovations in several critical fields. Below are some key applications where these developments are making a significant impact. Aerospace and Aviation In aerospace applications, the performance and weight reduction of polymer composites are crucial. The development of high-performance adhesives has enabled better bonding of composite structures, such as fuselage panels, wings, and interior components. Advances in adhesive technologies have also led to improvements in the durability of these materials under extreme temperature fluctuations, mechanical stresses, and environmental conditions. This chapter delves into the latest technological advancements in adhesive technologies for polymer composites, exploring cutting-edge techniques and their practical applications. It examines the types of adhesives commonly used, the methods for enhancing adhesion, and the real-world applications where these innovations have made significant contributions. By understanding these developments, engineers and material scientists can better tailor adhesive solutions to meet the ever-growing demands of modern composite materials

Automotive Industry The automotive sector benefits significantly from the lightweight nature of polymer composites, which help improve fuel efficiency and performance. Recent adhesive innovations have made it possible to bond composite materials to metal substrates, enhancing structural integrity and reducing the need for mechanical fasteners. These adhesives also offer better resistance to harsh chemicals, UV radiation, and moisture, ensuring long-term reliability in automotive parts like body panels, bumpers, and chassis components.

Wind energy polymer composites are widely used in wind turbine blades due to their high strength-to-weight ratio. Adhesive technologies have played a key role in the efficient assembly and repair of these large structures. Recent developments in adhesive bonding have improved the adhesion between different composite materials used in turbine blades, providing better performance, reduced weight, and increased lifespan of these critical components.

Construction and Infrastructure In construction, the use of polymer composites for reinforcement and repair of concrete structures has grown substantially. New adhesive technologies allow for better bonding between composites and concrete, increasing the efficiency of repairs and ensuring that the composite materials retain their integrity under heavy loads. These adhesives are also used in prefabricated structures, where they enhance the bonding of different composite components, offering faster construction times and more reliable results.

Marine Industry The marine industry also benefits from the advancements in adhesive technologies for polymer composites, particularly in the construction and repair of boats, ships, and offshore structures. These adhesives provide strong, water-resistant bonds that are essential in marine environments where exposure to saltwater, moisture, and UV radiation can compromise the durability of materials. Additionally, these adhesives allow for the joining of dissimilar materials, improving the overall design and performance of marine vessels.

Electronics and Consumer Goods Polymer composites and adhesives are increasingly used in the electronics industry, particularly in the production of lightweight, durable, and heat-resistant components. Adhesive technologies are critical in the assembly of devices such as smartphones, laptops, and wearables, where strong, reliable bonds are needed to hold components in place while maintaining performance under various conditions. New adhesives also offer improved electrical and thermal conductivity, essential for advanced electronics packaging.

Medical Devices In the medical field, polymer composites combined with specialized adhesives are used to produce lightweight, high-strength components for medical devices and implants. These adhesives not only provide strong bonding but also ensure biocompatibility and long-term reliability in medical applications. Recent advancements have led to adhesives that can bond various biomaterials used in surgical instruments, prosthetics, and implantable devices, ensuring both performance and safety.

Sports and Recreation Polymer composites have gained popularity in the sports and recreation industry, especially in the manufacturing of equipment such as bicycles, tennis rackets, golf clubs, and skis. The development of advanced adhesive technologies has improved the bonding of composite materials to metal, rubber, and plastic parts, enhancing the strength, performance, and durability of these products. Lightweight, high-strength adhesives are essential for optimizing performance in high-stress activities.

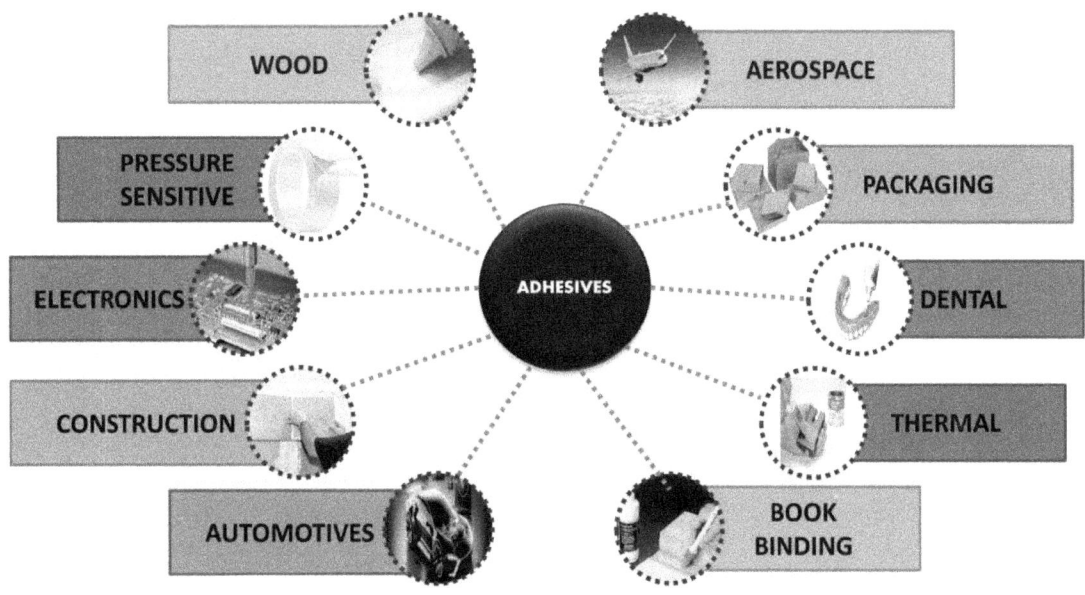

The synthesized adhesives are thoroughly characterized in the study, with important characteristics like mechanical strength, thermal stability, and chemical resistance being examined. In order to assess these materials' practicability, they are also tested for adhesion on a range of industrial substrates.

The findings from this research are expected to provide valuable insights into the design and development of next-generation silicon polymer adhesives, offering significant improvements in both the reliability and efficiency of industrial applications.

Silicone polymer adhesives have become an integral part of modern industrial applications due to their unique combination of properties, such as high thermal stability, flexibility and resistance to various environmental factors. These adhesives are essential in sectors ranging from aerospace to electronics, where the demand for materials that can withstand extreme conditions without compromising performance is constantly growing.

Silicone polymers, particularly those based on polydimethylsiloxane (PDMS), have gained prominence due to their remarkable thermal and oxidative stability, low glass transition temperature and excellent electrical insulation properties. These characteristics make them ideal for use in applications that require long-term durability and reliability under harsh conditions. In addition, their inherent flexibility allows excellent adhesion to a wide variety of substrates, including metals, plastics and glass, further broadening their applicability.

The development of high-performance silicone polymer adhesives is focused on enhancing their mechanical strength, adhesion properties and resistance to environmental factors such as moisture, UV radiation and chemical exposure. Recent advances in materials science have enabled silicone polymers to be modified at the molecular level, significantly improving their performance characteristics. These modifications often include functional fillers, cross-linking agents and other additives that enhance the overall performance of the adhesive.

The aim of this study is to analyse the current state of high-performance silicone polymer adhesives, explore progress in their development and challenges faced in optimizing their properties for industrial applications. The research will also take a closer look at the various test methods employed to evaluate the performance of these adhesives and how these tests relate to real-world application scenarios. By understanding these factors, the study seeks to contribute to ongoing efforts to develop more effective and reliable silicone polymer adhesives for a wide range of industrial applications.

The 1970s and 2021s saw significant advances in the manufacture and application of silicone polymers. Researchers developed new types of silicone elastomers, resins, and liquids with enhanced properties to suit specific industrial needs. For example, high-consistency rubber (HCR) and liquid silicone rubber (LSR) became widely used in the automotive and medical industries due to their durability and biocompatibility. In recent decades, the development of high-performance silicone polymers has focused on improving their mechanical strength, adhesion, and resistance to environmental factors. Innovations such as the incorporation of functional fillers, cross-linking agents, and nano-scale modifications have expanded the range of applications of silicone, including advanced electronics, aerospace, and renewable energy technologies. Today, silicone polymers are ubiquitous in modern life, found in everything from household products and cosmetics to sophisticated industrial components. Their continued evolution reflects ongoing research and development efforts aimed at meeting the demands of increasingly complex and challenging applications.

## General Classification of Adhesives

The adhesives can be classified according their origin, chemical structure and curing method [1-4]. A flow chart showing the classification of adhesives is given below.

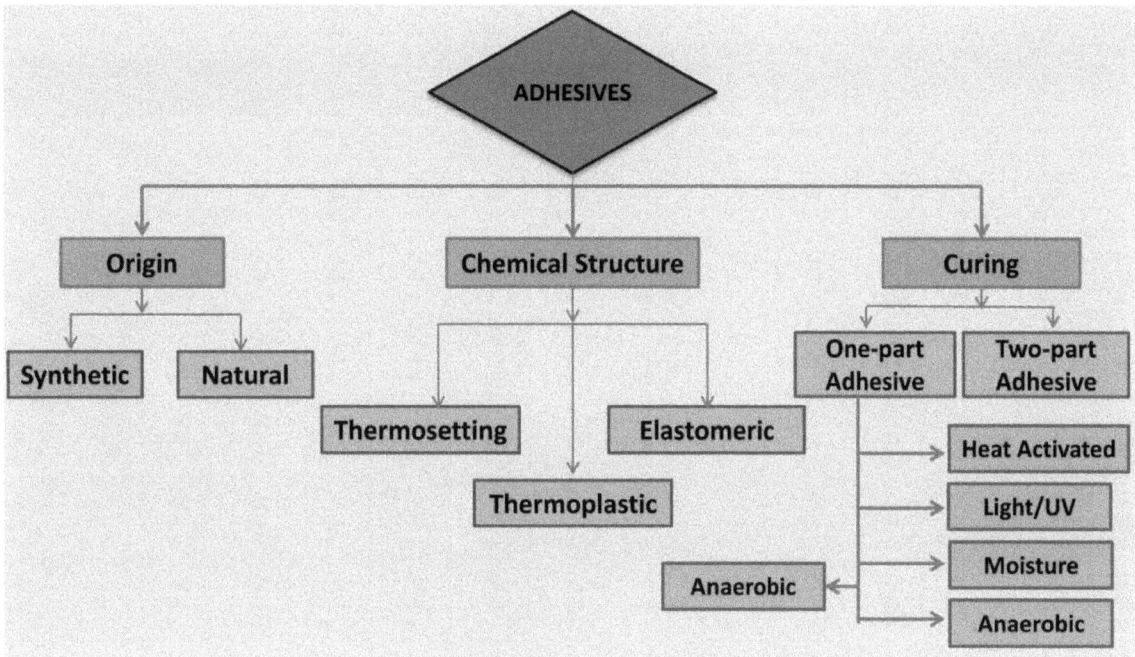

**Classification of adhesives**

## Synthesis of epoxidized polysiloxane using ether-terminated polydimethylsiloxane (PDMS-DGE)

Initially, PDMS-DGE was subjected to a pre-reaction with the hardener 1,2-diaminocyclohexane (DCH). During this stage, the oxirane groups in PDMS-DGE were consumed through the reaction with DCH, leaving only the amine groups of DCH available for subsequent interactions. Once this pre-reaction was complete, the resulting mixture was mixed with diglycidyl ether of bisphenol-A (DGEBA). The final blend was then cured, resulting in nanocomposites with significantly improved flexural mechanical properties. The reaction mechanism is shown in the schematic representation in **Scheme 1**.

It is significant to note that both the epoxy resin DGEBA and the PDMS-DGE elastomer feature oxirane rings as their functional end groups. Consequently, during the curing process, the curing agent DCH is expected to react with both the DGEBA epoxy system and the PDMS-DGE elastomer. This reaction involves the opening of the oxirane rings, and any unreacted rings will interact with other diamine molecules to form a molecular network. It is proposed that this network chemically bonds the elastomer to the resin, effectively integrating the elastomer within the polymeric matrix.

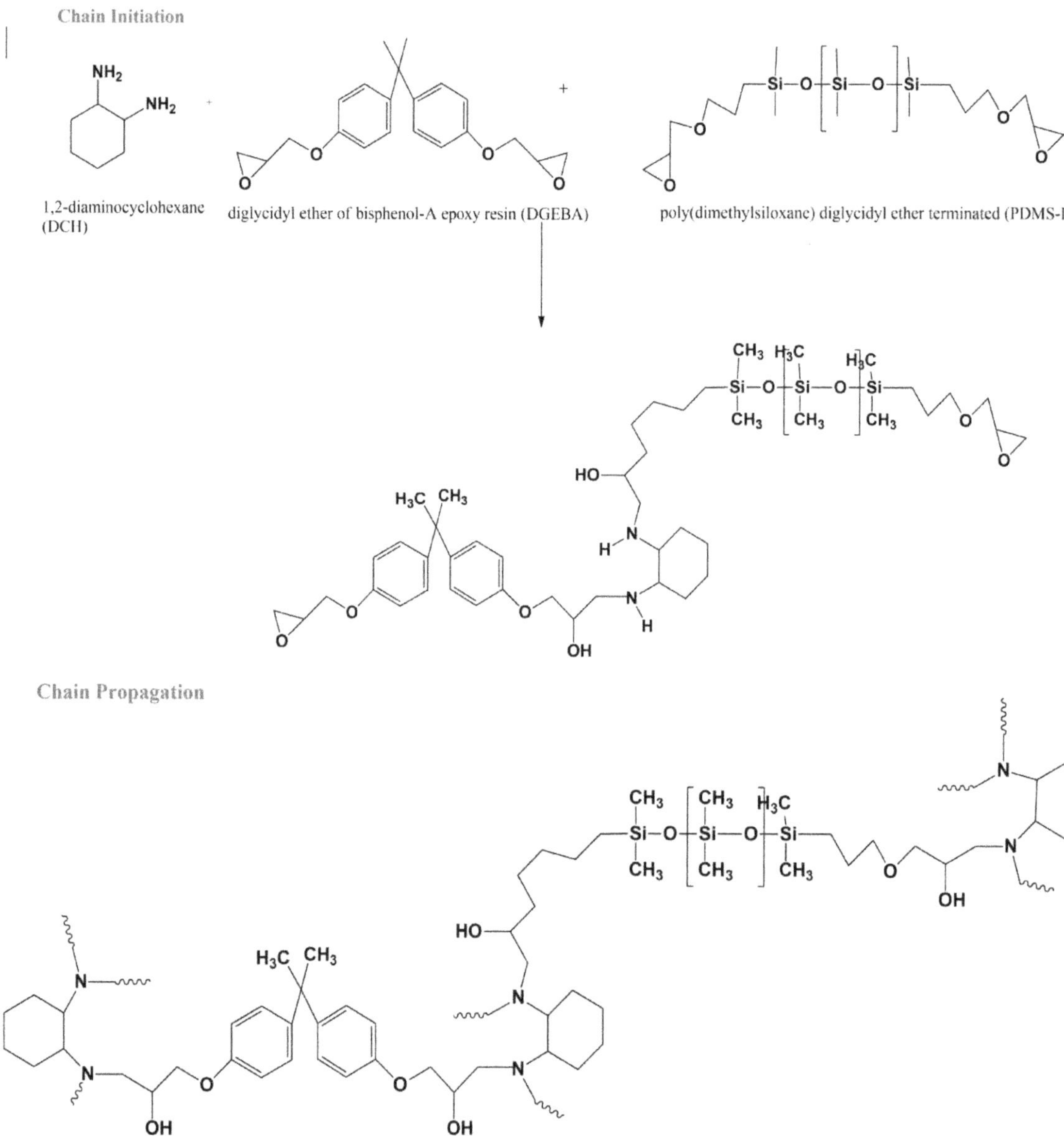

**Scheme 1. The schematic representation of reaction mechanism for synthesis of epoxidized polysiloxane using ether-terminated polydimethylsiloxane (PDMS-DGE)**

## FT-IR Studies

The FT-IR studies were performed to understand the chemical structure of the epoxidized polysiloxane. Figure below shows the FT-IR spectrum of the epoxidized polysiloxane synthesized using ether-terminated polydimethylsiloxane (PDMS-DGE). The FT-IR studies were performed to understand the chemical structure of the epoxidized polysiloxane.

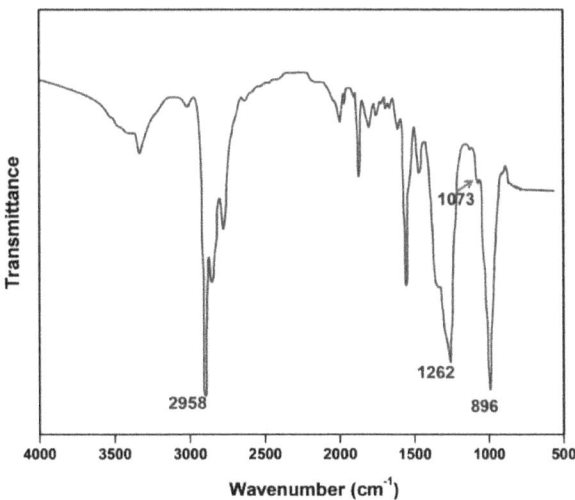

**FT-IR spectrum of the epoxidized polysiloxane synthesized using ether-terminated polydimethylsiloxane (PDMS-DGE)**

*TGA Studies*

The thermal stability of the composites was examined using thermogravimetric analysis (TGA) in both modulated mode and high resolution. The figure below illustrates the mass loss traces relative to the temperature for (a) neat epoxy, (b) epoxidized polysiloxane with ether-terminated polydimethylsiloxane (PDMS-DGE), and (c) epoxidized polysiloxane with GPTMS.

Overall, thermal studies indicate that epoxidized polysiloxane with GPTMS exhibits better thermal stability compared to the one with PDMS-DGE.

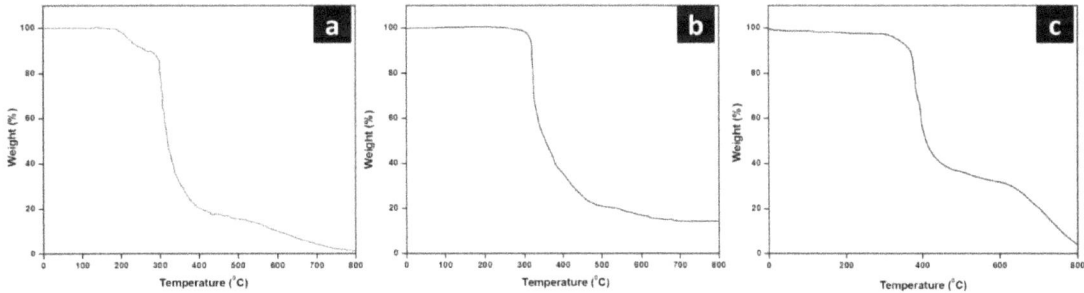

**TGA analysis of (a) neat epoxy, (b) epoxidized polysiloxane using ether-terminated polydimethylsiloxane (PDMS-DGE) and (c) epoxidized polysiloxane using GPTMS**

*DSC Studies*

The glass transition temperature (Tg) is a key indicator of the thermal stability of epoxy-based samples. The DSC analysis of epoxidized polysiloxane using ether-terminated polydimethylsiloxane (PDMS-DGE) and GPTMS are shown below.

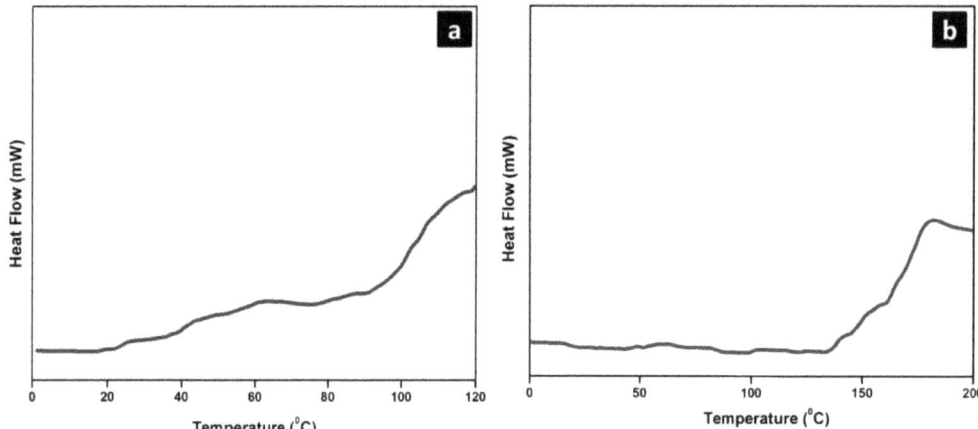

**DSC analysis of (a) epoxidized polysiloxane using ether-terminated polydimethylsiloxane (PDMS-DGE) and (b) epoxidized polysiloxane using GPTMS**

**Current Challenges in Silicone Polymers**

Despite their widespread use and numerous advantages, silicone polymers face several challenges that affect their performance, manufacturability, and widespread adoption across various industries. Addressing these challenges is critical to expanding the applications of silicones and increasing their overall effectiveness.

*1. Cost and Scalability*

Silicone polymers, especially high-performance variants, can be expensive to produce. Costs are affected by the need for raw materials, complex synthesis processes, and specialized equipment. Scaling up production while maintaining quality and consistency is a significant challenge, especially in industries that demand large quantities of material, such as construction and automotive. Reducing production costs without compromising silicone's unique properties remains a key focus area for manufacturers.

*2. Environmental and Sustainability Concerns*

Silicones are generally considered to be environmentally stable and non-toxic; however, their production involves energy-intensive processes and the use of non-renewable resources, primarily derived from petrochemicals. The environmental impact of silicone production and disposal is a growing concern, especially as industry and consumers are prioritizing sustainability. The development of greener synthesis methods, such as using bio-based or recyclable materials, is an ongoing challenge.

*3. Adhesion and bonding issues*

While silicones are known for their excellent thermal stability and flexibility, their inherent low surface energy can make adhesion to certain substrates challenging. This is particularly problematic in applications where strong bonding is critical, such as in electronics or medical devices. Improving their adhesive properties without sacrificing silicones' other beneficial properties is a complex task that requires innovative material modifications and surface treatments.

*4. Mechanical strength and durability*

Silicones are valued for their flexibility, but this can also be a drawback in applications requiring high mechanical strength and durability. In some cases, silicone materials can exhibit lower tensile strength, tear resistance, and abrasion resistance than other polymers. Increasing these mechanical properties without compromising silicone's inherent flexibility and thermal stability is a major challenge, especially for applications in harsh environments.

*5. Chemical Resistance and Degradation*

While silicones are generally resistant to many chemicals, they can be vulnerable to certain solvents, acids, and alkalis, which can cause degradation over time. In specific industrial environments such as chemical processing or oil and gas, this limitation can restrict the use of silicones. It is important to develop silicone formulations with increased chemical resistance to expand their applicability in these demanding areas.

*6. Regulatory and Health Concerns*

Silicones used in medical devices, personal care products, and food contact applications are subject to rigorous regulatory scrutiny. Concerns about the long-term biocompatibility and potential health effects of certain silicone compounds have increased the need for regulation and extensive testing. Navigating these regulatory landscapes and ensuring that silicone products meet all safety and performance standards is a significant challenge for manufacturers.

*7. Aging and long-term stability*

Although silicones are known for their long-term stability, they can undergo degradation over long periods of time, especially under extreme environmental conditions such as high UV exposure, ozone, or sustained mechanical stress. Predicting and improving the aging characteristics of silicone materials is important for applications that require long-lasting performance, such as in building sealants or automotive components.

*8. Innovation and customization*

The demand for specialized silicone materials tailored for specific applications is growing, especially in advanced technologies such as electronics, aerospace, and renewable energy. However, customizing silicone materials to meet these specific requirements can be challenging, requiring sophisticated research and development efforts and precise control over material properties. Balancing the need for innovation with practical manufacturability is an ongoing challenge.

Addressing these challenges requires continued research and development as well as collaboration between materials scientists, engineers, and manufacturers. As the demand for high-performance materials continues to grow across various industries, overcoming the limitations of silicone polymers will be essential to unleash their full potential and expand their use in existing and emerging applications.

**Improving Silicone Adhesion**

Silicone polymers are prized for their unique properties, such as thermal stability, flexibility, and resistance to environmental factors. However, their low surface energy, which contributes to their non-stick nature, presents a significant challenge when strong adhesion to various substrates is required. Improving silicone adhesion is crucial for enhancing their performance in applications such as electronics, medical devices, automotive components, and construction. Several strategies have been developed to address this challenge, focusing on both surface treatment of substrates and modification of silicone formulations.

**1. Surface Treatment of Substrates**

One of the most effective ways to enhance silicone adhesion is by modifying the surface of the substrate to increase its surface energy, thereby promoting better bonding with the silicone.

Plasma Treatment: Plasma treatment is a common technique used to increase the surface energy of substrates. It involves exposing the substrate to a plasma field, which generates reactive species that modify the surface chemistry. This process can introduce polar functional groups to the surface, improving the wettability and adhesion of silicone to materials such as plastics, metals, and glass.

Chemical Primers: Chemical primers are often used to improve adhesion by creating a chemically compatible layer between the silicone and the substrate. These primers typically contain silanes or other reactive compounds that can bond with both the substrate and the silicone. Applying a primer before the silicone adhesive ensures better adhesion, especially on difficult-to-bond surfaces like polyethylene, polypropylene, and certain metals.

Mechanical Abrasion: Mechanical abrasion, such as sanding or grit blasting, can increase surface roughness, providing more mechanical interlocking sites for the silicone adhesive. This technique is particularly useful for bonding to metals and hard plastics, where a roughened surface can significantly enhance the adhesion strength.

UV/Ozone Treatment: UV/ozone treatment is another surface modification technique that can enhance adhesion. This process involves exposing the substrate to ultraviolet light in the presence of ozone, which oxidizes the surface and increases its polarity. This treatment is effective for improving silicone adhesion to materials like glass and ceramics.

**2. Modification of Silicone Formulations**

Improving the adhesion of silicone itself can be achieved by modifying its chemical structure or by incorporating additives that enhance bonding.

Incorporation of Adhesion Promoters: Adhesion promoters, such as silane coupling agents, can be added directly to the silicone formulation. These agents contain functional groups that can interact with both the silicone polymer and the substrate, forming strong chemical bonds. This method is widely used in the formulation of silicone adhesives for industrial and medical applications.

Cross-Linking Enhancements: Modifying the cross-linking density of silicone polymers can also improve adhesion. By adjusting the degree of cross-linking, manufacturers can tailor the silicone's mechanical properties, such as flexibility and strength, to better suit the bonding requirements. Additionally, the use of specific cross-linking agents that interact with the substrate can further enhance adhesion.

Nanocomposites and Fillers: The incorporation of nanoparticles or functional fillers into silicone can significantly improve its adhesion properties. For example, adding silica nanoparticles or other reinforcing agents can increase the surface area and provide additional bonding sites. These fillers can also modify the rheological properties of the silicone, improving its wetting and spreading on the substrate.

Curing Process Optimization: The curing process plays a critical role in the adhesion of silicone adhesives. Optimizing curing conditions, such as temperature, time, and the presence of moisture (for moisture-cured silicones), can enhance the adhesion. For instance, heat curing often improves the adhesion of silicone to metals by promoting better polymer-substrate interaction.

### 3. Hybrid Silicone Formulations

Developing hybrid formulations that combine silicone with other polymers or resins can create materials that offer the best of both worlds—retaining the desirable properties of silicone while improving adhesion. For example, silicone-polyurethane or silicone-epoxy hybrids can offer enhanced adhesion to a wider range of substrates while maintaining flexibility and environmental resistance.

### 4. Innovative Bonding Techniques

Emerging bonding techniques, such as the use of self-assembled monolayers (SAMs) and advanced polymer grafting methods, are being explored to improve silicone adhesion at the molecular level. These techniques involve creating highly ordered and functionalized surfaces that can interact more effectively with silicone polymers, leading to stronger and more durable bonds.

Improving silicone adhesion is a multifaceted challenge that requires a combination of surface treatment, chemical modification, and process optimization. By leveraging these strategies, manufacturers can enhance the bonding performance of silicone adhesives, expanding their applicability in demanding industrial environments and advancing the development of new silicone-based products.

### Future Trends in Silicone Polymers

Silicone polymers are poised for significant advancements as industries continue to demand materials with enhanced performance, sustainability, and functionality. Several emerging trends are shaping the future of silicones, driven by innovations in material science, environmental considerations, and the growing need for high-performance materials in advanced applications. Here are some key trends expected to influence the future of silicone polymers:

1. Sustainability and Green Chemistry

As environmental concerns become increasingly central to material development, the silicone industry is focusing on more sustainable production methods and eco-friendly formulations.

*Bio-based Silicones:* Research is underway to develop silicones derived from renewable resources, such as bio-based precursors. These materials aim to reduce reliance on petrochemicals and lower the carbon footprint of silicone production.

*Recyclability and Circular Economy:* Efforts to improve the recyclability of silicone products are gaining momentum. This includes designing silicone materials that can be more easily recycled at the end of their life cycle or developing processes for reclaiming and reusing silicone waste.

*Green Manufacturing Processes*: Innovations in manufacturing processes, such as using less energy-intensive methods or environmentally friendly solvents, are expected to reduce the environmental impact of silicone production.

## 2. Advanced Silicone Composites

The development of silicone-based composites is a growing area of interest, particularly for applications requiring enhanced mechanical properties, electrical conductivity, or thermal management.

*Nanocomposites*: Incorporating nanoparticles like graphene, carbon nanotubes, or silica into silicone matrices can significantly improve properties such as strength, thermal conductivity, and electrical performance. These materials are particularly promising for use in electronics, aerospace, and automotive industries.

*Hybrid Materials:* Combining silicone with other polymers or materials can create hybrids that offer a balance of properties, such as the flexibility of silicone with the strength of epoxies or the conductivity of metals. These hybrids are likely to find applications in areas like flexible electronics and wearable devices.

## 3. Smart and Functional Silicones

The integration of smart functionalities into silicone materials is an exciting frontier, particularly for applications in healthcare, electronics, and responsive systems.

*Self-Healing Silicones:* Research is advancing in the development of silicones that can self-repair minor damages, extending their lifespan and reliability in critical applications like aerospace, automotive, and consumer electronics.

*Responsive Silicones*: Silicones that respond to external stimuli such as temperature, light, or pH changes are being developed for applications in sensors, actuators, and controlled drug delivery systems.

*Antimicrobial and Biocompatible Silicones:* The demand for antimicrobial silicones, particularly in medical devices and healthcare, is growing. These materials can prevent bacterial growth and improve patient outcomes. Additionally, silicones with enhanced biocompatibility are being developed for advanced medical implants and prosthetics.

## 4. Enhanced Adhesion and Processing Techniques

Improving the adhesion of silicones to various substrates and refining processing techniques are ongoing areas of focus to expand their application range.

*Surface Modification Innovations:* New surface treatment technologies, such as advanced plasma treatments or the use of nanocoating, are being explored to improve silicone adhesion to difficult-to-bond surfaces like metals and plastics.

*3D Printing of Silicones:* Additive manufacturing, or 3D printing, of silicone materials is a rapidly evolving area. Advances in this field are enabling the production of complex, customized silicone components for medical devices, automotive parts, and wearable technology.

*Low-Temperature Curing Silicones:* Development of silicones that cure at lower temperatures without compromising performance is underway, which would allow for energy savings during manufacturing and enable their use in heat-sensitive applications.

### 5. High-Performance and Specialized Applications

The demand for silicones in high-performance and specialized applications is expected to grow, driven by advancements in various industries.

*Electronics and Energy:* The increasing complexity of electronic devices and the shift towards renewable energy sources are driving demand for high-performance silicones with superior thermal management, electrical insulation, and environmental resistance.

*Aerospace and Automotive:* The aerospace and automotive industries are focusing on lightweight, durable materials that can withstand extreme conditions. High-performance silicones are likely to play a crucial role in developing next-generation vehicles and aircraft.

*Medical and Healthcare*: With the aging population and the rise of personalized medicine, silicones will continue to be critical in medical devices, implants, and wearable health technologies, requiring continuous innovation in biocompatibility and functionality.

### 6. Regulatory and Safety Innovations

As regulatory scrutiny increases, particularly in healthcare and consumer goods, the silicone industry is expected to focus more on compliance with safety standards and the development of safer, non-toxic materials.

*Non-leachable Additives*: The trend towards non-leachable additives in silicone formulations is likely to grow, particularly in applications involving direct contact with food, pharmaceuticals, or the human body.

*Compliance with Global Standards*: The industry will need to navigate increasingly stringent global regulations, which will drive innovations in silicone formulations that meet or exceed these standards, particularly concerning environmental and health impacts.

The future of silicone polymers is shaped by a combination of technological innovation, environmental responsibility, and the need for materials that meet the demands of advanced applications. As these trends continue to evolve, silicones are likely to play an increasingly important role in industries ranging from electronics and healthcare to aerospace and renewable energy, driven by their unique combination of properties and the ongoing development of new functionalities.

### Exploring the Potential of Bio-Based Silicones in Modern Applications

Bio-based silicones represent an exciting frontier in material science, combining the advantageous properties of traditional silicones with the sustainability of renewable resources. As industries increasingly seek eco-friendly alternatives without compromising on performance, bio-based silicones offer innovative solutions across a range of applications. This exploration highlights the potential of bio-based silicones and their transformative impact on various sectors.

## 1. Healthcare and Medical Devices

Biocompatible Implants: Bio-based silicones are finding significant use in medical implants due to their biocompatibility, flexibility, and long-term stability. These materials are increasingly chosen for implants such as breast implants, pacemakers, and dental devices, offering a safer and more sustainable option for patients and healthcare providers. In wound management, bio-based silicones are utilized in dressings and scar management products. Their gentle adhesion, moisture control, and reduced risk of irritation make them ideal for sensitive applications, aligning with the growing demand for sustainable medical solutions. Bio-based silicones are employed in medical tubing and catheters, where flexibility and chemical resistance are crucial. These materials support improved patient care by providing reliable performance in critical medical procedures while contributing to environmental sustainability.

## 2. Personal Care and Cosmetics

Eco-Friendly Skin Care: Bio-based silicones are increasingly incorporated into skin care formulations, where they enhance texture and provide a smooth, silky feel. Their use in creams, lotions, and serums reflects a growing preference for natural and sustainable ingredients in the beauty industry. Innovative Hair Care: In hair care products, bio-based silicones offer benefits such as shine, smoothness, and frizz control. Their inclusion in conditioners, shampoos, and styling products supports the trend towards environmentally conscious beauty solutions.

Sustainable Makeup: Bio-based silicones are used in makeup formulations to achieve desirable textures and long-lasting effects. Their presence in foundations, primers, and lipsticks highlights the move towards sustainable and ethical beauty products.

## 3. Electronics and Electrical Applications

Thermal Management Solutions: Bio-based silicones are utilized as thermal interface materials (TIMs) in electronic devices, efficiently dissipating heat from components like CPUs and GPUs. These materials provide a sustainable alternative while maintaining high performance in thermal management applications. In electronics, bio-based silicones serve as encapsulants and potting compounds, protecting sensitive components from moisture and mechanical stress. Their use helps to improve the longevity and reliability of electronic devices while supporting greener manufacturing practices. The flexibility and durability of bio-based silicones make them suitable for flexible electronics, such as wearable devices and flexible displays. These materials contribute to the development of next-generation electronics with sustainable attributes.

## 4. Automotive and Transportation

Sustainable Seals and Gaskets: Bio-based silicones are increasingly used in automotive seals and gaskets, providing durability and resistance to temperature extremes and chemicals. Their application supports the automotive industry's efforts to adopt more sustainable manufacturing practices.

High-Performance Hoses and Tubing: In the automotive sector, bio-based silicones are employed for hoses and tubing that need to withstand exposure to fluids, oils, and extreme temperatures. These materials offer a balance of performance and environmental responsibility.

Eco-Friendly Interior Components: Bio-based silicones are used in automotive interiors, such as dashboard coatings and seat cushions, providing durability and aesthetic appeal. Their use aligns with the growing emphasis on sustainable materials in vehicle design.

### 5. Construction and Building Materials

Sustainable Sealants and Adhesives: Bio-based silicones are used as sealants and adhesives in construction, offering weatherproofing and insulation properties. Their application supports greener building practices and contributes to energy-efficient construction.

Protective Coatings: In construction, bio-based silicones are used in protective coatings that shield surfaces from environmental damage, UV radiation, and chemical exposure. These coatings offer a sustainable alternative to traditional solutions.

Insulation Solutions: Bio-based silicones are utilized in insulation materials, providing thermal stability and moisture resistance. These materials contribute to energy efficiency in buildings, supporting sustainable construction practices.

### 6. Textiles and Fashion

Bio-based silicones are employed in performance fabrics for outdoor gear, sportswear, and footwear. They provide water repellences, flexibility, and durability, meeting the demand for eco-friendly and high-performance textiles. In the fashion industry, bio-based silicones are used as soft touch coatings on fabrics, enhancing their feel and appearance while supporting sustainability goals. These coatings are popular in high-end clothing and accessories.

Sustainable Printing Inks: Bio-based silicone inks are used in textile printing, offering vibrant colours and durability. Their use in the fashion industry reflects a commitment to sustainable practices in textile production.

### 7. Food and Beverage

Food-Grade Sealants: Bio-based silicones are employed as food-grade sealants in food processing and packaging, ensuring safety and performance while reducing environmental impact. These materials provide effective sealing and protection for food products. Bio-based silicones are used in bakeware, kitchenware and cooking utensils, offering non-stick properties, heat resistance, and flexibility. Their application supports the shift towards more sustainable kitchen products.

Bio-based silicones are paving the way for innovative solutions across a diverse range of industries. By combining the performance characteristics of traditional silicones with the benefits of renewable resources, bio-based silicones offer a sustainable alternative that meets the growing demand for environmentally responsible materials. As technology advances and production scales up, the potential for bio-based silicones to transform various sectors will continue to expand, driving progress towards a more sustainable future.

### Environmental Benefits of Bio-Based Silicones

Bio-based silicones offer significant environmental benefits, marking a shift towards more sustainable material practices. Unlike traditional silicones, which rely on finite petrochemical resources, bio-based silicones are derived from renewable raw materials, such as plant oils and sugars. This transition reduces dependence on fossil fuels, helping to conserve non-renewable resources and mitigate resource depletion.

One of the primary environmental advantages is the reduced carbon footprint associated with bio-based silicones. The production process for these materials generally results in lower greenhouse gas emissions compared to conventional silicones. This reduction is partly because bio-based feedstocks absorb carbon dioxide during their growth, partially offsetting the emissions produced during manufacturing.

Additionally, the production of bio-based silicones can involve cleaner and less toxic processes. Many bio-based formulations are designed to be less harmful to the environment and human health, with reduced toxicity and fewer hazardous by-products. This shift contributes to a decrease in environmental pollution during production and lowers the risk of adverse effects on ecosystems. Bio-based silicones can also offer improved biodegradability, although this depends on the specific formulation. Some bio-based silicones are designed to break down more readily than their traditional counterparts, which helps reduce the accumulation of non-degradable waste in landfills and natural habitats. Furthermore, certain bio-based silicones are compatible with existing recycling systems, promoting a circular economy where materials are reused rather than disposed of.

The production of bio-based silicones often requires fewer resources, such as water and energy, compared to conventional silicones. Sustainable agricultural practices used to grow bio-based feedstocks can also contribute to reduced water usage, less soil erosion, and minimized use of harmful chemicals. Bio-based silicones tend to emit fewer volatile organic compounds (VOCs), which are known to contribute to air pollution and have harmful effects on both human health and the environment. By reducing VOC emissions, bio-based silicones help improve air quality and support a healthier environment. Hence, bio-based silicones represent a more sustainable option that aligns with broader environmental goals. Their use contributes to resource conservation, reduced greenhouse gas emissions, and less environmental pollution, supporting a shift towards greener material practices across various industries.

**Cost comparison details**

When comparing the costs of bio-based silicones to traditional, petrochemical-based silicones, several factors come into play, including raw material costs, production processes, market scale, and end-use applications. Here's a detailed look at these factors:

**1. Raw Material Costs**

***Bio-Based Feedstocks:*** Bio-based silicones are derived from renewable resources like plant oils and sugars, which can be more expensive to cultivate and process compared to fossil fuels. The cost of bio-based feedstocks can vary based on the type of crop, agricultural practices, and regional factors such as climate and land availability. Additionally, fluctuations in the agricultural markets, due to weather or geopolitical factors, can impact the cost of these feedstocks.

***Petrochemical Feedstocks:*** Traditional silicones are made from silica (derived from sand) and various petrochemicals. The cost of petrochemical feedstocks is influenced by global oil prices, which tend to be volatile. However, large-scale extraction and refining processes for petrochemicals have been optimized over decades, leading to relatively stable and lower costs in comparison to bio-based materials.

## 2. Production Processes

***Bio-Based Production***: The production of bio-based silicones often requires specialized processing techniques to convert biological feedstocks into the desired silicone polymers. These processes can be more complex and costly due to the need for bio-refining technologies, the use of specific catalysts, and the management of biological raw materials. Additionally, bio-based silicone production is still in a relatively early stage of industrial development, which means economies of scale have not yet been fully realized, keeping production costs higher.

***Conventional Silicone Production:*** The production of traditional silicones is well-established, with highly efficient industrial processes. These processes benefit from decades of optimization, large-scale production facilities, and established supply chains. As a result, the production costs of conventional silicones are generally lower compared to bio-based alternatives.

## 3. Market Scale and Availability

***Bio-Based Silicones:*** The market for bio-based silicones is still emerging, which means that production volumes are lower and supply chains are less developed. Lower production volumes lead to higher per-unit costs due to the lack of economies of scale. Additionally, limited availability of bio-based silicones in the market can drive up prices as demand begins to grow faster than supply.

***Traditional Silicones:*** The market for conventional silicones is mature, with large-scale production and a well-established global supply chain. High production volumes enable manufacturers to benefit from economies of scale, reducing the per-unit cost of traditional silicones. Furthermore, the widespread availability of traditional silicones ensures competitive pricing in the market.

## 4. End-Use Applications

***Specialized Applications:*** In some cases, bio-based silicones may offer unique performance characteristics that justify their higher cost, particularly in applications where sustainability is a key selling point. Industries focused on eco-friendly products, such as cosmetics, personal care, and certain medical devices, may be willing to pay a premium for bio-based silicones due to their renewable origin and lower environmental impact.

***Commodity Applications***: In more cost-sensitive applications, such as general industrial use or construction, the higher cost of bio-based silicones may be a barrier to adoption. Here, the cost-effectiveness of traditional silicones often makes them the preferred choice, unless environmental regulations or consumer demand shifts towards more sustainable alternatives.

## 5. Long-Term Cost Trends

***Technological Advancements:*** As bio-based silicone production technologies advance and scale up, costs are expected to decrease over time. Innovations in bio-refining, improved agricultural practices, and more efficient production processes could help lower the overall cost of bio-based silicones, making them more competitive with traditional silicones.

***Market Dynamics:*** As consumer demand for sustainable products grows and regulatory pressures increase, the market for bio-based silicones is likely to expand. This could lead to greater investment in production infrastructure, further driving down costs and increasing the competitiveness of bio-based silicones.

Currently, bio-based silicones are generally more expensive to produce than traditional silicones, primarily due to higher raw material costs, less mature production processes, and smaller market scale. However, the gap in costs is expected to narrow as technology advances and economies of scale are achieved. While traditional silicones remain more cost-effective for many applications, bio-based silicones offer compelling environmental benefits that may justify their higher cost in markets where sustainability is a critical factor. Here is a cost comparison graph between traditional silicones and bio-based silicones across various categories, such as raw material costs, production processes, market scale, and end-use applications. The graph illustrates how bio-based silicones currently tend to be more expensive in each category, reflecting the challenges and higher costs associated with producing these more sustainable materials.

## Conclusion

The development and analysis of high-performance silicon polymer adhesives for industrial applications demonstrate the material's potential to revolutionize various industries. Silicon polymers, known for their excellent thermal stability, chemical resistance, and flexibility, offer superior adhesive properties that meet the demands of modern industrial applications. The research and innovations in this field have led to the creation of adhesives that not only withstand harsh environmental conditions but also maintain strong and durable bonds across a wide range of substrates. Advancements in silicon-based polymer formulations have enabled the production of adhesives with enhanced performance characteristics, such as improved adhesion like aerospace, automotive, electronics, and construction to different surfaces, increased durability, and resistance to extreme temperatures and chemicals. Moreover, the integration of bio-based components into silicon polymer adhesives presents an opportunity to align with global sustainability goals. The environmental benefits of bio-based silicon polymers—such as reduced carbon footprints and reliance on renewable resources—make them an attractive option for eco-friendly industries. As industrial applications continue to evolve, the demand for high-performance adhesives will grow, driving further innovation in silicon polymer technology. Future developments may focus on enhancing the environmental profile of these adhesives, improving their performance under increasingly demanding conditions, and expanding their applicability across emerging industries.

In conclusion, silicon polymer adhesives are poised to play a critical role in the future of industrial applications, offering a combination of high performance, versatility, and potential sustainability that makes them indispensable in the pursuit of advanced manufacturing and construction technologies. The ongoing research and development efforts will ensure that these materials continue to meet the ever-changing needs of industry, paving the way for new innovations and applications.

**References**

1. Sancaktar, E. (2018). Classification of adhesive and sealant materials. In *Handbook of adhesion technology*.

2. Ardu, S., Braut, V., Uhac, I., Benbachir, N., Feilzer, A. J., & Krejci, I. (2010). A new classification of resin-based aesthetic adhesive materials. *Collegium antropologicum*, *34*(3), 1045-1050.

3. Li, J., Gopalakrishnan, K., Piao, G., Pacha, R., Walia, P., Deng, Y., & Chakrapani, S. K. (2023). Classification of adhesive bonding between thermoplastic composites using ultrasonic testing aided by machine learning. *International Journal of Adhesion and Adhesives*, *125*, 103427.

4. De Lollis, N. J. (1962). Structural adhesives—characteristics and application. *Journal of Applied Polymer Science*, *6*(20), 155-160.

5. Davis, K. M., & Tomozawa, M. (1996). An infrared spectroscopic study of water-related species in silica glasses. *Journal of Non-Crystalline Solids*, *201*(3), 177-198.

6. Chen, C., Jia, Z., Wang, X., Lu, H., Guan, Z., & Yang, C. (2015). Micro characterization and degradation mechanism of liquid silicone rubber used for external insulation. *IEEE Transactions on Dielectrics and Electrical Insulation*, *22*(1), 313-321.

7. Fan, J., Wang, Z., Zhang, X., Deng, Z., Fan, X., & Zhang, G. (2019). High moisture accelerated mechanical behavior degradation of phosphor/silicone composites used in white light-emitting diodes. *Polymers*, *11*(8), 1277.

8. Mojsiewicz-Pienkowska, K., Jamrógiewicz, M., Zebrowska, M., Sznitowska, M., & Centkowska, K. (2011). Technology of an adhesive silicone film as drug carrier in transdermal therapy. I: Analytical methods used for characterization and design of the universal elastomer layers. *J. Pharm. Biomed. Anal*, *56*(1), 131-138.

9. Yang, L., Feng, J., Zhang, W., & Qu, J. E. (2010). Experimental and computational study on hydrolysis and condensation kinetics of γ-glycidoxypropyltrimethoxysilane (γ-GPS). *Applied surface science*, *257*(3), 990-996.

10. Borovin, E., Callone, E., Ribot, F., & Diré, S. (2016). Mechanism and kinetics of oligosilsesquioxane growth in the in situ water production sol–gel route: dependence on water availability. *European Journal of Inorganic Chemistry*, *2016*(13-14), 2166-2174.

11. Issa, A. A., & Luyt, A. S. (2019). Kinetics of alkoxysilanes and organoalkoxysilanes polymerization: A review. *Polymers*, *11*(3), 537.

12. Gandhimathi, R., & Dhanasekaran, R. (2014). Synthesis, growth and characterization of 4-dimethylaminobenzaldehyde-4-nitrophenylhydrazone single crystals. *Optik*, *125*(12), 2912-2917.

13. Coates, J. (2000). Interpretation of infrared spectra, a practical approach. *Encyclopedia of analytical chemistry*, *12*, 10815-10837.

14. Liu, H., Cash, G., Birtwhistle, D., & George, G. (2005). Characterization of a severely degraded silicone elastomer HV insulator-an aid to development of lifetime assessment techniques. *IEEE Transactions on Dielectrics and Electrical Insulation*, *12*(3), 478-486.

15. Fang, C., Luo, Y., & Naidu, R. (2023). Raman imaging for the analysis of silicone microplastics and nanoplastics released from a kitchen sealant. *Frontiers in Chemistry*, *11*, 1165523.

# Chapter-3

# Catalytic Advances in Polymer Composites

Dattatraya N. Pansare[1*]

Pravin N. Chavan[2]

Rohini N. Shelke[3]

Dhanraj Kamble[4]

Mubarak H. Shaikh[5]

Devidas S. Bhagat[6]

**Abstract:** Polymer composites, which are formed by integrating polymers with materials such as fibers or particles, have seen significant advancements, largely due to the influence of catalysis. These composites are increasingly favored across diverse industries because they offer improved mechanical, thermal, and chemical properties, resulting from the combination of the distinct characteristics of both polymers and reinforcing agents. The introduction of catalysts has been crucial in enhancing the synthesis, processing, and overall performance of polymer composites, leading to noteworthy progress in the field. Catalysts serve as essential components in numerous biological and chemical processes, accelerating reactions to improve efficiency. They are prevalent in industrial applications, transforming raw materials into valuable products, such as converting milk into yogurt or crude oil into plastic containers. In biological systems, these catalysts are known as enzymes, facilitating various functions such as signaling and digestion. Due to their high surface area, porosity, surface functionality, and resistance to extreme conditions, polymers have traditionally been utilized as supports for catalytic compounds. More recently, there has been a growing focus on employing polymer materials themselves as catalysts or in combination with other substances to enhance catalytic activity synergistically.

**Role of Catalysts in Polymer Composite Synthesis**

Catalysts play a crucial role in polymerization reactions by facilitating or accelerating the conversion of monomers into polymers under less extreme conditions. In polymer composites, they are not only used for polymerization but also to improve the interaction between the polymer matrix and reinforcing agents, which can greatly impact the composite's overall properties. For example,

---

[1] *Department of Chemistry, Deogiri College Chhatrapati Sambhajinagar, 431005, Maharashtra, India*
*Corresponding author E-mail: dattatraya.pansare7@gmail.com

[2] *Department of Chemistry, Doshi Vakil Arts College, and G. C. U. B. Science & Commerce College, Goregaon, Raigad 402103, MS, India.*

[3] *Department of Chemistry, R. K. M. M. Ahmednagar, 414001, Maharashtra, India*

[4] *Department of Chemistry, S. B.E.S. College of Science, Aurangabad 431001, Maharashtra, India*

[5] *Department of Chemistry, Radhabai Kale Mahila Mahavidyalaya Ahemadnagar, 414001, MS, India.*

[6] *Department of Forensic Chemistry and Toxicology, Government Institute of Forensic Science, Aurangabad 431004,*

transition-metal catalysts, such as Ziegler-Natta and metallocene types, have been widely applied in the production of polyolefins, leading to the creation of high-performance composites. These catalysts offer greater control over polymer microstructure, allowing precise adjustment of properties like crystallinity, molecular weight, and strength [1].

**Advances in Nano-catalysts for Polymer Composites**

One of the key advancements in polymer composites has been the incorporation of nanocatalysts. Nanoparticles like metal oxides and carbon-based materials act as catalysts to enhance the interfacial adhesion between the polymer matrix and the fillers. The larger surface area provided by these nanocatalysts facilitates improved dispersion of fillers, resulting in enhanced mechanical properties. For instance, nanoparticles such as titanium dioxide ($TiO_2$) and zinc oxide (ZnO) have been utilized to boost the thermal stability and UV resistance of polymer composites, making them ideal for use in challenging environments [2].

**Catalytic Curing of Polymer Composites**

Advancements in catalysis have significantly influenced the curing process, which involves hardening the polymer matrix. Catalysts incorporated into curing agents for thermosetting polymers, like epoxy resins, can greatly speed up the process and enhance crosslinking density. Organometallic catalysts, particularly tin-based compounds, are often employed to achieve this. These catalysts play a vital role in producing composites with improved mechanical and thermal properties, making them essential for use in industries such as aerospace, automotive, and construction [3].

**Sustainable Catalytic Strategies**

Due to increasing environmental concerns, there is a growing trend toward creating sustainable catalytic methods for polymer composites. Scientists are concentrating on biocatalysts and eco-friendly catalysts to minimize the environmental footprint of composite manufacturing. Enzymatic polymerization, for instance, provides a more sustainable option by employing enzymes to produce biodegradable polymer composites. Furthermore, integrating renewable resources like bio-based monomers and fillers with sustainable catalysts is contributing to the development of greener composite materials [4].

Polymeric catalysts have found applications across various fields, including medical uses such as antibacterial treatments and wound healing, environmental applications like pollutant breakdown and sustainable chemical synthesis, as well as in the energy sector for sustainable energy production and storage. This review highlights the platforms developed for these key areas, while also addressing challenges and emerging research directions [5]. Catalysis plays an essential role in both industrial and biological processes by enabling reactions to proceed faster and more efficiently through the use of catalysts—substances that speed up chemical reactions without being consumed. [6]. These catalysts work by altering the reaction pathway, lowering the activation energy, and selectively enhancing certain reactions. In 2020, the global catalyst market was valued at approximately $35.5 billion and is projected to grow to $57.5 billion by 2030, with the largest market shares in petroleum refining, chemical production, polymers, petrochemicals, and environmental applications [7]. The rising demand for catalysts in these and other sectors is driving the need for more efficient solutions that enhance process optimization, boost yield, and reduce both costs and energy consumption.

Catalysts are generally classified into three categories: homogeneous, heterogeneous, and biocatalysts. [8].

The book Polymer Nanocomposites: From Fabrication to Applications provides a comprehensive and current analysis of different polymer nanocomposite materials and technologies through critical evaluations. It explores the latest developments in nanomaterials, polymers, biopolymers, and processing techniques, starting with the synthesis, fabrication, and characterization of nanomaterials, and progressing to the manufacturing and practical applications of polymer-based nanocomposites. The primary emphasis is on polymer matrix nanocomposites and their emerging trends in the engineering field. [9].

Polymers by themselves have limited application in product manufacturing and structural design due to their relatively low performance compared to materials like metals. However, their properties can be significantly improved when combined with reinforcing materials, forming a composite. The overall characteristics of these composites are heavily influenced by the filler material, particularly its size. When the filler is on the nanoscale, the resulting material is a polymer nanocomposite (PNC), a key aspect of nanotechnology. The field of nanotechnology in polymer composites has garnered significant attention, with its potential to improve our quality of life and contribute to a better future. [10].

Nanotechnology has become a prominent field for research and innovation, with polymer nanocomposites (PNCs) being one of the key areas of focus. This research spans a broad array of topics, including nano-electronics, polymeric bio-nanomaterials, reinforced PNCs, and nanocomposite-based drug delivery systems, among others. [11].

In the current context, composite materials find extensive application in industries such as automotive, aerospace, and various engineering fields due to their exceptional strength-to-weight and stiffness-to-weight ratios. The fibre reinforcements in composites typically consist of thin continuous fibres or short fibre segments. For the latter, fibres with a high aspect ratio, meaning a high length-to-diameter ratio, are commonly used. Continuous fibre-reinforced composites are often preferred for high-performance structural applications because of their superior specific strength (strength-to-density ratio) and stiffness (modulus-to-density ratio). Carbon fibre-reinforced composites, in particular, outperform conventional metal alloys in both strength and stiffness. Furthermore, polymer composites, when tailored with specific fibre alignments and orientations, exhibit remarkable structural and mechanical properties, making them suitable for customized applications. In civil engineering, polymer concrete is now widely used for constructing structures that can withstand highly corrosive environments. These polymer-based materials, thanks to their excellent strength-to-weight ratio and non-corrosive characteristics, offer a cost-effective solution for high-performance structures [12].

# TYPES OF POLYMER COMPOSITES

## 1. Green Composites

Researchers are actively working on developing a new generation of fully biodegradable green composites by combining plant fibers with natural resins. The key appeal of these composites lies in their eco-friendly, completely biodegradable, and sustainable properties.

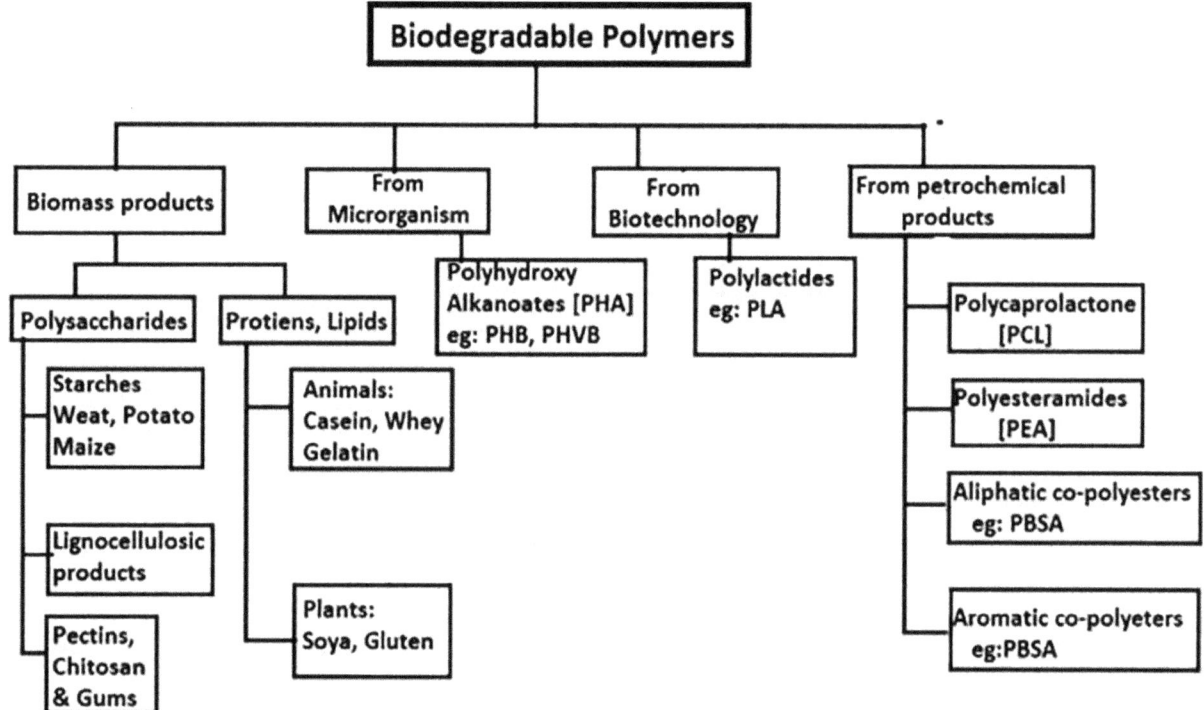

Figure 1. Classification of biodegradable polymers

These materials demonstrate that they are genuinely sustainable in every respect. At the end of their lifecycle, these green composites can be completely disposed of or composted without harming the environment. Figure 1 illustrates the classification of biodegradable polymers into four categories. Except for the fourth category, which is derived from fossil sources, the other polymers (categories one through three) are sourced from renewable materials, specifically biomass. The first category comprises biodegradable polymers derived from agriculture, such as polysaccharides sourced from biomass. The second and third categories consist of semi-synthetic fibers typically produced through the biofermentation of agricultural byproducts or through biological modification of plants. Examples include polyhydroxyalkanoate (PHA) and polylactic acid (PLA), which is chemically synthesized from monomers derived from biowaste. Finally, the fourth category includes polyesters entirely synthesized from petrochemical sources, including polyester amide (PEA), polycaprolactone (PCL), and aliphatic or aromatic copolyesters. [13].

## Hybrid Composites

Hybrid composites consist of multiple types of fibers integrated into a single matrix. The overall performance of these composites is influenced by the unique properties of the individual fibers, leading to a balance of advantages and disadvantages. Utilizing hybrid composites is advantageous because the different fibers can complement each other, compensating for any deficiencies in essential properties. This can result in a favorable balance between cost and performance through thoughtful material design. The characteristics of hybrid composites primarily depend on factors such as fiber content, fiber type, the quantity of fibers used, fiber orientation, bonding between fibers and matrix, and fiber alignment. Additionally, the overall strength of hybrid composites is closely related to the failure strain of the individual fibers, with optimal properties achieved when the fibers are under significant stress. The concept of hybrid effect refers to deviations in properties—either positive or negative—compared to the expected behavior of a simple mixture. This effect illustrates the synergistic enhancement in the physicochemical properties of a composite that includes at least two fiber types. The selection of fiber types for hybrid composite fabrication is influenced by the intended purpose of hybridization, material requirements, and the design objectives for the composite. Therefore, carefully choosing viable fibers and understanding their properties is crucial in the design, engineering, and production of hybrid composites. The effective application of hybrid composites relies not only on their mechanical, physical, and chemical stability but also on the compatibility of the fiber-matrix system. [14].

**Application of Polymer Composites**

Fibre-reinforced composites find applications across nearly all engineering disciplines. For instance, three-layer particle boards have been produced using sunflower and poplar wood stalks combined with varying proportions of urea formaldehyde adhesive. Additionally, cellulose fibers mixed with soy oil-based resin have been crafted into sheets for roofing structures, demonstrating adequate stiffness and strength to meet construction standards. Furthermore, flame-retardant composites have been developed by incorporating phosphorus into polypropylene (PP) or polyurethane (PUR) matrices containing waste biofillers and recycled polyol, proving effective in enhancing flame resistance.

Low dielectric constant materials have also been created using epoxidized soybean oil and hollow keratin fibers, showing promise for applications in electronic devices. These cost-effective vegetable oils may serve as substitutes for traditional dielectrics in circuit boards and microchips as the demand for electronic materials grows. Moreover, plastic-wood composites are widely employed in the production of docks, decks, window frames, and molded panel components, with production increasing from approximately 460 million pounds in 1999 to 750 million pounds by 2002. In the civil construction sector, bamboo fiber has been used as reinforcement in structural concrete elements. While biocomposites have gained significant traction in the furniture market, the use of biofibers in construction has a long history. Currently, the application of natural fibers as reinforcement is expanding primarily within the packaging and automotive industries. [14].

Polyolefins (POs) are polymers derived from simple or substituted alkenes, such as ethylene (PE), propylene (PP), vinyl chloride (PVC), and styrene (PS). These four types of polyolefins dominate contemporary plastic production. In 2021, polyethylene made up approximately 27% of total plastic output, which includes both low-density polyethylene (LDPE) and high-density polyethylene (HDPE). Meanwhile, polypropylene accounted for around 20%, vinyl chloride for about 13%, and styrene for roughly 5% [15]. Together, polyolefins constitute nearly two-thirds of all plastic production and a comparable share of plastic waste [16]. The large scale of production, along with the low price of plastic objects (POs), has resulted in a significant increase in short-term applications and a corresponding rise in waste, with an estimated 353 million metric tons of plastic waste generated in

2019 alone. Approximately 49% of this waste is disposed of in landfills globally. Around 19% is incinerated, which can recover some energy but also releases carbon dioxide and potentially harmful organic compounds into the environment. Traditional recycling efforts, which account for only 9% of plastic waste, have not yet proven to be an effective solution to these challenges. [17]. Approximately 22% of waste is not managed properly, resulting in leakage into natural environments such as rivers and oceans. This contamination introduces microplastics and nanoplastics into water sources, raising significant public health concerns. It is important to note, however, that an earlier estimate regarding the quantities of these tiny plastic particles consumed by humans has since been proven to be vastly overstated [18], providing an important cautionary tale [19,20] about hasty and/or unreproducible science [21].

Plastic waste can be recycled mechanically, chemically, or via hybrid chemomechanical processes [22–24]. Mechanical recycling refers to the process of re-manufacturing products using waste materials without disassembling or altering the polymer chains. This method is most effective with high-purity, known-composition materials, such as industrial scrap, rather than post-consumer waste. However, it often results in a reduction of the original polymer's mechanical properties (like strength and toughness) due to unintentional chemical changes and the presence of impurities, which may not be fully understood. In contrast, chemical recycling involves partially breaking down the polymers into monomers or oligomers, which can then be purified chemically and reassembled or repurposed [25]. This approach is most readily applied to heteroatom-containing polymers like polyesters, such as polyethylene terephthalate (PET), with hydrolysable ester linkages [26].

**Conclusion**

Recent advancements in catalytic methods have expanded the range of applications for polymer composites. Industries such as aerospace, automotive, electronics, and packaging are reaping the benefits of these materials, which are known for their lightweight nature, high strength, and durability. For example, carbon fiber-reinforced polymer composites, created with the assistance of catalysts, are commonly utilized in aerospace due to their remarkable strength-to-weight ratio. Likewise, composites modified with catalysts to enhance electrical conductivity are increasingly used in electronic devices. These catalytic developments have profoundly influenced the polymer composites sector, resulting in materials that possess superior properties and a wider range of uses. Innovations such as nanocatalysts that improve interfacial bonding and catalysts that optimize curing processes have propelled the evolution of high-performance composites. Additionally, the trend towards sustainable catalysis reflects the increasing demand for eco-friendly materials. As research progresses, further breakthroughs in catalytic approaches are anticipated to unlock new possibilities in polymer composite technology.

# References

1. Zheng, X., Wang, J., & Zhou, H. (2022). Catalytic polymerization for high-performance polymer composites: A review. *Polymer Chemistry, 13*(6), 453-478.

2. Liu, Y., Chen, Q., & Zhao, F. (2020). Nanocatalysts in polymer composites: Advances and applications. *Journal of Materials Science, 55*(10), 3578-3592.

3. Patel, M. K., & Sinha, S. (2019). Advances in catalytic curing of thermosetting polymer composites. *Progress in Organic Coatings, 137*, 105358.

4. Mori, H., & Tanaka, M. (2021). Sustainable catalysis in polymer composites: Current trends and future directions. *Green Chemistry, 23*(7), 2324-2341.

5. Federico Mazur, Andy-Hoai Pham, Rona Chandrawati, Polymer materials as catalysts for medical, environmental, and energy applications. Applied Materials Today, 35, 2023, 101937.

6. Y.H. Lin, et al., J. Am. Soc. Mass Spectrom. 34 (2023) 109–118.

7. Allied Market Research, Catalyst Market Statistics, Trends: Industry Analysis 2030. https://www.alliedmarketresearch.com/catalysts-market, 2023 (accessed 22 March 2023).

8. E. Roduner, Chem. Soc. Rev. 43 (2014) 8226–8239.

9. Rajesh Kumar Verma, Shivi Kesarwani, Jinyang Xu, J. Paulo Davim. Polymer Nanocomposites, Fabrication to Applications. 2023, 320, ISBN9781003343912. https://doi.org/10.1201/9781003343912

10. Delides, C. G. "Everyday life applications of polymer nanocomposites." Technological Educational Institute of Western Macedonia (2016): 1–8.

11. Paul, D. R., and L. M. Robeson. "Polymer nanotechnology: Nanocomposites." Polymer 49, no. 15 (2008): 3187–3204.

12. Hariharan, A. B. A., and H. P. S. Abdul Khalil. "Lignocellulose-based hybrid bilayer laminate composite: Part I-Studies on tensile and impact behavior of oil palm fiber-glass fiber-reinforced epoxy resin." Journal of Composite Materials 39, no. 8 (2005): 663–684.

13. Khan, A., R. A. Khan, S. Salmieri, C. Le Tien, B. Riedl, J. Bouchard, G. Chauve, V. Tan, M. R. Kamal, and M. Lacroix. "Mechanical and barrier properties of nanocrystalline cellulose reinforced chitosan based nanocomposite films." Carbohydrate Polymers 90, no. 4 (2012): 1601–1608.

14. Jadhav, N. C., and A. C. Jadhav. "Synthesis of acrylate epoxidized rice bran oil (AERBO) and its modification using styrene and Shellac to study its properties as a composite material." Polymer Bulletin 80, no. 5 (2022): 5023–5045.

15. Plastics Europe. Plastics The Facts 2022, Plastics Europe: Brussels, 2022. https://plasticseurope.org/knowledge-hub/plasticsthe-facts-2022/ (accessed 2023-11-27).

16. Tang, K. Y.; Chan, C. Y.; Chai, C. H. T.; Low, B. Q. L.; Toh, Z. Y.; Wong, B. W. L.; Heng, J. Z. X.; Li, Z.; Lee, C.-L. K.; Loh, X. J.; Wang, C.-H.; Ye, E. Thermochemical Valorization of Waste

Plastic for Production of Synthetic Fuels, Fine Chemicals, and Carbon Nanotubes. ACS Sustainable Chem. Eng. 2024, 12, 1769−1796.

17. Lange, J.-P. Managing Plastic Waste-Sorting, Recycling, Disposal, and Product Redesign. ACS Sustain. Chem. Eng. 2021, 9, 15722−15738.

18. Pletz, M. Ingested Microplastics: Do Humans Eat One Credit Card per Week? J. Hazard. Mater. Lett. 2022, 3, 100071.

19. Mohamed Nor, N. H.; Kooi, M.; Diepens, N. J.; Koelmans, A. A. Lifetime Accumulation of Microplastic in Children and Adults. Environ. Sci. Technol. 2021, 55, 5084−5096.

20. Jones, M. Microplastics are bad, but ignoring science is worse. R&D World, March 20, 2024. https://www.rdworldonline.com/microplastics-are-bad-but-ignoring-science-is-worse/ (accessed 2024-05-03).

21. Scott, S. L.; Gunnoe, T. B.; Fornasiero, P.; Crudden, C. M. To Err Is Human; To Reproduce Takes Time. ACS Catal. 2022, 12, 3644−3650.

22. Al-Salem, S. M.; Lettieri, P.; Baeyens, J. Recycling and Recovery Routes of Plastic Solid Waste (PSW): A Review. Waste Manag. 2009, 29, 2625−2643.

23. Martey, S.; Addison, B.; Wilson, N.; Tan, B.; Yu, J.; Dorgan, J. R.; Sobkowicz, M. J. Hybrid Chemomechanical Plastics Recycling: Solvent-Free, High-Speed Reactive Extrusion of Low-Density Polyethylene. ChemSusChem 2021, 14, 4280−4290.

24. Lange, J.-P.; Kersten, S. R. A.; De Meester, S.; van Eijk, M. C. P.; Ragaert, K. Plastic Recycling Stripped Naked − from Circular Product to Circular Industry with Recycling Cascade. Chem Sus Chem 2024, e202301320.

25. Ellis, L. D.; Rorrer, N. A.; Sullivan, K. P.; Otto, M.; McGeehan, J. E.; Román-Leshkov, Y.; Wierckx, N.; Beckham, G. T. Chemical and Biological Catalysis for Plastics Recycling and Upcycling. Nat. Catal. 2021, 4, 539−556.

26. Smith, R. L.; Takkellapati, S.; Riegerix, R. C. Recycling of Plastics in the United States: Plastic Material Flows and Polyethylene Terephthalate (PET) Recycling Processes. ACS Sustain. Chem. Eng. 2022, 10, 2084−2096.

# Chapter-4

# 3D Painting Innovations in Composite Materials

Pravin Chavan[1]

Harshad Sonawane[2]

Jaydeep Deore[3]

Shrikrishna Tupare[4]

**Abstract-** Nowadays, this paper explores the innovation of 3D painting in composite polymer materials, focusing on advanced techniques for applying colors, textures, and functional coatings directly to three-dimensional objects. By integrating traditional painting methods with modern 3D printing and coating technologies, this innovation enhances both the aesthetic appeal and performance of composite materials. Key benefits include increased customization options, improved durability through functional coatings, and sustainable materials that reduce environmental impact. The implications of this technology extend across various industries, such as automotive, aerospace, and consumer products, promising to revolutionize design and manufacturing processes [1-5]. As the field continues to evolve, 3D painting represents a significant advancement in applying composite polymers.

Keywords: 3D painting, composite polymer, printing materials, application of polymers.

## Introduction

Recently, 3D painting has become very popular due to their beauty. Day by day the demand for 3D painting is increasing in several fields such as car painting, home walls, wood, plastics, etc. The advent of 3D painting technologies marks a significant shift in the way composite polymer materials are utilized across various industries. Composite polymers, known for their lightweight and durable characteristics, are increasingly being enhanced through innovative painting techniques that allow for the direct application of colors, textures, and functional coatings. This integration of advanced 3D printing and coating technologies with traditional painting methods not only improves the aesthetic quality of products but also enhances their functional properties, such as UV resistance, scratch protection, and even self-healing capabilities. As consumer demand for customization grows, 3D painting offers unprecedented opportunities for personalization, enabling designers and manufacturers to create unique, tailored solutions. Furthermore, the use of sustainable materials in this process aligns

---

[1] *Department of Chemistry, Doshi Vakil Arts College and G.C.U.B. Science & Commerce College, Goregaon-Raigad 402103, Maharashtra, India.*

[2] *Department of Chemistry, G. M. Vedak College of Science, Tala-Raigad, 402111, Maharashtra, India,*

[3] *Department of Chemistry, G. M. Vedak College of Science, Tala-Raigad, 402111, Maharashtra, India,*

[4] *Department of Chemistry, AP Science College, Nagothane-Raigad, 402106, Maharashtra, India.*

Correspondences: *chemistryp141286@gmail.com*

with global efforts to reduce environmental impact and promote eco-friendly practices in manufacturing [1-3].

This introduction sets the stage for a comprehensive exploration of the various techniques involved in 3D painting, the benefits it brings to composite polymer applications, and its implications for the future of design and manufacturing in diverse sectors, including automotive, aerospace, and consumer products. Through this innovation, the potential for enhanced product performance and aesthetic appeal is transforming the landscape of composite materials [4, 5].

Various types of 3D painting are available in the market due to technology and research in the field of composite polymers. Some of the most common are as follows-

### 1. Direct Inkjet Printing:

Direct Inkjet Printing is a cutting-edge technique used to apply colors and designs directly onto three-dimensional objects. This method utilizes inkjet technology, which involves the precise ejection of ink droplets onto the surface of the material. Here's a detailed description of the process and its features:

Direct inkjet printing on materials, especially in the context of 3D painting and composite materials, involves several critical steps to ensure optimal results. Proper preparation enhances adhesion, color accuracy, and overall print quality [6].

***Technology Overview***: *Inkjet Mechanism*: The printer uses a series of tiny nozzles to spray liquid ink onto the object's surface, allowing for detailed and high-resolution images. *And Layer-by-Layer Application*: The printing occurs in layers, allowing for complex designs and gradations of color.

***Material Compatibility***: Direct inkjet printing can be applied to various materials, including plastics, metals, ceramics, and composite polymers. Specialized inks are available to enhance adhesion and durability on different surfaces.

***Customization***: This technique allows for extensive customization options, making it ideal for personalized products, prototypes, and small-batch manufacturing. Users can easily change designs, colors, and graphics without the need for extensive setup.

***Efficiency***: Direct inkjet printing is generally faster than traditional painting methods since it requires fewer manual processes. The ability to print directly onto finished or partially finished objects streamlines production workflows.

***Environmental Considerations***: Many ink formulations are eco-friendly, using water-based or biodegradable inks, which reduce the environmental impact compared to solvent-based paints.

***Applications:*** Commonly used in industries such as automotive, consumer electronics, packaging, and promotional products. Ideal for creating intricate patterns, logos, and full-color images on a variety of products.

***Post-Processing Options***: Printed surfaces can be further enhanced with protective coatings to improve durability and resistance to wear and tear.

***Advantages:*** *High Resolution*: Produces sharp and vibrant images. *Flexibility*: Capable of printing complex designs that may be difficult to achieve with traditional methods. *Speed:* Reduces production time for custom designs.

***Drawbacks:*** *Material Limitations*: Some materials may require special treatment to ensure proper ink adhesion. *Durability*: Depending on the inks used, printed designs may need additional protective coatings to enhance longevity [6, 7].

## 2. Stereolithography (SLA)

Stereolithography (SLA) is a popular additive manufacturing technique that utilizes a laser to cure liquid resin into solid objects layer by layer. It is known for its high precision and ability to produce intricate designs, making it widely used in various industries, including prototyping, dental, and jewelry. Stereolithography (SLA) is an advanced 3D printing technology that uses a laser to cure liquid resin into solid objects layer by layer. Proper preparation is essential to achieve high-quality prints with accurate dimensions and excellent surface finish [8].

*Process Overview:*

- *Resin Tank*: The SLA process begins with a tank filled with liquid photopolymer resin.
- *Laser Curing*: A UV laser beam selectively cures the resin according to the design, solidifying it layer by layer. The laser traces the cross-section of the object based on a digital model.
- *Build Platform:* The build platform is submerged in the resin tank. After each layer is cured, the platform moves down slightly to allow for the next layer to be added.

**High Precision and Detail**: SLA is capable of producing parts with exceptional detail and smooth surface finishes, making it suitable for applications that require intricate designs. The layer thickness can be adjusted, allowing for fine resolutions and complex geometries.

*Material Options*: A variety of photopolymer resins are available, including standard, flexible, durable, and high-temperature materials. Specialized resins can be used for specific applications, such as biocompatible materials for dental and medical uses.

*Speed:* While SLA is generally faster than some other methods of 3D printing, the total time depends on the size and complexity of the part, as well as the layer thickness settings.

*Post-Processing*: After printing, the parts typically require post-curing under UV light to ensure full hardness and durability. Additional steps may include cleaning to remove uncured resin and finishing processes like sanding or painting [8, 9].

Applications:

- *Prototyping:* Creating functional prototypes for testing and design validation.
- *Dental*: Producing dental models, aligners, and surgical guides.
- *Jewellery:* Crafting intricate designs and molds for casting.

*Advantages:*

- *High Detail and Accuracy*: Produces parts with very fine details and smooth finishes.
- *Versatile Material Choices:* A wide range of resins tailored for different applications.
- *Rapid Prototyping*: Facilitates quick iterations in product development.

*Drawbacks:*

- *Material Properties*: SLA parts may be less durable than those produced with some other techniques like FDM, particularly in terms of impact resistance.
- *Support Structures*: Complex designs may require support structures, which need to be removed post-printing.
- *Cost*: SLA printers and materials can be more expensive compared to other 3D printing technologies [8,9].

## 3. Fused Deposition Modelling (FDM)

Fused Deposition Modelling (FDM) is a widely used 3D printing technology known for its simplicity and versatility. It works by extruding thermoplastic filament to create objects layer by layer. Fused Deposition Modeling (FDM) is a popular 3D printing technology that uses thermoplastic materials to build objects layer by layer. Proper preparation is essential to ensure successful prints with good adhesion, accuracy, and surface quality [10].

*Process*: FDM uses spools of thermoplastic filament, which are fed into a heated nozzle. The nozzle heats the filament until it melts, then extrudes it onto a build platform in a controlled manner. The printer lays down the melted filament in thin layers, fusing each layer to the one below it as it cools and solidifies [11].

*Material Options*: FDM can utilize a variety of thermoplastic materials, including:

- PLA (Polylactic Acid): Biodegradable and easy to print, suitable for beginners.
- ABS (Acrylonitrile Butadiene Styrene): Strong and heat-resistant, commonly used for functional parts.
- PETG (Polyethylene Terephthalate Glycol-Modified): Offers a balance of strength and flexibility.
- TPU (Thermoplastic Polyurethane): Flexible and rubber-like, ideal for applications requiring elasticity.

*Build Size*: FDM printers come in various sizes, allowing for the production of small to large parts. The build volume is a key consideration when choosing a printer.

*Layer Height and Resolution*: The layer height can be adjusted, allowing users to choose between faster prints with thicker layers or finer details with thinner layers. Common layer heights range from 0.1 mm to 0.3 mm.

*Cost-Effectiveness*: FDM technology is often more affordable than other 3D printing methods, both in terms of printer cost and material expenses, making it accessible for hobbyists and small businesses.

*Post-Processing*: Depending on the desired finish, FDM parts may require post-processing, such as sanding, painting, or assembly of multiple parts.

*Benefits:*

- User-Friendly: Generally easy to set up and operate, making it suitable for beginners.

- ❖ Material Variety: A wide selection of materials, including specialty filaments for specific applications.
- ❖ Robustness: FDM prints can produce functional parts suitable for prototyping and end-use applications.

***Drawbacks:*** Surface Finish: FDM prints can have visible layer lines, which may require finishing for aesthetic purposes. Strength Limitations: Parts may have anisotropic properties, meaning strength can vary depending on the layer orientation. Warping and Adhesion: Certain materials can warp during printing, requiring careful management of print settings and environments [10-12].

## 4. Multi-material Printing

Multi-material Printing is an advanced 3D printing technique that enables the simultaneous use of different materials in a single build process. This capability allows for the creation of complex, functional parts that combine various properties, such as strength, flexibility, and aesthetic appeal. Multi-material printing allows for the simultaneous use of different materials or colors in a single print, enhancing the functionality and aesthetic appeal of the final product. Proper preparation is essential to ensure compatibility, adhesion, and overall print quality.

***Process:*** Printer Configuration: Multi-material printers can have multiple extruders or print heads, each capable of handling different materials. Some systems use a single nozzle with multiple feed lines. Layered Approach: During printing, different materials are deposited layer by layer according to the design specifications, allowing for precise control over material placement [13].

***Material Variety:*** Multi-material printing can incorporate a range of materials, including:

- ❖ Rigid Plastics: For structural components.
- ❖ Flexible Materials: Such as thermoplastic elastomers for soft or rubber-like parts.
- ❖ Composites: Materials enhanced with fibers or other additives for improved mechanical properties.
- ❖ Support Materials: Soluble supports can be used to create complex geometries without visible artifacts once removed.

***Applications:***

- ❖ Functional Prototypes: Ideal for creating prototypes that require varying properties within the same part.
- ❖ Consumer Products: Used in products that require different textures or functionalities, like grip surfaces or aesthetic details.
- ❖ Medical Devices: Custom implants or tools that combine rigidity and flexibility can be produced.

***Design Flexibility:*** Designers can optimize parts by strategically using materials where they are most needed, enhancing performance and reducing weight. Multi-material printing allows for intricate designs that would be difficult or impossible to achieve with single-material printing.

***Enhanced Aesthetics:*** The ability to mix colors and materials creates visually appealing products, enabling unique designs and branding opportunities.

***Benefits:*** Performance Optimization: Combines the best properties of different materials within a single part, enhancing overall functionality. Reduced Assembly: Parts that would traditionally require multiple components can be printed as a single unit, simplifying assembly and reducing potential failure points. Customizability: Facilitates the production of bespoke items tailored to specific user needs.

***Drawbacks:*** Complexity: Requires sophisticated printers and may involve more complex design and setup processes. Material Compatibility: Not all materials bond well with each other, which can limit combinations. Cost: Multi-material printers and the associated materials can be more expensive than traditional single-material systems.

Multi-material Printing is a transformative 3D printing technology that allows for the integration of various materials in a single print. This capability enhances design flexibility, improves product functionality, and opens new possibilities across a range of industries, from automotive to healthcare and consumer goods [13].

## 5. 3D Airbrushing

3D Airbrushing is a technique used to apply paint and other finishes directly onto three-dimensional objects, enhancing their aesthetics and surface quality. This method leverages the precision and control of airbrush technology to create intricate designs, textures, and color gradients. 3D airbrushing is an innovative technique used to apply detailed colors and textures to three-dimensional objects, enhancing their aesthetics and providing a professional finish. Proper preparation is essential to achieve smooth and even coverage.

***Process:*** Airbrush Tool: A specialized airbrush gun is used, which atomizes paint into fine particles and propels them onto the object's surface using compressed air. Control: The artist can control the flow of paint, air pressure, and nozzle size, allowing for detailed work and varying spray patterns. Layering: Multiple layers can be applied to achieve depth, shading, and complex effects, similar to traditional painting techniques [14].

***Material Compatibility:*** 3D airbrushing can be used on various materials, including plastics, metals, ceramics, and even some types of resin. Different types of paint can be used, such as acrylics, enamels, and specialty paints designed for specific finishes.

***Customization and Detail:*** This technique is ideal for custom designs, enabling artists to create unique patterns, textures, and gradients that enhance the visual appeal of the object. Intricate details can be achieved, making it suitable for applications in art, model-making, and product design.

***Applications:***

- ❖ Hobbyist and Art Projects: Popular among artists and model enthusiasts for custom painting figurines, models, and sculptures.

- ❖ Automotive: Used in custom vehicle painting and detailing, allowing for personalized designs and finishes.

- ❖ Prototyping and Product Design: Enhances prototypes with realistic finishes to better visualize the final product [14].

*Finishing Techniques*: After airbrushing, additional treatments such as clear coats can be applied to protect the finish and enhance durability. Techniques like masking can be used to create sharp lines and defined areas of color.

**Benefits:** Precision: Offers high levels of control, enabling detailed work and smooth transitions between colors. Versatility: Can be used for a wide range of applications, from fine art to industrial design. Customizability: Ideal for personalized or one-off projects, allowing for creative expression.

**Limitations:** Skill Level: Requires practice and skill to master, particularly for achieving specific effects and maintaining consistency. Setup Time: The setup process can be more involved compared to simpler painting methods. Ventilation: Proper ventilation is necessary when working with certain paints to avoid inhaling fumes.

3D airbrushing is a versatile and precise technique that enhances the aesthetic qualities of three-dimensional objects. Its ability to create intricate designs and textures makes it valuable in various fields, from art and modeling to automotive customization and product design [14].

## 6. Hydrographic Printing (Water Transfer Printing)

Hydrographic Printing, also known as Water Transfer Printing or Hydrographics, is a technique used to apply intricate patterns, images, or textures onto three-dimensional objects. This method involves a unique process where a design is transferred from a special film onto a surface using water [15].

*Process*:

- Preparation: The object to be printed is first cleaned and prepped, ensuring the surface is smooth and free of contaminants.
- Film Selection: A specialized hydrographic film, which contains the desired design, is chosen. This film is printed with water-soluble ink.
- Activation: The film is laid on the surface of water in a tank. A chemical activator is then sprayed onto the film, causing the ink to dissolve and the design to become floating.
- Transfer: The prepared object is dipped into the water, where the floating ink wraps around the surface, conforming to its shape.
- Curing: After the transfer, the object is removed, rinsed to remove excess film, and then cured, usually by applying a clear coat to protect the design.

*Material Compatibility*: Hydrographic printing can be applied to a wide range of materials, including plastics, metals, wood, and ceramics, making it highly versatile.

*Design Versatility*: This technique allows for the application of complex patterns, such as carbon fiber, camouflage, wood grain, and other decorative finishes that would be difficult to achieve through traditional painting methods. Custom designs can be created, allowing for the personalization of products.

*Applications*:

- ❖ Automotive: Commonly used for customizing vehicle interiors, exterior parts, and accessories with unique finishes.
- ❖ Consumer Products: Applied to items such as electronics, sporting goods, and home decor.
- ❖ Industrial: Used for creating branded products and promotional items with visually appealing graphics.

***Benefits:*** Aesthetic Appeal: Provides a high-quality, professional finish with detailed designs. Wide Range of Designs: Can replicate intricate patterns that would be challenging to paint manually. Customization: Ideal for creating one-of-a-kind items tailored to individual preferences.

***Drawbacks:*** Surface Preparation: Requires thorough preparation to ensure a smooth transfer and adherence of the design. Complexity: The process can be more complex and time-consuming compared to traditional painting techniques. Limitations on Size: The size of the water tank can limit the size of the objects that can be printed.

Hydrographic Printing is a versatile and effective method for applying intricate designs and textures to three-dimensional objects. Its ability to produce detailed and vibrant finishes makes it a popular choice across various industries, from automotive customization to consumer products and artistic applications [15-16].

## 7. Laser Etching and Engraving

In this study, Laser Etching and Engraving are advanced manufacturing processes that utilize laser technology to create designs, patterns, or inscriptions on various materials. These techniques are widely used in a range of applications, including industrial marking, artistic designs, and product customization. Laser etching and engraving are precise techniques used to create detailed designs, patterns, or text on a variety of materials. Proper preparation is essential to ensure high-quality results and to maximize the effectiveness of the laser process [17].

***Techniques:***

- ❖ Laser Technology: A focused beam of laser light is directed onto the material's surface. The intensity and focus of the laser can be adjusted based on the desired effect.
- ❖ Etching: Involves removing a thin layer of material from the surface to create a design or pattern. This process typically results in a lighter mark compared to engraving.
- ❖ Engraving: Involves deeper penetration of the laser into the material, resulting in a more pronounced and permanent marking. This can create a three-dimensional effect.

***Material Compatibility:*** Laser etching and engraving can be performed on a wide variety of materials, including:

- ❖ Metals: Such as aluminum, stainless steel, and brass.
- ❖ Plastics: Various types can be etched or engraved for branding or design purposes.
- ❖ Wood: Ideal for creating intricate designs and personalized items.
- ❖ Glass and Ceramics: Used for decorative items and awards.

*Applications*:

- ❖ Industrial Marking: Used for barcodes, serial numbers, and company logos on products.
- ❖ Custom Products: Ideal for personalized gifts, trophies, and promotional items.
- ❖ Art and Design: Artists use laser engraving to create detailed works on various substrates.

***Speed and Efficiency***: Laser engraving and etching are generally faster than manual methods, enabling quick production and customization. Minimal setup time is required, particularly for digital designs, making it suitable for small-batch production.

**Benefits:** High Precision: Capable of producing detailed and accurate markings. Versatility: Applicable to a wide range of materials and suitable for various applications. Minimal Waste: The laser process reduces material waste compared to traditional cutting or engraving methods.

*Drawbacks:*

- ❖ Material Limitations: Not all materials are suitable for laser etching or engraving; some may require special handling.
- ❖ Cost of Equipment: High-quality laser engraving machines can be expensive, which may be a barrier for small businesses or hobbyists.
- ❖ Heat-Affected Zone: The heat generated during the process can affect the material properties, especially in sensitive materials.

Laser Etching and Engraving are powerful techniques that leverage laser technology to create precise and detailed designs on various materials. Their versatility and efficiency make them popular choices for industrial applications, product customization, and artistic endeavors [17, 18].

## 8. Electrostatic Painting

Electrostatic Painting is a method of applying paint or coatings to surfaces using electrostatic charges to enhance adhesion and achieve a uniform finish. This technique is widely used in industrial applications, particularly for metal surfaces, but can also be applied to various materials. Electrostatic painting is a technique that uses electrical charges to apply paint to surfaces, resulting in a uniform and efficient coating. Proper preparation is crucial for achieving optimal adhesion, finish quality, and overall effectiveness of the process.

***Techniques***: Electrostatic Charge: In this process, the paint particles are electrically charged, typically using an electrostatic spray gun. The surface to be painted is grounded or given an opposite charge. Attraction: The charged paint particles are attracted to the oppositely charged surface, allowing for an even application and reducing overspray. Application: The paint is sprayed onto the object, where it adheres due to the electrostatic force, ensuring a uniform coating with minimal waste [19].

***Material Compatibility***: Electrostatic painting is primarily used on metals, such as steel and aluminum, but it can also be effective on some plastics and other conductive materials. Various types of paints and coatings can be used, including powder coatings and liquid paints.

*Benefits:*

- ❖ Efficient Material Use: The process reduces overspray and paint waste, making it a cost-effective option.
- ❖ Uniform Finish: The electrostatic attraction helps achieve a consistent and smooth coating, even in complex geometries.
- ❖ Environmentally Friendly: Many electrostatic painting processes use low-VOC (volatile organic compounds) paints, making it a greener choice compared to traditional spraying methods.
- ❖ Durability: Electrostatic coatings often have excellent adhesion and resistance to chipping, scratching, and corrosion, resulting in long-lasting finishes.

*Applications:*

- ❖ Industrial Coating: Commonly used for coating metal components in manufacturing, automotive, and appliance industries.
- ❖ Furniture and Fixtures: Used in the finishing of furniture, light fixtures, and other decorative elements.
- ❖ Architectural Applications: Effective for outdoor structures, railings, and metal siding, providing protection and aesthetic appeal.

***Equipment and Setup:*** The electrostatic painting process requires specialized equipment, including spray guns with electrostatic capabilities, a grounding system for the workpieces, and spray booths for containment. Proper training is essential to operate the equipment effectively and safely.

***Drawbacks:*** Surface Preparation: Thorough cleaning and preparation of the surface are necessary to ensure good adhesion. Material Restrictions: Non-conductive materials may not be suitable for electrostatic painting unless specially treated. Equipment Costs: Initial investment in electrostatic equipment can be higher than traditional painting systems.

In summary, Electrostatic Painting is an efficient and effective method for applying coatings to a variety of surfaces. Its ability to create uniform finishes with minimal waste makes it a popular choice in many industrial applications, contributing to both aesthetic and protective qualities in the final product [19].

## 9. Textured Coatings

Textured Coatings are specialized finishes applied to surfaces to create a tactile, three-dimensional effect. These coatings enhance both the visual and functional aspects of a variety of materials, offering improved aesthetics, durability, and grip. Textured coatings are used to enhance the aesthetic appeal and functionality of surfaces by providing a three-dimensional texture. This preparation guide outlines the steps necessary to achieve a successful application of textured coatings [20].

***Methodology:*** Application Methods: Textured coatings can be applied using various techniques, including spraying, rolling, brushing, or trowelling, depending on the desired texture and finish. Materials: They can be made from a range of substances, including paints, polymers, and specialty compounds that incorporate additives for texture.

*Textures types*:

- ❖ Rough Textures: Created using coarse aggregates or materials that provide a rugged surface, enhancing grip and slip resistance.
- ❖ Smooth Textures: Offer a subtle, soft finish while still adding visual interest, often used for decorative purposes.
- ❖ Patterned Textures: Involve specific patterns or designs, which can be achieved through stencils or textured rollers, allowing for creative customization.

*Material Compatibility*: Textured coatings can be applied to various substrates, including wood, metal, concrete, and plastic, making them versatile for different applications.

*Applications*:

- ❖ Architectural: Used on walls, ceilings, and exteriors to create visually appealing finishes while improving durability.
- ❖ Industrial: Often applied to surfaces requiring high levels of abrasion resistance or slip resistance, such as flooring and machinery.
- ❖ Automotive: Utilized in vehicle interiors and exteriors for aesthetic enhancement and improved grip on surfaces like dashboards and handles.
- ❖ Consumer Products: Found in items such as furniture, appliances, and electronic devices to improve tactile feel and visual appeal.

*Benefits:* Customization: Offers a wide range of textures and finishes, allowing for creative expression in design. Versatile Applications: Suitable for both indoor and outdoor use, across various industries and products. Ease of Maintenance: Many textured coatings are designed to be easy to clean and maintain, making them practical for everyday use.

*Limitations*: Application Complexity: Achieving a uniform texture may require skill and experience, especially for intricate designs. Drying Time: Some textured coatings may require longer drying or curing times, impacting project timelines. Cost: Depending on the materials and techniques used, textured coatings can be more expensive than standard finishes.

Textured Coatings are an effective way to enhance both the appearance and functionality of various surfaces. Their versatility and aesthetic appeal make them popular in numerous applications, from architectural and industrial uses to consumer products and automotive finishes [20].

## 10. Augmented Reality (AR) Painting

Augmented Reality (AR) Painting is an innovative technique that blends the physical and digital worlds, allowing users to create and interact with art in immersive environments. Using AR technology, artists and users can visualize, manipulate, and enhance their artwork through digital overlays that augment their real-world surroundings. Augmented Reality (AR) painting combines digital creativity with real-world environments, allowing artists to create immersive experiences. Preparing for AR painting involves both technical and creative steps to ensure seamless integration of digital elements [21].

***Methodology:*** AR Devices: AR painting typically uses smartphones, tablets, or AR glasses equipped with cameras and display screens to overlay digital images onto the real world. Software Applications: Specialized AR painting applications allow users to create, edit, and interact with their artwork in real-time, using intuitive gestures and controls.

***Layering and Depth:*** AR painting allows for the layering of digital elements, adding depth and complexity to the artwork. Artists can incorporate various textures, colors, and effects that might not be achievable on a physical canvas. The ability to manipulate and reposition elements in a 3D space provides a unique level of creative freedom.

***Interactive Experience:*** Users can paint in a 3D space, where their movements are tracked, enabling them to create large-scale or intricate designs that extend beyond traditional canvases. The technology allows for real-time feedback, enabling artists to see their creations immediately and adjust them as needed.

***Collaboration and Sharing***: Many AR painting platforms enable collaborative work, where multiple users can contribute to a single piece of artwork, regardless of their physical location. Finished pieces can be easily shared on social media or exported for printing, allowing for wider dissemination of digital art.

***Applications:***

- Art and Design: Artists can explore new creative possibilities and experiment with designs in a virtual space.
- Education: AR painting can be used in educational settings to teach art techniques and concepts interactively.
- Marketing and Advertising: Brands can create engaging campaigns that allow consumers to interact with products in augmented reality, enhancing brand experiences.

***Benefits:***

- Creative Freedom: Offers a limitless canvas for artists, enabling them to push the boundaries of traditional art forms.
- Engagement: The interactive nature of AR painting can attract and engage audiences, making art more accessible and appealing.
- Innovation: Combines traditional artistic techniques with modern technology, fostering new styles and methods of expression.

***Drawbacks:*** Technical Skills: Users may need some familiarity with technology and software to fully leverage AR painting tools. Equipment Dependency: Requires access to compatible devices and software, which may not be available to everyone. User Experience: The quality of the experience can vary based on the device used and the app's capabilities, potentially affecting the artistic process.

Augmented Reality (AR) Painting is a groundbreaking approach that merges the digital and physical realms, offering artists and users new avenues for creativity and expression. Its interactive features and immersive experiences make it an exciting tool for art creation, education, and marketing, paving the way for innovative artistic possibilities [21, 22].

## Conclusion

We concluded that the innovation of 3D painting in composite polymer materials represents a significant advancement in manufacturing and design, merging aesthetic appeal with functional enhancement. By leveraging various techniques such as direct inkjet printing, stereolithography, multi-material printing, and electrostatic painting, this technology allows for the creation of intricate designs and customized finishes on complex geometries. 3D painting not only elevates the visual aspects of composite polymer products but also contributes to their performance characteristics, such as durability and surface integrity. The ability to apply textures, colors, and functional coatings directly onto composite materials opens up new avenues for creativity in industries ranging from automotive and aerospace to consumer goods and medical devices. As technology continues to evolve, the potential for 3D painting in composite polymer materials will expand further, facilitating more sustainable practices, reducing waste, and enabling greater personalization. This intersection of artistry and engineering not only enhances product appeal but also meets the growing demand for customized solutions in today's market. Embracing these innovative techniques will undoubtedly lead to transformative applications and a new era of design in composite materials.

## References

1. Velu, R., Raspall, F., & Singamneni, S. (2019). 3D printing technologies and composite materials for structural applications. In *Green composites for automotive applications* (pp. 171-196). Woodhead Publishing.

2. Park, S., Shou, W., Makatura, L., Matusik, W., & Fu, K. K. (2022). 3D printing of polymer composites: Materials, processes, and applications. *Matter*, *5*(1), 43-76.

3. Bhong, M., Khan, T. K., Devade, K., Krishna, B. V., Sura, S., Eftikhaar, H. K., ... & Gupta, N. (2023). Review of composite materials and applications. *Materials Today: Proceedings*.

4. Iftekar, S. F., Aabid, A., Amir, A., & Baig, M. (2023). Advancements and limitations in 3D printing materials and technologies: a critical review. *Polymers*, *15*(11), 2519.

5. Zhang, L., Du, W., Nautiyal, A., Liu, Z., & Zhang, X. (2018). Recent progress on nanostructured conducting polymers and composites: synthesis, application and future aspects. *Sci. China Mater*, *61*(3), 303-352.

6. Lee, K. J., Jun, B. H., Kim, T. H., & Joung, J. (2006). Direct synthesis and inkjetting of silver nanocrystals toward printed electronics. *Nanotechnology*, *17*(9), 2424.

7. Lee, Y., Choi, J. R., Lee, K. J., Stott, N. E., & Kim, D. (2008). Large-scale synthesis of copper nanoparticles by chemically controlled reduction for applications of inkjet-printed electronics. *Nanotechnology*, *19*(41), 415604.

8. Oliaei, S. N. B., & Nasseri, B. (2020). 6. Stereolithography and its applications. *Additive and Subtractive Manufacturing*, *1*, 229-250.

9. Kushwaha, A. K., Rahman, M. H., Hart, D., Hughes, B., Saldana, D. A., Zollars, C., ... & Menezes, P. L. (2022). Fundamentals of stereolithography: techniques, properties, and applications. In *Tribology of Additively Manufactured Materials* (pp. 87-106). Elsevier.

10. Cano-Vicent, A., Tambuwala, M. M., Hassan, S. S., Barh, D., Aljabali, A. A., Birkett, M., ... & Serrano-Aroca, Á. (2021). Fused deposition modelling: Current status, methodology, applications and future prospects. *Additive manufacturing*, *47*, 102378.

11. Mohan, N., Senthil, P., Vinodh, S., & Jayanth, N. (2017). A review on composite materials and process parameters optimisation for the fused deposition modelling process. *Virtual and Physical Prototyping*, *12*(1), 47-59.

12. Long, J., Gholizadeh, H., Lu, J., Bunt, C., & Seyfoddin, A. (2017). Application of fused deposition modelling (FDM) method of 3D printing in drug delivery. *Current pharmaceutical design*, *23*(3), 433-439.

13. Shaukat, U., Rossegger, E., & Schlögl, S. (2022). A review of multi-material 3D printing of functional materials via vat photopolymerization. *Polymers*, *14*(12), 2449.

14. Schneider, R., Facure, M. H., Chagas, P. A., Andre, R. S., dos Santos, D. M., & Correa, D. S. (2021). Tailoring the surface properties of micro/nanofibers using 0D, 1D, 2D, and 3D nanostructures: a review on post-modification methods. *Advanced Materials Interfaces*, *8*(13), 2100430.

15. Sarkodie, B., Tawiah, B., Agbo, C., & Wizi, J. (2018). Status and development of transfer printing in textiles—A review. *AATCC Journal of Research*, *5*(2), 1-18.

16. Li, X., Chen, L., Ma, Y., Weng, D., Li, Z., Song, L., ... & Wang, J. (2022). Ultrafast Fabrication of Large-Area Colloidal Crystal Micropatterns via Self-Assembly and Transfer Printing. *Advanced Functional Materials*, *32*(45), 2205462.

17. Sarkar, S. K. (2022). Lasers in Materials Processing and Synthesis. *Handbook on Synthesis Strategies for Advanced Materials: Volume-II: Processing and Functionalization of Materials*, 791-831.

18. Cao, Y., Zeng, X., Cai, Z., & Duan, J. (2010). Laser micro/nano-fabrication techniques and their applications in electronics. In *Advances in Laser Materials Processing* (pp. 629-670). Woodhead Publishing.

19. Prasad, L. K., McGinity, J. W., & Williams III, R. O. (2016). Electrostatic powder coating: Principles and pharmaceutical applications. *International journal of pharmaceutics*, *505*(1-2), 289-302.

20. Nguyen-Tri, P., Tran, H. N., Plamondon, C. O., Tuduri, L., Vo, D. V. N., Nanda, S., ... & Bajpai, A. K. (2019). Recent progress in the preparation, properties and applications of superhydrophobic nano-based coatings and surfaces: A review. *Progress in organic coatings*, *132*, 235-256.

21. Sahu, C. K., Young, C., & Rai, R. (2021). Artificial intelligence (AI) in augmented reality (AR)-assisted manufacturing applications: a review. *International Journal of Production Research*, *59*(16), 4903-4959.

22. Dargan, S., Bansal, S., Kumar, M., Mittal, A., & Kumar, K. (2023). Augmented reality: A comprehensive review. *Archives of Computational Methods in Engineering*, *30*(2), 1057-1080

# Chapter-5

# Predicting the Next Decade in Polymer Composite Technologies: the Role of Islamic Endowment

Adamu Abubakar Muhammad[1]

Adam Muhammad Ardo[2]

Musa Hamza[3]

Ibrahim Dahiru Idriss[4]

## Abstract

This chapter examines the prospects for polymer composite technologies over the next years, highlighting the vital role that Islamic endowments, or Waqf, will play in promoting sustainability and innovation in the industry. The need for strong, lightweight, and environmentally friendly materials is driving acceleration in polymer composites research and development. The integration of nanotechnology, the growth of bio-based composites, and the creation of smart materials are just a few of the current developments covered in this chapter. It demonstrates how Waqf may make a substantial difference by sponsoring research and development (R&D), helping startups, encouraging education and training, and encouraging cooperation amongst different stakeholders. The chapter demonstrates the beneficial effects of Waqf on economic growth and technological advancement through an analysis of successful case studies. In the end, it offers a picture of a future when moral standards will direct the creation of polymer composites, in line with Islamic beliefs and tackling major international issues related to sustainability and innovation.

Keywords: **Decade, Islamic Endowment, Polymer Composite, Technologie.**

## Introduction

Over the past few decades, there has been a significant shift in the field of polymer composite technology. The importance of polymer composites is only increasing as businesses look for materials that are strong, lightweight, and environmentally friendly (Asyraf, et al., 2022). The upcoming years hold the possibility of novel developments propelled not just by scientific breakthroughs but also by socio-economic variables, such as the distinct impact of Islamic endowments (Waqf). Potential advancements in polymer composite technologies are examined in this chapter; along with the critical

---

[1] Department of Religious Studies, Faculty of Humanities, Federal University of Kashere, Gombe State Nigeria
E-mail: abubakaradamu1980@gmail.com,

[2] Modibbo Yusufa Foundation, New GRA Gombe State, Nigeria

[3] Department of Islamic Studies, Federal University of Education Zaria, Kaduna State Nigeria

[4] Federal College of Education (Technical) Potiskum, Yobe State Nigeria

role Islamic endowments can play in promoting research, development, and implementation. Polymer composites, owing to their special qualities including high strength-to-weight ratios, resistance to corrosion, and adaptability in a range of applications, have become essential materials for a number of sectors (Delvere, et al., 2019). Thanks to developments in polymer composite technologies over the last few decades, these materials are now widely used in a variety of industries, including electronics, automotive, aerospace, and building (Kumar et al., 2020). Innovations like bio-based composites and smart materials that react to environmental stimuli are the result of these materials being progressively customized to fulfill specific performance needs (Mohanty et al., 2021; Zhang et al., 2019).

On the other hand, serious difficulties are presented by the quick development of polymer composite technologies. These include the creation of high-performance composites that can satisfy demanding industry standards, the necessity of sustainable production techniques, and the effective recycling of composite materials (Khan et al., 2022; Ather et al., 2021). Researchers and industry are being forced to look for new and creative solutions as the need for eco-friendly materials and procedures increases along with the global awareness of environmental challenges.

Islamic endowments, or Waqfs, are a distinct type of socioeconomic organization that could have an impact on developments in polymer composite technology. In the past, Waqf has been essential in providing funds for infrastructure, healthcare, and education, which has promoted innovation and community development (Ali, S.N & Oseni, 2021).

By channeling resources into research and development, Waqf can greatly impact the growth of sustainable polymer composite technologies, harmonizing with both Islamic ideals of stewardship and the worldwide push for sustainability.

The potential improvements in polymer composite technologies notwithstanding, little is known about how ethical finance systems and innovation interact. It is not well understood how Islamic endowments might best support the advancement and use of these technologies, especially in terms of encouraging sustainability and moral behavior. The majority of the literature currently in publication concentrates on the technical aspects of polymer composites, with little attention paid to the socio-economic aspects, such as Waqf's role in promoting research, helping startups, and encouraging cooperation between academia and industry (El-Gayar et al., 2021; Ali & Al-Otaibi, 2020).

The following inquiries are the focus of this study: In what ways might Islamic endowments help the advancement of technology involving polymer composites? What particular tactics can be used to make the most of Waqf resources for long-term innovation in this area? By examining these issues, the research hopes to offer a framework for fusing moral funding sources with cutting-edge scientific discoveries, ultimately paving the way for a more sustainable future for polymer composites.

**Methodology**

The properties, composition, and uses of polymer composites are being studied methodically in polymer composite research. The methods and techniques used to collect and process the study's data are described in this section.

1. Research Design

The present investigation used an exploratory research design to examine the attributes, varieties, benefits, and obstacles associated with polymer composites. Exploratory research is appropriate because it offers insight into different materials, their qualities, and their applications while enabling a thorough understanding of a rather large topic.

## 2. Review of Literature

The principal approach of gathering data is a thorough examination of scholarly works on polymer composites. Books, industry reports, and pertinent peer-reviewed journal papers were compiled to offer insights into:

i. Types of polymer composite.

ii. Physical and mechanical characteristics.

iii. Applications in the construction, automotive, and aerospace industries.

iv. Obstacles like price and recyclable nature.

v. Upcoming developments in composite polymer materials.

We used databases including Science Direct, Google Scholar, and Scopus to find pertinent papers published between 2014 and 2024. To locate relevant research, search phrases like fiber-reinforced composites, particle composites, polymer nanocomposites, and natural fiber composites were employed. The list contained only English-language publications.

## 3. Material Selection Criteria

A portion of the study concentrates on examining particular polymer composite systems according to their reinforcement (particles or fibers) and matrix (thermoplastic or thermoset). The following criteria were used to choose studies on these systems:

a. Composition of polymer composites: Studies that specify the precise kind of polymer matrix (such as epoxy or polypropylene) and the reinforcement materials (such as glass, carbon, or natural fibers) that are used in polymer composites. Metrics for measuring mechanical performance include impact resistance, flexural strength, and tensile strength.

b. Environmental considerations: Articles that talk about how polymer composite systems affect the environment, are sustainable, or can be recycled.

## 4. Methods of Data Analysis

An analysis of the qualitative content was performed on the information gathered from the literature review. Using this approach, the text can be carefully examined to find recurrent themes, trends, and patterns related to the application and functionality of polymer composites. The essential actions consist of:

i. Data extraction: Important details about polymer composites, such as their mechanical characteristics, uses, benefits, and drawbacks, were retrieved and compiled for comparison.

ii. Categorization: The themes of varieties of polymer composites, their benefits, their applications in various industries, and future developments were used to categorize the extracted data.

iii. Synthesis of findings: The data were combined to give readers a clear and thorough grasp of the many facets of polymer composites, including present developments and untapped potential for further study.

5. Authenticity and Trustworthiness

The following procedures were followed by the study to guarantee the validity and reliability of the results:

i. Triangulation: In order to confirm the consistency of findings across several investigations, data from several sources were compared and contrasted.

ii. References that have undergone peer review: To ensure the academic rigor and dependability of the data, only articles from reputable, peer-reviewed journals were taken into consideration.

6. Ethical Considerations

Since this study only uses secondary data from other publications, there were no explicit ethical issues with using human or animal subjects. However, in order to prevent plagiarism and to provide correct acknowledgment to the original writers, appropriate academic reference and referencing guidelines were followed.

7. Limitations of the Study

This study's main limitation is its reliance on secondary data, which can be limited by the volume and accessibility of the body of current research. Furthermore, although the research strategy is exploratory, polymer composites are not tested in real-world settings or through experimental validation.

This technique provides a thorough literature analysis as a means of outlining an organized procedure for obtaining and evaluating data on polymer composites. The methodology enables an in-depth examination of the subject while guaranteeing the incorporation of many sources and viewpoints, offering a strong basis for comprehending the characteristics, uses, and potential developments of polymer composites.

**Literature Review**

1. Introduction to Polymer Composites

Materials called polymer composites are created by mixing polymers with additional materials typically fillers or fibers to improve the materials' mechanical, thermal, or chemical characteristics (AL-Oqla et al., 2023). Because of their great strength, low weight, and adaptability, these materials have drawn a lot of interest from a variety of industries, they offer a balance between performances, and weight reduction, and cost-effectiveness, polymer composites have transformed engineering sectors (Pati, et al., 2014).

2. Definition and Composition of Polymer Composites

In essence, a polymer composite is a multi-phase material consisting of a polymer matrix and a dispersed reinforcing phase, typically in the form of fibers or particles. Glass, carbon, aramid, or natural fibers like sisal and jute are frequently used as reinforcing materials, whereas the matrix can be constructed of thermoplastic or thermosetting polymers. When these two elements are combined, a material produced has better qualities than any of the elements by itself (Andrew & Dhakal, 2022).

The polymer matrix transfers weight between fibers, acts as a binder to hold the reinforcing components together, and shields the fibers from external elements including moisture and chemical damage (Hubbe & Grigsby, 2020). Conversely, the strength, stiffness, and overall mechanical performance of the composite material are greatly enhanced by the reinforcing phase (Hubbe, et al., 2008).

Polymer composites have become more popular because of how strong, lightweight, and adaptable they are. Polymers' mechanical and thermal properties are improved when they are combined with reinforcing agents, including fibers or nanoparticles (Hubbe, 2020). In order to customize composites for particular applications in sectors including aerospace, automotive, and construction, researchers have investigated a variety of matrix and filler materials (Nassar, et al., 2021). Composites are used to reduce weight and improve performance, which is crucial in industries where durability and efficiency are important.

3. Types of Polymer Composites

In general, polymer composites can be classified according on the kind of reinforcement that is employed.

i. Fiber-Reinforced Polymer Composites (FRPC): These are made of a polymer matrix with long or short fibers incorporated in it. Carbon, aramid, and glass are examples of common fibers. Because of their excellent strength-to-weight ratios, FRPCs are frequently utilized in the construction, automotive, and aerospace industries (Khalid, et al., 2021).

ii. Particles Reinforced Polymer Composites: These composites are reinforced with particles rather than fibers. Particles dispersed throughout the polymer matrix may consist of metals, ceramics, or organic compounds. Applications needing wear resistance, like coatings and automotive parts, use this kind of composite (Delvere et al., 2019).

iii. Hybrid Composites: This particles attempt to combine the benefits of several reinforcements to customize the material's qualities for particular applications. They are composed of two or more types of reinforcements, such as fibers and particles, in the same matrix (Seile et al., 2022).

4. Recent Advances in Polymer Composite Technologies

i. Sustainable Composites: Concerns about sustainability are becoming central to the development of polymer composites. Study on bio-based composites made of renewable materials has increased as a result of growing concerns about environmental effect. The possibility of utilizing natural fibers and biodegradable matrices to produce sustainable materials that lessen dependency on petroleum-based goods is covered by Seile, et al. (2022). The necessity for environmentally acceptable alternatives that satisfy consumer and regulatory standards for sustainability is what spurs innovation in this field.

ii. Nanotechnology in Polymer Composites: One major trend that has evolved is the incorporation of nanoparticles into polymer composites. Mechanical characteristics, thermal stability, and electrical conductivity can all be greatly improved by the inclusion of nanoparticles (Lunetto et al., 2023). For example, Khalid, et al. (2021) highlight developments in carbon nanotube-reinforced composites, which show exceptional conductivity and strength-to-weight ratios, is making them appropriate for use in electronics and aerospace. In addition to increasing efficiency, the application of nanotechnology creates new opportunities for intelligent materials that are responsive to changes in their surroundings.

iii. Smart and Multifunctional Materials: Another fascinating field of study is the development of smart materials, which are materials that can react to external stimuli like light, moisture, or temperature (Kumar et al., 2023). For instance, self-healing polymers are made to repair damage on their own, extending the lifetime of composite materials (Bari et al., 2021). Smart composites have potential applications in biomedical devices to aerospace, where adaptability and resilience are essential.

5. Advantages of Polymer Composites

The excellent strength-to-weight ratio of polymer composites is one of its main benefits. For industries like aerospace and automotive to reduce emissions and improve fuel efficiency, weight reduction is essential. Without compromising mechanical strength, polymer composites offer a lightweight substitute for metals (Rajeshkumar, et al., 2021). Furthermore, polymer composites are very versatile materials since they may have their properties customized by changing the kind, direction, and quantity of reinforcement (Hubbe, et al., 2021).

Corrosion resistance is one of the other main advantages; this is important in situations where traditional materials, like metals, could deteriorate from exposure to severe environments. Additionally well-known for their superior fatigue resistance, polymer composites are perfect for usage in components that are subjected to cyclic loading (Adekomaya & Majozi, 2019).

6. Applications of Polymer Composites

Due to their performance advantages and adaptable qualities, polymer composites are used in a wide range of sectors. Because of their exceptional strength and low weight, composite materials are utilized in the aerospace sector to build aircraft parts including wings, fuselage sections, and tail assemblies, which increase cargo capacity and fuel efficiency (Kamarudin, et al., 2022). Polymer composites are also used in the automotive industry to lighten vehicles, which improves fuel efficiency and lowers pollutants. Car bodies, bumpers, and interior parts are frequently made of composite materials (Khalid et al 2022).

Polymer composites are being utilized more frequently in the building sector to fabricate structural elements like bridge decks, columns, and beams. They are appealing substitutes for conventional building materials due to their resistance to corrosion and capacity to tolerate environmental deterioration (Vazquez-Nunez, et al., 2021).

7. Challenges in Polymer Composite Technologies

Notwithstanding notable progress, the polymer composite sector encounters various obstacles. One significant problem, which frequently makes end-of-life management more complex, is the difficulty in recycling composite materials (Oliaei et al., 2021). Because of the intricate architecture of composites, traditional recycling techniques are frequently useless. To meet this problem, researchers are looking into cutting-edge recycling methods include mechanical processing and chemical recycling.

The procedures used to produce composites can be energy-intensive and harmful to the environment, which presents another difficulty (Antov et al., 2020). In order for the industry to meet global sustainability targets and lessen its carbon impact, sustainable manufacturing techniques are essential.

Even with all of its benefits, polymer composites have drawbacks. Their high production costs are one of their main drawbacks, especially for advanced composites reinforced with aramid or carbon fibers. Layup, pultrusion, and resin transfer molding are examples of manufacturing methods that can be expensive and difficult, which prevents them from being widely used in areas where costs are a concern (Jagadeesh, et al., 2022).

The complexity of recycling polymer composites presents another obstacle. The basic components are difficult to extract and separate due to the mixture of polymer matrices with different types of reinforcing elements. This raises environmental issues, especially in sectors of the economy where end-of-life planning and sustainability are vital (Jagadeesh, et al., 2022).

## 8. The Role of Islamic Endowments in Technological Advancement

Islamic endowments, or Waqfs, offer a special means of promoting polymer composite technology research and innovation. In the past, Waqf has provided support to a number of industries, such as community development, healthcare, and education (Sulistyowati (2023). Current research highlights Waqf's capacity to finance research projects, assist new ventures, and improve polymer sciences-related educational activities.

i. Funding Research and Development

Waqf can give academic institutions and research centers financial resources, enabling state-of-the-art studies in polymer composites. Technological advancements can be facilitated by Waqf through the establishment of research centers or specific financing. Successful case studies where Waqf-funded research projects have resulted in notable improvements in materials science are covered by Fatoni (2021).

Waqf also can support innovative research in polymer composite technologies by setting up specialized research centers and awards. These monies can be used to support innovative projects that are consistent with moral and sustainable behavior at universities and research facilities.

Islamic endowments can provide the funding required for polymer composites development and commercialization by investing in businesses in this field. By bridging the gap between theory and practice, this support can promote local economic development.

ii. Promoting Education and Skills Development

Putting money into education and training is essential to creating a workforce with the necessary skills for polymer composite technology. Bassiouni, (2012) emphasize the value of Waqf-supported training programs and scholarships because they may foster talent and provide a consistent supply of engineers and researchers who are prepared to take on new challenges.

By creating networks between academic institutions, business partners, and government agencies, Waqf can support cooperative projects that foster innovation and knowledge exchange. Similarly, by providing scholarships and educational opportunities, Waqf can help engineers and researchers in the field of polymer technology develop their skill sets and guarantee a consistent supply of skilled labor ready to take on new challenges.

## 9. Case Studies: Successful Applications of Waqf in Technology

We can look at a few successful case studies to show the possible influence of Islamic endowments in the field of polymer composite technologies:

i. Research Institutes Funded by Waqf: The creation of research institutes supported by Waqf in nations like Malaysia and Turkey is one prominent example (Kamarubahrin & Ayedh, 2018). These institutes have played a key role in the advancement of polymer composites and materials science, which has resulted in advances in bio-composites and sustainable materials.

ii. Programs for Incubation: Innovative polymer composite goods have been commercialized as a result of incubation programs for tech entrepreneurs established under certain Waqf initiatives (Wadi & Nurzaman, 2020). These initiatives have helped regional business owners while also bringing cutting-edge solutions to the international market.

iii. Public-Private Partnerships: Partnerships aimed at creating high-performance polymer composites have been established as a result of cooperation between Waqf entities and private sector businesses. These collaborations have been effective in turning research into goods that are ready for market.

## 10. Outlook for Polymer Composite Technologies in the Future

The field of polymer composites research is still developing, with an emphasis on cost reduction, performance enhancement, and sustainability issues. Natural fiber-reinforced composites are becoming more and more popular as a greener substitute for synthetic fibers. While being renewable and biodegradable, materials like flax, hemp, and jute have mechanical qualities that are similar to those of glass fibers (Rajeshkumar et al., 2021). Furthermore, improved mechanical, thermal, and barrier properties with low filler concentration are possible with the creation of nanocomposites, in which nanoparticles are scattered inside the polymer matrix (Bari, et al., 2021).

Several trends in polymer composite technologies are expected in the upcoming years, including:

i. Intelligent and Versatile Composites: Smart materials that react to environmental cues will become more common in the future. Waqf investments have the potential to spur the advancement of these technologies, which have a wide range of industrial uses.

ii. International Cooperation: Research and development will become more integrated in the future, with Waqf acting as a link for cross-border cooperation. This will increase the influence of polymer composite technology by facilitating cross-border collaboration and knowledge sharing.

iii. A Greater Emphasis on Sustainability: Innovation in bio-based and recyclable composites will be propelled by the demand for sustainable materials. By providing financing for studies that support Islamic stewardship and environmental responsibility, Waqf can have an impact on this trend.

iv. Ethical Production Procedures: The polymer composites sector will see a movement in favor of ethical sourcing and manufacturing techniques. Islamic endowments have the opportunity to set an example by encouraging accountability and openness in the manufacturing process.

With innovation and sustainability at its core, polymer composite technologies have enormous potential for the following years ahead. In this context, Islamic endowments have a special chance to make a significant impact. Waqf can advance the field of polymer composites and make a positive impact on sustainable development that aligns with Islamic ideals by means of financial support, education, and partnership. Adopting these values going forward will be essential for a future that strikes a balance between ethical duty and technological growth.

Therefore, the above literature presents a dynamic picture of polymer composite technologies, with the growth of smart materials, sustainability, and nanotechnology driving the field. Even if there have been great improvements, recycling and sustainable production methods still face difficulties. Incorporating Islamic endowments offers a viable way to support research, encourage creativity, and improve education in this area. Achieving sustainable growth in polymer composite technologies will depend on matching ethical funding channels with technological advancement as the industry develops.

**Gaps in the Literature**

Finding gaps in the literature can aid in forming sensible suggestions for businesses, Waqf institutions, and governmental organizations. The following list of typical gaps is accompanied by suggestions:

1. Restricted Empirical Research: A lot of research on Waqf institutions is theoretical, with little empirical evidence to back up conclusions.
2. Interdisciplinary Approaches: There is a dearth of interdisciplinary study on Waqf that integrates sociology, economics, and religious studies.
3. Impact Assessment: Not enough information has been gathered about how Waqf affects communities socially and economically.
4. Technology Integration: A cursory investigation of how technology can improve Waqf institutions' operational and administrative effectiveness by using technology is limited in the field.
5. Regulatory Framework: The effects of current legislative frameworks on Waqf operations have not been sufficiently examined.

**Discussion of Findings**

1. Summary of Developments in Polymer Composites

The review of the literature focuses on important developments in polymer composite technologies, especially in the fields of sustainability, nanotechnology, and the creation of intelligent materials. The findings show a clear trend toward high-performance, environmentally friendly materials that may satisfy the needs of contemporary industry. According to Lunetto, et al. (2023) and Kumar et al. (2023), the development of bio-based composites which lessen dependency on fossil fuels and also help reduce carbon footprints has been prompted by the demand for sustainable materials.

2. Sustainability in Polymer Composite

The results show that sustainability is a motivating factor for research and development as well as a legal necessity. Sustainable practices are becoming an essential part of the polymer composite lifecycle, from procuring raw materials to managing end-of-life issues, according to Maiti, et al. (2022). The use of natural fibers and biodegradable matrices are two innovations that highlight the industry's dedication to environmental responsibility.

Composite material recycling still faces difficulties, despite encouraging advancements. According to Hubbe, et al. (2021), conventional recycling techniques are made more difficult by the intricate architectures of composite materials. This suggests that in order to improve material recovery and lower waste, further study is required into cutting-edge recycling strategies including chemical recycling and up cycling.

3. The Function of Nanotechnology

The mechanical and thermal properties of polymer composites have been improved as a result of the use of nanotechnology. According to Hubbe & Grigsby (2020), the application of nanomaterials, such as grapheme and carbon nanotubes, can improve strength and conductivity, opening up new possibilities in industries like electronics and aerospace. These results imply that more performance improvements in polymer composites may be possible if funding for nanotechnology research is maintained.

However, concerns regarding environmental effect and safety are also raised by the application of nanotechnology. Comprehensive risk evaluations and regulatory frameworks are necessary to address the long-term consequences of nanomaterials on human health and ecosystems.

4. Ingenious and Versatile Substances

One of the most intriguing discoveries in the literature is the creation of smart materials that can react to external stimuli. According to Nassar et al., (2021) the development of self-healing polymers is a noteworthy advancement. These materials, especially in demanding industries like aerospace and automotive, have the potential to lower maintenance costs and increase the lifespan of composite products.

The results point to a rising demand for multipurpose materials that can handle multiple jobs at once. For example, composite materials having the ability to sense their surroundings and give structural support could completely change how intelligent systems are designed. In order to fully achieve the promise of smart composites, this movement emphasizes the necessity of interdisciplinary collaboration across materials science, engineering, and electronics.

5. Impact of Islamic Endowment on Polymer Composite Technology

Furthermore, a substantial knowledge vacuum exists on the ways in which Islamic endowments, or Waqf can promote developments in polymer composite technology. Researches by Harahap et al., (2023), and Ferdous & Uddin (2011) shows that Waqf can be very helpful in assisting businesses, financing research, and advancing education in this area. According to the findings, creating research centers supported by the Waqf could spur innovation by offering tools for interdisciplinary cooperation.

On the other hand, there is a paucity of actual data regarding the Waqf projects' ability to propel scientific advancements in polymer composites. Case studies evaluating the effect of Waqf on research outcomes, new technology commercialization, and workforce development should be the main focus of future study.

Therefore, the results of the literature review point to a strong and developing field of polymer composite technologies that is defined by sustainability, the use of nanotechnology, and the creation of intelligent materials. To guarantee the industry's sustained expansion, however, issues with recycling and regulatory worries about nanoparticles must be resolved.

**Conclusion**

By fusing polymers with reinforcements to produce a family of materials with improved mechanical, thermal, and chemical properties, polymer composites have become a revolutionary material. This study has demonstrated the great versatility and wide range of uses of polymer composites, especially those that are fiber- and particle-reinforced, in a variety of industries, including construction, automotive, and aerospace. These materials are perfect for demanding applications where weight reduction and performance are crucial because of their lightweight nature, high strength, and resistance to corrosion, and fatigue endurance. Polymer composites are anticipated to be essential in meeting industry demands as the need for high-performance, lightweight materials increases. This is particularly true in terms of lowering energy consumption and improving environmental sustainability. Future studies will probably explore new areas in nanocomposites and biodegradable materials while addressing current constraints, such as lowering costs and enhancing recycling procedures. To sum up, polymer composites are revolutionary materials with great potential for the advancement of engineering and technology. Sustained progress in research and development is expected to augment their potential for application, propelling innovation throughout global industries.

**Recommendations**

For the Government

1. Fund Research Initiatives to provide financial support for and promote empirical research on the socioeconomic effects of Waqf.

2. Develop Regulatory Frameworks to guarantee accountability and transparency, establish explicit rules for the management of Waqf institutions.

3. Promote Awareness and start initiatives to inform the general public and possible contributors about the advantages of Waqf.

For Industries

1. Corporate Social Responsibility (CSR): As part of their CSR initiatives, industries should be encouraged to collaborate with Waqf institutions.

2. Innovation and Technology: Make technological investments to improve Waqf institutions' outreach and management.

3. Capacity Building: Work with Waqf institutions to offer resources and training for improved financial management and governance.

For Waqf Institutions

1. Data Collection and Analysis: Put in place mechanisms to gather data in order to more accurately evaluate impact and guide strategic planning.

2. Community Engagement: Develop close relationships with nearby communities to learn about their needs and adjust Waqf initiatives as necessary.

3. Interdisciplinary Collaboration: Join forces with educational establishments to take use of a range of specialized knowledge to enhance Waqf management.

Moreover, communities and economies stand to gain from improved waqf institutions due to their increased efficacy and sustainability as a result of resolving these gaps and putting the recommendations into practice.

**References**

1. Ali, S.N & Oseni, U. A. 2021,Waqf Development and Innovation: Socio-Economic and Legal Perspectives, Book 1st Edition, Pp 302, ISBN9781003158073

2. Adekomaya, O., & Majozi, T. (2019). Sustainability of surface treatment of natural fibre in composite formation: challenges of environment-friendly option. The International Journal of Advanced Manufacturing Technology, 105(7), 3183-3195.

3. AL-Oqla, F. M., Hayajneh, M. T., & Nawafleh, N. (2023). Advanced synthetic and biobased composite materials in sustainable applications: a comprehensive review. Emergent Materials, 6(3), 809-826.

4. Andrew, J. J., & Dhakal, H. N. (2022). Sustainable biobased composites for advanced applications: recent trends and future opportunities–A critical review. Composites Part C: Open Access, 7, 100220.

5. Antov, P., Savov, V., & Neykov, N. (2020). Sustainable bio-based adhesives for eco-friendly wood composites. A review. Wood Res, 65(1), 51-62.

6. Asyraf, M. R. M., Syamsir, A., Zahari, N. M., Supian, A. B. M., Ishak, M. R., Sapuan, S. M., ... & Rashid, M. Z. A. (2022). Product development of natural fibre-composites for various applications: Design for sustainability. Polymers, 14(5), 920.

7. Bari, E., Sistani, A., Morrell, J. J., Pizzi, A., Akbari, M. R., & Ribera, J. (2021). Current strategies for the production of sustainable biopolymer composites. Polymers, 13(17), 2878.

8. Bassiouni, C. (2012). "Islamic civilization get involved Islamic civilized" middle East Institute file:///J:/SCIENTIFIC TECHNOLOGICAL DEVT/ISLAMIC civilization middle East institute htm retrieved 5/12/19.

9. Delvere, I., Iltina, M., Shanbayev, M., Abildayeva, A., Kuzhamberdieva, S., & Blumberga, D. (2019). Evaluation of polymer matrix composite waste recycling methods. Environmental and Climate Technologies, 23(1), 168-187.

10. Fatoni, A. 2021, Initiating The Integrated Cash Waqf Model Among OIC Countries, International Journal of Waqf, Vol 1(1), Pp. 1-6.

11. Ferdous, F. & M.A. Uddin (2011) "Towards Islamization of Science and Technology" IIUC studies Vo 9 Dec. 2011 DOI: https://doi.org/10.3329/iiucs.v9i0.24029

12. Harahap, B.; Risfandy, T.; Futri, I.N. Islamic Law, Islamic Finance, and Sustainable Development Goals: A Systematic Literature Review. Sustainability 2023, 15, 6626. https://doi.org/10.3390/su15086626

13. Hubbe, Martin A. 2023. "Sustainable Composites: A Review with Critical Questions to Guide Future Initiatives" Sustainability 15, no. 14: 11088. https://doi.org/10.3390/su151411088

14. Hubbe, M. A., Rojas, O. J., Lucia, L. A., & Sain, M. (2008). Cellulosic nanocomposites: a review. BioResources, 3(3), 929-980.

15. Hubbe, M. A., Lavoine, N., Lucia, L. A., & Dou, C. (2021). Formulating Bioplastic Composites for Biodegradability, Recycling, and Performance: A Review. BioResources, 16(1).

16. Hubbe, M. A., & Grigsby, W. (2020). From Nanocellulose to Wood Particles: A Review of Particle Size vs. the Properties of Plastic Composites Reinforced with Cellulose-based Entities. BioResources, 15(1).

17. Jagadeesh, P., Mavinkere Rangappa, S., Siengchin, S., Puttegowda, M., Thiagamani, S. M. K., Hemath Kumar, M., ... & Moure Cuadrado, M. M. (2022). Sustainable recycling technologies for thermoplastic polymers and their composites: A review of the state of the art. Polymer Composites, 43(9), 5831-5862.

18. Krauklis, A. E., Karl, C. W., Gagani, A. I., & Jørgensen, J. K. (2021). Composite material recycling technology—state-of-the-art and sustainable development for the 2020s. Journal of Composites Science, 5(1), 28.

19. Khalid, M. Y., Al Rashid, A., Arif, Z. U., Ahmed, W., Arshad, H., & Zaidi, A. A. (2021). Natural fiber reinforced composites: Sustainable materials for emerging applications. Results in Engineering, 11, 100263.

20. Kamarudin, S. H., Mohd Basri, M. S., Rayung, M., Abu, F., Ahmad, S. B., Norizan, M. N., ... & Abdullah, L. C. (2022). A review on natural fiber reinforced polymer composites (NFRPC) for sustainable industrial applications. Polymers, 14(17), 3698.

21. Khalid, M. Y., Arif, Z. U., Ahmed, W., & Arshad, H. (2022). Recent trends in recycling and reusing techniques of different plastic polymers and their composite materials. Sustainable Materials and Technologies, 31, e00382.

22. Kamarubahrin, A. F. & Ayedh, A. M. A. 2018, Critical Review on Waqf Experiences: Lessons from Muslim and Non-Muslim Countries, IQTISHADIA Jurnal Kajian Ekonomi dan Binis Islam, Vol. 11(2), Pp. 332-353, DOI: https://doi.10.21043/iqtishadia.v11i2.3272

23. Kola-Aderoju, S. A. (2023). The Muslim world and the development of science and technology: phase in history. South Florida Journal of Development, 4(2), 737–754. https://doi.org/10.46932/sfjdv4n2-009

24. Kumar, J. A., Sathish, S., Prabu, D., Renita, A. A., Saravanan, A., Deivayanai, V. C., ... & Hosseini-Bandegharaei, A. (2023). Agricultural waste biomass for sustainable bioenergy production: Feedstock, characterization and pre-treatment methodologies. Chemosphere, 331, 138680.

25. Lunetto, V., Galati, M., Settineri, L., & Iuliano, L. (2023). Sustainability in the manufacturing of composite materials: A literature review and directions for future research. Journal of Manufacturing Processes, 85, 858-874.

26. Maiti, S., Islam, M. R., Uddin, M. A., Afroj, S., Eichhorn, S. J., & Karim, N. (2022). Sustainable fiber-reinforced composites: a Review. Advanced Sustainable Systems, 6(11), 2200258.

27. Nassar, M. M., Alzebdeh, K. I., Pervez, T., Al-Hinai, N., & Munam, A. (2021). Progress and challenges in sustainability, compatibility, and production of eco-composites: A state-of-art review. Journal of Applied Polymer Science, 138(43), 51284.

28. Oliaei, E., Lindström, T., & Berglund, L. A. (2021). Sustainable development of hot-pressed all-lignocellulose composites—comparing wood fibers and nanofibers. Polymers, 13(16), 2747.

29. Pati, P., McGinnis, S., & Vikesland, P. J. (2014). Life cycle assessment of "green" nanoparticle synthesis methods. Environmental Engineering Science, 31(7), 410-420.

30. Rajeshkumar, G., Seshadri, S. A., Devnani, G. L., Sanjay, M. R., Siengchin, S., Maran, J. P., ... & Anuf, A. R. (2021). Environment friendly, renewable and sustainable poly lactic acid (PLA) based natural fiber reinforced composites–A comprehensive review. Journal of Cleaner Production, 310, 127483.

31. Seile, A., Spurina, E., & Sinka, M. (2022). Reducing global warming potential impact of bio-based composites based of LCA. Fibers, 10(9), 79.

32. Sulistyowati (2023). Encouraging The Islamic Endowment's Achievement Through Digital Technology. International Journal of Management Studies and Social Science Research (IJMSSSR 2023), VOLUME 5 ISSUE 2, 24-31. DOI: https://doi.org/10.56293/IJMSSSR.2022.4571

33. Wadi, D.A. & Nurzaman, M.S. 2020, Millennials Behaviour towards Digital Waqf Innovation, International Journal of Islamic Economics and Finance (IJIEF), Vol. 3(2), Pp. 1-30, Special Issue: Islamic Social Finance and Ethics.

34. Vazquez-Nunez, E., Avecilla-Ramirez, A. M., Vergara-Porras, B., & López-Cuellar, M. D. R. (2021). Green composites and their contribution toward sustainability: a review. Polymers and Polymer Composites, 29(9_suppl), S1588-S1608.

# Chapter-6

# Development of Biodegradable and Bio-based Composite

Mithu Maiti Jana[1]

Surjit Kaur[2],

Nizamul Haque Ansari[3]

Honey Sharma[4]

**Abstract**

The demand for biodegradable bio-composite materials for use in packaging, farming, medicine and other fields has significantly increased in recent years. Polymer bio-composite materials are produced to minimize the demand for synthetic polymer manufacture (thus lowering pollution) at a cheap cost, having a favorable impact on both the economy and the environment. Humans have recently needed to raise awareness and responsibility for the reduction of agricultural waste due to the growing population, carbon overload and environmental discomfort. It is an intriguing discovery to use agricultural waste as filler in reinforced polymers. Although the physical and mechanical properties of the polymer composite are affected, treatments or alterations of fiber surface properties often increase the adhesion properties of fibers which use as a better reinforcement material for developing biodegradable composites.

**Keywords:** Green composite, Natural fiber, Thermal behaviour, Eco-friendly.

## 1. Introduction

During the industrial revolution, humans utilized few resources, but as technology advanced, the demand for better materials increased. The scientific community developed artificial materials known as composites. To reduce costs, scientists began looking for previously discarded materials. Rice husk, an abundant agricultural waste, fulfills all the conditions described above and has been extensively utilized to produce biocomposites. The growing interest in natural and biodegradable materials due to ecological concerns has increased awareness of issues like biodegradability and environmental safety.[1] When developing new products, a wider range of materials are being designed with a focus on sustainability, or eco-design. It is for this reason that environmentally friendly material alternatives, such as natural fibers and biodegradable polymers, might be regarded as valuable options for the

---

[1] *Department of Physical Sciences, Associate Professor, Sant Baba Bhag Singh University, Jalandhar, Punjab - 144030, India.*
[2] *Department of Physical Sciences, Research Scholar, Sant Baba Bhag Singh University, Jalandhar, Punjab - 144030, India.*
[3] *Department of Physical Sciences (Chemistry), Professor, Sant Baba Bhag Singh University, Jalandhar, Punjab - 144030, India.*
[4] *Department of Physical Sciences, Associate Professor, Sant Baba Bhag Singh University, Jalandhar, Punjab - 144030, India.*
E-mail address: nizamulchem@gmail.com, honeyshrma777@gmail.com

production of new biodegradable composites. In the current era of renewable energy usage in place of petrochemical sources, the development of natural biodegradable polymer composites is a significant research area. Nowadays, there is an increasing demand for looking into a new environmentally friendly, sustainable product to replace current ones as industry attempts to reduce its dependency on petroleum-based fuels and materials. Natural fibers are a desirable filler material due to their wide variety and developed surface that enhances matrix adhesion. In fiber-reinforced composites, the fibers act as reinforcement by providing strength and stiffness to the structure, while the polymer matrix maintains the fibers in place so that acceptable structural composites may be developed. Natural fibers provide a number of benefits over synthetic ones, such as less environmental impact, enhanced energy recovery and biodegradability, low density, superior toughness, appropriate specific strength, reduced respiratory irritation, low cost, and the availability of renewable resources.[2,3] Composites manufactured from natural fibers are lightweight, rigid and have an excellent strength-to-weight ratio. The cost gap among biocomposite and synthetic composite is very high which also encourage the development of bio-composite.

## 2. Composites

The composite materials are heterogeneous substances made up of two or more solid phases that are in close contact with one another on a microscopic level. On a microscopic level, they can also be viewed of as homogeneous materials because any part of them will share the same physical characteristics.[4] Straw and mud were the first man-made composite materials, and they were used to make bricks for buildings. Nowadays, composite materials are widely utilized in a wide range of industrial applications, from simple household items to offshore constructions used by the petroleum industry.[5,6] Individual materials, referred generally as constituent materials, are the building blocks of composites. Wood is a naturally occuring composite material made of cellulose fibres embedded in a lignin matrix.[7] The composites should not be considered of as a simply mixture of two materials. The combination has special qualities on a larger scale. It is superior to either one of the components alone or vastly different from either one of them in terms of strength, heat resistance, or some other desirable feature.[8] "The composites are compound materials which differ from alloys by the fact that the individual components retain their features but are thus integrated into the composite to take benefit solely of their assets and not of their weaknesses", in order to obtain a superior material.[9] Two types of constituent materials are available: matrix and reinforcement. The reinforcing materials are surrounded by the matrix materials, which hold them in place by maintaining their relative locations. To improve the matrix's features, the reinforcement adds their distinct mechanical and physical characteristics. The wide range of matrix and strengthening substances enables the designer of the product or structure to select the ideal combination, while a synergism creates material qualities unavailable from the individual constituent materials. It is necessary to shape engineered composite materials. Before or after the reinforcement material is inserted into the mold cavity or onto the mold surface, the matrix material may be added to the reinforcement. Produced composites use a polymer matrix material that is frequently referred to as a resin solution, and this moulding event may occur depending on the nature of the matrix material. most frequently through a variety of processes, like chemical polymerization or solidification from a molten state. Polyester, vinyl ester, epoxy, phenolic, polyimide, polyamide, polypropylene etc. are used most widely commercially for the matrix production.[10,11] Fibers are frequently used as reinforcing materials, although ground materials are also frequently used. To increase the fiber content or decrease the resin content in the finished product, numerous techniques have been designed. The ratio of fiber to resin considerably affects the product's strength.[12] There are two basic groups of fiber-reinforced composite materials: continuous fiber-reinforced materials and short fiber-reinforced materials. Layered or laminated structures are frequently made of continuous fiber-reinforced materials. Fibre-reinforced polymers (FRPS) include wood (comprising cellulose fibers in a lignin and hemicellulose matrix), carbon-fiber reinforced plastic (CFRP), and glass- reinforced plastic (GRP).[10] High performance composites called shape memory polymer composites are perfect for applications including lightweight, rigid, deployable constructions, quick manufacturing, and dynamic reinforcing.[13] Composite materials have become more and more popular in high-performance products that need to be lightweight but strong enough to withstand challenging loading conditions, such as aerospace components (tails, wings, fuselages, propellers), boat and scull hulls, bicycle frames, and racing car bodies.[14] Due to pulp mill competition for fiber, decreased harvesting and production, and decreased log quality, there is a perceived shortage of wood fiber for composite products. Additionally, environmentalists are pushing for regulations on how to dispose of agricultural fibers and to decrease the usage of forests.[15] For example, any possibility to reduce field burning is beneficial to the environment and helps to find a solution to the issue of restricted open burning. Agricultural biomass is readily available in enormous amounts for non-agricultural purposes like paper and composite materials. Each year, North America produces a total of around 365,000,000 dry tons of non-wood fiber.[16] The amount of cereal straw that can be used for non-agricultural purposes is only about one-third of the total amount produced each year according to estimates, but if wood-based composites were produced on the basis of volume alone, the available agricultural residues could replace more than all of them. Agriculture residues-based composite products may have the potential to be sold as premium items, or they may be marketed in other ways depending on environmental factors (formaldehyde-free, sustainable, and green certification) and features (moisture resistance, machining properties, low density). Agricultural biomass, including wheat straw, barley and oats is the source of many different fibers. It has been demonstrated that potential materials for the polymer composite include hemp, oil seed flax, rice straw, and bagasse. Wheat straw has the potential to be used in the production of a variety of board products, such as a medium density fiberboard-type product, a structural particle board alternative, and medium quality interior particle board.[17] There is growing interest in using agricultural wastes for the production of composite panels despite Canada's sizeable timber industry and the availability of vast volumes of wood residues for the composite industry. In order to successfully produce wheat straw-based composite, extensive technological development was needed to overcome handling and processing issues. However, the end product is of high quality and will encourage the consideration and development of other value-added building materials made from agricultural residues.[18] Composite materials made from forest resources will have a highly dynamic and interesting future. Traditions, trends, expenses, performance, the accessibility of resources, and regulation will all influence it. However, ideas about sustainable development are altering the economic structure so that it now places more emphasis on establishing sustainable industries than just profit margins. On the one hand, there is an increasing demand to generate employment, increase recreational possibilities, and raise living standards. On the other hand, there are worries over the use of energy, the growth of the global population, the preservation of wilderness areas, environmental cleanup, and the preservation of our natural resources. Resources that are recyclable, renewable, and sustainable will be essential to future global development. The materials of this dynamic future will include composite materials and forestry resources.[19] Sustainability is defined by the UN world commission on "Environment and development in our future" as development that satisfies present demands without compromising the capacity of future generations to satisfy their own needs. It is important to understand the utilization of biomass that is annually renewable, such as wheat, rice, barley and oats. This approach is based on the production and manufacturing of goods from cellulose and starch, two sources that are both sustainable and biodegradable. The use of biodegradable polymers is increasing. There are numerous biodegradable polymers that have been manufactured or developed naturally during all organisms' growth cycles.[20] These various biodegradable polymers can be divided into two major families: the agro polymers and the biodegradable polymers. Biopolymers are plastics created by living things. Examples of biopolymers with monomeric units that are sugars, amino acids, and nucleotides include cellulose and starch, protein and peptides, DNA, and RNA. The most frequent organic compound on earth as well as the most frequent biopolymer is cellulose. Cellulose makes up about 33% of all plant matter (the cellulose content of cotton is 90% and that of wood is 50%).[21] Different cellulose contents can be measured based on botanical species. It is a reasonably priced semi-crystalline substance that is used to make paper and as a stabilizing component in polymer matrices. The primary source of storage in plant resources is starch (Cereals, legumes and tubers). On earth, it is a commonly accessible raw resource. It provides several industrial uses for the field, including those for food, paper, textiles, and glue.

## 2.1 Classification of composites

Composites are divided into three categories based on their matrix materials: metal matrix composites, ceramic matrix composites, and polymer matrix composites. In terms of reinforcement, they can be further divided into three categories: fiber reinforced, particulate reinforced or structural composites.[22]

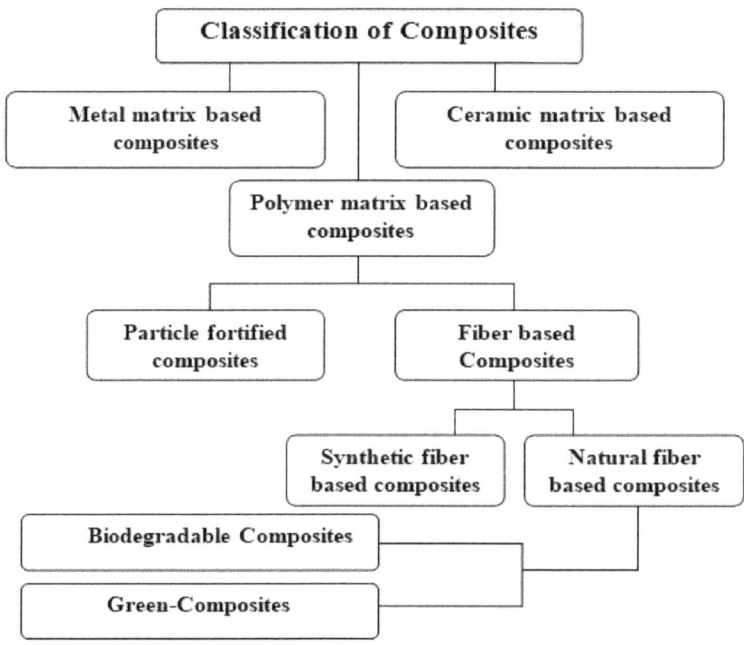

**2.1.1 Metal matrix composites:** Metal grids provide higher quality, crack resistance, and stiffness. Compared to polymer composites, metal lattice can resist higher temperatures under damaging conditions. The currently popular grid metals are titanium, aluminum, and magnesium, which are especially useful for applications involving flying machines. Due to these qualities, metal lattice composites are being considered for a wide range of applications, including the burning chamber spout (in rockets and space transportation), hotels, tubes, linkages, heat exchangers, auxiliary personnel, and more.[23]

**2.1.2 Ceramic matrix composites:** Building durability is one of the main goals while delivering burned lattice composites. Typically, it is believed and undoubtedly frequently observed that ceramic matrix composites are becoming better in terms of both quality and strength.[24] They are mostly acceptable for high temperature applications, such as thermal protection systems for the nose caps of re-entry vehicles and components in thrust-producing portions of rocket or missile systems.[25] In general, aerospace applications demand for high thrust-to-weight ratios, better cruising speeds, higher altitudes and better flying performance.[26]

**2.1.3 Polymer matrix composites:** The most often used matrix materials in polymer matrix composites are polymeric. The physical and mechanical qualities of polymers are typically insufficient for some fundamental tasks. Particularly, in comparison to the manufacturing of metals and pottery, their quality and solidity are poor. These difficulties are overcome by adding polymers to various materials. Additionally, handling polymer grid composites does not require high temperatures or weights. Similarly, the equipment needed to assemble polymer grid composites is simpler. As a result, polymer lattice composites expanded swiftly and soon became common place for auxiliary purposes.[27]

**2.1.3.1 Particle fortified composites:** The components that are used for fortification include those used in the production of ceramics and glassware, such as tiny mineral particles, metal particles like aluminum, and cloudy materials like polymers and carbon black. Particles used to construct the framework's modules and reduce the malleability of the network.[28] Thakur & Singha have examined the physio-chemical and mechanical characteristics of natural fiber and particle-fortified polymer composites produced with the three different types of fibers (particulate, short and long). The findings shown that when compared to short and long fiber composites, polymer composites reinforced with particles have superior mechanical characteristics. The outcomes also demonstrated that particle reinforced composites exhibit increased moisture absorption, swelling resistance and chemical resistance behavior.[29]

**2.1.3.2 Fiber based Composites:** Natural fibers are beneficent materials because they are abundant, affordable, fully or partially recyclable, and biodegradable.[30] This is a new phase of improvements and fortifications for polymer-based materials. Plant-based fibers such as cotton, hemp, jute, sisal, pineapple, ramie, bamboo, banana, and so forth are used as reinforcement in polymer grid composites, along with wood and flax seeds. They are desirable alternative fortifications to glass, carbon, and other synthetic strands because of their accessibility, low thickness, affordable price, and acceptable mechanical features.[31] Natural fibers are a type of substance that resembles hair and is continuously transformed into fibers, much to how fragments of string are transformed into fibers. In light of their origins as plant, animal, and mineral interpretations, common filaments were grouped into a variety of types. In a variety of designing applications, this reasonable and environmentally friendly strand has been used to replace glass and other produced filaments.[32] Natural fibers are biodegradable, which means they can lower the problem of massive strong wastes and the weight on landfills if they are used to replace other non-degradable materials for product development. This is in accordance with the concept of ecological consciousness.[33] Furthermore, because they are less susceptible to machine device damage and health dangers during production, as shown by their inherent qualities, natural filaments are flexible for handling. Due to the risks to the environment, natural strands could be traded for artificial filaments in the selection of a material. Increasing awareness of the limits of fossil energy resources and limiting the emissions of greenhouse gasses like $CO_2$ into the atmosphere have led to the development of new materials that are entirely based on sustainable resources.[34]

**2.1.3.2.1 Synthetic fiber based composites:** The most important material category for fiber-reinforced composites nowadays is synthetic fibers, especially for industries that place a high value on the mechanical, thermal, and material soundness of the material, like aviation, automotive, or energy shift.[35] The process of making the material, the resulting fiber structure and characteristics, as well as the composite material's application fields, are all condensed for each class of material. Materials used to make the manufactured filaments included glass, basalt, charcoal, artistic pottery (oxide and non-oxide), and polymeric filaments (aramides). The necessary calculations of a composite's solidity and elasticity have determined the selection of suitable filaments. Additional requirements for the suitable fortifying strands include elongation at despair thermal security adhesion of filaments and network, dynamic conduct long-time conduct price, and preparation costs. The high handling costs of fiber made from produced polymers, the inability of synthetic fibers to breakdown after transfer, etc. Common fiber has been developed as an economical alternative for manufactured strands due to the contamination caused by this synthetic waste and its effects on the environment.[36] Since synthetic fiber composite's characteristics have been found to be superior to those of natural fiber, their usage is unavoidable in the manufacturing and production sectors. High-performance polymer matrix composite products including fiber reinforced plastic (FRP) tanks, aircraft components, vehicle parts, and building panels have all been developed with synthetic fiber. Glass, carbon and aramid are three notable synthetic fibers that are frequently utilized in the composites industry.[37] **2.1.3.2.2 Natural fiber based composites:** There has been an exponential increase in the use of natural fiber composites over the past 20 years, and there is enormous potential for future growth in this area from both a mechanical application and a research aspect. The common fiber composites can be easily disposed of because they are made of biodegradable materials (Green Composites). Ongoing research into regular fiber composites offers notable advancements in resources from endless sources, with improved assistance for global manageability.[38] Natural fiber using as a reinforcing material because (i) They are easily producible with little effort, which makes them interesting (ii) Using renewable sources, which utilize carbon dioxide and oxygen to produce their products, consumes little energy during production (iii) Reduced tooling wear, better operating condition and no skin irritation. They are eco-friendly materials in terms of manufacture, processing and waste (iv)While produced strands mess with ignition heaters, thermal reuse is theoretically possible (v) They provide effective thermal and acoustic insulation. Since ancient times, people have used natural fibers for a variety of purposes, including as building materials. The usage of natural fibers from various plants, such as bagasse, cereal straw, corn stem, cotton stalk, rice husk/rice straw, etc., has been investigated by users in the majority of the world's nations. Researchers now have a new perspective on natural fibers in more specialized domains thanks to the majority of fibers that have been utilized for centuries. As a result of this need, interest in synthetic fibers like glass fibers has grown, and they are gradually taking the place of natural fiber in a variety of applications. Energy consumption increased as a result of the change in the raw material and manufacturing procedure for composites made with synthetic fibers. Pollution-related environmental damage has once again raised awareness of the benefits of using natural fibers. The renewed interest led to new techniques for modifying and using natural fibers, bringing them up to equality with or even exceeding synthetic fibers.[39] The use of natural fibers as a reinforcing ingredient in composite matrices is becoming more popular for a variety of low-cost building materials. Locally, there is an abundance of natural fiber that is derived from renewable resources. India produces more than 400 million tons of natural fibers at the moment.[40]

**2.1.3.2.2.1 Biodegradable Polymers:** In the 1970s, increasing oil prices stimulated an early interest in biodegradable materials, and today, worries about the decreasing number of garbage sites are reigniting that interest. Scientists have been presented with a viable solution by biodegradable polymers for the issues with waste disposal that are related to conventional plastics made from petroleum. Biodegradable plastics and polymers, which were first developed in the 1980s and are utilized in films, molded products, sheers, etc., are a relatively new product category. Renewable and non-renewable resources are frequently categorized in this manner. Resources that can replace themselves at a rate that is roughly equal to their rate of extraction are typically referred to as renewable resources.[41] Water, wind, tides and solar radiation are examples of renewable non-living natural resources; compare to renewable energy. Renewable resources are typically all-natural resources that do not become depleted when exploited by humans. Plastics, gasoline, coal and other products made from fossil fuels are non-renewable because the resource is exhausted and can only be used once. Recent research on biocomposites shows that, for the most part, these materials's particular mechanical properties are equal to those of common glass fiber reinforced plastics. Biocomposites have been used to construct a variety of complicated structures, including tubes, sandwich plates, vehicle door inside paneling etc. According to the results of numerous studies, biocomposites have successfully replaced glass fiber reinforced plastics (GFRP) in many applications.[42] There are many applications that demand for additional characteristics in addition to satisfying mechanical requirements. Biocomposites are flammable since they are made of organic components. Therefore, a specific level of flame resistance is one of the most crucial requirements for biocomposites to be utilized as paneling in trains or on airplanes. Different forms of polymer flame-retardants based on halogens (Cl, Br), heavy and transition metals (Zn, V, Pb, Sb) or phosphorus organic compounds may cause ecological difficulties in the current polymer industry while reducing risk during polymer combustion and pyrolysis. There is still an upward tendency in the use of halogenated flame retardants and environmental concerns have started a serious research for eco-friendly polymer additives. New features of a polymer flame retardant system that is environmentally beneficial have been revealed.[43] According to the most recent studies on natural fiber and matrix combinations and environmentally friendly flame-retardants, biocomposites can often replace glass fiber reinforced plastic. The novel building materials are ideal for anisotropic and specifically designed lightweight structural parts as well as for automotive paneling components. Current research activities are focused on the possible uses of biocomposites in the fields of railway, aircraft, irrigation, furniture, sports equipment, and leisure products.[42]

**2.1.3.2.2.2 Green Composites:** Generally speaking, "green-composites" are composite materials manufactured from petroleum-derived non-degradable polymers (Polypropylene, Polyethylene) or biodegradable polymers with natural/bio-based fiber (Poly lactic acid, Polyhydroxyalkanoate). Biocomposites developed from plant-based fibers (natural/bio-based fiber) and crop- or bio-derived plastics (bio polymers/bioplastics) are expected to become more environmentally friendly in the future and are known as "green composites. "The production of green composites began in the late 1980s and today the market is filled with biodegradable polymers that don't yet fulfill all of the parameters for biocomposites. A variety of biodegradable polymers, including Biopolm, polycaprolacton, Bioceta, Mater Bi, Sconacell and others [44], have been studied in order to evaluate their properties, with a focus on whether or not they would be suitable for use as a matrix material in the creation of green composites. To produce high-quality biocomposites, these matrix polymers must have low viscosities at processing temperatures, good mechanical properties for the matrix and reinforcing fiber, and strong fiber-matrix adhesion. Since ancient times, people have been aware of and used biodegradable type composites, or "green-composites." Their use dates back to ancient times, as evidenced by the construction of the great wall of China, which began in 200 B.C. as earthworks connected and strengthened by clay bricks made of local materials, first with gravel and red willow twigs during the Han dynasty (209 B.C. ), and later with clay, stone, willow branches, reeds, and sand during the Qin dynasty (221-206 B.C.).[45] The Mongolians utilized bows made of laminates of animal horns and tendons, wood, or silk in 1200 A.D. as yet another example. Since paper, silk, and other natural polymers have been used since ancient times, using them is not a novel idea. Natural polymers were less frequently used between 1940 and 1980 as a variety of synthetic polymers were produced using cheap petroleum-based polymers as the basis for their raw materials. However, since the 1990s, more focus has been given to the usage of lignocellulose fibers and natural polymers. All organisms's growth cycles in nature result in the formation of biopolymers. The most distinctive group of these natural polymers is the polysaccharide family, which includes starch and cellulose. Biopolymers are organic, biodegradable polymers. There are numerous kinds of biopolymers that exist naturally. While some of the polymers are currently in use in industry, others are still only being studied experimentally. Proteins and other natural polymers can be combined to produce biodegradable products. There are two primary sources of biopolymers that are renewable. Lipids are another resource. Natural polymers are frequently chemically synthesized in order to enhance the mechanical properties of such polymers or to change the rate at which they degrade. There is a large selection of naturally occurring polymers that come from renewable resources that can be used in material applications. New possibilities for the use of polymers from renewable resources are being addressed because to the rapid improvement in our understanding of basic biosynthetic pathways and the alternatives to modify or customize these pathways through genetic modifications.[46] For a several years, biopolymers's production and research have advanced at the fastest rates. Garbage and grocery bags [47], edible films [48], adhesives in particleboard and plywood [49] are just a few examples of the uses of soy protein and wheat protein based polymers. Both soy protein isolate (SPI) and whey protein isolate (WPI) films are commonly utilized in meat, fruit, and vegetable goods as packaging films or coatings because they are biodegradable, nutritious, reasonably transparent, and have excellent gas, lipid, and aroma barrio features. Drug delivery devices have also utilized soy protein isolate (SPI) and whey protein isolate (WPI) films.[50] Why green composites are needed: Natural resources are once again in demand, and the development of new materials and products now places a greater emphasis on safety and recyclable materials. Petroleum-based materials are poisonous and non-biodegradable, like thermoset resins. The resins and fibers used in green composites break down when they are discharged into the environment due to microorganisms. They are transformed into water and carbon dioxide. These $CO_2$ and $H_2O$ are absorbed by plant systems. Natural composites are made by combining plant fibers and natural resins. Composites are a specific kind of composite when at least one of the components, like the reinforcement or matrix, is made from natural resources. Biocomposites, eco composites, and green composites all refer to the same category of materials. Straw was utilized in ancient Egypt as a mud-based wall material's reinforcement method three thousand years ago. Mud bricks strengthened with straw were used to build its walls.[51]

## 2.2 Properties of composite materials

**2.2.1 Mechanical properties:** There are many criteria that must be met before a material may be used in biomedical applications, but one of them is that it must be structurally and mechanically sound enough to replace load-bearing structures. In order to prove the excellent reliability and mechanical qualities of the graft, this material should provide a comparable or greater mechanical stability. The microstructure of ceramics determines their physical characteristics, which may be described in terms of the number and types of phases present, the relative amounts of each, and the size, shape, and orientation of each phase.[52]

**2.2.1.1 Elastic modulus:** When a tensile or compressive force is applied, the elastic modulus shows the thickness and stiffness of the material within the elastic range. The fact that it suggests that the chosen materials and the biomaterial have similar deformable qualities to the material being replaced makes it clinically significant. In order to determine the elastic modulus of these materials, the nano-indentation test is utilized. This technique is highly accurate, precise, and practical for small sample sizes. Destructive and nondestructive methods, such as laser ultrasonic technology, are also used to determine elastic modulus. Due to its simplicity and repeatability in light of the fact that materials are deteriorating, it is also a very crucial clinical technique.

**2.2.1.2 Hardness:** One of the most crucial factors for comparing the characteristics of different materials is hardness, which is a measure of plastic deformation and is defined as the force per unit area of indentation or penetration. It is used to determine whether biopolymers and biomaterials are appropriate for use in clinical settings and has a beneficial impact on the resistance to heat and mechanical degradation. Similar to bone hardness, biomaterial hardness is beneficial. Due to the fact that the biomaterial needs to be harder than the base to penetrate the bone. Due to the extremely small size of the samples for biomaterials, micro- and nanoscale hardness tests (using Diamond Knoop and Vickers indenters) are used. Due to the non-yielding nature of ceramics and glasses, it is quite challenging to apply a conventional hardness test on them (no plastic deformation). In order to increase the microhardness and develop a fine microstructure, hydroxyapatite (HA) can be mixed with 0.2 weight percent of Lithium. A key engineering design area is the use of ceramic materials to develop self-standing implants that can endure tensile pressures. Applications include reinforcing ceramics, coating materials, and using fracture mechanics. Due to their resemblance to the natural bone minerals, as well as their outstanding biocompatibility and bioactivity but low fatigue resistance and strength, hydroxyapatite, calcium phosphates, biocomposites, and bioceramics are essential for the regeneration of hard tissues.

**2.2.1.3 Fracture toughness:** To protect ceramics from cracking, ceramics must have a high level of fracture toughness. It is used to evaluate the biomaterial's use, effectiveness, and long-term biological and therapeutic success. In comparison to low fracture toughness materials, it has been demonstrated that high breakage toughness materials have improved clinical and medicinal performance and reliable measurement. These are crucial factors that determine caliber toughness. Human bone has a fracture toughness of 2–12 MPa.m1/2, whereas hydroxyapatite (HA) has a fracture toughness of 1 MPa.m1/2. One way to increase the mechanical properties is to densify the HA by adding (5 wt.%) $K_2CO_3$, $Na_2CO_3$.[53]

**Table 1: Mechanical properties of some natural and synthetic fibre [34]**

| Fibre | Length (mm) | Density (g/cm$^3$) | Tensile strength (MPa) | Failure strain (%) |
|---|---|---|---|---|
| Jute | 1.5-120 | 1.3-1.5 | 393-800 | 1.5-1.8 |
| Hemp | 5-55 | 1.5 | 550-1110 | 1.6 |
| Flax | 5-900 | 1.5 | 345-1830 | 1.2-3.2 |
| Ramie | 900-1200 | 1.5 | 400-938 | 2.0-3.8 |
| Cotton | 10-60 | 1.5-1.6 | 287-800 | 3.0-10 |
| Sisal | 900 | 1.3-1.5 | 107-855 | 2.0-2.5 |
| Coir | 20-150 | 1.2 | 131-220 | 15-30 |
| Wool | 38-152 | 1.3 | 50-315 | 13.2-35 |
| Silk | Continuous | 1.3 | 100-1500 | 15-60 |
| Feather | 10-30 | 0.5 | 100-203 | 6.9 |
| E-glass | Continuous | 2.5 | 2000-3000 | 2.5 |

Table 1 shows the characteristics of different natural fibers and the most common form of glass fiber (E-glass). Although it should be noted that there is a lot of variation in the literature, it can be observed that flax, hemp, and ramie fiber are some of the cellulose-based natural fibers with the highest specific tensile strengths. Usually, geography has a significant impact on fiber selection in terms of availability. For instance, flax fiber has received a lot of attention in Europe, whereas hemp, jute, ramie, kenaf and sisal have attracted more attention in Asia. In general, higher performance is obtained with varieties that contain more cellulose and with cellulose micro fibrils that are more aligned in the direction of the fiber, which is more common in bast fibers (such as flax, hemp, kenaf, jute, and ramie) that have higher structural requirements for supporting the plant's stalk. The chemical composition and structure of natural fibers, which are related to the type of fiber as well as growth conditions, harvesting timing, extraction technique, treatment, and storage techniques, greatly influence their qualities. The strength of natural fibers is often lower than that of glass fiber.

## Conclusion

Using petroleum-based products has been associated with a number of problems, such as increased costs and environmental harm from extraction, processing and disposal. As a result, bio-composites have been the focus of recent research efforts. Utilising bio-composites instead of materials derived from petroleum helps the agriculture sector become more profitable while lowering carbon dioxide emissions and dependence on foreign oil. In order to achieve this goal, more multidisciplinary research in the fields of engineering, biology, agriculture and economy will be necessary. Additionally, the government will need to provide support in the form of educational programmes, tax breaks and subsidies. Developing countries can make use of their own natural resources by making composite materials from natural fibres. A combination of natural/biofibre surface modifications, the development of bioplastic as a viable matrix for composite fabrication and processing techniques are required for developing and manufacturing bio-composites of commercial consequence. There are many advantages to using bio-composites as building materials, including the fact that they are more affordable, lighter, eco-friendly, bio-renewable and durable. Bio-plastics derived from renewable resources are already being manufactured, but additional research is still required to get beyond the performance barrier.

## Acknowledgments

The authors acknowledge financial support from Sant Baba Bhag Singh University, Jalandhar,

Punjab, India.

## References

1. Yu, W. R., Lee, B. H., and Kim, H. J., **2009**. Fabrication of Long and discontinuous natural fibre reinforced polypropylene biocomposites and their mechanical properties. *Fibres and Polymer,* 10(1), pp.83-90.

2. Mohanty, A. K., Misra, M., and Drzal, L. T., eds., **2005**. Natural fibres, biopolymers and bio composites. CRC Press UK, Taylor & Francis Group. pp.1-876.

3. Fowler, P. A., Hughes, M. J., and Elias, R. M., **2006**. Review bio composites: technology, environmental credentials and market forces. *Journal of the Science Food and Agriculture,* 86, pp.1781-1789.

4. Van Suchtelen, J., **1972**. Philips Research Reports. Product Properties: A New Application of Composite Materials. 27, pp.28-37.

5. Winkle, I. E., Cowling, M. J., Hashim, S. A., and Smith, E. M., **1991**. What can adhesives offer to shipbuilding? *Journal of ship production.* 7(3), pp.137-152.

6. Gibson, R. F., **1994**. Principles of composite materials mechanics. McGraw. Hill, New York. (Chapter-I), pp.1-417.

7. Hon, DN., S., and Shiraishi, N., **2001**. Wood and cellulosic chemistry. 2nd ed. New York : Marcel Dekker. pp.1-923.

8. Sperling, L. H. (Ed.). **1986**. Renewable-resource Materials: New Polymer Sources: *2nd International Symposium on Polymeric Renewable Resource Materials: 189th Meeting*. Plenum.

9. Qureshi, S., Manson, J. A., Sperling, L. H., and Murphy, C. J. **1983**. Polymer applications of renewable-resource materials. *Plenum Press, New York, NY*, pp.249-71.

10. Maldas, D., and Kokta, B. V., **1995**. Composite Molded Products Based on Recycled Thermoplastics and Waste Cellulosics. II. Kenaf Fiber-Recycled PE Composites. *Journal of Reinforced Plastic and Composite,* 14(5), pp.458-470.

11. Feldman, D., Banu, D., Luchian, C., and Wang, J., **1991**. Epoxy- lignin polyblends: correlation between polymer interaction and curing temperature. *Journal of Applied Polymer Sci*ence, 42(5), pp.1307-1318.

12. Apsar, G., Musthak, M., and Ahmed, J. **2020**. Study of factors affecting tape-wound composite helical spring prepared by E-glass/epoxy by using taguchi method and statistical distributions. *International Journal of Composite Materials*, 10(1), pp.10-17.

13. Jones, R. M. **2018**. Mechanics of composite materials. CRC press.

14. Tenney, D. R., Sykes, G. F., and Bowles, D. E. **1985**. Composite materials for space structures. *In ESA Proceedings of 3rd European Symposium on Spacecraft Materials in Space Environments.*

15. Pande, H., **1998**. Non wood fibres and global fibre supply. *Unasylva*. 49, pp.44-50.

16. Lengel, D. E. **1999**. AG-fibers: They Look Like Fibers-They Act Like Fibers. Why not Make Fiberboards. In *The Meeting of the Eastern Canadian Section of the Forest Products Society (May 19-20), Winnipeg, Manitoba, Canada.*

17. Bach, L. **1999**. Structural board manufactured from split straw. In *The Meeting of the Eastern Canadian Section of the Forest Products Society (May 19-20), Winnipeg, Manitoba, Canada.*

18. Cooper, P. A., Balatinecz, J. J., and Flannery, S. J. **1999**. Agricultural waste materials for composites: A Canadian reality. In *Center for Management Technology Global Panel Based Conference, Kuala Lumpur.*

19. Rowell, R. M., **2007**. Composite materials from forest biomass: a review of current practices, science and technology. *Journal of the American Chemical Society,* pp.76-92.

20. Kaplan, D. L., **1998**. Biopolymers from renewable resources. *Springer. Berlin. Heidelberg.* pp.1-417.

21. Zafar, M., Najeeb, S., Khurshid, Z., Vazirzadeh, M., Zohaib, S., Najeeb, B., and Sefat, F. **2016**. Potential of electrospun nanofibers for biomedical and dental applications. *Materials*, 9(2), pp.73.

22. Zagho, M. M., Hussein, E. A., and Elzatahry, A. A., **2018**. Recent overviews in functional polymer composites for biomedical applications. *Polymers*. 10(7), pp.1-21.

23. Rawal, S. P., **2001**. Metal-matrix composites for space applications. *Journal of the Minerals, Metals and Materials Society,* 53(4), pp.14-17.

24. Descamps, P., Tirlocq, J., and Cambier, F., **1991**. Ceramic Matrix Composites: Properties and Applications. *Riley. F. L. (eds) 3rd European Symposium on Engineering Ceramics.* pp.109-125.

25. Triantou, K., Perez, B., Marinou, A., Florez, S., Mergia, K., Vekinis, G., Barcena, J., Rotärmel, W., Zuber, C., and Montbrun, De. À., **2017**. Performance of cork and ceramic matrix composite joints for re-entry thermal protection structures. *Composites Part B: Engineering*, 108, pp.270-278.

26. Naslain, R., Guette, A., Rebillat, F., Pailler, R., Langlais, F., and Bourrat, X., **2004**. Boron-bearing species in ceramic matrix composites for long-term aerospace applications. *Journal of Solid State Chemistry*, 177(2), pp.449-456.

27. Gupta, N., and Paramsothy, M., **2014**. Metal- and polymer-matrix composites: Functional Lightweight Materials for High-Performance Structures. *Journal of the Minerals, Metals and Materials Society*, 66(6), pp.862-865.

28. Masuelli, M., ed., **2013**. Fiber reinforced polymers - the technology applied for concrete repair. *IntechOpen*. pp.1-240.

29. Thakur, V. K., and Singha, A. S., **2010**. Physico-Chemical and Mechanical Characterization of Natural Fibre Reinforced Polymer Composites. *Iranian Polymer Journal*, 19(1), pp.3–16.

30. Beg, M. D. H., and Pickering, K. L., **2008**. Mechanical performance of Kraft fiber reinforced polypropylene composites: influence of fiber length, fibre beating and hygrothermal ageing. *Composites Part A: Applied Science and Manufacturing*, 39(11), pp.1748-1755.

31. Saba, N., Paridah, M. T., and Jawaid, M., **2015**. Mechanical properties of kenaf fiber reinforced polymer Composite: A review. *Construction and Building Materials*, 76, pp.87-96.

32. Peças, P., Carvalho, H., Salman, H., and Leite, M., **2018**. Natural fibre composites and their applications: A Review. *Journal of Composites Science*, 2(4), pp.2-20.

33. Song, J. H., Murphy, R. J., Narayan, R., and Davies, G. B. H., **2009**. Biodegradable and compostable alternatives to conventional plastics. *Philosophical Transactions of the Royal Society B*, 364(1526), pp.2127-2139.

34. Pickering, K. L., Efendy, M. G. A., and Le, T. M., **2016**. A review of recent developments in natural fibre composites and their mechanical performance. *Composites Part A: Applied Science and Manufacturing*, 83, pp.98-112.

35. Unterweger, C., Brüggemann, O., and Furst, C., **2014**. Synthetic fibers and thermoplastic short-fiber-reinforced polymers: Properties and characterization. *Polymer Composites*, 35(2), pp.227-236.

36. Manikandan, A., and Rajkumar, R., **2016**. Evaluation of mechanical properties of synthetic fiber reinforced polymer composites by mixture design analysis. *Polymers & Polymer Composites*, 24(7), pp.455-462.

37. Thakur, V. K., Thakur, M. K., and Pappu, A., eds., **2017**. Hybrid polymer composite materials: applications. Woodhead publishing series in composites science and engineering. *Elsevier Science*. pp.1-423.

38. Sangthong, S., Pongprayoon, T., and Yanumet, N., **2009**. Mechanical property improvement of unsaturated polyester composite reinforced with admicellar- treated sisal fibers. *Composites Part A: Applied Science and Manufacturing*, 40(6-7), pp.687-694.

39. Rai, M. **1998**. Building materials in India, 50 years: a commemorative volume. Building Materials & Technology Promotion.

40. Megelski, S., Stephens, J. S., Chase, D. B., and Rabolt, J. F. **2002**. Micro-and nanostructured surface morphology on electrospun polymer fibers. *Macromolecules*, 35(22), pp.8456-8466.

41. Beach, E. D., and Price, J. M. **1993**. The effects of expanding biodegradable polymer production on the farm sector. *Industrial uses of agricultural materials. Situation and outlook report*, (6), pp.41-48.

42. Beach, E. D., Boyd, R., and Uri, N. D., **1996**. Expanding biodegradable polymer resin use: assessing the aggregate impact on the US economy. *Applied Mathematical Modeling*, 20(5), pp.388-398.

43. Calmon-Decriaud, A., Bellon-Maurel, V., and Silvestre, F., **1999**. Standard Methods for Testing the Aerobic Biodegradation of Polymeric Materials. Review and Perspectives. *Advances in Polymer Sciences.* 135, pp.207-226.

44. Herrmann, A. S., Nickel, J., and Riedel, U., **1998**. Construction Materials Based upon Biologically Renewable Resources - From Components to Finished Parts. *Polymer Degradation and Stability,* 59(1-3), pp.251-261.

45. Subramanian, M. N. **2017**. *Polymer blends and composites: chemistry and technology.* John Wiley & Sons.

46. Rowell, R. M., and Banks, W. B. **1985**. Water repellency and dimensional stability of wood. *Gen. Tech. Rep. FPL-50. Madison, WI: US Department of Agriculture, Forest Service, Forest Products Laboratory;* 50, pp.24.

47. Kester, J. J., and Fennema, O. R., **1986**. Edible Films and Coatings: A Review. *Food Technology (Chicago)*. 40(12), pp.47-59.

48. Gennadios, A., Ghorpade, V. M., Weller, C. L., and Hanna, M. A., **1996**. Heat curing of soy protein films.*Trans. ASABE*. 39(2), pp.575-579.

49. Sun, X., and Bian, K., **1999**. Shear strength and water resistance of modified soy protein adhesives. *Journal of American Oil Chemists Society,* 76(8), pp.977-980.

50. Chen, L., Remondetto, G., Rouabhia, M., and Subirade, M., **2008**. Kinetics of the breakdown of cross-linked soy protein films for drug delivery. *Biomaterials,* 29(27), pp.3750-3756.

51. Kondpal, B. C., Chaurasia, R., and Khurana, V., **2015**. Recent advances in green composites–a review. *International Journal for technological Research in Engineering*, 2(7), pp.742-747.

52. Zdanowicz, K., Kotynia, R., and Marx, S., **2019**. Prestressing concrete members with fibre-reinforced polymer reinforcement: State of research. *Structural Concrete*, 20(3), pp.872-885.

53. Garcez, M. R., Meneghetti, L. C., and Teixeira, R. M., **2019**. The effect of FRP prestressing on the fatigue performance of strengthened RC beams. *Structural Concrete*, 22(1), pp.6-2

# Chapter-7

# Polymer Composite in Energy Storage and Conversion

Honey Sharma[1],

Nizamul Haque Ansari[2]

Mithu Maiti Jana[3]

**Abstract:** This present chapter highlights the importance of polymer composite materials and their application in energy storage and energy conversion. Polymer composites are a desirable alternative for energy storage because of their great flexibility, low cost, and light weight. Many kinds of polymer composites such as carbon based composites, metal oxide and conductive based composites, biopolymer based composite that are employed for energy storage are discussed. The several energy storage devices such as batteries, supercapacitors, dielectric capacitors, redox flow batteries, flexible and wearable energy storage devices are also covered. Polymers composites which are increasingly used in energy conversion applications are also discussed.

**Keywords:** Polymers Composites, Energy Storage, Energy Conversion.

## 1. Introduction

Polymer composites are a class of highly effective and adaptable material composed of a combination of several phases of materials, with polymers often making up at least one of the phases as the matrix [1]. The combination of these components work together to provide distinct mechanical and thermal properties that are not possible to accomplish with a single material. The two primary stages that are crucial for creating polymer composites are matrix and reinforcement. Typically, these two stages consist of fiber serving as reinforcement and organic polymers acting as the matrix. In polymer composites, the fiber is primarily the load-bearing element as its strength and stiffness are often far higher than those of the matrix material. However, by evenly distributing the applied force to the fiber, the matrix acts as a load distributor. Consequently, in order to provide an effective load transfer and improve the mechanical properties of the polymer composites, the matrix needs to hold the fiber securely.

---

[1] *Department of Physical Sciences, Associate Professor, Sant Baba Bhag Singh University, Jalandhar, Punjab - 144030, India.*
[2] *Department of Physical Sciences (Chemistry), Professor, Sant Baba Bhag Singh University, Jalandhar, Punjab - 144030, India.*
[3] *Department of Physical Sciences, Associate Professor, Sant Baba Bhag Singh University, Jalandhar, Punjab - 144030, India.*
Email. Id: nizamulchem@gmail.com, maiti.mithu@gmail.com

Polymer composites' overall performance is usually determined by:

1. The properties of the fiber

2. The properties of the polymer matrix

3. The ratio of the fiber to the polymer matrix in the composite (fiber volume fraction)

4. The geometry and orientation of the fiber in the composite

The mechanical characteristics of polymer composites are commonly used to describe the performance. It is thought to be the most significant of the polymer composite's chemical and physical characteristics. Various reinforcing types are employed in various composites based on their intended applications. Polymers and their composites have garnered a lot of interest in the electronics industry over the past few decades. Many researchers [2] use them as a material because of their great strength, stiffness, ease of processing, and low weight. In accordance with the required application, several combinations and variations have been used as these characteristics may also be readily changed by adding fibers, nanoparticles, or just mixing them with other polymers. A cobalt complex and polypyrrole (PPy) composite thin film was created by Parnell et al., [3] for use as supercapacitor electrodes. Greater accumulation inside the PPy films was made possible by the unique redox feature of the cobalt complex, which enhanced the films's total capacitance and charge storage. According to the data as a whole, energy storage devices are essential to the shift to a cleaner, more sustainable energy system [4]. Because of their unique attributes and probable applications polymer composites have drawn a lot of interest in the field of energy storage devices [5]. Polymer composites can be made with high porosity and surface areas, which makes them ideal for energy storage devices like supercapacitors. Additionally, polymer composites may be designed to have certain conductive properties, which enable them to function as current collectors or electrodes in energy storage devices. For instance, conductive polymer composites are a desirable alternative for use in batteries because they may be made with low resistance and great electrical conductivity. Because polymer composites are affordable and lightweight, they are ideal for energy storage and energy conversion applications in portable electronics and transportation. Polymer composites may drastically lower the weight and cost of energy storage devices when compared to conventional metal-based materials, increasing their usefulness and accessibility. Overall, the special range of properties that polymer composites provide makes them desirable materials for energy storage devices and energy conversion, especially for uses requiring high performance, adaptability, and affordability. With ongoing research and advancement, polymer composites are probably going to become more significant in energy storage technologies in the future. One may learn more about the special benefits and drawbacks of polymer composites for energy storage by investigating their applicability, performance, and potential applications.

## 2. Applicability

**2.1. Carbon-Based Polymer Composites:** Carbon-based polymer composite's huge surface area, excellent conductivity, and electrochemical stability has made them a popular choice for energy storage devices, especially supercapacitors. Numerous methods, including sol-gel, hydrothermal, and electrochemical deposition methods, may be used to synthesize these materials, and can be modified to have specific properties [6-7]. Controlling the synthesis parameters, such as temperature and reaction time, and employing carbon precursors with a high degree of graphitization can both improve the surface area. The large surface area of carbon-based polymer composites makes ion transport more effective and increases supercapacitors ability to store energy [8].

**2.2. Metal Oxide-Based Polymer Composites:** Metal oxide-based polymer composites have also been studied as possible materials for energy storage devices. Metal oxides that may conduct reversible redox processes [9], such as $MnO_2$, $Fe_2O_3$, and $CO_3O_4$, offer significant theoretical capabilities for energy storage. The enhanced electrical conductivity of metal oxide-based polymer composites is an additional benefit, as it is essential for rapid charge and discharge cycles in energy storage devices. The addition of conducting polymer matrices, such polypyrrole or polythiophene, to metal oxide-based polymer composites might increase their conductivity. The conducting polymer matrix can facilitate the pathway for electron transport and enhance the metal oxide's electrochemical activity [10].

**2.3. Conductive Polymer Composites:** One kind of composite material that has been extensively researched for application in energy storage devices, especially batteries and supercapacitors, is conductive polymer composite. These materials consist of a conductive polymer matrix, such polyaniline, polypyrrole, or polythiophene which is reinforced by a filler material, such graphene or carbon nanotubes. The resultant material is appropriate for energy storage applications due to a number of unique properties. A major benefit of conductive polymer composites is their high electrical conductivity, which is essential to efficient charge and discharge in energy storage devices. The conductive polymer matrix offered a path for electron transport, while additional ion transport pathways are provided by the filler material, which also enhances the surface area. This results in quicker charging and discharging periods as well as an increased energy storage capacity [11].

## 3. Performance

**3.1. Energy Density:** Energy density, a measurement of the quantity of energy stored per unit mass or volume of the material may be used to assess the performance characteristics of polymer composite materials in energy storage devices. The unique properties of polymer composite materials make them capable of achieving high energy densities in energy storage devices. For example the energy storage capacity of carbon-based polymer composites, such as graphene-reinforced polymer composites and carbon nanotubes, can be enhanced by their high electrical conductivity and surface area. For supercapacitors, these materials can reach energy densities of up to 400 Wh/kg, whereas for batteries, they can reach up to 200 Wh/kg. The large potential energy storage capacity of metal oxide-based polymer composites contributes to their high energy densities. For example the energy densities of $Fe_2O_3$ based polymer composites may reach up to 180 Wh/kg, whereas those of $MnO_2$-based polymer composites can reach up to 120 Wh/kg. Because of their strong electrical conductivity and ion transport characteristics, conductive polymer composites, including polyaniline or polypyrrole-reinforced polymer composites, also show high energy densities. These materials have the potential to provide energy densities of up to 180 Wh/kg for batteries and 120 Wh/kg for supercapacitors [12].

**3.2. Power density:** The power density of polymer composite materials, which determines the rate at which energy may be released from the device, is another crucial performance feature of these materials in energy storage devices. Applications requiring fast charging and discharging, such as high-speed data processing or electric vehicles need a high power density. The unique features of polymer composite materials make them capable of achieving large power densities in energy storage devices. Power densities of up to 20 kW/kg for supercapacitors and 5 kW/kg for batteries may be attained using these materials. Because of their quick ion diffusion and rapid charge-transfer rates, metal oxide-based polymer composites also have high power densities. For example power densities of up to 10 kW/kg may be attained by $TiO_2$-based polymer composites, for instance, while $Fe_2O_3$ based polymer composites can only reach up to 3 kW/kg [13].

**3.3. Durability:** Metal oxide-based polymer composites show excellent durability owing to their high stablility under challenging conditions and their capacity to sustain their performance over time. For example polymer composites based on $Fe_2O_3$ can sustain 80% of their initial capacity after 1000 cycles of charge and discharge, whereas those based on $TiO_2$ can sustain 90% of their initial capacity after 500 cycles. Conductive polymer composite like polyaniline or polypyrrole-reinforced polymer composites show excellent durability owing to their capability to maintain their mechanical and electrical properties over time. Additionally, these materials can continue to perform well in challenging chemical conditions at high temperatures [14-15]. The lightweight and flexibility of polymer composite materials, in addition to their durability, are important attributes for wearable and portable energy storage devices. However, in order to increase the durability of polymer composite materials in energy storage devices, a few issues still need to be resolved. These include creating novel materials with improved chemical and mechanical stability, enhancing the composite materials and electrodes interfacial characteristics, and extending the devices' cycle life and safety [16].

**3.4. Cost Effectiveness:** One crucial performance feature of polymer composite materials in energy storage devices is their cost-effectiveness, which is the capacity of the materials to offer excellent performance at an affordable cost. Conductive polymer composites, including polypyrrole-reinforced polymer composites or polyaniline, can also be economical due to their high electrical conductivity and comparatively cheap production costs, which can result in a lower cost per unit of power. Besides being economical, polymer composite materials are also lightweight and flexible, which can result in reduced installation and maintenance costs, especially for wearable and portable energy storage devices. To further increase the cost-effectiveness of polymer composite materials in energy storage devices, a few issues still need to be resolved. These include lowering production costs, enhancing device's energy and power densities, and extending their cycle life and safety [17].

**4. Future and Development:** Future developments in the field of polymer composite energy storage applications present both major challenges and great opportunities. Advanced energy storage devices with better energy densities and quicker charging times are ready for investigation alongside a commitment to sustainability through eco-friendly materials. One important way to improve energy efficiency is to combine polymer composites with renewable energy sources like solar and wind power [18-19]. More advancement in the design of electrochemical devices will be crucial, especially in the fields of energy management systems and smart grids. Lightweight and high-capacity polymer composites are also necessary for electric vehicles (EVs) in order to increase range and reduce charging times. Recycling techniques and sustainable manufacturing procedures will support environmentally friendly production. In order to reduce hazards and provide reliable monitoring methods, safety and durability factors demand constant study. Collaborations across disciplines and stakeholders are vital for achieving full capability of these materials. Since energy density continues to be a challenge, collaboration will be essential to bridging the gap and advancing polymer composite energy storage toward a sustainable and cutting-edge energy future.

The need for more environmentally friendly materials led to the development of biopolymers in recent years. Biopolymers are polymer-based molecules made up of single units joined by covalent bonds to create larger molecules [20]. This transition to green energy is essential as the long-term use of polymers derived from synthetic fossil fuels has accelerated climate change and continuously impacted the environment. The non-biodegradable nature of these synthetic polymers and their manufacture method, which uses hazardous substances or produces toxic byproducts, are what cause their adverse effects [21]. Multiple studies have emphasized the significance and relevance of employing polymer composites obtained from bioresources as a remarkable substitute for synthetic polymers. A biopolymer membrane was created by Kumar et al., [22] using lithium chloride as the dopant and tamarind seed polysaccharides as the primary polymer, respectively. Kumar et al., [22] discovered that adding lithium chloride dopant enhanced the ionic conductivity by enabling temporary cross-linking to develop between the segments of the polymer chain. Additionally, biomass-derived carbon has been widely employed as carbon precursors in supercapacitors [23-26] due to the cost-effectiveness and abundance of carbon resources on Earth. High performance can be achieved by using carbon derived from renewable resources as a natural binder-free electrode material for supercapacitors by enhancing the specific capacitances of carbon materials, particularly the carbon porous structure, physical and chemical activation, and heteroatom addition [27-29].

## 5. Energy Storage Applications:

Energy storage is the process of storing energy which can then be extracted at a later time to perform the necessary task. The use of polymers derived from bioresources for a variety of electrochemical devices has been emphasized by researchers. This is mostly due to the biodegradable and biocompatible properties of biopolymers, which may be used to enhance the functionality of other biologically active molecules in a device.

This section covers the latest developments in energy storage devices based on biopolymers, namely batteries, supercapacitors.

**5.1. Batteries:** The battery is a type of chemical power cell that provides the device with power or current [30]. While the number of cells linked in series determines a battery's nominal voltage, the size of the cells determines its discharge capacity rate. Traditional metal and inorganic materials have demonstrated successful and consistent outcomes and hold significant potential for use in commercial applications [31]. Lithium-ion and nickel-cadmium batteries are two of the most widely used types of batteries in the market today. However, these devices have safety problems including poisonous leaks, which might endanger users. Despite the use of several methods, such as recycling battery waste, the most recent effort to create environmentally friendly batteries is the use of biomaterials, particularly biopolymers. Some of the environmentally friendly biopolymer-based composites are as follows.

**5.1.1. Cellulose:** One of the most often utilized biopolymers in battery applications is cellulose. Natural cellulose fibers may be derived from a variety of plant-based bioresources, including wheat, corn cobs, cotton, bananas, and maize. Bacterial fermentation-derived cellulose has drawn attention mainly as a precursor for high-rate lithium-ion batteries, which produce carbonaceous fiber material when pyrolyzed at high temperatures. A more porous structure, a greater surface area, superior biodegradability, the capacity to produce cellulose on a wide scale, and the presence of several hydroxyl groups [32-33] are some of the clear benefits that bacterial cellulose precursors have over conventional precursors. These advantages turn bacterial cellulose into an adaptable, flexible scaffold biomaterial that sparks interest in creating a highly adaptable three-dimensional carbon nanomaterial because of its extremely potent interactions with different added chemicals and its finely thinner morphology in comparison to plant cellulose[34-35]. For use as an elastic electrode in lithium-sulfur batteries, Huang et al., [36] created a three-dimensional (3D) carbonaceous aerogel produced from bacterial cellulose. Due to the inherent microporous structure, significant sulfur loading is made possible, which enhances electrical conductivity and mechanical stability. A high discharge capacity of 1134 mA h/g, long-lasting cycle stability of 700 mA h/g at 400 mA/g, and good rate capability were the outcomes of the cellulose-sulfur combination. The porous membrane of bacterial cellulose nanocrystals coupled with a polymer matrix was also used by Ajkidkarn et al., [37] as a lithium-ion battery separator. According to the Ajkidkarn et al.,[37] these bacterial cellulose-based separators have good electrolyte absorption and wettability. They also showed ionic conductivity between $10^{-2}$ and $10^{-3}$ S/cm at 56.8% porosity. Additionally, Li et al., [38] showed how to employ cellulose-encapsulated carbon-sulfur core shells for lithium-sulfur batteries. The elastic shape of cellulose makes it a suitable shell because it can support volumetric expansion, has strong ion conductivity, and may serve as a deterrent to stop sulfur from decomposing in the electrolyte. Thus, the shell provides an excellent coulombic efficiency over 99%, a high initial discharge capacity of more than 1200 mA $hg^{-1}$, and a degradation rate of around 0.12% over 3000 cycles at low capacity. Lithium sulfur (Li–S) batteries are essentially unique in their energy storage mechanism due to their great energy density of around 2675 W h $kg^{-1}$ (or about 2800 W h $L^{-1}$), affordability, and speed of generation. This rechargeable device employs lithium as the anode and sulfur as the cathode. Lithium sulfur batteries have a considerably higher energy density than lithium-ion batteries. Even though sulfur is inexpensive, plentiful, and environmentally benign, there are a few technological obstacles that must be overcome before lithium sulfur can be commercialized. These include the insulator surface of sulfur, rapid capacity degradation, and significant volumetric expansion that might cause structural damage to the electrode. For the anode material of lithium-ion batteries, Yu et al.,[39] synthesized carbon nanospheres using cellulose waste maize straw. According to their research, carbon nanospheres made from cellulose enhanced the specific surface area, allowing for the injection of lithium ions into more active areas. After 100 cycles, the material provided a specific capacity of 577 mA h/g when integrated into a lithium-ion battery.

**5.1.2. Chitosan:** Chitosan is another popular biopolymer utilized in battery applications. Shellfish bioresources including prawns, crabs, lobsters, and even some types of mushrooms are typically the source of waste chitin [40]. Tang et al., [40] used chitosan oligosaccharides to create a $Li_2ZnTi_3O_8$ electrode binder for lithium-ion batteries. According to their research, the energy cell's improved electrochemical performance was caused by the properties of the binder, which inhibited electrode inflammation in the electrolyte solution and allowed for the formation of strong hydrogen bonds between the active material's hydroxyl groups and the current collector. The system shows a superior initial discharge capacity of 215.6 mA $hg^{-1}$, a higher coulombic efficiency of 93.6%, and a better charge retention rate of 33.6% after 1000 cycles compared to the traditional polyvinylidene fluoride (PVDF) binder. In order to create porous nitrogen-doped carbon materials for use as anodes in lithium-ion batteries, Wang et al.,[41] used abundant chitosan biomass. Their research revealed remarkable lithium-ion storage characteristics, including outstanding cyclic stability over 1100 cycles and a high specific capacity of 460 mA h/g at a current density of 50 mA/g.

**5.1.3. Lignin:** Another biopolymer that is regularly studied for battery applications is lignin. Likewise, plant-based bioresources including vegetable stalks and other straw grains may be used to make lignin. Lu et al., [42] used lignin as the binder material to create graphite-negative and LiFePO$_4$ positive electrodes for lithium batteries. Lu et al., [42] found that the positive electrode had an excellent reversible capacity of 148 mA h/g while the negative electrode had 305 mA h/g. Additionally, strong rate capabilities were found for the positive electrode at 117 mA h/g and the negative electrode at 160 mA h/g. Low ohmic resistance was also made possible by good binder functioning. Furthermore, Chen et al., [43] used lignin as a conductive additive and binder to create a silicon-nanoparticle-based composite for lithium-ion batteries. The carbon black component and the traditional polymer binder were both replaced with lignin. After 100 cycles, the composite electrode's initial discharge capacity of 3086 mA h/g and its sustained capacity of 2378 mA h/g demonstrated exceptional electrochemical capabilities. The electrode also demonstrated good rate capability and performance in a whole cell arrangement. To absorb the liquid electrolyte, Liu et al., [44] created a lignin-polyvinyl pyrrolidone membrane. It was noted from the final composite that the membrane had improved mechanical qualities and thermal security. Additionally, at room temperature, it had a high ionic conductivity of $2.52 \times 10^{-3}$ S cm$^{-1}$.

**5.1.3. Pectin:** Pectin is another biopolymer that is commonly utilized in battery construction. The peel of the majority of citrus fruits, namely oranges and apples, contains natural pectin. Perumal et al., [45] created a biopolymer electrolyte based on pectin that is adaptable and has different lithium chloride (LiCl) compositions. According to their research, a 50:50 Mwt% composite electrolyte produced the maximum ionic conductivity of $2.08 \times 10^{-3}$ S cm$^{-1}$. In comparison to the standard lithium chloride integrated electrolyte, both pectin-based biopolymer electrolytes demonstrate exceptional mechanical strength and reliable cycle performance.

**5.1.4. Carrageenan.:** Another biopolymer utilized in batteries is carrageenan. Priya et al., [46] developed a biopolymer electrolyte that can conduct magnesium ions for battery applications using iota carrageenan and various magnesium nitrate (Mg(NO$_3$)$_2$) salt compositions.

**5.1.5. Polysaccharides:** In the creation of biopolymer-based batteries, polysaccharides like those in tamarind fruit seeds are used. To enable it to serve as the electrolyte in lithium-ion batteries, Premalatha et al., [47] synthesized a pure tamarind seed polysaccharide (TSP) membrane and doped it with lithium bromide. For proton batteries, Premalatha et al., [48] created biopolymer membranes using TSP complexed with varying ammonium bromide (NH$_4$Br) concentrations.

Using biopolymer-based composites that contain cellulose, chitosan, lignin, pectin, and carrageenan generally greatly improves batteries capacity to store energy.

**6. Supercapacitors:** Chemical energy storage devices known as supercapacitors store and release energy by using the reversible adsorption and desorption of ions from the boundary between electrolytes and electrodes [49]. Supercapacitors can be broadly classified into two categories: electrical double-layer capacitors (EDLCs) and electrochemical pseudocapacitors. By assimilating charged ions at the interface between the electrolyte and the conducting electrodes, EDLCs are able to store electrical energy. Through reversible redox processes, pseudocapacitors transfer charge between the electrode and electrolyte, storing electrical energy. Additionally, hybrid supercapacitors with double-layer capacitive charging and discharging schemes [31] and pseudocapacitive are also available. The high energy conversion rate, rapid charge speed, and exceptional recyclability of supercapacitors make them potentially great energy storage devices. Supercapacitors employ conventional binders, which are hazardous and have poor mechanical properties. Biopolymers have emerged as a viable substitute due to their exceptional electrical conductivity and biodegradability. Similar to batteries, supercapacitors' capacity to store energy is significantly increased by the use of biopolymer-based composites (cellulose, chitosan, lignin). It is evident that using biopolymers allows for better specific capacitance in the majority of applications. Additionally, there was a significant improvement in the initial capacitance retention across thousands of cycles.

## 7. Some More Energy Storage Devices

### 7.1. Dielectric Capacitors:

**7.1.1. High-k Dielectric Composites:** Dielectric capacitors use an electric field to store energy. High dielectric constant (high-k) polymer composites provide higher energy density. PVDF and polypropylene (PP) are common polymers that are frequently mixed with ceramic fillers like titanium dioxide ($TiO_2$) or barium titanate ($BaTiO_3$) to increase energy storage and discharge efficiency [50].

**7.1.2. Flexible Dielectric Films:** Metal oxides or ferroelectric particles combined with polymer composites can create flexible films for small, bendable capacitors. Silver or zinc oxide (ZnO) nanoparticles are added to films to improve their dielectric properties while maintaining their flexibility and light weight [51].

### 7.2. Redox Flow Batteries (RFBs):

**7.2.1. Ion Selectivity Membranes:** The two compartments in RFBs are separated by polymer composite membranes, including those based on Nafion, which allows ions to flow through only while blocking cross-mixing. The mechanical strength, ion selectivity, and stability of these membranes are enhanced by the addition of fillers such as metal oxides or silica [52].

**7.2.2. Electrodes:** By increasing the electrode's surface area and conductivity in RFBs, carbon-based composites like carbon felt embedded in a polymer matrix improve battery efficiency and charge-discharge rate [53].

### 7.3. Flexible and Wearable Energy Storage Devices:
Polymer composites provide lightweight, stretchy, and flexible alternatives for wearable technology applications. Materials that can stretch and bend while retaining conductivity and charge storage are produced by combining polymers like PDMS (polydimethylsiloxane) with conductive fillers like graphene, silver nanowires, or carbon nanotubes.

**7.3.1. Self-Healing Composites:** In order to preserve the durability and effectiveness of the device, recent research has concentrated on polymers having self-healing attributes, such as polyurethanes or polyacrylates mixed with conductive elements [54].

The potential of polymer composites for energy storage is enormous since they may be tailored to enhance characteristics like charge capacity, flexibility, and ionic conductivity. Enhancing energy density, cycle stability, and environmental resilience are still the main goals of their research in order to satisfy the rising demand for high-performance energy storage systems.

## 8. Characteristics of Polymer Composite Materials for Energy Conversion/ Energy Harvesting

8.1. Mechanical Properties: When choosing composite materials for energy harvesting in electric vehicles, mechanical characteristics are essential. The capacity of the materials to tolerate the mechanical stress and strain produced during energy conversion is critical to the performance of energy harvesting devices. Depending on the matrix and reinforcing components utilized, composite materials have different mechanical properties. Good toughness and ductility are characteristics of polymer-based composites, which are made up of a polymer matrix and reinforcing materials like carbon, glass, or ceramic fibers. Therefore, in order to obtain maximum performance, mechanical attributes and energy conversion properties, such as electrical conductivity and thermal stability, must be taken into account while developing and characterizing composite materials for energy harvesting in electric vehicles [55-59].

8.2. Electrical Conductivity: A key component of composite materials for energy harvesting in electric vehicles is electrical conductivity. Energy harvesting is made feasible by these material's efficient electrical conductivity. The mix of matrix and reinforcing components utilized determines the electrical conductivity of composite materials. Electrical conductivity is often higher in metal-based composites and lower in polymer-based composites. Nonetheless, including conductive fibers or fillers into the composite structure can increase the electrical conductivity of polymer-based composites. It's crucial to remember that electrical conductivity might not be sufficient to assess a composite material's capability for energy harvesting [60-66].

8.3. Thermal Stability: One of the most important properties of composite materials for energy harvesting in electric vehicles is thermal stability. In electric vehicles, energy harvesting systems have the potential to produce heat, and composite materials need to be able to tolerate the thermal stress that comes with these processes. Additionally, the matrix and reinforcing elements employed in composite materials affect their thermal stability. For example, composites made of metal have strong thermal stability, but composites made of polymers often have less thermal stability [67-77].

## 9. Polymer Composite Materials in Energy Conversion:

Polymer composites are becoming more and more popular in energy conversion applications because of their adaptable qualities, which can be adjusted by changing the filler components as well as the polymer matrix. The structural and dielectric qualities of polymers are combined with the functional benefits of fillers such as metal oxides, ceramics, and carbon nanomaterials in these composites to provide a range of energy conversion systems. Some uses are as follows:

### 9.1. Solar Energy Conversion:

**9.1.1. Organic Photovoltaics (OPVs)**: In organic photovoltaics (OPVs), polymer composites can serve as the active layer. The polymer matrix in OPVs absorbs light, while fillers (such as non-fullerene acceptors or fullerene derivatives) enable effective charge separation and transport. The materials used in OPVs are frequently donor-acceptor polymers such as poly(3-hexylthiophene) (P3HT) [78].

**9.1.2. Perovskite Solar Cells:** Reliability and efficiency are improved by certain polymer composites. Improved charge transfer, decreased hysteresis, and improved moisture resistance of the perovskite layer can all be achieved using a polymer matrix including filler components [79].

### 9.2. Thermoelectric Energy Conversion:

Temperature gradients may be converted into electric voltage and vice versa using thermoelectric polymer composites. To achieve high electrical conductivity and low thermal conductivity ideal for thermoelectric applications polymers such as poly(3,4-ethylenedioxythiophene) (PEDOT) and polyaniline (PANI) are frequently combined with fillers like carbon nanotubes (CNTs), graphene, or metallic nanoparticles [80-81].

### 9.3. Piezoelectric and Triboelectric Energy Harvesting:

**9.3.1. Piezoelectric Polymer Composites**: Piezoelectric polymers, such poly (vinylidene fluoride) (PVDF), produce an electrical charge when they undergo mechanical deformation. To improve their piezoelectric performance, these polymers are frequently mixed with piezoelectric fillers such as lead zirconate titanate (PZT) or barium titanate ($BaTiO_3$) [82].

**9.3.2. Triboelectric Nanogenerators (TENGs):** TENGs use the triboelectric effect to capture mechanical motion energy. To improve the efficiency of charge transfer, TENGs employ composite materials such PDMS (polydimethylsiloxane) with metal oxide fillers [83].

**9.4. Fuel Cells and Electrolytes in Batteries:** In fuel cells, polymer composites can be used as proton exchange membranes. Materials such as Nafion with embedded nanoparticles enhance ion conductivity, mechanical strength, and longevity. For improved ionic conductivity and thermal stability, solid polymer electrolytes with ceramic fillers are also used in lithium-ion and other batteries [84-85].

**9.5. Capacitive Energy Storage:** Capacitors benefit from dielectric polymer composites because of their high dielectric constant, which allows them to store more electrical energy. High-k dielectric fillers like titanium dioxide ($TiO_2$) or barium titanate are typically mixed with polymers like polypropylene (PP) or polycarbonate (PC) to create composites that are appropriate for high-energy-density capacitors [86-87].

Because of their adjustable mechanical and electrical characteristics, polymer composites offer enormous promise in energy conversion, and research is moving quickly to increase their scalability, stability, and efficiency.

**Conclusion:** The large specific surface areas, mechanical flexibilities, and adjustable electrochemical characteristics of polymer composite materials have made them attractive options for energy storage applications. Because of their adjustable mechanical and electrical characteristics, polymer composites offer enormous promise in energy conversion.

**References:**

1. M.A. Masuelli, Introduction of fibre-reinforced polymers_ polymers and composites: concepts, properties and processes, Fiber Reinforced Polymers-The Technology Applied for Concrete Repair, Intech, (2013).

2. D. Ponnamma, K.K. Sadasivuni, M.A. AlMaadeed, Introduction of biopolymer composites: what to do in electronics? , Biopolymer Composites in Electronics Elsevier, (2017).

3. C.M. Parnell, B.P. Chhetri, T.B. Mitchell, F. Watanabe, G. Kannarpady, A. B. RanguMagar, H. Zhou, K.M. Alghazali, A.S. Biris, A. Ghosh, Simultaneous electrochemical deposition of cobalt complex and poly(pyrrole) thin films for supercapacitor electrodes, Sci. Rep. 9 (2019) 5650.

4. L. da Silva Lima, M. Quartier, A. Buchmayr, D. Sanjuan-Delmás, H. Laget, D. Corbisier, J. Mertens, J. Dewulf, Life cycle assessment of lithium-ion batteries and vanadium redox flow batteries-based renewable energy storage systems, Sustain. Energy Technol. Assess 46 (2021) 101286.

5. Q.K Feng, S.L. Zhong, J.Y. Pei, Y. Zhao, D.L. Zhang, D.F. Liu, Y.X. Zhang, Z.M. Dang, Recent Progress and Future Prospects on All-Organic Polymer Dielectrics for Energy Storage Capacitors, Chem. Rev. 122 (2022) 3820–3878.

6. J. Iyyadurai, F.S. Arockiasamy, T. Manickam, S. Rajaram, I. Suyambulingam, S. Siengchin, Experimental Investigation on Mechanical, Thermal, Viscoelastic, Water Absorption, and Biodegradability Behavior of Sansevieria Ehrenbergii Fiber Reinforced Novel Polymeric Composite with the Addition of Coconut Shell Ash Powder, J. Inorg. Organomet. Polym. Mater. 33 (2023) 796–809.

7. M. Ramesh, C. Deepa, M. Tamil Selvan, K.H. Reddy, Effect of Alkalization on Characterization of Ripe Bulrush (Typha Domingensis) Grass Fiber Reinforced Epoxy Composites, J. Nat. Fibers 19 (2022) 931–942.

8. K. Sheoran, V.K. Thakur, S.S. Siwal, Synthesis and overview of carbon-based materials for high performance energy storage application, A review. Mater. Today Proc. 56 (2022) 9–17.

9. B.S. Dakshayini, K.R. Reddy, A. Mishra, N.P. Shetti, S.J. Malode, S. Basu, S. Naveen, A.V. Raghu, Role of conducting polymer and metal oxide-based hybrids for applications in ampereometric sensors and biosensors, Microchem. J. 147 (2019) 7–24.

10. V. Mani, K. Krishnaswamy, F.S. Arockiasamy, T.S. Manickam, Mechanical and dielectric properties of Cissus Quadrangularis fiber-reinforced epoxy/$TiB_2$ hybrid composites, Int. Polym. Process (2023).

11. K. Shahapurkar, M. Gelaw, V.Tirth, M.E.M. Soudagar, P. Shahapurkar, M.C.K. Mujtaba, G.M.S. Ahmed, Comprehensive review on polymer composites as electromagnetic interference shielding materials, Polym. Polym. Compos. 30 (2020) 09673911221102127.

12. Y. Zhao, H. Hao, T. Song, X. Wang, C. Li, W. Li, High energy-power density Zn-ion hybrid supercapacitors with N/P co-doped graphene cathode, J. Power Sources 521 (2022) 230941.

13. G. Zhu, L. Ma, H. Lin, P. Zhao, L. Wang, Y. Hu, R. Chen, T. Chen, Y. Wang, Z. Tie, High-performance Li-ion capacitor based on black-$TiO_2$−x/graphene aerogel anode and biomass-derived microporous carbon cathode, Nano Res. 12 (2019) 1713–1719.

14. T. Manickam, J. Iyyadurai, M. Jaganathan, A. Babuchellam, M. Mayakrishnan, F.S. Arockiasamy, Effect of stacking sequence on mechanical, water absorption, and biodegradable properties of novel hybrid composites for structural applications, Int. Polym. Process. 38 (2022) 88–96.

15. M. Ramesh, M. Tamil Selvan, K. Niranjana, Hygrothermal Aging, Kinetics of Moisture Absorption, Degradation Mechanism and Their Influence on Performance of the Natural Fibre Reinforced Composites, In Aging Effects on Natural Fiber-Reinforced Polyme Composites; Springer: Cham, Switzwerland, (2022) 257–277.

16. M. Bhar, S. Ghosh, S.K. Martha, Designing freestanding electrodes with $Fe_2O_3$-based conversion type anode material for sodium-ion batteries, J. Alloys Compd. 948 (2023) 169670.

17. A.G. Olabi, Q. Abbas, A. Al Makky, M.A. Abdelkareem, Supercapacitors as next generation energy storage devices, Properties and applications, Energy 248 (2022) 123617.

18. A.F. Sahayaraj, I. Jenish, M. Tamilselvan, M. Muthukrishnan, B.A. Kumar, Mechanical and morphological characterization of sisal/kenaf/pineapple mat reinforced hybrid composites, Int. Polym. Process 37 (2022)581–588.

19. M. Ramesh, M.T. Selvan, K. Niranjana, Thermal characterization and hygrothermal aging of lignocellulosic Agave Cantala fiber reinforced polylactide composites, Polym. Compos. 43 (2022)6453–6463.

20. S. Mohan, O.S. Oluwafemi, N. Kalarikkal, S. Thomas, S.P. Songca, Biopolymers – application in nanoscience and nanotechnology, Recent Advances in Biopolymers, In Tech, (2016).

21. D. Ibrahim, E.R. Sadiku, T. Jamiru, Y. Hamam, Y. Alayli, A.A. Eze, W.K. Kupolati, Biopolymer Composites and Bionanocomposites for Energy Applications (2019).

22. L.S. Kumar, P.C. Selvin, S. Selvasekarapandian, R. Manjuladevi, S. Monisha, P. Perumal, Tamarind seed polysaccharide biopolymer membrane for lithium-ion conducting battery, Ionics 24 (2018).

23. T.N.J.I. Edison, R. Atchudan, M.G. Sethuraman, Y.R. Lee, Supercapacitor performance of carbon supported Co3O4 nanoparticles synthesized using Terminalia chebula fruit, J. Taiwan Inst. Chem. Eng. 68 (2016) 489–495.

24. R. Atchudan, T.N.J.I. Edison, S. Perumal, Y.R. Lee, Green synthesis of nitrogen-doped graphitic carbon sheets with use of Prunus persica for supercapacitor applications, Appl. Surf. Sci. 393 (2017) 276–286.

25. R. Atchudan, T.N.J.I. Edison, S. Perumal, P. Thirukumaran, R. Vinodh, Y.R. Lee, Green synthesis of nitrogen-doped carbon nanograss for supercapacitors, J. Taiwan Inst. Chem. Eng. 102 (2019).

26. T.N. Jebakumar Immanuel Edison, R. Atchudan, Y.R. Lee, Facile synthesis of carbon encapsulated $RuO_2$ nanorods for supercapacitor and electrocatalytic hydrogen evolution reaction, Int. J. Hydrog. Energy 44 (2019) 2323–2329.

27. Y. Wang, Q. Qu, S. Gao, G. Tang, K. Liu, S. He, C. Huang, Biomass derived carbon as binder-free electrode materials for supercapacitors, Carbon 155 (2019) 706–726.

28. S. Ghosh, R. Santhosh, S. Jeniffer, V. Raghavan, G. Jacob, K. Nanaji, P. Kollu, S. K. Jeong, A.N. Grace, Natural biomass derived hard carbon and activated carbons as electrochemical supercapacitor electrodes, Sci. Rep. 9 (2019) 16315.

29. D.R. Kumar, I. Kanagaraj, G. Dhakal, A.S. Prakash, J.J. Shim, Palmyra palm tree biomass-derived carbon low-voltage plateau region capacity on Na-ion battery and its full cell performance, J. Environ. Chem. Eng. 9 (2021) 105698.

30. J.P. Nelson, W.D. Bolin, Basics and advances in battery systems, IEEE Trans. Ind. Appl. 31 (1995) 419–428.

31. R. Singh, H.W. Rhee, The rise of bio-inspired energy devices, Energy Storage Mater. 23 (2019).

32. M.P. Illa, M. Khandelwal, C.S. Sharma, Bacterial cellulose-derived carbon nanofibers as anode for lithium-ion batteries, Emerg. Mater. 1 (2018) 105–120.

33. M.P. Illa, A.D. Pathak, C.S. Sharma, M. Khandelwal, Bacterial cellulose–polyaniline composite derived hierarchical nitrogen-doped porous carbon nanofibers as anode for high-rate lithium-ion batteries, ACS Appl. Energy Mater. 3 (2020) 8676–8687.

34. D.A. Gregory, L. Tripathi, A.T.R. Fricker, E. Asare, I. Orlando, V. Raghavendran, I. Roy, Bacterial cellulose: a smart biomaterial with diverse applications, Mater. Sci. Eng. R Rep. 145 (2021) 100623.

35. L. Ma, Z. Bi, Y. Xue, W. Zhang, Q. Huang, L. Zhang, Y. Huang, Bacterial cellulose: an encouraging eco-friendly nano-candidate for energy storage and energy conversion, J. Mater. Chem. A 8 (2020) 5812–5842.

36. Y. Huang, M. Zheng, Z. Lin, B. Zhao, S. Zhang, J. Yang, C. Zhu, H. Zhang, D. Sun, Y. Shi, Flexible cathodes and multifunctional interlayers based on carbonized bacterial cellulose for high-performance lithium–sulfur batteries, J. Mater. Chem. A 3 (2015).

37. P. Ajkidkarn, H. Manuspiya, Novel bacterial cellulose nanocrystals/polyether block amide microporous membranes as separators for lithium-ion batteries, Int. J. Biol. Macromol. 164 (2020) 3580–3588.

38. C. Li, H. Yue, Q. Wang, J. Li, J. Zhang, H. Dong, Y. Yin, S. Yang, A novel composite solid polymer electrolyte based on copolymer P(LA-co-TMC) for all-solid-state lithium ionic batteries, Solid State Ion. 321 (2018) 8–14.

39. K. Yu, J. Wang, K. Song, X. Wang, C. Liang, Y. Dou, Hydrothermal synthesis of cellulose-derived carbon nanospheres from corn straw as anode materials for lithium ion batteries, Nanomaterials 9 (2019) 93.

40. H. Tang, Q. Weng, Z. Tang, Chitosan oligosaccharides: a novel and efficient water soluble binder for lithium zinc titanate anode in lithium-ion batteries, Electrochim. Acta 151 (2015) 27–34.

41. Y.Y. Wang, B.H. Hou, H.Y. Lü, F. Wan, J. Wang, X.L. Wu, Porous N-doped carbon material derived from prolific chitosan biomass as a high-performance electrode for energy storage, RSC Adv. 5 (2015).

42. H. Lu, A. Cornell, F. Alvarado, M. Behm, S. Leijonmarck, J. Li, P. Tomani, G. Lindbergh, Lignin as a binder material for eco-friendly Li-ion batteries, Materials 9 (2016) 127.

43. T. Chen, Q. Zhang, J. Pan, J. Xu, Y. Liu, M. Al-Shroofy, Y.T. Cheng, Low-temperature treated lignin as both binder and conductive additive for silicon nanoparticle composite electrodes in lithium-ion batteries, ACS Appl. Mater. Interfaces 8 (2016) 32341–32348.

44. B. Liu, Y. Huang, H. Cao, A. Song, Y. Lin, M. Wang, X. Li, A high-performance and environment-friendly gel polymer electrolyte for lithium ion battery based on composited lignin membrane, J. Solid State Electrochem. 22 (2018) 807–816.

45. P. Perumal, P. Christopher Selvin, S. Selvasekarapandian, Characterization of biopolymer pectin with lithium chloride and its applications to electrochemical devices, Ionics 24 (2018).

46. S. Shanmuga Priya, M. Karthika, S. Selvasekarapandian, R. Manjuladevi, Preparation and characterization of polymer electrolyte based on biopolymer I-carrageenan with magnesium nitrate, Solid State Ion. 327 (2018) 136–149.

47. M. Premalatha, T. Mathavan, S. Selvasekarapandian, S. Monisha, S. Selvalakshmi, D. Vinoth Pandi, Tamarind seed polysaccharide (TSP)-based Li-ion conducting membranes, Ionics 23 (2017).

48. M. Premalatha, T. Mathavan, S. Selvasekarapandian, S. Selvalakshmi, S. Monisha, Incorporation of NH4Br in tamarind seed polysaccharide biopolymer and its potential use in electrochemical energy storage devices, Org. Electron. 50 (2017) 418–425.

49. Q. Li, N. Mahmood, J. Zhu, Y. Hou, S. Sun, Graphene and its composites with nanoparticles for electrochemical energy applications, Nano Today 9 (2014) 668–683.

50. Z. M. Dang, J.K. Yuan, S.H. Yao, and R.J. Liao, Flexible nanodielectric materials with high permittivity for energy storage, Advanced Materials, 25(44) (2013) 6334–6365.

51. B. Chu, X. Zhou, K. Ren, B. Neese, M. Lin, Q. Wang, F. Bauer, Q.M. Zhang, A dielectric polymer with high electric energy density and fast discharge speed, Science 313(2006) 334–336.

52. J. Winsberg, T. Hagemann, T. Janoschka, M.D. Hager and U.S. Schubert, Redox-flow batteries: From metals to organic redox-active materials, Angewandte Chemie International Edition 56(3) (2017) 686–711.

53. M. Skyllas-Kazacos, and M. Kazacos, State of charge monitoring and electrolyte rebalancing for all-vanadium redox flow battery, Journal of Power Sources, 196(20) (2011) 8822–8827.

54. X. Pu, M. Liu, X. Chen, J. Sun, C. Du, Y. Zhang, and Z. L. Wang, Ultrastretchable, transparent triboelectric nanogenerator as electronic skin for biomechanical energy harvesting and tactile sensing, Science Advances, 2(11) (2016) e1501779.

55. J. Chen, Y. Zhu, Self-healing polymers and their application in energy storage devices, Advanced Polymer Technology, 35(4) (2016) 407–419.

56. F. Yildiz, Potential Ambient Energy-Harvesting Sources and Techniques, J. Technol. Stud. 35 (2009) 40–48.

57. J. I. Roscow, H. Pearce, H. Khanbareh, S. Kar-Narayan, C.R. Bowen, Modified energy harvesting figures of merit for stress- and strain-driven piezoelectric systems, Eur. Phys. J. Spec. Top. 228 (2019) 1537–1554.

58. D.A.Van Den Ende, H. J. Van De Wiel, W.A. Groen, S. Van Der Zwaag, Direct strain energy harvesting in automobile tires using piezoelectric PZT-polymer composites. Smart Mater. Struct. 21 (2012) 015011.

59. M. Borowiec, J. Gawryluk, M. Bochenski, Influence of mechanical couplings on the dynamical behavior and energy harvesting of a composite structure, Polymers 13 (2021) 66.

60. D. Ibrahim, E.R. Sadiku, T. Jamiru, Y. Hamam, Y. Alayli, A.A. Eze, Prospects of nanostructured composite materials for energy harvesting and storage, J. King Saud. Univ.-Sci. 32 (2020) 758–764.

61. S. Ahmad, M. Abdul Mujeebu, M.A. Farooqi, Energy harvesting from pavements and roadways: A comprehensive review of technologies, materials, and challenges. Int. J. Energy Res. 43 (2019)1974–2015.

62. J. Chen, X. Gao, Thermal and electrical anisotropy of polymer matrix composite materials reinforced with graphene nanoplatelets and aluminum-based particles, Diam. Relat. Mater. 100 (2019) 107571.

63. P.J. Brigandi, J.M. Cogen, R.A.Pearson, Electrically conductive multiphase polymer blend carbon-based composites, Polym. Eng. Sci. 54 (2014) 1–16.

64. S.K. Bhattacharya, A.C.D. Chaklader, Review on metal-filled plastics. Part1. Electrical conductivity, Polym.-Plast. Technol. Eng. 19 (1982) 21–51.

65. L.Wang, F. Aslani, A review on material design, performance, and practical application of electrically conductive cementitious composites, Constr. Build. Mater. 229 (2019) 116892.

66. H. Liu, Q. Li, S. Zhang, R. Yin, X. Liu, Y. He, K. Dai, C. Shan, J. Guo, C. Liu, Electrically conductive polymer composites for smart flexible strain sensors: A critical review. J. Mater. Chem. C 6 (2018) 12121–12141.

67. N.A. Mohd Radzuan, A.B. Sulong, J. Sahari, A review of electrical conductivity models for conductive polymer composite, Int. J. Hydrogen Energy 42 (2017) 9262–9273.

68. R. Hsissou, R. Seghiri, Z. Benzekri, M. Hilali, M. Rafik, A. Elharfi, Polymer composite materials: A comprehensive review, Compos. Struct. 262 (2021)113640.

69. M. Asim, M.T. Paridah, M. Chandrasekar, R.M. Shahroze, M. Jawaid, M. Nasir, R. Siakeng, Thermal stability of natural fibers and their polymer composites, Iran. Polym. J. 29 (2020) 625–648.

70. A.N. Burger, A. Laachachi, M. Ferriol, M. Lutz, V. Toniazzo, D. Ruch, Review of thermal conductivity in composites: Mechanisms, parameters and theory, Prog. Polym. Sci. 61(2016) 1–28.

71. K.I. Parashivamurthy, R.K. Kumar, S. Seetharamu, M.N. Chandrasekharaiah, Review on TiC reinforced steel composites, J. Mater. Sci. 36 (2001)4519–4530.

72. Y. Jiang, M. Liu, Y. Sun, Review on the development of high temperature phase change material composites for solar thermal energy storage, Sol. Energy Mater. Sol. Cells 203 (2019) 110164.

73. S.S. Sidhu, S. Kumar, A. Batish, Metal Matrix Composites for Thermal Management: A Review, Crit. Rev. Solid State Mater. Sci. 41 (2016) 132–157.

74. I.A. Ibrahim, F.A. Mohamed, E.J. Lavernia, Particulate reinforced metal matrix composites: A review, J. Mater. Sci. 26 (1991)1137–1156.

75. Sommers, Q. Wang, X. Han, C. T'Joen, Y. Park, A. Jacobi, Ceramics and ceramic matrix composites for heat exchangers in advanced thermal systems-A review, Appl. Therm. Eng. 30 (2010) 1277–1291.

76. Z. Wu, J. Wang, Y. Liu, S. Hou, X. Liu, Q. Zhang, F. Cao, A review of spectral controlling for renewable energy harvesting and conserving, Mater. Today Phys. 18 (2021)100388.

77. G. Hu, X. Ning, M. Hussain, U. Sajjad, M. Sultan, H.M. Ali, T.R. Shah, H. Ahmad, Potential evaluation of hybrid nanofluids for solar thermal energy harvesting: A review of recent advances, Sustain. Energy Technol. Assess. 48 (2021) 101651.

78. G. Li, R. Zhu, Y. Yang, Polymer solar cells, Nature Photonics, 6(3)( (2012) 153–161.

79. M.A. Green, A. Ho-Baillie, H.J. Snaith, The emergence of perovskite solar cells. Nature Photonics, 8(7) ((2014) 506–514.

80. J. He, T.M. Tritt, Advances in thermoelectric materials research: Looking back and moving forward, Science, 357(2017) eaak9997.

81. Q. Zhang, Y. Sun, W. Xu, D. Zhu, Organic thermoelectric materials: Emerging green energy materials converting heat to electricity directly and efficiently, Advanced Materials, 26(40) (2014) 6829–6851.

82. Z.L. Wang, W. Wu, Nanotechnology-enabled energy harvesting for self-powered micro-/nanosystems, Angewandte Chemie International Edition, 51(47) (2012) 11700–11721.

83. F.R. Fan, Z.Q. Tian, Z.L.Wang, Flexible triboelectric generator, Nano Energy, 1(2) (2012) 328–334.

84. J. Xie, X. Zhao, Fuel cell membranes and polybenzimidazole composites: Synthesis, characterization, and performance, Journal of Membrane Science, 435 (2013)123–138. Details the use of polymer composites in fuel cell membranes.

85. Q. Zhang, R. He, N.J. Bjerrum, Polybenzimidazole membranes for high-temperature proton exchange membrane fuel cells. Journal of Materials Chemistry, 13(4) (2003) 654–661.

86. Z.M. Dang, J.K. Yuan, J.W. Zha, T. Zhou, S.T. Li, G.H. Hu, Fundamentals, processes and applications of high-permittivity polymer-matrix composites, Progress in Materials Science, 57(4) (2012) 660–723.

87. B. Chu, X. Zhou, K. Ren, B. Neese, M. Lin, Q. Wang, F. Bauer, Q.M. Zhang, A dielectric polymer with high electric energy density and fast discharge speed, Science, 313(5785) (2006) 334–336.

# Chapter-8

# Nanocomposites Based on Polyaniline: A Pathway to High-Performance Supercapacitors

Dr. Apoorv Saraswat[1]

**Abstract**: Since intrinsic conductive polymers provide several advantages over traditional materials, extensive research has been done on them. Due to its significant mechanical, optical, and electrical properties, polyaniline has become the subject of extensive research as an intrinsic conducting polymer, increasing its potential applications. A multifunctional polyaniline composite with improved performance employing various energy supply devices was created by combining pristine polyaniline with inorganic electrolytes that opens up new pathways for the development of futuristic energy gadgets such as high-performance supercapacitors. For this reason, in this chapter, we have examined current advancements in polyaniline and its nanocomposites using different inorganic electrolytes such as sulphuric acid perchloric acid, and sodium sulphate which will be helpful to the electrochemical research community.

**Keywords:** Conducting polymers; Polyaniline; Composites; Supercapacitor

## 1. Introduction

These organic polymers were initially thought to be insulators, which limited their use in day-to-day activities. However, Nobel grads M. Shirakawa and Heeger made the astounding discovery of the doping phenomena at polyacetylene [1–3] introducing a groundbreaking concept in electrical conductivity, for which they received the 2000 Nobel Prize. Reversible doping, often known as de-doping, is a phenomenon that made this intriguing hypothesis possible [4] that transforms the conducting polymers from the insulating undoped polymers [5] that cause the material's electrical conductivity. Electronic band theory, which includes conjugated electron-dense π links that are highly delocalized and polarized and create intrinsically conducting polymers, could help explain this doping mechanism. [6–11].

These conducting polymers have a wide range of innovative applications such as supercapacitors [12], chemical sensors [13], light-emitting-diode [14], and electrochromic displays [15]. Among these polyanilines, one was identified as an intriguing and unpredictable subordinate of the group of π conducting polymers conjugated [16–18] that have a positive, life-altering influence on society. Since its creation in 1862, it has been the subject of in-depth research as a conducting polymer. [19,20]

The combination of nitrogen heteroatom moieties between phenyl rings in a polyaniline pillar provides chemical flexibility, facile tunability, processability, and environmentally friendly stability [21]

---

[1] *Department of Chemistry, Ramashray Baleshwar College, Dalsingsarai (A Constituent Unit of Lalit Narayan Mithila University, Darbhanga), Samastipur-848114, Bihar, India*

*Email ID: apoorvsaraswat@gmail.com*

Comfort of synthesis, thermal stability, and electroluminescence provide important mechanical, optical, and electrical resources in the spine of the chain supporting the myriad cutting-edge applications as electrode modifier in chemical sensors, heavy metal detection, rechargeable batteries, solar cells, and OLEDs, among other cutting-edge uses. [22–24]

## 2. Supercapacitor

In this chapter concerning the present era, there is an urgent need to develop a source of energy conversion or storage device that may be the substitute for fossil fuel, super-capacitors, lithium batteries, and fuel cells that may rightly fit into this category [25–27]. A great deal of research and development has gone into creating improved supercapacitors because of their high power and energy density, which are essential for digital communication and electric car applications. [28–33]. In addition to the active materials themselves, the electrode-electrolyte interface also undergoes rapid and reversible redox processes, which are consistent with the charge storage mechanism of conducting polymers. Consequently, the development of various nanostructured conducting polymers is gaining attention. In general, oxidized cathode and reduced anode are present during the charging process, and the opposite occurs during the discharging process, as in the cases of both secondary batteries and electrochemical supercapacitors. Such charging and discharging resembled the electrode material's redox process. [34–36]. Therefore, the potential electrode material's electrochemical performance offers a crucial and accessible option for use as an energy storage capacity. [37]. Pure polyaniline has good pseudocapacitive properties and can be used as a supercapacitor electrode in an aqueous electrolyte with a high specific capacitance of about 600 F/g. [38,39]. High electrochemical activity often favors a large specific capacitance value for polyaniline-based supercapacitors, according to literature reports. [40–42].

## 3. High capacitive behavior of the polyaniline nano-composite using inorganic electrolyte

### 3.1. Polyaniline nano-composite using in 0.1 M $H_2SO_4$ as inorganic electrolyte

Using rectangular-shaped cyclic voltammetry in 0.1 M $H_2SO_4$ at a scan rate of 10 mV/s, Lei et al. [19] demonstrated the electrochemical performance of polyaniline nanobelt electrodes. This showed a potential window in the range of -0.24 to 0.78 V versus SCE with high overall current (galvanostatic electrolysis), which supports the highly capacitive behavior of the polyaniline nanobelts. When such PANI nanobelt material is fabricated as electrodes, it shows a high specific capacitance value of about 873 F/g, which is significantly larger than that of PANI nanospheres, which are found to have a value of only about 382 F/g. It also shows good cyclic stability, maintaining its electrochemical performance, or capacitive behavior, over a 1000 cycle.

### 3.2. Polyaniline nano-composite using in 1 M $HClO_4$ as inorganic electrolyte

Polyaniline nano-wire array material, as demonstrated by Wang et al. [19], can be fabricated into electrodes with a high specific capacitance value of 950 F/g, which is significantly bigger than that of pure polyaniline. Additionally, they used cyclic voltammetry in 1 M $HClO_4$ to describe the electrochemical performance of the polyaniline nano-wire arrays at a different scan rate. This method shows a potential window in the range of -0.2 to 0.85 V versus SCE with an overall high current that supports the polyaniline nano-wire array's virtuous rate capacity.

### 3.3. Polyaniline nano-composite using in 1M $Na_2SO_4$ as inorganic electrolyte

With a cyclic voltammeter in 1M $Na_2SO_4$ aqueous solution as the electrolyte and a scan rate of 2 mV/s, Rawal et al. [19] demonstrated the electrochemical performance of the polyaniline/activated carbon composite (PANI/AC) (APA-29.4) electrode with a high overall current density that supports the enhanced capacitive behavior of the polyaniline composite. The resultant polyaniline/activated carbon composite demonstrated a good performance of reversibility at various scan rates as well as an increased electrochemical specific capacitance of 947 F g-1 (polyaniline's pseudo-capacitive behavior).

### 3.4. Polyaniline nano-composite using in 1 M $H_2SO_4$ as inorganic electrolyte

An anodic polymerization process was used by Wang et al. [19] to fabricate graphene/polyaniline composite paper (GPCP-900s) in-situ with desired flexibility and electrochemical activity. In comparison to G-paper, the resultant graphene/polyaniline composite paper demonstrated a higher volumetric capacitance of 135 F/cm, a higher electrochemical specific capacitance of 233 F g-1 (a 58 % improvement), and a 43% increase in mechanical strength. Cyclic voltammetry was used to study the electrochemical performance of nano-composite material in a 1 M $H_2SO_4$ dopant with a potential window ranging from -0.2 to 0.8 V versus SCE at a scan rate from 2 to 20 mV s-1. This resulted in an interesting comparison between conventional G-paper and GPCP-900s nanostructure.

### 4. Conclusion and Future Outlook

Polyaniline assembly nano-composites are latent materials that find a foundation in several applications and meet the new needs arising from scientific advancements. In order to integrate and advance them into a technological application, pristine polyaniline can be filled inorganic electrolyte that improve its performance. Such polyaniline nanocomposite would be promising candidates for developing high performance supercapacitor energy supply systems.

### 5. Reference

1. C.K. Chiang, Y.W. Park, A.J. Heeger, H. Shirakawa, E.J. Louis, A.G. MacDiarmid, Conducting polymers: Halogen doped polyacetylene, J Chem Phys 69 (1978) 5098–5104. https://doi.org/10.1063/1.436503.

2. A.G. MacDiarmid, "Synthetic metals": a novel role for organic polymers, Current Applied Physics 1 (2001) 269–279. https://doi.org/10.1016/S1567-1739(01)00051-7.

3. A.J. Heeger, Semiconducting and Metallic Polymers: The Fourth Generation of Polymeric Materials, J Phys Chem B 105 (2001) 8475–8491. https://doi.org/10.1021/jp011611w.

4. T.-H. Le, Y. Kim, H. Yoon, Electrical and Electrochemical Properties of Conducting Polymers, Polymers (Basel) 9 (2017) 150. https://doi.org/10.3390/polym9040150.

5. M.-C. Lee, G. Simkovich, Electrical conduction, Metallurgical Transactions A 18 (1987) 485–486. https://doi.org/10.1007/BF02648811.

6. M.S. AlSalhi, J. Alam, L.A. Dass, M. Raja, Recent Advances in Conjugated Polymers for Light Emitting Devices, Int J Mol Sci 12 (2011) 2036–2054. https://doi.org/10.3390/ijms12032036.

7. N. K, C.S. Rout, Conducting polymers: a comprehensive review on recent advances in synthesis, properties and applications, RSC Adv 11 (2021) 5659–5697. https://doi.org/10.1039/D0RA07800J.

8. T. Nezakati, A. Seifalian, A. Tan, A.M. Seifalian, Conductive Polymers: Opportunities and Challenges in Biomedical Applications, Chem Rev 118 (2018) 6766–6843. https://doi.org/10.1021/acs.chemrev.6b00275.

9. S. Kumar, P.K. Yadav, P. Maiti, Renewable cathode materials dependent on conjugated polymer composite systems, in: Conjugated Polymers for Next-Generation Applications, Elsevier, 2022: pp. 55–90. https://doi.org/10.1016/B978-0-12-824094-6.00002-9.

10. S. Kumar, R. Prakash, P. Maiti, Redox mediation through integrating chain extenders in active ionomer polyurethane hard segments in CdS quantum dot sensitized solar cell, Solar Energy 231 (2022) 985–1001. https://doi.org/10.1016/j.solener.2021.12.043.

11. S. Kumar, S. Kumar, R.N. Rai, Y. Lee, T. Hong Chuong Nguyen, S. Young Kim, Q. van Le, L. Singh, Recent development in two-dimensional material-based advanced photoanodes for high-performance dye-sensitized solar cells, Solar Energy 249 (2023) 606–623. https://doi.org/10.1016/j.solener.2022.12.013.

12. M. Mastragostino, C. Arbizzani, F. Soavi, Polymer-based supercapacitors, J Power Sources 97–98 (2001) 812–815. https://doi.org/10.1016/S0378-7753(01)00613-9.

13. D.T. McQuade, A.E. Pullen, T.M. Swager, Conjugated Polymer-Based Chemical Sensors, Chem Rev 100 (2000) 2537–2574. https://doi.org/10.1021/cr9801014.

14. J.H. Burroughes, D.D.C. Bradley, A.R. Brown, R.N. Marks, K. Mackay, R.H. Friend, P.L. Burns, A.B. Holmes, Light-emitting diodes based on conjugated polymers, Nature 347 (1990) 539–541. https://doi.org/10.1038/347539a0.

15. P.M. Beaujuge, J.R. Reynolds, Color Control in π-Conjugated Organic Polymers for Use in Electrochromic Devices, Chem Rev 110 (2010) 268–320. https://doi.org/10.1021/cr900129a.

16. A.G. Macdiarmid, J.-C. Chiang, M. Halpern, W.-S. Huang, S.-L. Mu, L.D. Nanaxakkara, S.W. Wu, S.I. Yaniger, "Polyaniline": Interconversion of Metallic and Insulating Forms, Molecular Crystals and Liquid Crystals 121 (1985) 173–180. https://doi.org/10.1080/00268948508074857.

17. A.F. Diaz, B. Hall, Mechanical Properties of Electrochemically Prepared Polypyrrole Films, IBM J Res Dev 27 (1983) 342–347. https://doi.org/10.1147/rd.274.0342.

18. W.W. Focke, G.E. Wnek, Yen. Wei, Influence of oxidation state, pH, and counterion on the conductivity of polyaniline, J Phys Chem 91 (1987) 5813–5818. https://doi.org/10.1021/j100306a059.

19. H. Letheby, XXIX.—On the production of a blue substance by the electrolysis of sulphate of aniline, J. Chem. Soc. 15 (1862) 161–163. https://doi.org/10.1039/JS8621500161.

20. A.F. Diaz, J.A. Logan, Electroactive polyaniline films, J Electroanal Chem Interfacial Electrochem 111 (1980) 111–114. https://doi.org/10.1016/S0022-0728(80)80081-7.

21. D.E. Stilwell, S. Park, Electrochemistry of Conductive Polymers: II . Electrochemical Studies on Growth Properties of Polyaniline, J Electrochem Soc 135 (1988) 2254–2262. https://doi.org/10.1149/1.2096248.

22. J. Bhadra, A. Alkareem, N. Al-Thani, A review of advances in the preparation and application of polyaniline based thermoset blends and composites, Journal of Polymer Research 27 (2020) 122. https://doi.org/10.1007/s10965-020-02052-1.

23. E.N. Zare, P. Makvandi, B. Ashtari, F. Rossi, A. Motahari, G. Perale, Progress in Conductive Polyaniline-Based Nanocomposites for Biomedical Applications: A Review, J Med Chem 63 (2020) 1–22. https://doi.org/10.1021/acs.jmedchem.9b00803.

24. C.O. Baker, X. Huang, W. Nelson, R.B. Kaner, Polyaniline nanofibers: broadening applications for conducting polymers, Chem Soc Rev 46 (2017) 1510–1525. https://doi.org/10.1039/C6CS00555A.

25. C.-C. Hu, K.-H. Chang, M.-C. Lin, Y.-T. Wu, Design and Tailoring of the Nanotubular Arrayed Architecture of Hydrous $RuO_2$ for Next Generation Supercapacitors, Nano Lett 6 (2006) 2690–2695. https://doi.org/10.1021/nl061576a.

26. E. Kim, P.F. Weck, N. Balakrishnan, C. Bae, Nanoscale Building Blocks for the Development of Novel Proton Exchange Membrane Fuel Cells, J Phys Chem B 112 (2008) 3283–3286. https://doi.org/10.1021/jp711568f.

27. J. Xiao, N.A. Chernova, M.S. Whittingham, Layered Mixed Transition Metal Oxide Cathodes with Reduced Cobalt Content for Lithium Ion Batteries, Chemistry of Materials 20 (2008) 7454–7464. https://doi.org/10.1021/cm802316d.

28. L. Athouël, F. Moser, R. Dugas, O. Crosnier, D. Bélanger, T. Brousse, Variation of the $MnO_2$ Birnessite Structure upon Charge/Discharge in an Electrochemical Supercapacitor Electrode in Aqueous $Na_2SO_4$ Electrolyte, The Journal of Physical Chemistry C 112 (2008) 7270–7277. https://doi.org/10.1021/jp0773029.

29. R.K. Selvan, I. Perelshtein, N. Perkas, A. Gedanken, Synthesis of Hexagonal-Shaped $SnO_2$ Nanocrystals and $SnO_2$@C Nanocomposites for Electrochemical Redox Supercapacitors, The Journal of Physical Chemistry C 112 (2008) 1825–1830. https://doi.org/10.1021/jp076995q.

30. G.M. Suppes, B.A. Deore, M.S. Freund, Porous Conducting Polymer/Heteropolyoxometalate Hybrid Material for Electrochemical Supercapacitor Applications, Langmuir 24 (2008) 1064–1069. https://doi.org/10.1021/la702837j.

31. K.S. Ryu, S.K. Jeong, J. Joo, K.M. Kim, Polyaniline Doped with Dimethyl Sulfate as a Nucleophilic Dopant and Its Electrochemical Properties as an Electrode in a Lithium Secondary Battery and a Redox Supercapacitor, J Phys Chem B 111 (2007) 731–739. https://doi.org/10.1021/jp064243a.

32. D. Hulicova, M. Kodama, H. Hatori, Electrochemical Performance of Nitrogen-Enriched Carbons in Aqueous and Non-Aqueous Supercapacitors, Chemistry of Materials 18 (2006) 2318–2326. https://doi.org/10.1021/cm060146i.

33. C. Zhou, S. Kumar, C.D. Doyle, J.M. Tour, Functionalized Single Wall Carbon Nanotubes Treated with Pyrrole for Electrochemical Supercapacitor Membranes, Chemistry of Materials 17 (2005) 1997–2002. https://doi.org/10.1021/cm047882b.

34. B.E. Conway, W.G. Pell, Double-layer and pseudocapacitance types of electrochemical capacitors and their applications to the development of hybrid devices, Journal of Solid State Electrochemistry 7 (2003) 637–644. https://doi.org/10.1007/s10008-003-0395-7.

35. M. Armand, J.-M. Tarascon, Building better batteries, Nature 451 (2008) 652–657. https://doi.org/10.1038/451652a.

36. J.-H. Kim, K. Zhu, Y. Yan, C.L. Perkins, A.J. Frank, Microstructure and Pseudocapacitive Properties of Electrodes Constructed of Oriented NiO-TiO 2 Nanotube Arrays, Nano Lett 10 (2010) 4099–4104. https://doi.org/10.1021/nl102203s.

37. A. Rudge, J. Davey, I. Raistrick, S. Gottesfeld, J.P. Ferraris, Conducting polymers as active materials in electrochemical capacitors, J Power Sources 47 (1994) 89–107. https://doi.org/10.1016/0378-7753(94)80053-7.

38. H. Zhou, H. Chen, S. Luo, G. Lu, W. Wei, Y. Kuang, The effect of the polyaniline morphology on the performance of polyaniline supercapacitors, Journal of Solid State Electrochemistry 9 (2005) 574–580. https://doi.org/10.1007/s10008-004-0594-x.

39. H. Li, J. Wang, Q. Chu, Z. Wang, F. Zhang, S. Wang, Theoretical and experimental specific capacitance of polyaniline in sulfuric acid, J Power Sources 190 (2009) 578–586. https://doi.org/10.1016/j.jpowsour.2009.01.052.

40. A. Sumboja, X. Wang, J. Yan, P.S. Lee, Nanoarchitectured current collector for high rate capability of polyaniline based supercapacitor electrode, Electrochim Acta 65 (2012) 190–195. https://doi.org/10.1016/j.electacta.2012.01.046.

41. K. Chen, L. Chen, Y. Chen, H. Bai, L. Li, Three-dimensional porous graphene-based composite materials: electrochemical synthesis and application, J Mater Chem 22 (2012) 20968. https://doi.org/10.1039/c2jm34816k.

42. S. He, X. Hu, S. Chen, H. Hu, M. Hanif, H. Hou, Needle-like polyaniline nanowires on graphite nanofibers: hierarchical micro/nano-architecture for high performance supercapacitors, J Mater Chem 22 (2012) 5114. https://doi.org/10.1039/c2jm15668g.

# Chapter-9

# Rheological studies of Ecofriendly and Multifunctional materials

Sangeeta kandpal[1]

A.K.Saxena[2]

**Abstract:** To maintain sustainability of technological growth, now day's research and development activities are mainly focused towards the synthesis of eco friendly and multifunctional materials. As organosilanes and silicone dendrimers meet both the requirements hence recently drawn the attention of researchers to a greater extent to prepare and characterize these derivatives. In view of it, in the present chapter, we have discuss about some dendrimers, oligomers which are having high potential to be used for a number of high tech applications specially where high temperature, excellent solubility and easy processing conditions are required and about the curing of these materials and study in respect of rhelogy. we discuss the different rheological advance study related to these multifunctional materials. in the present chapter rheological studies in the field of dendrimers, oligomers, polymers are discussed.

**Keywords**: dendrimers, hydrosilation, rheology, epoxy resin

## 1. Introduction

Metals, Ceramics and Organic Polymers are most commonly used materials for various domestic and technological applications. But these materials have their own advantages and disadvantage thus limiting their applications. For instance, metals are very heavy in weight, prone to corrosion and high thermal expansion coefficient whereas ceramics are brittle in nature and non- tractable therefore making complicated engineering structures is very cumbersome. Similarly, the poor thermo-oxidative stability and susceptibility to radiations and solvents etc., of organic polymers restricts their application for a number of uses. To overcome these problems, the researchers now days have shown considerable interest in inorganic polymers [1], hybrid polymers and dendrimers[2]

Despite of several advantages the literature survey revealed that compared to organic polymers and dendrimers the inorganic polymers and dendrimers are very scarcely studied. The reason may be attributed to the sophisticated handling of the reactants which in most cases are very susceptible to air and moisture and the yields of the products are also comparatively poorer which minimizes the cost effectiveness of the materials. But it could be overcome with the use of appropriate synthetic methods, reaction conditions and proper catalyst, etc.

---

[1]*Asst. Prof. in CSJMU Kanpur,*
[2]*Ex-Director and Outstanding Scientist, DMSRDE (DRDO) Kanpur, General President (Elect) Indian Science Congress Association, Kolkata.*
*\*Corresponding Author Email: kandpalsangeeta@gmail.com*

*Keeping in view the versatile functional properties of inorganic polymers and dendrimers, the present study is focused to the synthesis and study the properties of organosilicone compounds for various applications. Herein, some novel functional organosilicone dendrimers have been prepared and characterized. These functional organosilicone dendrimers have been evaluated as diluents and modifier of organic resins, base stock solution for developing complete neutral lubricants and high thermo-oxidative resin matrix for composites etc.*

## 2. Dendrimers

Dendrimer may be defined by various definitions but the most accepted definition is "A dendrimer is a regularly branched tree- like monodisperse polymer molecule emanating from a central core." The name dendrimer comes from the Greek word "dedndron" meaning "tree" and "meros" meaning "parts". Dendrimers are highly branched, star shaped or globular or spheroid macromolecules with nanometer-scale dimensions. In general, dendrimers are monodisperse molecule that possesses a fascinating regular and highly branched three dimensional architecture, which differs significantly from that of linear polymers. The structure of dendrimers mainly consists of three components namely:

(i) A central core

(ii) An interior dendritic structure (the branches)

(iii) An exterior surface with functional surface groups.

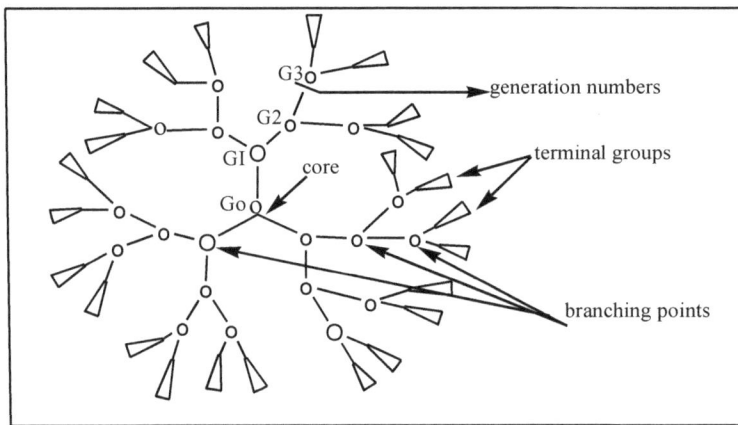

**Figure 1 : Dendrimer**

Dendrimers have been synthesized by step- wise chemical method to give distinct generations ($G_0$, $G_1$, $G_2$,...) of molecules with narrow molecular weight distribution, uniform size, shape and multiple (multivalent) surface groups.

The dendrimer builts up one monomer layer at a time, referred to as a "generation", starting from a core molecule, known as "Generation 0", each repeated layer along the branch is numbered from that core molecule. Dendrimers of lower generations (0, 1 and 2)

have highly asymmetric shape and possess more open structures as compared to higher generation dendrimers. As the chains grow from the core molecule, these become longer and more branched (in 4 and higher generations) and adopt a globular [2] and densely packed structure. When a critical branched state is reached dendrimers cannot grow because of a lack of space. This is called the 'starbust effect' [3] e.g., in PAMAM dendrimer synthesis it has been observed after tenth generation, the rate of reaction drops suddenly and further reaction of the end groups cannot occur. The tenth generation PAMAM contains 6141 monomer units. [4].

Due to their unique physical, chemical properties and potential application in various fields from drug-delivery to coating, interest in hyperbranched polymer is growing rapidly

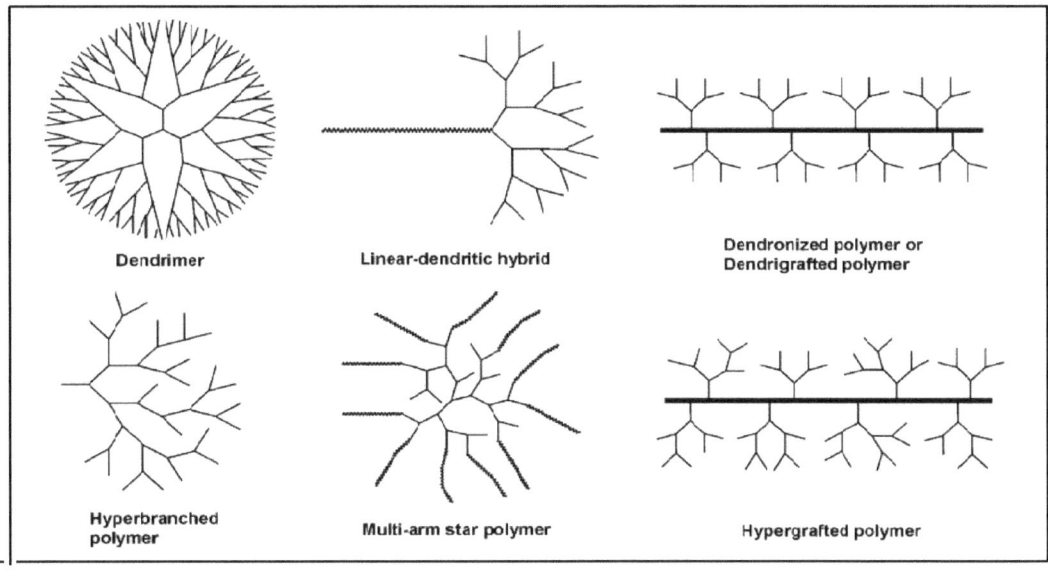

**Figure 2: Schematic description of dendritic polymer [5].**

Recently, carbosilane as well as carbosiloxane dendrimer have appeared as one of the important families of dendritic macromolecules [6]. Carbosilane dendrimers are the most important class of silicon-containing dendrimers, due to their excellent chemical and thermal stability and to the possibility of synthesizing these molecules to high generations [7]. The synthetic method of silicone-containing dendrimers was reported by a great number of researchers who used the simple repeating procedures such as hydrosilation, dehydrocoupling, alkenylation as well as alcoholysis [8]. The divergent method introduced by van der Made [9], Roovers [10] and Seyferth [11] is the most common and efficient route to synthesize carbosilane dendrimers by repetitive alkenylation- hydrosilylation cycles. Silicone tetra chloride is used as core in most case to produce carbosilane dendrimers. Kim's group has reported carbosilane dendrimers with other cores, such as (Me $(CH_2=CH)$ $SiO)_4$ and $((CH_2=CHCH_2O)SiCH_2)_2$ [12, 13].

## 3. Synthesis of Dendrimers

The strategies for the design of dendrimers are mainly based on the convergent, divergent or double-stage convergent growth methods [14, 15]. The precise formation of the corresponding fundamental architecture can be controlled on the basis of only a few type of reactions, involving, e.g., repetitive hydrosilylation-alkylation or hydrosilylation- alcoholysis cycles [16-18].

## 4. Properties of Dendrimers

Dendrimers are well defined, highly branched macromolecules that radiate from a central core and are synthesized through a stepwise, repetitive reaction sequence that guarantees complete shells for each generation, leading to polymers that are monodisperse. Some of the characteristics of dendrimers are:

(i) Monodispersity: Dendrimers are the class of dendritic polymers that can be constructed with a well-defined molecular structure, i.e. being mono-disperse, unlike to linear polymers. Monodispersity offers researchers the possibility to work with a tool for well defined scalable size.

(ii) Nanoscale size and shape: These fundamental properties have in fact lead to their commercial use for gene therapy, immunodiagnostics and variety of other biological applications.

(iii) Polyvalency: Polyvalency shows the outward presentation of reactive groups on the dendrimer nanostructure exterior. This creates more connections between surfaces and bulk materials for applications such as adhesives, surface coatings, or polymer cross-linking. The product, a topical vaginal microbicide called Vivagel™, prevents infection by HIV and other sexually transmitted diseases during intercourse takes advantage of dendrimers polyvalent properties.

(iv) Physicochemical properties of dendrimers: The use of dendrimers as protein mimics has been encouraged scientists to investigate the physicochemical properties of dendrimers in comparison to proteins shows that dendrimers, similar to protein, can adapt "native" (e.g. tighter) or "denatured" (e.g. extended) conformations dependent on the polarity, ionic strength and pH of the solvent.

(v) Biocompatibility of dendrimers: In order to utilize dendrimers as biological agents, they have to fulfill certain biological demands. The dendrimer should be: nontoxic, non-immunogenic, able to cross biobarriers (biopermeable), able to stay in circulation for the time needed to have a clinical effect and able to target to specific structures. The cytotoxicity of dendrimers has been primarily evaluated in vitro; however, a few in vivo studies have been published [19, 20].

## 5. Application of dendrimers

A number of applications of organosilicone dendrimers based on the terminal functional groups and polysiloxy carbosilane core have also been enumerated in the literature [21-24].

surface groups. These surface-modified dendrimers were predicted to enhance pilocarpine bioavailability [25, 26]. Ideal ocular drug-delivery systems should be nonirritating, sterile, isotonic, biocompatible, does not run out from the eye and biodegradable.

## 6. Rheological Studies of Dendrimers

Rheology can be defined as 'the science of the deformation and flow of matter', which means that it is concerned with relationship between viscosity, stress, strain, rate of strain and time [27]. Many materials of industrial interest behave in a way such as to bring their study within the scope of rheology, and included in these epoxy resins [28]. Newtonian behaviour of medium and highly concentrated solution of Polyamidoamine dendrimers in ethlene di amine solvent were studied using Rheology[29].Rheological is an indispensable characterization tool for the study of dendrimers under steady shear, creep, dynamic oscillatory shear [30 ], Carbosilane dendrimer with various type of end group [31 ], Polybenzyl ether dendrimers and its co-polymer and blends [32 ]and star shaped Polydimethylsiloxane[33].

## 7. Ecofriendly Multifunctional Dendrimers

This section described the synthesis and characterization of different generation's novel Si-H functional silicone dendrimers and hydrosilylation of these dendrimers with allyl glycidyl ether in presence of Speier's catalyst to produce its oxirane derivatives. Thus oxirane terminal dendrimers were synthesized and the curing of the different generation's oxirane dendrimers was carried out using aliphatic hardener. The curing phenomenon and thermal behaviour of all the cured dendrimers were studied. Further application of the oxirane dendrimers as diluents with commercially available resin LY556 were carried out and change in its thermal behaviours, comparative to neat LY556 were also studied.

This section is divided in five sub-sections.

7.1 Introduction

7.2 Synthesis of Si-H functional dendrimer

7.3 Synthesis of oxirane functional dendrimer

7.4 Curing of oxirane dendrimers

7.5 Characterization of dendrimers

**7.1 Introduction**

Epoxy resins, one of the most important thermosetting polymers are currently used in advanced composites, coatings, structural adhesives and microelectronics, due to their high stiffness, high strength, good chemical resistance, dimensional stability and excellent electrical insulation properties [34,35]. Epoxy resins were known for their high performance, especially with respect to thermal and dimensional stabilities combined with high stiffness and strength at low creep. As a consequence of their highly cross-linked structure, these materials tended to suffer from brittle behavior, poor crack resistance and low fracture toughness.

Keeping in view the current interest of researcher, in the current section, is to synthesize and characterize different generations' novel Si-H functional silicone dendrimers and hydrosilylation of these dendrimers with allyl glycidyl ether in presence of Speier's catalyst to synthesized oxirane terminated dendrimers and curing of the different generation's oxirane dendrimers were carried out using aliphatic hardener. Applications of oxirane dendrimer's different percentage as diluents in LY556 resin were carried out and their curing and thermal behaviors were studied.

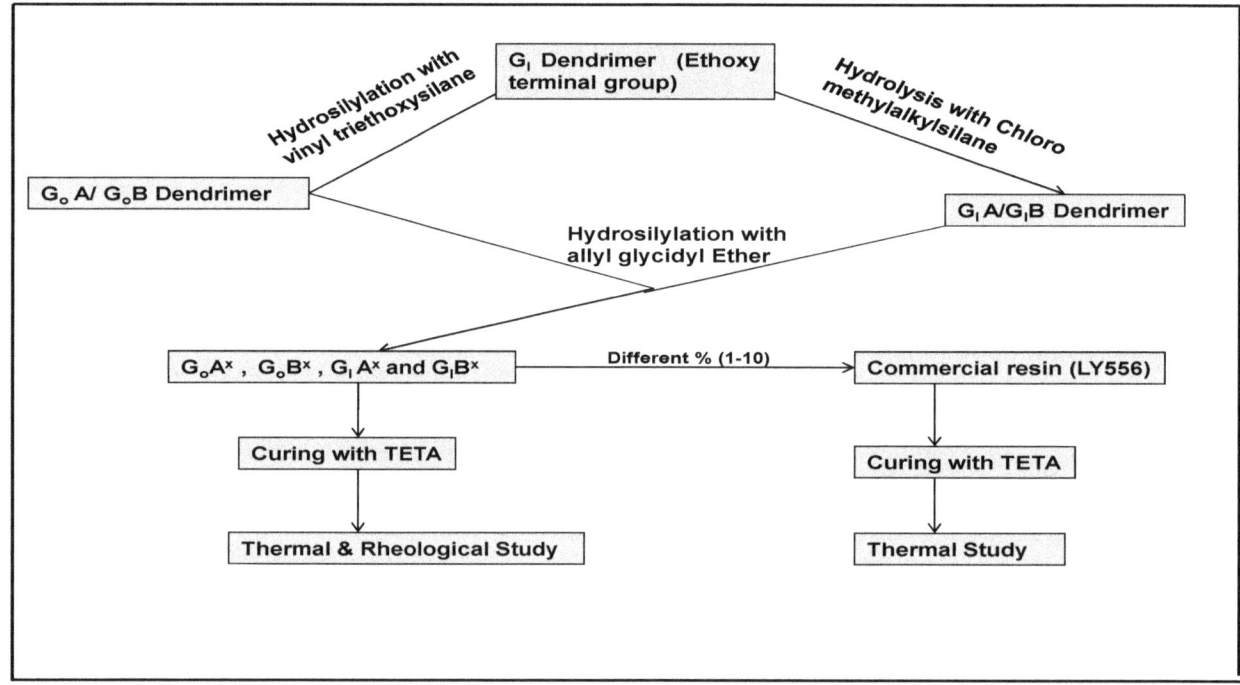

Figure 3: Flow chart of study of Si-H and Oxirane terminal dendrimers.

## 7.2 Synthesis of Si-H Functional Dendrimers

The synthesis of zero and first generation Si-H terminal dendrimers using controlled hydrolysis and hydrosilylation reactions. [36]

### 7.2.1 G₀A dendrimer [Tetrakis(dimethylsiloxy)silane]

A solution of TEOS (7.34 g, 0.03 mol), ethyl alcohol (6.57 g, 0.14 mol) and water (4.0 g, 0.21 mol) was taken in a three necked round bottom flask equipped with magnetic stirrer, thermometer, condenser, dropping funnel and stirred for 30 minutes. Into the above solution chlorodimethylsilane (16.67 g, 0.18 mol) was added drop wise within 3 to 4 hours under stirring. Afterward, few drops (0.2 ml) of concentrated $H_2SO_4$ were added in the solution and mixture was further stirred for 15 minutes. Later on, the solution was allowed A solution of TEOS (7.34 g, 0.03 mol), ethyl alcohol (6.57 g, 0.14 mol) and water (4.0 g, 0.21 mol) was taken in a three necked round bottom flask equipped with magnetic stirrer, thermometer, condenser, dropping funnel and stirred for 30 minutes. Into the above solution chlorodimethylsilane (16.67 g, 0.18 mol) was added drop wise within 3 to 4 hours under stirring. Afterward, few drops (0.2 ml) of concentrated $H_2SO_4$ were added in the solution and mixture was further stirred for 15 minutes. Later on, the solution was allowed to settle down and both silicone and aqueous layer were separated using separating funnel. The silicone layer was washed with distilled water till it became neutral. The aqueous layer was extracted with petroleum ether thrice (3x20 ml) and mixed with silicone layer. The silicone layer was then washed with brine solution (50 ml) and kept on anhydrous sodium sulphate overnight and filtered. The filtrate was distilled on water bath to remove petroleum ether. The residue was distilled on oil bath to collect dendrimer G₀A ($C_8H_{28}O_4Si_5$). Yield 28.0 g, 82.5%, b.p. 190°C. FTIR (KBr): 1077 (–SiOSi–), 2136 (–SiH) cm⁻¹; ¹H NMR (400MHz, CDCl₃, δ ppm): 0.22 (d, 24H, –Si–C$\underline{H}_3$), 4.74 (m, 4H, –Si–$\underline{H}$); elemental analysis (%) C 29.23, H 8.56

, Si 42.74 (calcd C 29.21, H 8.58 & Si 42.72 respectively). Mol wt (VPO): 320.14 (calcd 328.73). GPC: PDI value ($M_w/M_n$), 1.01 (315.14/312.01); Rt, 23.05 min. (Fig.4).

Similarly other reactions as mentioned below were carried out.

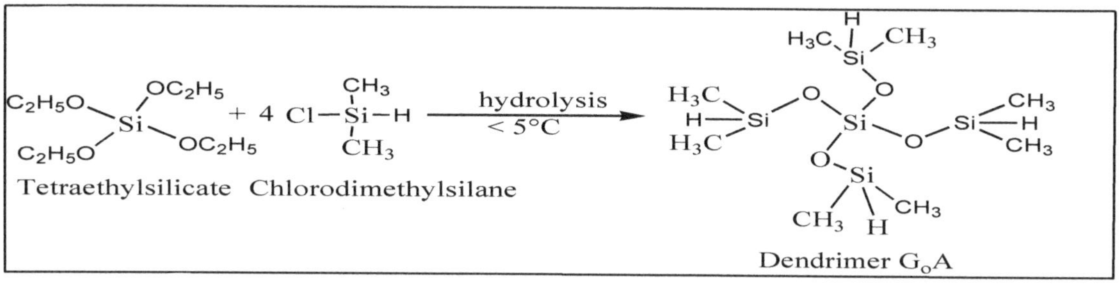

**Figure 4 : Synthesis of zero generation Si-H functional dendrimer $G_oA$.**

### 7.2.3 $G_oB$ dendrimer (Si-H terminated)

Reaction of TEOS (8.8 g, 0.04 mol), ethyl alcohol (6.5 g, 0.08 mol), water (4.0 g, 0.22 mol) & chloromethyl(phenyl)silane (31.3 g, 0.21 mol) was carried out as above to afford $G_oB$ dendrimer. Reaction mixture was distilled under vacuum (~26 mbar at 64°C) to remove unreacted reactants and disiloxanes (by-products of partial hydrolysis of chloromethyl(phenyl)silane. The pot residue was purified by column chromatography (silica gel as stationary phase and n-hexane as mobile phase) to afford colorless liquid $G_oB$ ($C_{28}H_{36}O_4Si_5$) dendrimer; Yield 18.7 g, 80%. FTIR (KBr): 1080 (–SiOSi–), 2139 (–SiH), 1456 (–Si-Ph) cm$^{-1}$; $^1$H NMR (400MHz, CDCl$_3$, δ ppm): 0.21 (d, 12H, –Si–C$\underline{H}_3$), 4.74 (m, 4H, –Si–$\underline{H}$), 7.1~7.3 (d, 20H, -Si-$\underline{Ph}$); elemental analysis (%) C 58.28, H 6.29, Si 24.31 (calcd. C 58.15, H 6.96 & Si 24.34 respectively). Mol wt (VPO): 512.21 (calcd. 576.15). GPC: PDI value ($M_w/M_n$), 1.01 (475.25/470.54); Rt, 22.32 min. (Fig. 5).

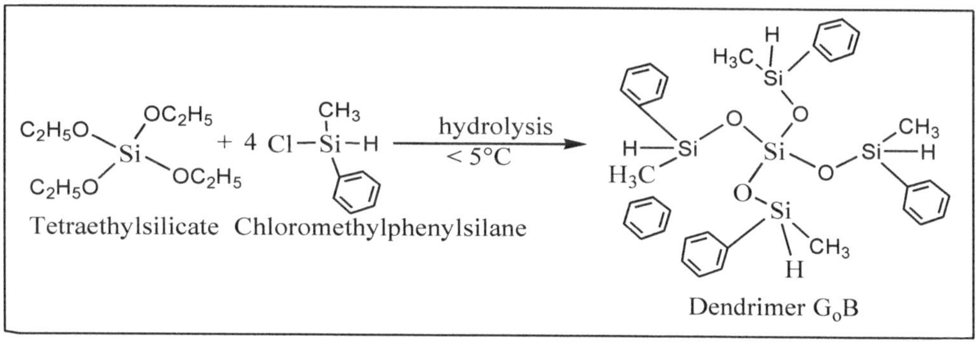

**Figure 5: Synthesis of zero generation Si-H functional dendrimer $G_oB$.**

### 7.2.4 dendrimer (Si-OC$_2$H$_5$ terminated)

A solution of $G_oA$ dendrimer (11.7 g, 0.035 mol) and speier's catalyst (0.03 mol %) in dry THF (50 ml) was taken in a three necked round bottom flask (100 ml) fitted with a dropping funnel containing vinyltriethoxysilane, magnetic stirrer, thermometer, condenser and heated up to 60°C in inert atmosphere. Vinyltriethoxysilane (27.09 g, 0.142 mol) was gradually added drop wise in $G_oA$ solution within 30 min. afterwards the solution was heated for an additional 4 hours and cooled to room temperature. The solution was distilled under reduced pressure (~26 mbar at 64°C) to remove unreacted vinyltriethoxysilane and solvent. The pot residue was column chromatographed (silica gel and n-hexane) to afford colourless & transparent $G_I$ ($C_{40}H_{100}O_{16}Si_9$) dendrimer; yield 30.14 g, 79%. FTIR (KBr): 1080 (–SiOSi–), 1254 (–SiCH$_3$) cm$^{-1}$; $^1$H NMR (400 MHz, CDCl$_3$, $\delta$ ppm): 0.22 (s, 24H, –Si–C$\underline{H}_3$), 0.31 (t, 16H, –Si–C$\underline{H}_2$–), 3.75 (q, 24H, –Si–O–C$\underline{H}_2$–), 1.57 (t, 36H, –Si–O–CH$_2$C$\underline{H}_3$); elemental nalysis (%) C 44.07, H 9.17, Si 23.14 (calcd C 43.95, H 9.02 and Si 23.19 respectively). Mol wt (VPO): 1001.27 (calcd 1089.98). GPC: PDI value (M$_w$/ M$_n$), 1.01 (909.25/ 900.24); Rt, 18.65 min. (Fig. 6).

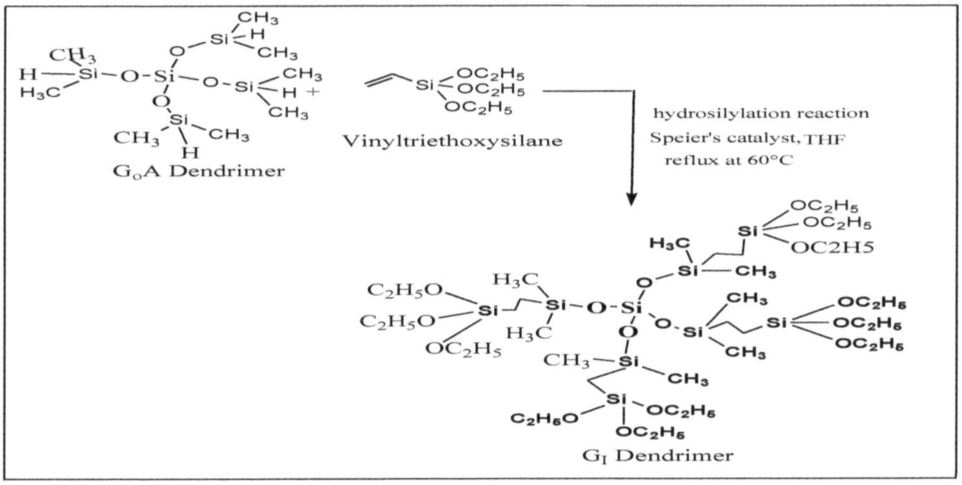

**Figure 6: Synthesis of first generation ethoxy functional dendrimer G$_I$.**

### 7.2.5 G$_I$A dendrimer (dimethyl Si-H terminated)

Reaction of G$_I$ dendrimer (7.69 g, 0.0071mol) in ethyl alcohol (2.13 g, 0.028 mol), water (0.76 g, 0.0426 mol) and chlorodimethylsilane (8.061 g, 0.0852 mol) was carried out similarly as the procedure adopted for the synthesis of dendrimer G$_0$A, which yielded colourless, transparent liquid dendrimer G$_I$A ($C_{40}H_{124}O_{16}Si_{21}$), yield 9.27 g, 90%. FTIR (KBr): 1075 (–SiOSi–), 2136 (–SiH) cm$^{-1}$. $^1$H NMR (400MHz, CDCl$_3$, $\delta$ ppm ): 0.24 (d, 72H, –Si–C$\underline{H}_3$), 4.74 (m, 12H, –Si–$\underline{H}$), 0.23 (s, 24H, –CH$_2$–Si–C$\underline{H}_3$), 0.64 (t, 16H, –Si– C$\underline{H}_2$–); elemental analysis (%) C 33.10, H 8.61 Si 40.59 (calcd C 33.06, H 8.23 and Si 40.64 respectively). Mol wt (VPO): 1360.18 (calcd 1451.19). GPC: PDI value (M$_w$/ M$_n$), 1.01 (1275.95/1263.31); Rt, 17.10 min. (Fig.7).

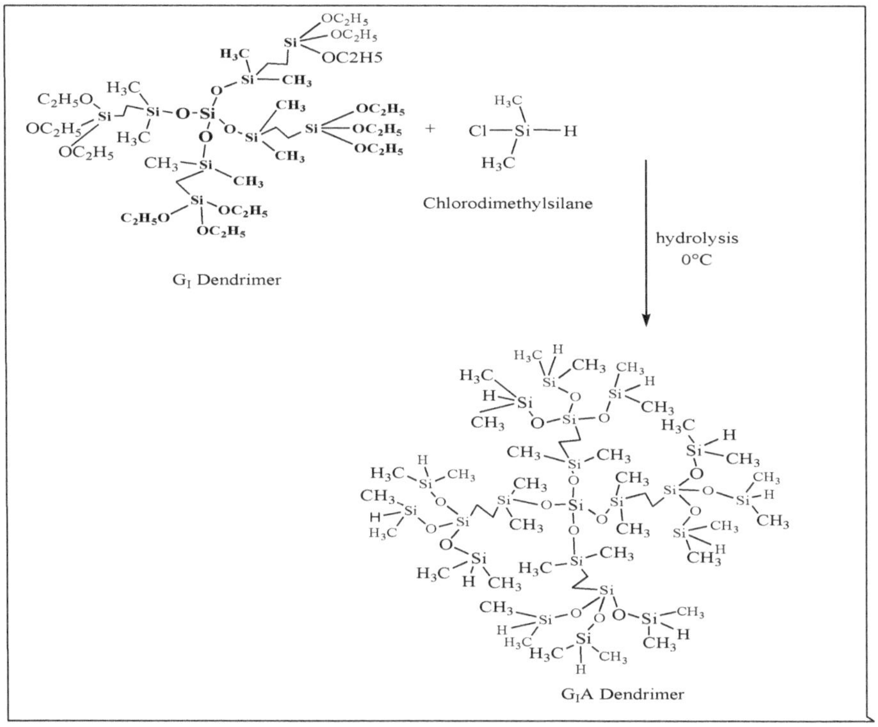

**Figure 7 : Synthesis of first generation Si-H functional dendrimer G₁A.**

## 7.2.6 G₁B dendrimer (methylphenyl Si- H terminated)

Similarly as above, the reaction of G₁ dendrimer (15.2 g, 0.014 mol) in ethyl alcohol (4.2 g, 0.056 mol), water (1.4 g, 0.08 mol) and chloromethyl(phenyl)silane (26.52 g, 0.168 mol) was carried out to afford colourless, transparent liquid dendrimer G₁B ($C_{100}H_{148}O_{16}Si_{21}$), Yield 27.0 g, 88%. FTIR (KBr): 1075 (–SiOSi–), 2139 (–SiH), 1457(–Si-Ph) cm$^{-1}$. $^1$H NMR (400MHz, CDCl$_3$, δ ppm) : 0.22 (m, 36H, –Si–C$\underline{H}_3$), 4.74 (m, 12H, –Si–$\underline{H}$), 0.23 (s, 24H, –CH$_2$–Si–C$\underline{H}_3$), 0.64 (t, 16H, –Si–C$\underline{H}_2$–), 7.1~7.3 (d, 60H, –Si–$\underline{Ph}$); elemental analysis (%) C 54.69, H 6.79 Si 26.61 (calcd. C 54.69, H 6.78 and Si 26.66 respectively). Mol Wt (VPO): 2085.48 (calcd. 2196.02). GPC: PDI value ($M_w/M_n$), 1.03 (1925.67/ 1869.58); Rt, 16.20 min. (Fig. 8).

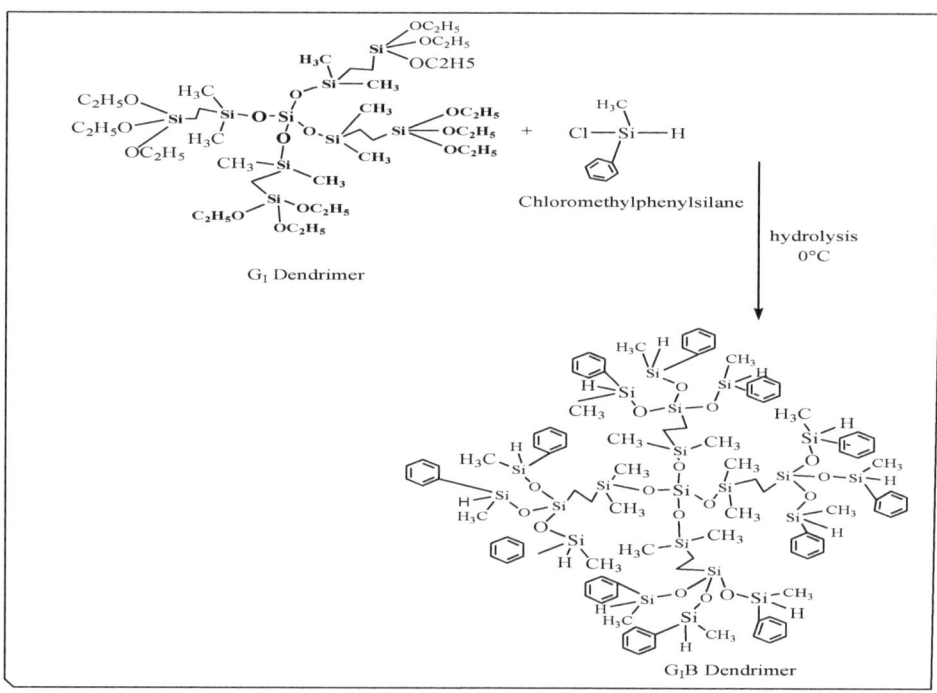

Figure 8 : Synthesis of first generation Si-H functional dendrimer G$_1$B.

## 7.3 Synthesis of Oxirane Functional Dendrimers

this section explained the synthesis of zero generation and first generation oxirane functional dendrimers using hydrosilylation reaction with Si-H functional dendrimers and allyl glycidyl ether in presence of Speier's catalyst.

### 7.3.1 G$_o$A$^x$ dendrimer (Si-oxirane terminated)

A solution of G$_o$A dendrimer (8.84 g, 0.027 mol) and speier's catalyst (0.03 mol %) in dry THF (50 ml) was taken in a three necked round bottom flask (100 ml) fitted with a dropping funnel containing allylglycidyl ether, magnetic stirrer, thermometer, condenser

and heated up to 60°C in inert atmosphere. Allylglycidyl ether (12.3 g, 0.11mol) was gradually added drop wise in G$_o$A solution within 30 min. afterwards the solution was heated for an additional 4 hours and cooled to room temperature. The solution was distilled under reduced pressure to remove unreacted allylglycidyl ether and solvent. The residue was purified by column chromatography (silica gel and n-hexane) to afford colorless, transparent liquid G$_o$A$^x$ dendrimer (C$_{32}$H$_{68}$O$_{12}$Si$_5$). Yield 19.08 g, 89%. FTIR (KBr): 913 (epoxy ring, asy), 1080 (–SiOSi–), 3050 (epoxy ring, sym) cm$^{-1}$. $^1$H NMR (400MHz, CDCl$_3$, δ ppm) : 0.07 (s, 24H, –Si–CH$_3$), 0.54 (t, 8H, –Si–CH$_2$ –), 1.82 (m, 8H, –CH$_2$–CH$_2$–CH$_2$–), 2.59 (d, 8H, epoxy ring, –CH$_2$–, *trans*), 2.77 (d, 8H, epoxy ring, –CH$_2$–, *cis*), 3.13 (m, 4H, epoxy ring, –CH–), 3.37 (d, 8H, –O–CH$_2$–epoxy ring, *cis*), 3.71 (d, 8H, –O–CH$_2$–epoxy ring, trans), 4.01 (t, 8H, –CH$_2$–CH$_2$–O–); elemental analysis (%) C 48.95, H 7.96, Si 17.83 (calcd. C 48.23, H 8.03 & Si 17.88 respectively). Mol wt (VPO): 712.93 (calcd. 785.3). GPC: PDI value (M$_w$/ M$_n$), 1.02 (625.73/613.46); Rt, 20.52 min. (Fig. 9).

Similarly other reactions as mentioned below were carried out.

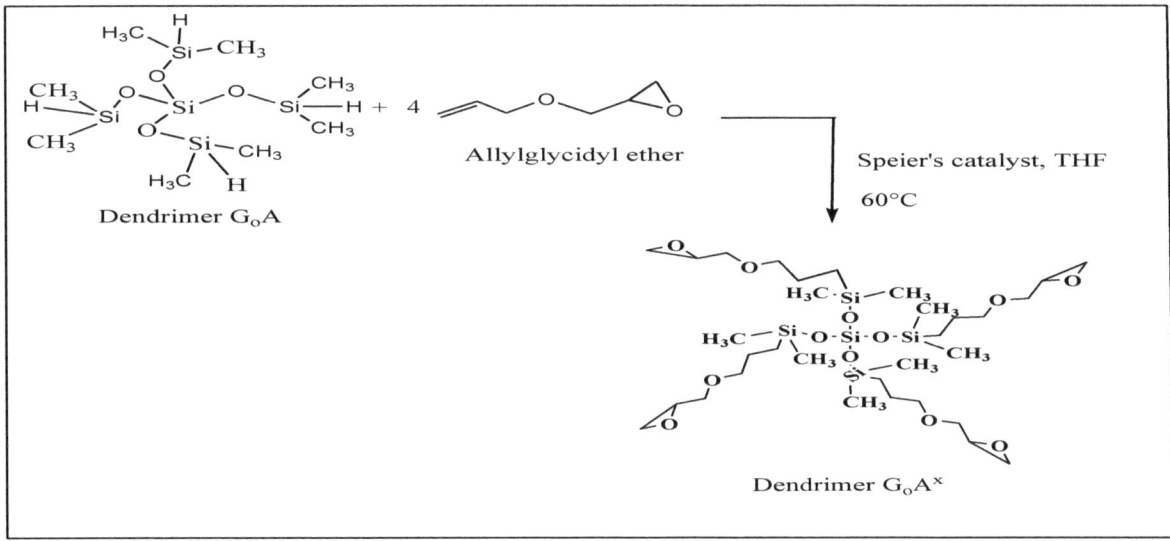

**Figure 9 : Synthesis of zero generation oxirane functional dendrimer $G_0A^x$.**

### 7.3.2 $G_0B^x$ dendrimer (Si-oxirane terminated)

Reaction of $G_0B$ dendrimer (4.18 g, 0.007 mol), Speier's catalyst (0.03 mol %) and allyl glycidyl ether (3.4 g, 0.03 mol) yielded a colourless, transparent liquid dendrimer $G_0B^x$ ($C_{52}H_{76}O_{12}Si_5$). Yield 6.20 g, 85%. FTIR (KBr): 913 (epoxy ring, asy), 1080 (–SiOSi–), 3050 (epoxy ring, sym) cm$^{-1}$. $^1$H NMR (400MHz, CDCl$_3$, δ ppm): 0.07 (s, 12H, –Si–C$\underline{H}_3$), 7.1 (d, 20H, –Si–$\underline{Ph}$), 0.54(t, 8H, –Si–C$\underline{H}_2$–), 1.82 (m, 8H, –CH$_2$–C$\underline{H}_2$–CH$_2$ –), 2.59 (d, 8H, epoxy ring, –C$\underline{H}_2$–, *trans*), 2.77 (d, 8H, epoxy ring, –C$\underline{H}_2$–, *cis*), 3.13 (m, 4H, epoxy ring, –C$\underline{H}$–), 3.37 (d, 8H, –O–C$\underline{H}_2$–epoxy ring, *cis*), 3.71 (d, 8H, –O–C$\underline{H}_2$ – epoxy ring, trans), 4.01 (t, 8H, –CH$_2$–C$\underline{H}_2$–O–); elemental analysis (%) C 60.43, H 7.41, Si 13.54 (calcd. C 61.02, H 7.15 & Si 13.59 respectively). Mol wt (VPO): 989.18 (calcd. 1032.42). GPC: PDI value ($M_w/ M_n$), 1.01 (825.08/816.91); Rt, 19.49 min. (Fig. 10).

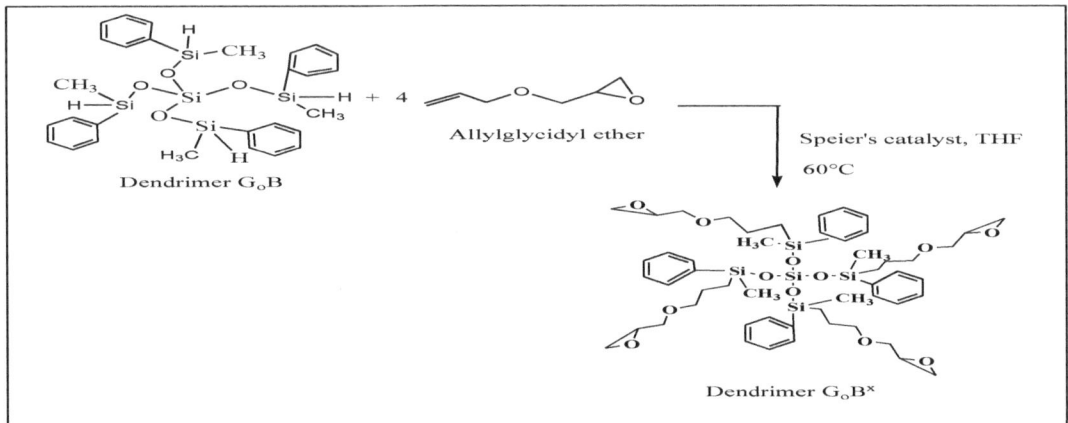

**Figure 10: Synthesis of zero generation oxirane functional dendrimer $G_0B^x$.**

### 7.3.3 G$_I$A$^x$ dendrimer (Si-oxirane terminated)

A solution of G$_I$A dendrimer (6.0 g, 0.0041 mol) and speier's catalyst (0.03 mol %) in dry THF (50 ml) was taken in a three necked round bottom flask (100 ml) fitted with a dropping funnel containing allylglycidyl ether, magnetic stirrer, thermometer, condenser and heated up to 60°C in inert atmosphere. Allylglycidyl ether (6.75 g, 0.0592 mol) was gradually added drop wise in G$_o$A solution within 30 min. afterwards the solution was heated for an additional 4 hours and cooled to room temperature. The solution was distilled under reduced pressure to remove unreacted allylglycidyl ether and solvent. The pot residue was yielded a dendrimer G$_I$A$^x$ (C$_{112}$H$_{244}$O$_{40}$Si$_{21}$) which was colourless & transparent liquid, yield 9.59 g, 85 %. FTIR (KBr): 913 (epoxy ring, asy), 1080 (–SiOSi–), 3050 (epoxy ring, sym) cm$^{-1}$. $^1$H NMR (400MHz, CDCl$_3$, δ ppm): 0.07 (s, 96H, –Si–C$\underline{H}_3$), 0.64 (t, 16H, –Si–C$\underline{H}_2$–) 0.54 (t, 24H, –Si–C$\underline{H}_2$–), 1.82 (m, 24H, –CH$_2$–C$\underline{H}_2$–CH$_2$–), 2.59 (d, 24H, epoxy ring, –CH$_2$–, *trans*), 2.77 (d, 24H, epoxy ring, –CH$_2$–, *cis*), 3.13 (m, 12H, epoxy ring, –CH–), 3.37 (d, 24H, –O–C$\underline{H}_2$–epoxy ring, *cis*), 3.71 (d, 24H, –O–C$\underline{H}_2$ –epoxy ring, trans), 4.01 (t, 24H, –CH$_2$–C$\underline{H}_2$–O–); elemental analysis (%) C 47.68, H 8.72, Si 20.90 (calcd. C 48.02, H 8.69 & Si 20.91 respectively). Mol wt (VPO): 2753.79 (calcd. 2820.91). GPC: PDI value (M$_w$/ M$_n$), 1.01 (2721.29/ 2694.34); Rt, 16.59 min. (Fig. 11).

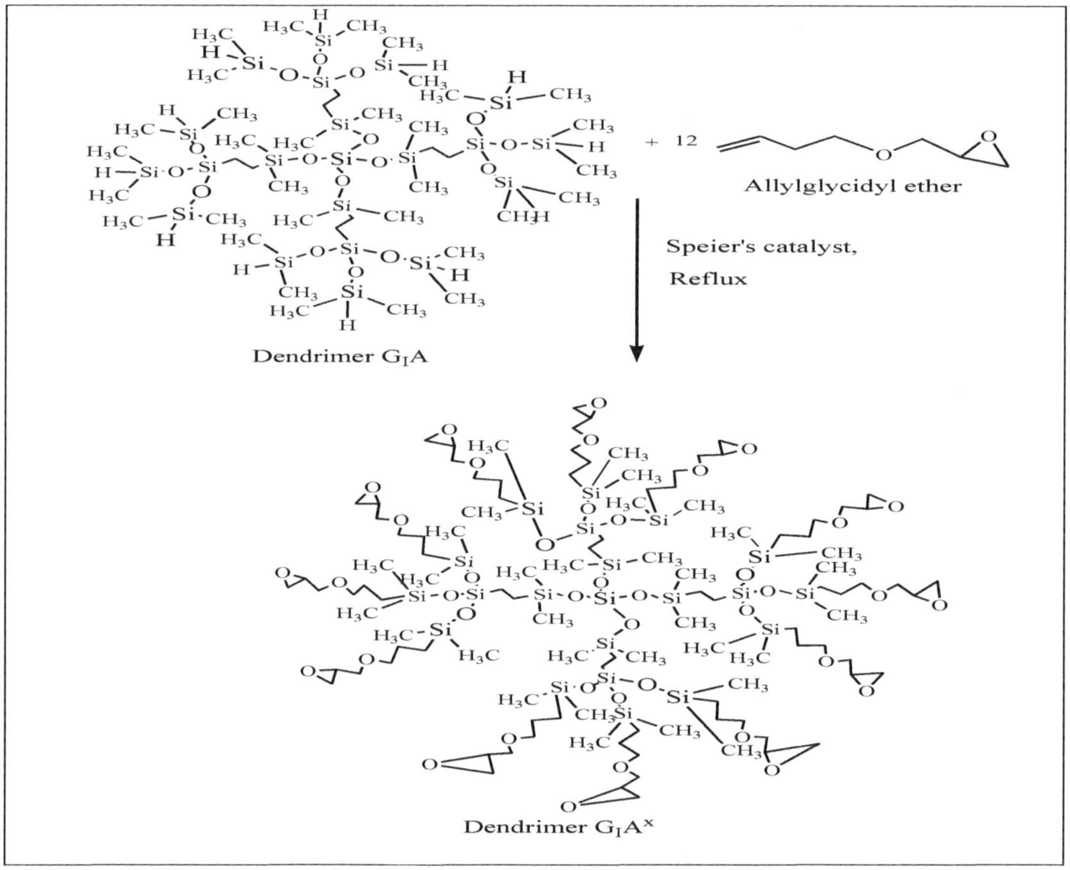

**Figure 1 1 : synthesis of first generation oxirane functional dendrimer G$_I$A$^x$.**

### 7.3.4 G₁Bˣ dendrimer (Si-oxirane terminated)

A solution of $G_1B$ dendrimer (4.0 g, 0.0018 mol) and speier's catalyst (0.03 mol %) in dry THF (50 ml) was taken in a three necked round bottom flask (100 ml) fitted with a dropping funnel containing allylglycidyl ether, magnetic stirrer, thermometer, condenser and heated up to 60°C in inert atmosphere. Allylglycidyl ether (2.5 g, 0.0218 mol) was gradually added drop wise in $G_0A$ solution within 30 min. afterwards the solution was heated for an additional 4 hours and cooled to room temperature. The solution was distilled under reduced pressure to remove unreacted allylglycidyl ether and solvent. The residue was purified by column chromatography (silica gel and n-hexane) to afford colorless, transparent liquid dendrimer $G_1B^x$ ($C_{172}H_{268}O_{40}Si_{21}$). Yield 5.7 g, 90%. FTIR (KBr): 913 (epoxy ring, asy), 1080 (–SiOSi–), 3050 (epoxy ring, sym) cm⁻¹. ¹H NMR (400MHz, CDCl₃, δ ppm) : 0.07 (s, 60H, –Si–C$\underline{H}_3$), 7.3 (d, 60H, –Si–$\underline{Ph}$) 0.64 (t, 16H, –Si–C$\underline{H}_2$–) 0.54 (t, 24H, –Si–C$\underline{H}_2$–), 1.82 (m, 24H, –CH₂–C$\underline{H}_2$–CH₂–), 2.59 (d, 24H, epoxy ring, –CH₂–, *trans*), 2.77 (d, 24H, epoxy ring, –CH₂–, *cis*), 3.13 (m, 12H, epoxy ring, –CH–), 3.37 (d, 24H, –O–C$\underline{H}_2$–epoxy ring, *cis*), 3.71 (d, 24H, –O–C$\underline{H}_2$ –epoxy ring, trans), 4.01 (t, 24H, –CH₂–CH₂–O–); elemental analysis (%) C 57.94, H 7.57, Si 16.52 (calcd. C 57.32, H 7.95 & Si 16.54 respectively). Mol wt (VPO): 3498.31 (calcd. 3565.74). GPC: PDI value ($M_w/M_n$), 1.01 (3285.63/ 3253.09); Rt, 16.18 min.

### 7.4 Curing of Oxirane Functional Dendrimers

This section explained the sample preparation of different generation oxirane dendrimers with aliphatic hardener TETA and further its hybrid compositions having different percentage (1-10%) of all oxirane terminated dendrimers and commercially available epoxy resin LY556 with TETA.

### 7.4.1 Sample Preparation

The oxirane dendrimers ($G_0A^x$, $G_0B^x$, $G_1A^x$ and $G_1B^x$) initially cured neat with stoichiometric amount of TETA using the formula as given below were kept at room temperature (28°C) for 24h.

$X = W_1N_2 / W_2N_1$

Where X = weight of amine required to cure 1 gm of epoxy compound.

$W_1$= weight of amine

$W_2$= weight of epoxy molecule

$N_1$= number of -NH group present in amine

$N_2$= number of –epoxy group present in epoxy compound.

The value for $N_1$ in case of TETA is 6. While the values of $N_2$ in case of zero generation dendrimer $G_0A^x$ and $G_0B^x$ is 4 and first generation dendrimers $G_1A^x$ and $G_1B^x$ it is 12. By using the formulation, all oxirane terminated dendrimers were cured with aliphatic amine TETA.

Rheological and differential scanning calorimetric analysis of this composition were also carried out to study the curing process. Afterwards the mixtures were heated for post curing at 50°C for 0.5 h, 70°C for 1 h, 85°C for 2 h and 101°C for 2 h. The thermal properties i.e., DSC & TGA were carried out for post cured resin matrix.

## 7.4.2 Modification of oxirane dendrimers with commercial resin

The oxirane dendrimers ($G_oA^x$, $G_oB^x$, $G_IA^x$ and $G_IB^x$) were taken in different percentage like 1%, 2%, 3%, 5% and 10% were mixed homogeneously with epoxy resin [Araldite LY556, EEW= 183- 192 g/eq, n=0.3) ( Bisphenol A diglycidyl ether)] then cured with TETA in stoichiometric amount and kept at room temperature (28°C) for 24h. Afterwards the mixtures were heated for post curing at 50°C for 0.5 h, 70°C for 1 h, 85°C for 2 h and 101°C for 2 h. The thermal gravimetric analysis was carried out for post cured resin matrix.

## 7.5 Characterization of Dendrimers:

Characterization of dendrimers were carried out by elemental analysis, FT-IR Spectroscopy, 1H- NMR Spectroscopy, GPC, VPO, DSC, TGA, Rheological Analysis.

## 7.5.1 FT-IR Spectroscopy

FT-IR spectroscopy provided valuable information about the reaction progress and the functional group attached on the dendrimers. In all the dendrimers an IR absorption peak (Figure 12) appeared at ~1080 cm$^{-1}$ which indicates the presence of ν Si-O-Si bond. The ν Si-H absorption peak appeared at ~ 2131 cm$^{-1}$ in dendrimers $G_oA$, $G_oB$, $G_IA$ and $G_IB$. When the hydrosilylation reaction of dendrimer $G_oA$ with vinyltriethoxysilane was carried out to prepare $G_I$ dendrimer, the ν Si-H peak at 2136 cm$^{-1}$ and ν $CH_2$=CH peak at 1600 cm$^{-1}$ disappeared which confirmed the addition of Si-H group on vinyl moiety.

The FT-IR spectrum (Figure 13) of the reaction product $G_oA^x$, $G_oB^x$, $G_IA^x$ and $G_IB^x$ showed the appearance of characteristic absorption peak of oxirane ring at 913 cm$^{-1}$ and 3054 cm$^{-1}$ and the disappearance of ν Si-H peak at 2136 cm$^{-1}$ which was very much prominent in dendrimers $G_oA$, $G_oB$, $G_IA$ and $G_IB$ respectively. Therefore, it was tentatively inferred that hydrosilylation of allyl glycidyl ether with all Si-H terminated dendrimers took place.

IR spectrum of cured resin matrix showed the peak of unsymmetrical stretching of ether linkage at ~1259 cm$^{-1}$ which showed the presence of ether linkage of allylglycidylether moiety due to crosslinking of allylglycidylether with TETA. The oxirane ring which appeared at 913 cm$^{-1}$ and 3054 cm$^{-1}$ disappeared and in the resin matrix secondary hydroxyl group appeared at ~3439 cm$^{-1}$ due to the reaction of amino group of TETA with dendrimer and LY556.

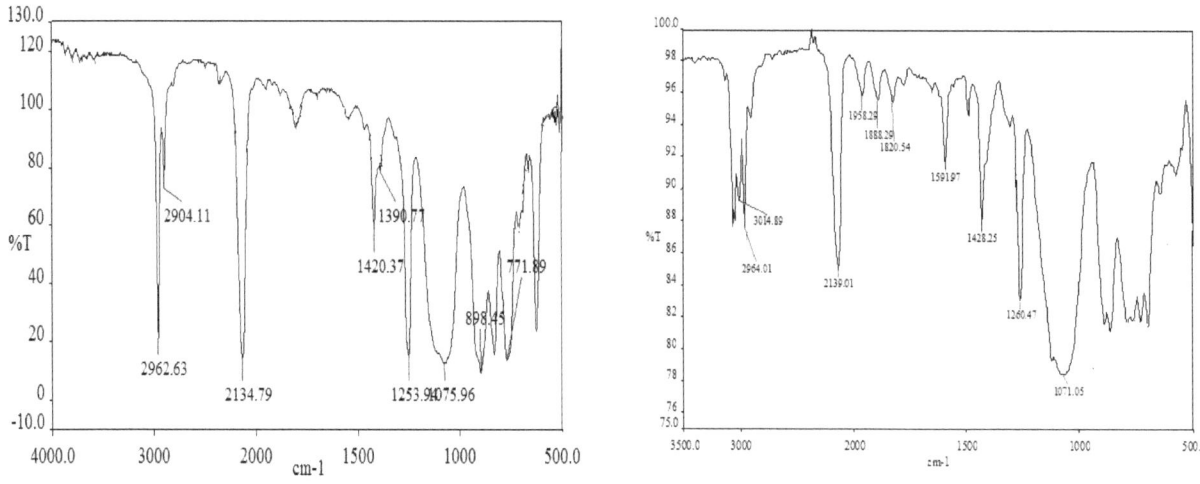

Figure 12 : FT-IR spectra of $G_0A$, $G_0B$ ( Si-H Functional) Dendrimer

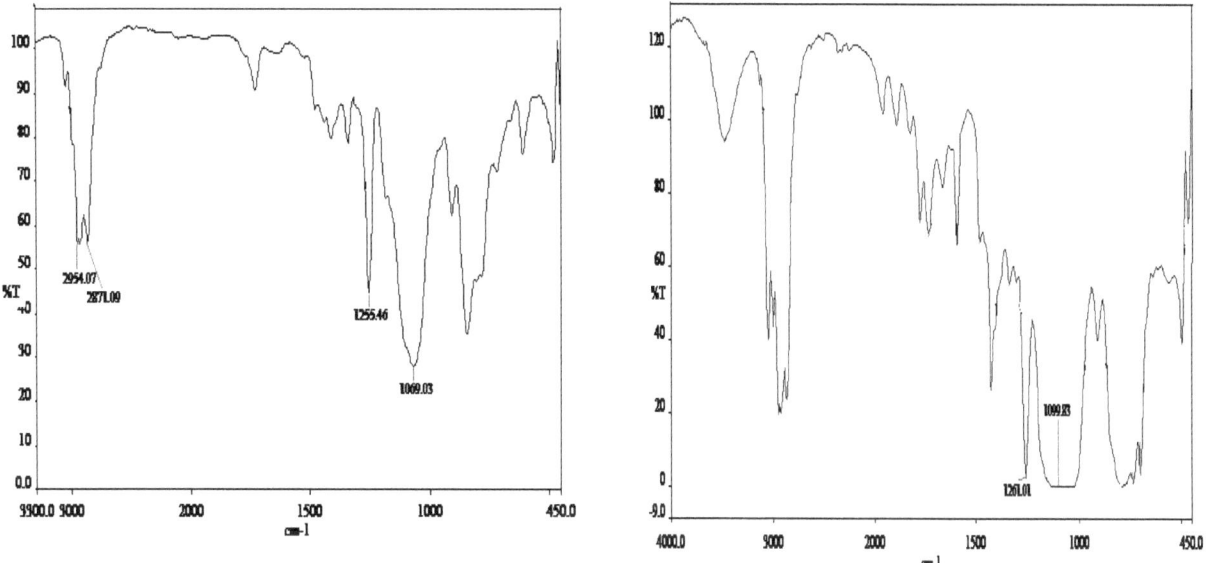

Figure 13: FT-IR spectra of $G_0A^x$, $G_0B^x$ ( Si-oxirane terminated )Dendrimer

## 7.5.2 $^1$H- N MR spectroscopy

The spectrum of dendrimers $G_0A$, $G_0B$, $G_1A$ and $G_1B$ respectively showed multiplet for δ Si-H at ~ 4.74 to 4.85 ppm due to coupling with Si-CH$_3$ protons and doublet for δ Si-CH$_3$ at 0.22 ppm due to coupling with protons of Si-H group.

The progress of hydrosilylation of the dendrimer $G_0A$ with vinyltriethoxysilane was confirmed by disappearance of δ SiH proton at 4.74 ppm and δ H$_2$C=CH proton at 5-6 ppm.

## 7.5.3 Gel Permeation Chromatography (GPC)

Gel permeation chromatography used to determine the number average molecular weight and the poly dispersity index (PDI) of dendrimers. The poly dispersity index or heterogeneity index or simply dispersity was a measure of the distribution of molecular mass in a given polymer sample. It was calculated by dividing weight average molecular weight ($M_w$) to number average molecular weight ($M_n$).

The values of $M_n$ for all the synthesized dendrimers were found in the range of 312- 825 gmol$^{-1}$ for zero generation dendrimers and its values for first generation dendrimers were observed in the range of 900-3286 gmol$^{-1}$. The value of PDI was in the range of 1.01- 1.02 which indicated the uniformity of dendrimers.

### 7.5.4 Vapor Pressure Osmometry (VPO)

The number average molecular weight ($M_n$) of the Si-H terminal zero and first generation and oxirane terminated zero and first generation silicone dednrimers under same experimental condition using toluene as solvent. It was observed from the results that the value of observed number average molecular weight from VPO and calculated values are close to each other.

### 7.5.5 Differential Scanning Calorimetry (DSC)

In DSC study a broad exotherm [3 6] was observed for all oxirane dendrmers when cured with aliphatic amine (TETA) in the temperature range of 60-178 °C. The characteristic curing temperatures summarized in table 3.1.4, which established that curing of oxirane dendrimers proceeded by nucleophilic attack of amine on the electrophile oxirane ring, so it was tentatively assumed that more oxirane centers will initiate the curing at low temperature with fast rate. Therefore, onset temperature of exotherm ($T_o$) may be used as a criterion for evaluating the relative reactivity of various oxirane terminal dendrimers (1%) and LY556. From the results it was evident that the lowest $T_o$ occurred with 1% $G_IA^x$ and LY556 due to maximum cross linking cites and less bulky group at periphery.

**Table 1 : DSC results of Curing of LY556 and dendimers hybrid composition with TETA**

| Epoxy | $T_o$ $^a$ (°C) | $T_p$ $^b$ (°C) | $T_f$ $^c$ (°C) |
|---|---|---|---|
| LY556 | 66.41 | 101.79 | 173.11 |
| 1%$G_oA^x$ + LY556 | 61.77 | 98.91 | 177.81 |
| 1% $G_IA^x$+ LY556 | 60.77 | 96.53 | 173.54 |
| 1% $G_oB^x$ + LY556 | 63.40 | 100.84 | 166.93 |
| 1% $G_IB^x$ + LY556 | 64.66 | 101.60 | 173.92 |

$^a$ $T_o$ (onset of exotherm), $^b$ $T_p$ (tem. of peak position of exotherm), $^c$ $T_f$ (tem. of end of exotherm).

Above results showed the value of the glass transition temperature ($T_g$) of TETA cured dendrimers $G_oA^x$, $G_oB^x$, $G_IA^x$ and $G_IB^x$. It was evident from the results that the value of Tg increased with the increase in silicone core which may be tentatively attributed to the fact that with the increase of crosslinking density, $T_g$ increases . The glass transition temperature obtained by DSC analysis showed that the $T_g$ of $G_oA^x$ is lower and $G_IB^x$ is higher among all dendrimers.

## 7.5.6 Thermal Gravimetric Analysis

The TGA graphs (Figure 14) of the TETA cured neat dendrimers $G_oA^x$, $G_oB^x$, $G_IA^x$ and $G_IB^x$ were shown a single step degradation process which reflects the formation of uniform structure and single component system. The onset temperature of decomposition ($T_o$), the temperature of maximum rate of mass loss ($T_{max}$) and the extrapolated final decomposition temperature ($T_{ef}$) were noted from TG traces and these were in the range of 360-375°C, 410-431°C and 450-500°C. The relative thermal stability of the cured resin was compared by determining % char yield at 800°C. Moreover, the char yields of resin matrix at 800°C were about 29%.

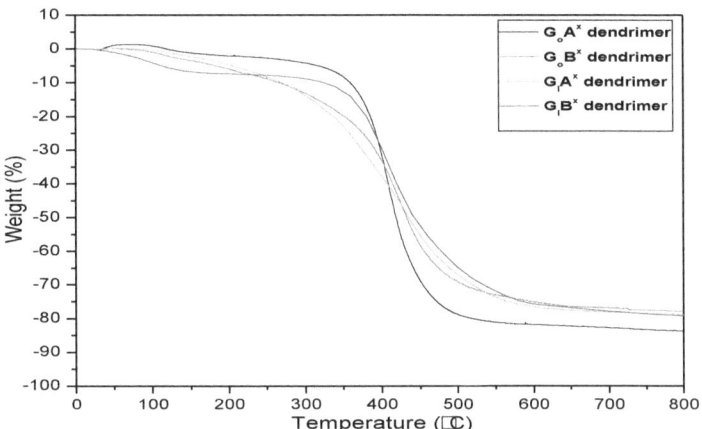

**Figure 14: Thermogravimetric analysis of cured dendrimers**

The TGA results of the TETA cured product of neat LY556 epoxy and the different percentages (1%-10%) of dendrimers with LY556 epoxy (hybrid compositions). All hybrid composition showed an enhancement of onset temperature of decomposition 15 ± 5 °C with respect to neat epoxy system. Whereas varied amount (1-10%) of dendrimers did not show any remarkable variation.

Conclusively the TGA studies of dendrimers modified LY556 resin showed that there was marginal yet distinct increase on onset temperature of degradation ($T_o$) in case of all epoxy composition while increasing the dendrimers from 1% to 3% a distinct effect of $T_o$ was observed but beyond it i.e., 4 % - 10%, no significant effect on $T_o$ could be noticed yet the char yield increased which may be attributed due to increased Si-O-Si quantities. The change in the value of maximum degradation temperature ($T_{max.}$) in case of addition of $G_IA^x$ dendrimer was found maximum (+10°C) which may be due to good synergistic effect of silicone and organic content present in the epoxy composition of this dendrimer. The char yield also increased in case a mixture of resins and it was more in case of $G_IB^x$ invariably in all ratios. Results were consistent with neat dendrimer results for char yields. The LOI of dendrimer containing resin matrix also increased distinctly, yet marginally due to –Si-O-Si- linkage as silicones on burning yields $SiO_2$ in air atmosphere, and also acted as self extinguishing material. So, it may be expected that with the increase of –Si-O-Si- groups containing dendrimers or their quantities may further enhance LOI and char yield of resin matrix to a certain extent.

## 7.5.7 Rheological Analysis

Epoxy resin exhibit both viscous and elastic properties. During the curing process, their viscosity increases quickly in the gel region. The viscosity can be related to degree of cure. Rheological analysis has been used to study the curing process of epoxy resin [37- 38] ike polymers; epoxy resin is a viscoelastic material. During a curing process under continuous stresses or strains, its viscoelastic characteristics change; this is reflected in the variations of the viscosity.

In the present study, all oxirane dendrimers were mixed with hardener TETA in *stoichiometric* ratio, to study the change in storage (G`) modulous and complex viscosity with respect to temperature (Figure 15,16 ]. As with the increase in temperature, the curing of resin matrix i.e., increase in crosslinking took place which increased the viscosity and rotation speed started diminishing and it was an indicator of changing the viscous emulsion into elastic cured network. It is shown in fig. 3.1.35 that the initial low value of complex viscosity of the system increased abruptly in the specific time range as the curing reaction proceeds. Graph reflects that initiation of curing has been started at 75°C for $G_IA^x$, at 80°C for $G_0A^x$, 95°C for $G_IB^x$ and 110°C for $G_0B^x$. There is substantial increase in the value of storage modulus which showed an increase from 10-20 Pascal to $10^5$ Pascal. Storage modulous and complex viscosity of $G_0B^x$ dendrimer increased slowly as compared to other dendrimers which showed that the dendrimer was least reactive among all. It may be due to less crosslinking units and hinderance in its structure due to bulky phenyl groups.

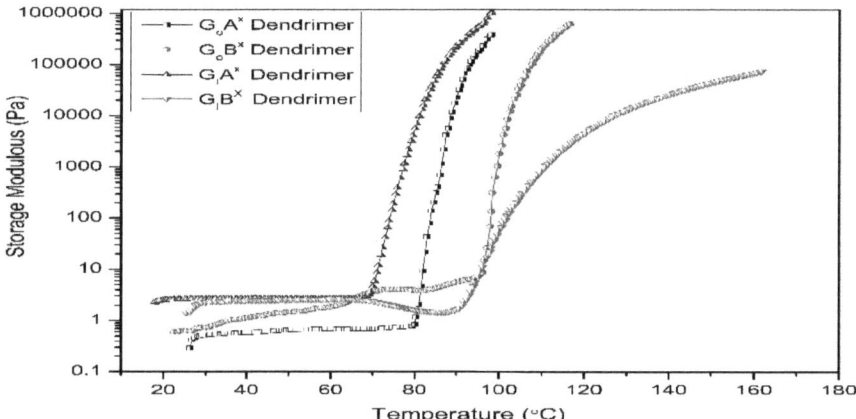

**Figure 15: Rheological plot of storage modulous against temperature for curing of dendrimers**

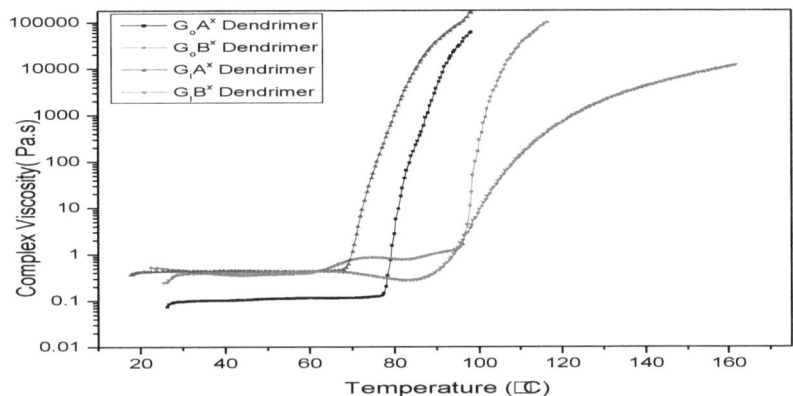

**Figure 1 6: Rheological plot of complex viscosity against temperature for curing of dendrimers**

Conclusively, the rheological results of all dendrimers curing showed that dendrimer $G_IA^x$ having maximum oxirane and dimethyl group at periphery, cured faster compared to other dendrimers ($G_0A^x$, $G_0B^x$, $G_IB^x$) due to more crosslinking units and less hindrance at terminals while dendrimer $G_0B^x$ having minimum oxirane methylphenyl groups at periphery took maximum time for curing.

## 8. Conclusions

*As most of the organosilicone oligomers and polymers have excellent manipulative structure property relationship hence it is considered worthwhile to study the synthesis and properties of multi generation organosilicone dendrimers for various high-tech applications. It is considered worthwhile to synthesize some new organosilicone dendrimer bearing terminal Si-H groups, epoxy groups, anhydride groups, ester group and imide groups in high yield and explore their application in different high-tech applications like, as diluents, additive to epoxy resin to improve thermal properties and as base stock for lubricants etc.*

In this study the different generations Si-H terminated dendrimers were successfully synthesized in high yield via a new alternative modified method. Hydrosilylation of dendrimers was done with allyl glycidyl ether using speier's catalyst to prepare novel oxirane terminated dendrimers. Rheological and differential scanning calorimetric studies of curing behavior of oxirane dendrimers were carried out with TETA. The results reflected that curing time is decreased as the number of oxirane unit increases in terminals and steric hinderance decreased in the system.

Thermal studies of the cured product of dendrimer were carried out. These dendrimers were further used as a modifier for up gradation of thermal properties of commercial epoxy LY556. Enhancement in thermal behavior and flame retardancy were observed after adding these dendrimers. It proves that these novel dendrimers can further used for modifier, diluents and in different High-Tech applications.

# REFRENCES

1. [1]. A. Mark, J.E., Allcock, H.R., West, R., *Inorganic Polymer*. Prentice Hall Englewood Cliffs, NJ. , 1992. Chap.3, 61500 p.

   Brook, M.A., *Silicone in organic, organometallic and polymer chemistry*, Johns Wiley & Sons, New York, 2000. 256 p. Knoll, W., *Chemistry & Technology of Silicones*, Acdemic Press, London, New York, 1968. 305-327 p.

2. Caminati, G., Turro, N.J., Tomalia, D.A., Photophysical investigation of starburst dendrimers and their interactions with anionic and cationic surfactants. *J. Am. Chem. Soc.*,1990. Vol. 112, 8515-8522 p. DOI.10.1021/ja00179a041

3. Fischer, M., Vogtle, F., Dendrimers: From design to application: A progress report. *Angew.Chem., Int. Edn.*, 1999. Vol. 38, Issue 7, 884-905 p. DOI: 10.1002/(SICI)1521-3773(19990401)38:7<884::AID-ANIE884>3.0.CO;2-K

4. Tomalia, D.A., Naylor, A.M., Goddard III, W.A., Starburst dendrimers: Molecular level control of size, shape, surface chemistry, topology, and flexibility from atoms to macroscopic matter. *Angew. Chem., Int. Edn.*, 1990. Vol.29, Issue 2, 138-175 p. DOI: 10.1002/anie.199001381

5. Gao, C., Yan, D., Hyperbranched polymers: from synthesis to applications. *Prog. Polym. Sci.*, 2004. Vol.29, 183-275 p. DOI:10.1016/j.progpolymsci.2003.12.002

6. a. Atherton, J.C.C., Jones, S., Diastereomeric control of photoinduced Diels-Alder reactions of 1-anthracen-9-yl-ethanol by hydrogen-bonding effects. *Tetrahedron Lett.*, 2001. Vol. 42, 8239-8241 p. DOI: 10.1016/S0040-4039(01)01742-7

   *b. Kumar, A., Pawar, S.S., The aqueous salt- promoted Diels- Alder reaction of anthracene- 9-carbinol with N-ethylmaleimide.* Tetrahedron, *2002. Vol. 58, Issue 9, 1745-1749 p. DOI:10.1016/S0040-4020(02)00035-2*

   c. Wiehe, A., Senge, M.O., Schafer, A., Speck, M., Tannert, S., Kurreck, H., Roader, B., Electron donar- acceptor compounds: Exploiting the triptycene geometry for the synthesis of porphyrin quinone diads, triads, and tetrad. *Tetrahedron*, 2001. Vol. 57, Issue 51, 10089-10110 p.

7. Majoral, J.P., Caminade, A.M., Dendrimers containing hetroatoms (Si, P, B, Ge or Bi). *Chem. Rev.*, 1999. Vol. 99, Issue 3, 845-880 p. DOI:10.1021/cr970414j

8. a. Turrin, C.O., Chiffre, J., Montauzon, D. de., Balavoine, G., Manoury, E., Caminade, A.M.,

   Majoral, J.P. , Behavior of an optically active ferrocene chiral shell located within phosphoruscontaining dendrimers. *Organometallics*, 2002. Vol. 21, 1891-1897 p. DOI: 10.1021/om010956y

   b. Hovestad, N.J., Ford, A., Jastrzebski, J.T.B.H., Koten, G. Van., Functionalized carbosilane dendritic species as soluble support in organic synthesis. *J. Org. Chem.*, 2000. Vol. 65, 6338-6344 p. DOI:10.1021/jo991726k

   c. Wijkens, P., Jastrzebski, Jj.t.b.h., Van der Schaarf, P.A., Kolly, R., Hafner, A., Van Koten, G., Synthesis of periphery functionalized dendritic molecules using polylithiated dendrimers as starting material. *Org. Lett.*, 2000. Vol. 2, Issue 11, 1621-1624 p. DOI: 1021/jo991726k

De Groot, D., Emmerink, P.G., Couke, C., Reek, J.N.H., Kamer, P.C.J., Van Leeuwen, P.W.N.M., Rhodium catalysed hydroformylation using diphenylphosphine functionalised carbosilane dendrimers. *Inorg. Chem. Commun.*, 2000. Vol. 3, Issue 12, 711-713 p. DOI: 10.1016/s1387-7003(00)00168-4

9. Van der Made, A.W., Van Leeuwen, P.W.N.M., Silane dendrimers. *J.Chem.Soc. Chem. Comm.*, 1992. 1400-1401 p. DOI: 10.1039/C39920001400

10. Zhou, L. L., Roovers, J. Synthesis of novel carbosilane dendritic macromolecules. *Macromolecules*, Vol.26, Issue26, 963-968p. DOI:10.1021/ma00057a013

11. Seyferth, D., Son, D.Y., Rheingold, A.L., Ostrander, R.L., Synthesis of an organosilicone dendrimer containing 324 Si-H bonds. *Organometallics*, 1994. Vol.13, Issue 7, 2682-2690 p. DOI: 10.1021/om00019a026

12. Kim, C., Kwon, A., Silane arborols- XV-A dendritic carbosilane based on siloxane tetramer. Synthesis. 1998. Issue 1, 105 p. DOI: 1o.1055/S-1998-2000.

13. Kim, C., Park, J., Preparation of dendritic carbosilanes containing propargyloxy groups. Synthesis. 1999. Issue 10, 1804-1808 p. DOI: 10.1016/S0022-328X (99)00335-6

14. Hawker, C., Fréchet, J. M. J. A new convergent approach to monodisperse dendritic macromolecules. *J. Chem. Soc., Chem. Commun., 1990.* Vol. 15, 1010-1013 p. DOI: org/10.1039/C39900001010

15. Chow, H.F., Mong, T.K.K., Nongrum, M.F., Wan, C.W., The synthesis and properties of novel functional dendritic molecules. *Tetrahedron*. 1998. Vol. 54, 8543-8660 p.

16. Bruning, K., Lang, H., Linear and branched carbosiloxane dendrimers by repetitive hydrosilylation-alcoholysis cycles. *Synthesis-S*, 1999. Vol. 11, 1931-1936 p.

17. Buschbeck, R., 1, 2-Branched 1st to 4th generation carbosiloxane dendrimers with a $Me_2SiO_2$ or $MeSiO_3$ Core. *Synthesis*, 2001. Vol. 15, 2289-2298 p.

18. Kim, C., Hong, J.H., Carbosilane and carbosiloxane dendrimers. *Molecules,* 2009. Vol. 14, 3719-3730 p. DOI: 10.3390/molecules14093719

19. Duncan, R., Izzo, L., Dendrimer biocompatibility and toxicity. *Adv. Drug Deliv. Rev.*, 2005. Vol. 57, 2215–2237 p.DOI: 10.1016/j.addr.2005.09.019.

20. Chen, H.T., Neerman, M.F., Simanek, E. E., Cytotoxicity, hemolysis and acute in vivo toxicity of dendrimers based on melamine, candidate vehicles for drug delivery, *J. Am. Chem. Soc.*, 2004. Vol. 126, 10044- 10048 p. DOI:10.1021/ja048548j

21. Newkome, R., Moorefield, C.N., Vogtle, F., *Dendritic Molecules, Concepts, Synthesis*, Perspective. VCH: Weinheim 1996.

22. Dvornic, P.R., Owen, M.J., *Silicon-Containing Dendritic Polymers.* 2009. Vol. 2 Springer: Amsterdam.

23. Bischoff, R., Cray, S.E., Polysiloxanes in macromolecular architecture. *Prog. Polym. Sci.*, 1999. Vol. 24, 185-219 p. DOI:10.1016/S0079-6700(99)00006-4

24. Muzafarov, A.M., Gorbatsevich, O.B., Rebrov, E.A., Ignateva, G.M., Chenskaya, T.B., Myakushev, V.D., Bulkin, A.F., Papkov, V.S., Organosilicon dendrimers : Volume-growing polyallylcarbosilanes. *Polym. Sci. (USSR) Engl.Trans*. 1993. Vol. 35, Issue 11, 1575-1580 p.

25. Vandamme, T. F., Brobeck, L., Poly(amidoamine) dendrimers as ophthalmic vehicles for ocular delivery of pilocarpine nitrate and tropicamide, *J. Control. Release*, 2005. Vol. 102, 23-38 p. DOI: 10.1016/j.jconrel.2004.09.015

26. Tolia, G.T., Choi, H.H., Ahsan, F., The role of dendrimers in drug delivery. *Pharmaceut. Tech.*, 2008. Vol.32, 88–98 p.

27. Van Wazer, J.R., Lyons, J.W., Kim, K.Y., Colwell, R.E., 1963. *Viscosity and Flow Measurement*. Jhon Wiley and sons, New York, NY.

28. Arnold, G. Fredrickson, 1963. *Principals and Application of Rheology*. Prentice-Hall Inc., Englewood Cliffs, NJ.

29. Srinivas Uppuluri, Steven E. Keinath, Donald A. Tomalia, Petar R. Dvornic, Rheology of Dendrimers. I. Newtonian Flow Behavior of Medium and Highly Concentrated Solutions of Polyamidoamine (PAMAM) Dendrimers in Ethylenediamine (EDA) Solvent, *Macromolecules* 1998, 31, 14, 4498–4510 p. DOI: 10.1021/ma971199b

30. Srinivas Uppuluri, Faith A. Morrison, Petar R. Dvornic, Macromolecules 2000, 33, 7, 2551–2560 p. DOI:10.1021/ma990634u

31. M. V. Mironova, A. V. Semakov, A. S. Tereshchenko, E. A. Tatarinova, E. V. Getmanova, A. M. Muzafarov & V. G. Kulichikhin *Polymer Science Series A*, 2000. volume 52, pages 1156–1162 p. DOI:10.1134/S0965545X1011009X

32. Haipeng Wang, George P. Simon, Craig Hawker, Carlos Tiu, Materials Research Innovations , 2002, vol. 6, issue 4, 160-166 p .DOI:10.1007/s10019-002-0179-1

33. Pavel A.Tikhonov[a] Nataliya G. Vasilenko[a] Georgii V.Cherkaev[a] Viktor G.Vasil'ev[b1] Nina V.Demchenko[a] Elena A.Tatarinova[a] Aziz M.Muzafarov[ab1], Mendeleev Communications, Vol. 29, Issue 6, 2019, 625-627 p. DOI: 10.1016/j.mencom.2019.11.006

34. May, C.A., 1988. *Epoxy Resins Chemistry and technology*. New York: Marcel Dekker, 1288pp. DOI: 10.1002/pol.1988.140261212.

35. Park, S. J., Jin, F. L., Lee, J.R. Thermal and mechanical properties of tetrafunctional epoxy resin toughened with epoxidized soybean oil. *Mater. Sci. Eng. A*, 2004. Vol. 374, Issue 1-2, 109-114 p. DOI:10.1016/j.msea.2004.01.002.

36. Sangeeta Kandpal and A.K.Saxena , Studies on the synthesis & reaction of silicone oxirane dendrimer & their thermal & rheological properties. Eur. Polym. Jou. 2014; vol. 58, 115-124 p. DOI:10.1016/j.eurpolymj.2014.06.009

37. Laza, J. M., Julian, C. A., Larrauri, E., Rodriguez, M., Leon, L. M., Thermal scanning rheometer analysis of curing kinetics of an epoxy resin: 2. An amine as curing agent. *Polymer, 1999*. Vol. 40, Issue 1, 35-45 p. DOI: 1016/S0032-3861(98)00217-1

38. Thomus, Rahu, Yumei, Ding, Yuelong, He, Yang, Le, Moldenaers, Paula, Weimin, Yang, Czigany, Tibor, Thomos, Sabu, Miscibility, morphology, thermal, and mechanical properties of a DGEBA based epoxy resin toughened with a liquid rubber. *Polymer, 2008.* Vol. 49, Issue 1, 278-94 p. DOI:1016/j.polymer.2007.11.030

39. Ampudia, J., Larrauri, E., Gil, E. M., Rodriguez, M., Leon, L. M., Thermal scanning rheometric analysis of curing kinetic of an epoxy resin. I. An anhydride as curing agent. *J. Appl. Polm. Sci., 1999.* Vol. 71, Issue 8, 1239-45 p. DOI: 10.1002/(SICI)1097-4628(19990222)71:8<1239::AID-APP4>3.0.CO;2-U

# Chapter-10

# The Impacts of Recycling of Polymers on Environment

Shambhavi Sharma[1]

Muhammad Jahanzaib[2]

Prashant kumar Rai[3]

Rajneesh Dwivedi[4]

Duckshin Park[5]

Shikha Mehta[6*]

**Abstract**

Recycling polymers significantly benefits the environment by reducing waste, conserving resources, and minimizing pollution. Plastics, being non-biodegradable, accumulate in landfills and oceans, causing long-term environmental harm. Recycling these materials decreases the demand for virgin polymer production, which requires substantial energy and fossil fuels. This process lowers greenhouse gas emissions and reduces the carbon footprint. Additionally, recycling helps prevent plastic from entering ecosystems, where it endangers wildlife and disrupts natural habitats.

Despite these benefits, challenges such as contamination and limited recycling infrastructure persist, hindering efficiency. Innovative technologies like chemical recycling and improved sorting systems are addressing these issues, promoting a circular economy for plastics. Public awareness and participation are crucial to enhancing recycling rates and fostering sustainable practices.

**Keywords:** recycling, polymers, environment, pollution, sustainability

---

[1]*Transportation Environmental Research Division, Korea Railroad Research Institute (KRRI), Chleodobangmulgwan-ro, Uiwang-si 16105, Republic of Korea.*
*Transportation System Engineering, University of Science & Technology (UST), 217 Gajeong-ro, Yuseong-gu, Daejeon (34113), Republic of Korea*
[2] *Transportation Environmental Research Division, Korea Railroad Research Institute (KRRI), Chleodobangmulgwan-ro, Uiwang-si 16105, Republic of Korea.*
*Transportation System Engineering, University of Science & Technology (UST), 217 Gajeong-ro, Yuseong-gu, Daejeon (34113), Republic of Korea*
[3] *Medicinal Reserarch Lab University of Allahabad, Allahabad UP, India 211002*
[4] *Kashi Naresh Govt. P.G. College, Gyanpur, Bhadohi. U.P. India*
[5] *Transportation Environmental Research Division, Korea Railroad Research Institute (KRRI), Chleodobangmulgwan-ro, Uiwang-si 16105, Republic of Korea.*
*Transportation System Engineering, University of Science & Technology (UST), 217 Gajeong-ro, Yuseong-gu, Daejeon (34113), Republic of Korea*
[6] *Kashi Naresh Govt. P.G. College, Gyanpur, Bhadohi. U.P. India*
*\*Correspondence: shikhamehta06@gmail.com*

# 1. Introduction

Polymers, particularly synthetic plastics (1-2), have become an indispensable part of modern life. Their lightweight, durable, and versatile properties have made them essential in various industries, from packaging and construction to automotive, electronics, and healthcare. However, this ubiquity has also given rise to significant environmental challenges. The rapid expansion of polymer production, inefficient waste management and low recycling rates, have led to widespread pollution and resource depletion. To address these concerns, it is crucial to explore the environmental impacts of polymer production and waste while investigating the potential of recycling as a sustainable solution. The environmental impacts of polymer production begin with the extraction of raw materials, most of which are derived from fossil fuels (3). The petrochemical processes involved in polymer synthesis are highly resource-intensive, contributing to greenhouse gas emissions, air and water pollution, and the depletion of non-renewable resources. As the demand for polymers continues to grow, particularly in sectors like packaging and consumer goods, the environmental burden of production is escalating. Moreover, the energy-intensive nature of polymer manufacturing, along with the release of toxic chemicals and pollutants during the production process, exacerbates the overall environmental footprint of polymers (4-6). These impacts are further compounded by the end-of-life challenges associated with polymer products, particularly plastics, which are often designed for single use and are discarded shortly after serving their purpose. One of the most pressing environmental concerns arising from the use of polymers is pollution caused by polymer waste. Synthetic plastics, being highly resistant to degradation, persist in the environment for centuries. When improperly managed, plastic waste accumulates in landfills and the natural environment, contributing to pollution in oceans, rivers, and soil. This pollution has devastating consequences for ecosystems, wildlife, and even human health. Marine pollution, in particular, has garnered significant attention in recent years, as plastics have been found to impact a wide range of marine organisms, from plankton to large mammals (7-9). The persistence of plastic waste has led to the formation of massive floating garbage patches in the world's oceans, posing a long-term threat to biodiversity. In addition to large plastic debris, microplastics—tiny particles formed through the fragmentation of larger plastic items—have emerged as a major environmental and health hazard. These microplastics are now ubiquitous in aquatic and terrestrial ecosystems, and their potential to enter food chains and affect both animal and human health is a growing area of concern.

Given the scale of polymer waste pollution, recycling has emerged as a key strategy to mitigate its environmental impacts. However, polymer recycling faces numerous challenges (10), which have limited its effectiveness on a global scale. One major challenge is the complexity of polymer waste streams, which often contain a wide variety of polymer types, colors, and additives that complicate the recycling process (11-12). Contamination from food, chemicals, and other non-polymeric materials further reduces the recyclability of plastic waste. Moreover, polymers can degrade in quality during the recycling process, resulting in materials that are less durable or have inferior mechanical properties compared to virgin polymers (13). This phenomenon, known as "downcycling," limits the number of times certain polymers can be recycled before they become unusable. Economic factors also play a significant role in the challenges of polymer recycling. In many cases, it is cheaper to produce new polymers from virgin raw materials than to collect, sort, and recycle existing polymer waste. This economic disparity, driven by the low cost of petrochemical raw materials and the energy efficiency of large-scale polymer production, has stifled investment in recycling infrastructure and innovation.Despite these challenges, a variety of recycling techniques have been developed to process polymer waste and reduce its environmental impact. Mechanical recycling, the most common method, involves the physical shredding, melting, and reprocessing of plastic waste into new products. While mechanical recycling is widely used, it is limited by the quality degradation of polymers and is typically suitable only for single-material streams. Chemical recycling, a more advanced technique, breaks polymers down into their monomers or other chemical building blocks, which can then be used to synthesize new polymers with properties equivalent to virgin materials. Although chemical recycling offers a potential solution to the quality degradation issue, it is currently less economically viable and has a larger environmental footprint due to the energy-intensive nature of the process. Emerging biological recycling methods, which involve the use of microorganisms or enzymes to degrade polymers into harmless byproducts, are also being explored as a way to address the limitations of mechanical and chemical recycling (15,16). While still in the early stages of development, these biological methods hold promise for the future of polymer recycling, particularly for difficult-to-recycle materials such as certain types of plastics.The environmental benefits of polymer recycling are substantial. Recycling diverts plastic waste from landfills and reduces the need for new raw materials, thereby conserving natural resources and reducing greenhouse gas emissions. It also helps to mitigate the pollution caused by polymer waste, particularly in marine environments, by reducing the amount of plastic debris that enters waterways and oceans. Moreover, by promoting a circular economy in which materials are continuously reused and repurposed, recycling offers a pathway towards more sustainable industrial practices. However, to fully realize these benefits, significant improvements in recycling technologies and infrastructure are needed, along with increased consumer participation and support from governments and industries.

Recent innovations in polymer recycling are helping to address some of the limitations of existing methods. Advances in sorting technologies, such as optical sorting and near-infrared spectroscopy, have improved the efficiency and accuracy of separating different polymer types, making recycling more viable. New depolymerization techniques are being developed to break down complex polymers into their chemical components, which can then be reused to create high-quality polymers with properties similar to those of virgin materials. Additionally, biodegradable and compostable polymers are gaining traction as alternatives to traditional plastics, particularly in applications where single-use products are necessary. These innovations, combined with efforts to improve the design of polymer products for easier recyclability, are paving the way for a more sustainable polymer industry.

Policy and regulatory measures also play a crucial role in promoting polymer recycling and reducing plastic pollution. Governments around the world have implemented a range of policies aimed at curbing plastic waste, including bans on single-use plastics, extended producer responsibility (EPR) schemes, and mandates for recycled content in products. These measures are designed to create economic incentives for industries to adopt more sustainable practices and reduce their reliance on virgin polymers. At the same time, global initiatives such as the European Union's Circular Economy Action Plan are pushing for systemic changes in how materials are produced, used, and disposed of, with a particular focus on increasing recycling rates and reducing plastic waste.Finally, consumers have a vital role to play in the success of recycling initiatives. Public awareness of the environmental impacts of plastics has grown in recent years, leading to changes in consumer behavior and increased demand for sustainable products. By adopting responsible consumption practices, such as reducing the use of single-use plastics, properly sorting waste for recycling, and supporting products made from recycled materials, consumers can drive the transition towards a more sustainable polymer industry.

## 2. Environmental Impacts of Polymer Production

The production of synthetic polymers, particularly plastics, has transformed industries globally, but it has also introduced significant environmental challenges throughout its life cycle. From raw material extraction to manufacturing and disposal, polymer production is associated with substantial environmental burdens. The processes involved in producing polymers are resource-intensive, contribute to greenhouse gas emissions, and result in both water and air pollution, all of which play a critical role in the environmental footprint of this material.

### 2.1 Raw Material Extraction and Energy Use

The primary raw materials for most synthetic polymers are derived from petrochemical sources such as crude oil and natural gas. The extraction of these fossil fuels is not only resource-depleting but also highly energy-intensive. Significant energy is required for the drilling, transportation, and refinement processes to convert these raw materials into polymer feedstocks like ethylene, propylene, and other monomers.

The energy use during polymer production is substantial. Cracking and polymerization processes, which convert monomers into polymers, require high temperatures and pressures, consuming vast amounts of energy, typically derived from fossil fuels (18). The reliance on non-renewable energy sources contributes to the overall environmental impact, as it accelerates the depletion of these resources while also emitting large quantities of carbon dioxide and other greenhouse gases.

In addition to the direct consumption of energy in the production phase, the life cycle of polymers involves significant indirect energy use. This includes the energy needed for the production and transportation of the chemicals and additives used in polymer synthesis, such as stabilizers, plasticizers, and flame retardants. Overall, the intensive energy demands of polymer production directly contribute to the environmental issues linked to fossil fuel dependency, particularly as global polymer demand continues to grow.

### 2.2 Greenhouse Gas Emissions

The polymer production process is a major contributor to global greenhouse gas emissions, which are a key driver of climate change. Carbon dioxide ($CO_2$) and methane ($CH_4$) are the two primary greenhouse gases emitted during the extraction, processing, and manufacturing stages of polymer production. The combustion of fossil fuels for energy in these stages releases substantial amounts of $CO_2$ into the atmosphere. Moreover, the refining of crude oil and natural gas also results in the release of methane, a potent greenhouse gas with a much higher global warming potential than $CO_2$ over a shorter time frame.

The production of polymers also indirectly contributes to greenhouse gas emissions through the energy required to manufacture the chemicals used in polymer production and through the life cycle of polymer products. For example, single-use plastics, which dominate global plastic production, are typically manufactured in energy-intensive processes that contribute significantly to the carbon footprint of the materials. While polymers themselves are not usually sources of emissions during their use phase, their end-of-life scenarios (e.g., incineration of plastic waste) can further exacerbate greenhouse gas emissions.

Additionally, polymer production facilities often utilize processes that involve the release of other industrial gases such as nitrous oxide ($N_2O$) and hydrofluorocarbons (HFCs), both of which have a much greater impact on global warming than $CO_2$. These emissions are particularly problematic in terms of their long-term environmental consequences and add to the growing concerns regarding the role of polymer production in accelerating climate change.

## 2.3 Water and Air Pollution

Beyond energy use and greenhouse gas emissions, polymer production contributes to both water and air pollution, further exacerbating its environmental impact. During the production of polymers, particularly in large-scale petrochemical plants, significant quantities of water are used for cooling, cleaning, and chemical processing. This process generates wastewater contaminated with various harmful chemicals, including solvents, residual monomers, and plasticizers. When not properly treated, this wastewater can be discharged into natural water bodies, leading to water pollution that affects ecosystems and human health.

Pollutants in the water can cause eutrophication, in which excess nutrients lead to the overgrowth of algae and the depletion of oxygen in water bodies, harming aquatic life. Moreover, the chemical additives used in polymer production(17), such as stabilizers and colorants, can leach into the environment and disrupt hormonal systems in both wildlife and humans. Many of these chemicals are persistent in the environment and bioaccumulate, leading to long-term ecological damage.

Air pollution is another major issue linked to polymer production. The refining and manufacturing processes release a variety of hazardous air pollutants, including volatile organic compounds (VOCs), particulate matter (PM), and sulfur and nitrogen oxides ($SO_x$ and $NO_x$). These pollutants contribute to smog formation, acid rain, and respiratory problems in humans. VOCs, in particular, are harmful not only because they contribute to air quality degradation but also because they are precursors to ozone formation, a pollutant that is harmful to both human health and the environment at ground level.Moreover, accidental releases or leakages of toxic gases, such as styrene, during the production process can have acute impacts on local air quality and present health risks to nearby communities. For example, styrene is a known neurotoxin and is classified as a possible carcinogen. The accumulation of these pollutants in the atmosphere from polymer production facilities significantly contributes to regional and global environmental degradation.

In conclusion, the environmental impacts of polymer production are extensive and multifaceted, involving the depletion of non-renewable resources, high energy consumption, substantial greenhouse gas emissions, and water and air pollution. As the demand for polymers continues to rise, driven by global economic and industrial growth, so too does the need for sustainable practices in polymer production. Reducing the environmental footprint of polymers requires not only technological innovation in energy efficiency and waste management but also systemic changes in how polymers are produced, used, and disposed of. Moving towards more sustainable production methods, such as the increased use of renewable energy sources, and improved pollution controls, is essential for mitigating the environmental impacts of polymer production. Addressing these challenges through policy, regulation, and technological advances will be critical to reducing the environmental costs of polymers in the future.

## 3. Pollution from Polymer Waste

Polymers, particularly synthetic plastics, have become indispensable materials in modern society, yet their environmental persistence presents significant challenges. The mass production and widespread use of polymers, often designed for single-use applications, have contributed to the growing problem of polymer waste pollution. As the global production of plastics continues to increase, the environmental burden of improperly managed polymer waste has become one of the most pressing issues of the 21st century. This section explores the environmental pollution caused by polymer waste, focusing on its accumulation in landfills, its role in marine pollution and microplastic formation, and its harmful impact on wildlife and ecosystems. In summary, polymer waste pollution is a multifaceted environmental issue with far-reaching consequences for land, marine environments, and wildlife. The persistence of polymers in landfills, their degradation into microplastics in oceans, and their detrimental effects on wildlife and ecosystems highlight the urgent need for more effective waste management strategies. By reducing polymer production, improving recycling systems, and adopting better waste disposal practices, it is possible to mitigate the long-term environmental impacts of polymer waste and protect global ecosystems from further harm.

### 3.1 Landfill Accumulation and Degradation Time

One of the most significant environmental impacts of polymer waste is its accumulation in landfills. Synthetic polymers, such as polyethylene, polypropylene, and polystyrene, are designed for durability and resistance to natural degradation processes. As a result, they can persist in the environment for hundreds to thousands of years. Unlike organic waste, which can decompose relatively quickly, most polymers are non-biodegradable. This means that when they are disposed of in landfills, they remain intact for extended periods, occupying valuable landfill space and contributing to long-term environmental pollution.

The accumulation of plastic waste in landfills(18) poses several environmental risks. First, as landfills reach capacity, there is an increasing need for more land to accommodate waste, which can lead to deforestation and the destruction of natural habitats. Second, landfill sites can generate harmful leachate—a toxic liquid that forms when rainwater percolates through waste materials. Leachate from plastic waste may contain hazardous chemicals, including additives like plasticizers, flame retardants, and stabilizers. These chemicals can seep into the soil and groundwater, contaminating local ecosystems and water sources.

Moreover, the degradation of polymers in landfills is an exceedingly slow process. While certain environmental conditions, such as UV exposure, can break down some polymers, most plastics degrade primarily through physical fragmentation rather than chemical decomposition. This process leads to the formation of smaller plastic particles known as microplastics, which persist in the environment and are much harder to manage. Microplastics can leach harmful substances into surrounding soils and water systems, further complicating the environmental management of polymer waste in landfills.

## 3.2 Marine Pollution and Microplastics

Perhaps the most visible and concerning aspect of polymer waste pollution is its impact on marine environments. Oceans have become the ultimate sink for a significant proportion of the world's plastic waste, with millions of tons of plastics entering the oceans each year. Poor waste management practices, littering, and the inadequacy of recycling systems (19) contribute to this issue, allowing plastic debris to be transported by rivers, winds, and coastal activities into marine ecosystems. This influx of polymer waste into oceans has led to the accumulation of vast amounts of debris in marine environments, including large items such as plastic bottles, bags, and fishing gear, as well as smaller fragments like microplastics.

Microplastics, which are particles of plastic less than 5 millimeters in size, are a particularly pervasive form of marine pollution. They are either directly manufactured for specific applications (e.g., microbeads in cosmetics) or result from the breakdown of larger plastic items through photodegradation, wave action, and mechanical wear. Once in the ocean, these microplastic particles can be transported over long distances by ocean currents, spreading the pollution across global marine environments.

The widespread presence of microplastics in marine ecosystems presents significant challenges for environmental management and marine life. Microplastics are easily ingested by a wide range of marine organisms, from plankton and small fish to larger animals such as seabirds and marine mammals. Once ingested, these particles can cause physical harm, block digestive tracts, and lead to malnutrition or death. In addition, microplastics have the ability to adsorb toxic chemicals from seawater, including persistent organic pollutants (POPs) such as polychlorinated biphenyls (PCBs) and pesticides like DDT. When ingested by marine organisms, these toxic chemicals can enter the food chain, potentially affecting the health of marine species and, ultimately, humans who consume seafood.

## 3.3 Impact on Wildlife and Ecosystems

The environmental impacts of polymer waste extend beyond marine environments and affect terrestrial wildlife and ecosystems as well. Plastic pollution is responsible for the direct harm of countless animal species, primarily through ingestion, entanglement, and habitat destruction. Many animals, particularly marine species, mistake plastic debris for food. For example, seabirds often consume plastic fragments floating on the water's surface, mistaking them for small fish or other prey. This ingestion of plastic can lead to blockages in the digestive system, starvation, and eventual death.

Marine mammals and reptiles, such as sea turtles, are also highly susceptible to the dangers posed by plastic pollution. Plastic bags, fishing nets, and other debris can entangle animals, leading to injury, restricted movement, drowning, or the inability to feed. Similarly, coral reefs, which provide essential habitat for a variety of marine species, are affected by plastic waste. Plastics that settle on coral reefs can cause physical damage to the delicate coral structures and increase the spread of disease among reef systems. This not only threatens marine biodiversity but also undermines the ecological health of ocean ecosystems that rely on coral reefs for shelter and sustenance.

On land, plastic waste poses significant threats to wildlife in both natural and urban environments. Many terrestrial animals, such as birds and mammals, encounter plastic waste while foraging for food.

Ingesting plastic can cause similar problems to those seen in marine species, including digestive blockages and exposure to toxic chemicals. Additionally, plastic debris that accumulates in natural habitats can alter ecosystems by introducing foreign materials into environments that are not adapted to accommodate synthetic waste(19). For instance, plastic waste in soil can disrupt natural processes such as nutrient cycling, water filtration, and plant growth.

Beyond the immediate effects on individual species, the presence of polymer waste in ecosystems can have broader ecological consequences. When key species are affected by plastic ingestion or entanglement, it can disrupt entire food webs and ecosystem dynamics. For example, the decline of certain seabird populations due to plastic ingestion can alter predator-prey relationships and impact the overall health of marine ecosystems. In addition, the chemicals leached from plastics—such as bisphenol A (BPA) and phthalates—can have hormone-disrupting effects on animals, leading to reproductive issues and population declines in affected species.

## 4. Challenges of Polymer Recycling

Recycling polymers, particularly plastics, has long been recognized as a crucial strategy for reducing plastic waste and its environmental impact (20). However, despite growing global awareness and advancements in recycling technologies, the recycling of polymers faces significant challenges that limit its effectiveness. These challenges range from the inherent properties of various polymer types to practical issues such as contamination, sorting, and economic feasibility. This section delves into the key obstacles that complicate polymer recycling, including the recyclability of different polymer types, the complexities of contamination and sorting, and the economic barriers to scaling up recycling efforts. In conclusion, polymer recycling faces numerous challenges that hinder its widespread implementation and efficiency. The inherent complexity of different polymer types, combined with contamination and sorting difficulties, makes it difficult to recycle plastics in a cost-effective and environmentally beneficial manner. While advances in technology and stronger policy frameworks can help mitigate some of these challenges, the economic viability of recycling remains a key hurdle. Overcoming these obstacles will require a combination of technological innovation, improved waste management systems, and economic incentives to make recycling a more attractive and sustainable solution to the growing problem of polymer waste.

### *4.1 Types of Polymers and Their Recyclability*

One of the primary challenges in polymer recycling is the diversity of polymer types, each of which has different properties, applications, and recyclability. Not all polymers are equally recyclable, and the chemical structure of a polymer largely determines whether and how it can be recycled. For example, thermoplastics—polymers such as polyethylene (PE), polypropylene (PP), and polyethylene terephthalate (PET)—can be melted and remolded multiple times without significant degradation of their properties, making them more suitable for mechanical recycling. These plastics dominate the packaging industry and represent the majority of recyclable plastics.

In contrast, thermosetting polymers, such as epoxy resins, polyurethanes, and vulcanized rubbers, undergo irreversible chemical changes during their initial processing. Once cured, thermosets cannot be remelted or reprocessed, which severely limits their recyclability through conventional mechanical means. These polymers are commonly used in durable goods, adhesives, and coatings, making them challenging to recycle without advanced chemical recycling technologies that break down the polymer chains into their original monomers.

Moreover, even within the thermoplastic category, differences in polymer grades, additives, and fillers complicate the recycling process. For instance, high-density polyethylene (HDPE) and low-density polyethylene (LDPE) are chemically similar but have different melting points and mechanical properties, which require them to be processed separately. Additionally, polymers often contain a variety of additives—such as plasticizers, stabilizers, colorants, and flame retardants—that can affect their recyclability and may lead to the formation of inferior products when mixed together. As a result, the inherent complexity of polymer materials poses a major challenge to creating an efficient and universal recycling system.

### *4.2 Contamination and Sorting Issues*

Effective polymer recycling depends heavily on the ability to properly sort and separate different types of plastic waste, yet this remains one of the most difficult aspects of the process. Contamination of polymer waste streams is a pervasive issue, and even small amounts of contaminants can render an entire batch of recycled plastic unusable. Contaminants can include food residues, chemicals, non-polymeric materials such as metals or paper, and incompatible plastics mixed into a single waste stream.

The difficulty of separating mixed polymers is exacerbated by the fact that many consumer products are made from multiple types of plastics, often bonded together or used in layers. For example, food packaging frequently combines several types of polymers, adhesives, and coatings to create barriers against moisture and oxygen. However, these multi-layered materials are nearly impossible to recycle without advanced technologies that can separate each layer for individual recycling. In most cases, such products are sent to landfills or incinerated rather than recycled.

Automated sorting systems, which rely on technologies such as infrared spectroscopy, can improve the accuracy of sorting different types of polymers, but these systems are expensive and not yet widely implemented in many regions. Furthermore, the presence of labels, dyes, and inks on plastics adds another layer of complexity to the sorting process. These surface treatments may not be compatible with the recycling process and can degrade the quality of the recycled material, leading to products that are unsuitable for high-quality applications. As a result, contaminated or poorly sorted plastic waste often ends up being downcycled into lower-value products, further reducing the efficiency of recycling efforts.

### *4.3 Economic Viability of Recycling*

The economic viability of polymer recycling remains one of the most significant barriers to its widespread adoption. In many cases, it is more cost-effective to produce new, virgin plastics from fossil fuel feedstocks than to collect, sort, and recycle existing plastic waste (21). This economic imbalance is driven by several factors, including the low cost of petrochemicals, the labor-intensive nature of waste collection and sorting, and the fluctuating demand for recycled materials.

One of the main challenges is that recycled polymers often have inferior mechanical properties compared to virgin materials, particularly if the polymers have been degraded during the recycling process. This can limit the range of applications for recycled plastics, reducing their market value and making it difficult for recycling companies to compete with the production of new plastics. In addition, the contamination of waste streams can result in higher processing costs and lower yields of high-quality recycled materials, further discouraging investment in recycling infrastructure.

Another economic consideration is the variability in market demand for recycled plastics. While there is growing interest in sustainable materials, the demand for recycled plastics is still heavily influenced by the price of oil, which directly affects the cost of producing virgin plastics (22). When oil prices are low, the cost of manufacturing new plastics drops, making it less economically attractive to invest in recycling. This price volatility creates uncertainty for recycling operations and can lead to fluctuations in recycling rates.

In many cases, government incentives, subsidies, or regulatory frameworks are necessary to make recycling economically viable. Extended producer responsibility (EPR) schemes, where manufacturers are required to take financial or physical responsibility for the recycling of their products, can help shift the economic balance in favor of recycling. Similarly, mandates for the use of recycled content in certain products, such as packaging, can drive demand for recycled polymers and encourage innovation in recycling technologies. However, without strong policy support, the economic barriers to polymer recycling will continue to limit its effectiveness (23).

## 5. Recycling Techniques for Polymers

The growing concern over plastic pollution and resource depletion has spurred the development of various recycling techniques aimed at reducing the environmental impact of polymer waste. Recycling plays a key role in the circular economy, where materials are continuously repurposed, thereby minimizing the need for virgin resources and reducing waste. However, recycling polymers presents distinct challenges due to the diversity of materials, contamination, and economic factors. Several techniques are employed to address these challenges, each with its own advantages and limitations. This section explores the primary recycling methods for polymers, including mechanical recycling, chemical recycling, and energy recovery through incineration. In conclusion, the recycling of polymers involves a range of techniques, each with distinct benefits and challenges. Mechanical recycling remains the most commonly used method but is limited by material degradation and contamination issues (24). Chemical recycling offers a more flexible and potentially higher-quality solution, although it is still in the developmental phase and faces economic and environmental hurdles. When recycling is not feasible, energy recovery through incineration provides an alternative, albeit with environmental trade-offs. Together, these techniques form a critical part of the strategy to reduce polymer waste and promote a more sustainable and circular economy.

### *5.1 Mechanical Recycling*

Mechanical recycling is the most widely used method for processing polymer waste. It involves the physical reprocessing of plastic waste into new materials without altering the polymer's chemical structure. The process typically begins with the collection and sorting of plastic waste, followed by cleaning, shredding, and melting the materials into granules or pellets that can be used to manufacture new products.

Mechanical recycling is most effective for thermoplastics—polymers like polyethylene (PE), polypropylene (PP), and polyethylene terephthalate (PET)—which can be repeatedly melted and remolded. This method is commonly used to recycle post-consumer plastics, such as beverage bottles, packaging, and household products. One of the key benefits of mechanical recycling is its relatively low cost compared to other recycling techniques. It is also energy-efficient since it requires less energy than the production of virgin polymers from fossil fuels.

However, mechanical recycling has several limitations. One major challenge is the degradation of polymer properties during the recycling process. Each time a polymer is melted and reprocessed, it can lose some of its mechanical strength, flexibility, and durability, resulting in lower-quality materials. This degradation limits the number of times a plastic can be recycled and often leads to downcycling, where recycled plastics are used to produce items of lower value and functionality, such as park benches or construction materials. Additionally, contamination from food residues, additives, or incompatible plastics can compromise the quality of the recycled material, making it unsuitable for high-performance applications.

Despite these challenges, mechanical recycling remains a crucial component of the global effort to reduce plastic waste. Innovations in sorting technologies and advancements in the design of recyclable products are helping to improve the efficiency and scalability of mechanical recycling. However, its limitations, particularly in terms of polymer degradation and contamination, have led to the exploration of alternative recycling methods.

### 5.2 Chemical Recycling

Chemical recycling is an emerging technique that addresses many of the limitations of mechanical recycling by breaking down polymers into their original chemical components, such as monomers, oligomers, or other feedstock chemicals. These recovered chemicals can then be used to synthesize new polymers with properties equivalent to those of virgin materials. Unlike mechanical recycling, chemical recycling can handle a wider variety of plastics (25), including those that are difficult to recycle mechanically, such as mixed or contaminated polymers and thermosetting plastics.

There are several methods of chemical recycling, including pyrolysis, gasification, and depolymerization. Pyrolysis involves heating polymers in the absence of oxygen to break them down into smaller hydrocarbon molecules, which can be further refined into fuels, chemicals, or new polymers. Gasification, a similar process, converts plastic waste into syngas (a mixture of hydrogen and carbon monoxide), which can be used to produce chemicals or energy. Depolymerization, on the other hand, breaks polymers down into their monomer building blocks, which can be purified and used to create new plastics.

One of the main advantages of chemical recycling is its ability to produce high-quality recycled materials that are comparable to virgin polymers. This method also offers greater flexibility in handling a broader range of plastic waste streams, including multi-layered and contaminated materials that are not suitable for mechanical recycling. Additionally, chemical recycling can contribute to the circular economy by recovering valuable chemical feedstocks from waste, reducing the need for new fossil-based resources.

However, chemical recycling faces several challenges, particularly related to cost and environmental impact. The process is energy-intensive and often requires high temperatures and advanced equipment, making it more expensive than mechanical recycling. Additionally, depending on the specific method used, chemical recycling can generate greenhouse gas emissions and other pollutants, which may offset some of the environmental benefits. As a result, chemical recycling is still in the early stages of commercialization, and further technological advancements and economic incentives will be necessary to make it a more viable and sustainable option on a large scale.

## *5.3 Energy Recovery and Incineration*

When recycling is not feasible, energy recovery through incineration is often considered as an alternative method for managing polymer waste. Incineration involves the combustion of plastic waste at high temperatures to produce energy in the form of heat or electricity. This process can significantly reduce the volume of plastic waste, diverting it from landfills and generating energy that can be used in industrial processes or to power homes and businesses.

Energy recovery offers several advantages. First, it can handle a wide range of plastic materials, including those that are contaminated, degraded, or otherwise unsuitable for mechanical or chemical recycling. Second, it provides an efficient way to recover energy from waste, potentially offsetting the use of fossil fuels. In waste-to-energy plants, the heat produced during incineration can be used to generate steam, which powers turbines to produce electricity. This energy can then be fed into the grid, contributing to the overall energy supply.

However, the environmental impact of incineration is a topic of significant debate. While modern waste-to-energy facilities are equipped with advanced filtration systems to capture harmful emissions, incineration still generates pollutants, including carbon dioxide ($CO_2$), particulate matter, and toxic compounds like dioxins and furans. These pollutants can contribute to air pollution and pose health risks to nearby communities. Moreover, incineration does not contribute to the circular economy in the same way that recycling does, as the polymer material is destroyed rather than reused.

Another issue with incineration is that it can disincentivize efforts to reduce plastic production and improve recycling. In regions where waste-to-energy plants are prevalent, the availability of incineration as a disposal option may reduce the urgency to develop more sustainable waste management practices. Critics argue that energy recovery should be viewed as a last resort, used only when recycling or reuse is not possible.

In summary, while energy recovery through incineration offers a way to reduce waste volumes and generate energy, it is not without environmental costs. To maximize the environmental benefits of polymer waste management, it is essential to prioritize recycling methods that retain the material value of polymers and reduce overall waste production.

## 6. Environmental Benefits of Polymer Recycling

Recycling polymers, especially plastics, offers numerous environmental benefits, playing a crucial role in mitigating the negative impacts of plastic waste and reducing the depletion of natural resources. In recent decades, polymer recycling has gained prominence as a key component of sustainable waste management, offering a viable solution to the growing environmental crisis associated with plastic production and disposal. By diverting waste from landfills, conserving natural resources, and lowering greenhouse gas emissions, polymer recycling contributes to reducing the environmental footprint of modern industrial processes. This section highlights the major environmental benefits of polymer recycling, focusing on its role in reducing the carbon footprint, conserving resources, and decreasing the amount of waste in landfills and oceans. In conclusion, polymer recycling offers a range of environmental benefits that are essential for addressing the global plastic waste crisis and promoting more sustainable industrial practices. By reducing carbon emissions, conserving natural resources, and decreasing the accumulation of plastic waste in landfills and oceans, recycling plays a pivotal role in mitigating the environmental impacts of polymer production and disposal. As recycling technologies continue to advance and public awareness of plastic pollution grows, the environmental benefits of polymer recycling will become even more pronounced, contributing to a cleaner and more sustainable future.

### *6.1 Reduction in Carbon Footprint*

One of the most significant environmental benefits of polymer recycling is its potential to reduce the carbon footprint of plastic production. The production of new polymers, particularly plastics derived from fossil fuels, is an energy-intensive process that releases substantial amounts of greenhouse gases, including carbon dioxide ($CO_2$) and methane ($CH_4$), into the atmosphere. These emissions contribute to global warming and climate change, exacerbating environmental degradation and impacting ecosystems worldwide.

Recycling polymers, on the other hand, requires far less energy than producing new plastics from raw materials. Mechanical recycling, which reprocesses plastics by shredding and remelting them, can cut energy consumption by up to 80% compared to the energy needed to produce virgin plastic. This substantial reduction in energy use directly translates to lower carbon emissions, making polymer recycling an effective way to reduce the overall carbon footprint of the plastics industry. By substituting recycled materials for virgin polymers, manufacturers can significantly reduce the amount of energy required for production, resulting in fewer greenhouse gas emissions across the supply chain.

Moreover, chemical recycling techniques, which break down plastics into their chemical components, offer additional opportunities to reduce carbon emissions by recovering valuable feedstock that can be used to produce new plastics. Although chemical recycling is more energy-intensive than mechanical recycling, it still offers a lower carbon footprint compared to the extraction, refining, and processing of fossil fuels for new plastic production. As recycling technologies continue to advance, the potential for even greater reductions in carbon emissions will increase, positioning polymer recycling as a critical tool in the fight against climate change.

### *6.2 Conservation of Resources*

Another key environmental benefit of polymer recycling is the conservation of natural resources, particularly fossil fuels, which are the primary raw materials for most synthetic plastics. The global demand for plastics has surged in recent decades, leading to increased pressure on non-renewable resources such as crude oil and natural gas. Each year, millions of barrels of oil are used to produce polymers, contributing to the depletion of these finite resources.

By recycling polymers, the demand for virgin materials is reduced, thereby conserving fossil fuels and extending the lifespan of these critical resources. Instead of relying on fresh feedstocks, manufacturers can use recycled plastics as a substitute, helping to reduce the extraction and consumption of petroleum-based raw materials. This conservation of resources not only decreases the environmental impact of raw material extraction, including land degradation and habitat destruction, but also helps to alleviate the geopolitical and economic risks associated with the reliance on fossil fuels.

Additionally, polymer recycling contributes to the conservation of other resources used in plastic production, such as water and energy. The manufacturing of virgin plastics requires large amounts of water for cooling and processing, and recycling plastics can significantly reduce this water consumption. By decreasing the demand for new plastic production, polymer recycling also helps to lower the environmental costs associated with the transportation, refining, and processing of raw materials, thereby promoting more efficient use of natural resources.

*6.3 Reduction in Landfill Use and Ocean Pollution*

One of the most visible environmental benefits of polymer recycling is its ability to reduce the amount of plastic waste that ends up in landfills and oceans. Plastic waste is a persistent problem due to its non-biodegradable nature, meaning it can take hundreds to thousands of years to break down in the environment. As a result, improperly managed plastic waste accumulates in landfills, takes up valuable space, and contributes to long-term pollution (26).

By recycling polymers, a significant portion of plastic waste can be diverted from landfills, reducing the environmental burden associated with waste disposal. Recycling decreases the volume of waste that needs to be managed by landfill sites, which in turn reduces the demand for new landfill space and helps to preserve land for other uses. Moreover, the reduction in landfill use helps to minimize the release of harmful chemicals from plastic degradation, such as microplastics and toxic additives, that can leach into the soil and groundwater, causing environmental contamination.

Polymer recycling also plays a crucial role in mitigating ocean pollution, particularly the problem of marine plastic debris. Oceans have become a major repository for plastic waste, with millions of tons of plastic entering marine ecosystems each year. This pollution threatens marine wildlife, damages ecosystems, and affects global fisheries. Recycling polymers prevents plastics from being improperly disposed of or littered, reducing the likelihood that they will enter waterways and ultimately the ocean. As recycling rates increase, the amount of plastic waste polluting marine environments can be significantly reduced, helping to protect marine life from the harmful effects of plastic debris, including ingestion and entanglement.

In addition, recycling helps to address the issue of microplastics—small plastic particles that result from the breakdown of larger plastic items. These microplastics are a pervasive pollutant, found in oceans, rivers, and even the air. By recycling polymers before they degrade into microplastics, the introduction of these particles into the environment can be mitigated. The reduction of both visible plastic debris and microplastic pollution represents a substantial environmental benefit of increased polymer recycling efforts.

## 7. Innovations in Polymer Recycling

As the world grapples with the growing plastic waste crisis, significant efforts are being made to develop new technologies and approaches that enhance the efficiency and sustainability of polymer recycling. Traditional recycling methods, while valuable, have inherent limitations that have spurred the need for innovative solutions. Emerging technologies, biodegradable and compostable polymers, and circular economy approaches are all contributing to the transformation of how polymers are managed and recycled. This section explores the cutting-edge advancements in polymer recycling, focusing on advanced recycling technologies, the development of biodegradable and compostable polymers, and the integration of circular economy principles into the life cycle of polymers. In conclusion, innovations in polymer recycling are transforming the way plastics are managed, with advanced recycling technologies, biodegradable materials, and circular economy approaches leading the charge. These advancements offer solutions to the limitations of traditional recycling methods, helping to create a more sustainable and resilient system for managing polymer waste. As these technologies and approaches continue to evolve, they hold the potential to significantly reduce the environmental footprint of plastics and pave the way for a more sustainable future.

*7.1 Advanced Recycling Technologies*

One of the most promising areas of innovation in polymer recycling lies in the development of advanced recycling technologies, particularly chemical recycling methods. While mechanical recycling has been the dominant method for decades, it struggles with limitations such as material degradation and contamination, which can result in lower-quality recycled products. In contrast, advanced chemical recycling technologies offer the potential to overcome these challenges by breaking down polymers into their fundamental chemical components, allowing for the production of new, high-quality polymers.

Chemical recycling techniques, such as pyrolysis, gasification, and depolymerization, are leading the way in advanced recycling. Pyrolysis involves heating plastic waste in the absence of oxygen to break down the long polymer chains into smaller hydrocarbons. These hydrocarbons can then be refined into fuels, chemicals, or new polymer feedstock. Gasification is a similar process that converts plastic waste into syngas, a mixture of hydrogen and carbon monoxide, which can be used as a precursor for various chemical processes. Depolymerization, on the other hand, breaks down polymers into their original monomers, which can be purified and re-polymerized into new materials with properties comparable to virgin plastics.

These technologies are particularly useful for recycling plastics that are difficult to process mechanically, such as multi-layered packaging or contaminated waste streams. By converting polymers back into their original chemical building blocks, advanced recycling enables the creation of new, high-quality plastics without the quality degradation associated with traditional methods. This not only helps to close the loop in polymer production but also reduces the need for virgin fossil fuel-based feedstocks, contributing to resource conservation and emissions reductions.

Despite their potential, advanced recycling technologies are still in the early stages of commercialization. High energy requirements and costs, along with the need for sophisticated infrastructure, pose challenges to widespread adoption. However, as these technologies continue to mature, they hold the promise of revolutionizing the way plastics are recycled and reused, making polymer recycling more efficient and sustainable.

*7.2 Biodegradable and Compostable Polymers*

Another significant innovation in polymer recycling is the development of biodegradable and compostable polymers. These materials are designed to break down more easily in natural environments, offering an alternative to traditional, non-biodegradable plastics that persist for hundreds of years. Biodegradable polymers, such as polylactic acid (PLA) and polyhydroxyalkanoates (PHA), are derived from renewable resources like corn starch or microbial fermentation and are engineered to decompose under specific environmental conditions, such as exposure to microbes, heat, and moisture.

Compostable polymers go a step further by breaking down into non-toxic components that can be absorbed by the soil, enriching it in the process. These materials are particularly suited for applications like single-use packaging, food service items, and agricultural films, where plastics are used briefly and then discarded. By replacing conventional plastics with compostable alternatives, the environmental impact of plastic waste can be significantly reduced, particularly in regions where proper waste management and recycling infrastructure are lacking.

However, while biodegradable and compostable polymers offer clear environmental advantages, they also present certain challenges. For one, the conditions required for proper degradation—such as industrial composting facilities with controlled temperature and humidity—are not always readily available. In many cases, biodegradable plastics that end up in landfills or oceans will not break down as intended, leading to continued environmental pollution. Additionally, the introduction of biodegradable materials into conventional recycling streams can cause contamination and complicate the recycling process.

To address these issues, ongoing research is focused on improving the performance and versatility of biodegradable and compostable polymers. Innovations in material science are leading to the development of polymers that can break down more efficiently under a wider range of conditions, as well as hybrid materials that combine the benefits of recyclability and biodegradability. These advancements hold great potential for reducing plastic waste and enhancing the sustainability of polymer use in various industries.

### *7.3 Circular Economy Approaches for Polymers*

At the heart of many innovations in polymer recycling is the concept of the circular economy, a systems approach that seeks to eliminate waste and continuously circulate materials through production cycles. In the traditional linear economy, materials are extracted, used to manufacture products, and then discarded as waste. In contrast, a circular economy aims to keep materials in use for as long as possible, extracting maximum value from them before they are recovered and regenerated.

For polymers, the transition to a circular economy involves rethinking the entire life cycle of plastic products, from design and production to use and disposal. One of the key innovations driving this shift is the development of design-for-recycling strategies, where products are designed with recycling in mind from the outset. This may involve using fewer materials, simplifying polymer blends, or ensuring that products can be easily disassembled and recycled. By improving product design, manufacturers can help ensure that plastics remain in circulation and are easier to recycle at the end of their life cycle.

Circular economy approaches also emphasize the importance of collaboration between stakeholders across the value chain, including manufacturers, consumers, and waste management companies. Extended producer responsibility (EPR) schemes, for example, require manufacturers to take responsibility for the end-of-life management of their products, incentivizing them to design for recyclability and invest in recycling infrastructure. Similarly, closed-loop systems are being implemented in industries such as packaging, where used plastic products are collected, recycled, and remanufactured into new products, creating a continuous loop of material use.

Incorporating circular economy principles into polymer recycling not only reduces waste and environmental pollution but also conserves resources and reduces reliance on virgin materials. By keeping polymers in use for longer and ensuring that they are effectively recycled, circular economy approaches can help minimize the environmental impact of plastic production and disposal.

## 8. Policy and Regulatory Measures

The global plastic waste crisis has prompted governments and regulatory bodies worldwide to implement policies aimed at reducing polymer waste and encouraging more sustainable practices. These policies play a crucial role in shaping the future of polymer recycling by creating a framework for waste management, incentivizing recycling, and holding producers accountable for their environmental impact. From government-led initiatives to bans on single-use plastics and producer responsibility schemes, a wide range of regulatory measures are being employed to combat plastic pollution and promote recycling. This section explores key policy and regulatory approaches, including government initiatives for recycling, bans on single-use plastics, and the role of producer responsibility and eco-labeling. In conclusion, policy and regulatory measures are essential for driving the global shift towards sustainable polymer management and recycling. Government initiatives that promote recycling infrastructure, bans on single-use plastics, and extended producer responsibility programs are key strategies for reducing plastic waste and minimizing environmental harm. As these policies continue to evolve, they will play an increasingly important role in shaping a future where polymers are used and recycled responsibly, contributing to the circular economy and reducing the overall environmental footprint of plastic production and consumption.

### *8.1 Government Initiatives for Recycling*

Governments around the world have increasingly recognized the importance of recycling as a means to reduce plastic waste and its environmental impact. Many countries have introduced comprehensive national recycling strategies that seek to enhance waste collection systems, improve recycling infrastructure, and encourage the use of recycled materials in manufacturing. These initiatives often involve a combination of legislative mandates, financial incentives, and public awareness campaigns designed to boost recycling rates and support the circular economy.

In Europe, for instance, the European Union (EU) has implemented several ambitious recycling targets as part of its Circular Economy Action Plan. The EU's Waste Framework Directive mandates that member states recycle at least 50% of their municipal waste by 2025, with higher targets set for packaging materials like plastic. This policy encourages the development of more efficient waste management systems and promotes the adoption of new recycling technologies. Additionally, the EU has introduced the Plastic Strategy, which aims to make all plastic packaging on the European market recyclable by 2030.

In other parts of the world, countries like Japan and South Korea have adopted advanced recycling systems that emphasize waste segregation and material recovery. Japan's Plastic Waste Management Law, for example, requires businesses and consumers to separate plastic waste at the source, making it easier to collect and recycle. These government-led initiatives have proven effective in increasing recycling rates and reducing the amount of plastic waste sent to landfills or incinerated.

Financial incentives also play a key role in promoting polymer recycling. Governments have introduced schemes such as deposit return systems (DRS), where consumers pay a small fee when purchasing plastic products and receive a refund when they return the item for recycling. Such initiatives not only encourage recycling but also reduce littering and improper disposal. Additionally, subsidies for recycling infrastructure development and tax incentives for companies that use recycled materials have further spurred investment in the recycling industry.

*8.2 Bans on Single-Use Plastics*

One of the most prominent regulatory measures in recent years has been the implementation of bans or restrictions on single-use plastics. Single-use plastics, such as straws, cutlery, plastic bags, and packaging, are among the most significant contributors to plastic waste, particularly in oceans and other natural environments. Due to their short lifecycle and poor recyclability, these items often end up as litter, causing widespread environmental damage.

In response, many countries have introduced bans on single-use plastics to curb their production and use. The European Union's Single-Use Plastics Directive, adopted in 2019, bans the sale of certain single-use plastic products, such as plastic straws, plates, and cutlery, and sets targets for reducing the consumption of other items, such as plastic food containers. The directive also mandates that plastic beverage bottles contain at least 25% recycled content by 2025. These regulations aim to shift consumer behavior towards reusable alternatives and promote the development of recyclable products.

Several other countries have followed suit with their own restrictions. For example, Canada has announced plans to ban the use of single-use plastic items, such as straws, stir sticks, and plastic bags, as part of its Zero Plastic Waste strategy. Similarly, India has introduced a phased ban on single-use plastics, targeting items like plastic bags, cups, and plates. These bans are often accompanied by public awareness campaigns and financial support for businesses transitioning to sustainable alternatives, such as paper or biodegradable materials.

Bans on single-use plastics have proven effective in reducing plastic waste, particularly in regions where waste management infrastructure is limited. However, the success of these measures depends on enforcement, the availability of sustainable alternatives, and consumer willingness to adopt reusable products. While these bans represent a significant step towards reducing plastic pollution, complementary strategies—such as improved recycling infrastructure and extended producer responsibility—are needed to achieve long-term sustainability.

*8.3 Producer Responsibility and Eco-Labeling*

A growing focus of regulatory measures is the concept of extended producer responsibility (EPR), which places the onus on producers to manage the environmental impact of their products throughout the entire lifecycle, from design to disposal. Under EPR schemes, manufacturers are required to take responsibility for the collection, recycling, and proper disposal of their products, often through financial contributions to waste management systems or by directly managing take-back programs.

EPR initiatives are designed to incentivize producers to design products that are easier to recycle, use fewer materials, and contain more recycled content. By holding manufacturers accountable for the end-of-life management of their products, these programs aim to reduce the overall environmental impact of polymer production and encourage more sustainable business practices. EPR has been successfully implemented in several countries, particularly in Europe, where industries such as packaging, electronics, and automotive parts are subject to producer responsibility laws.

In addition to EPR, eco-labeling has emerged as an important regulatory tool to promote environmentally responsible products. Eco-labels provide consumers with information about the environmental impact of a product, including its recyclability, carbon footprint, and use of sustainable materials. By offering transparency, eco-labeling encourages consumers to make informed choices and supports the demand for products with lower environmental impacts.

Many countries have introduced eco-labeling programs to promote sustainable products. For example, the EU's Eco-label scheme certifies products that meet stringent environmental standards throughout their life cycle, including the use of recycled materials and reduced energy consumption. In the United States, the Environmental Protection Agency's (EPA) "Safer Choice" label identifies products made with environmentally friendly ingredients and recyclable packaging. Eco-labeling not only helps consumers make greener choices but also drives competition among producers to develop more sustainable products.

By combining EPR with eco-labeling, governments are encouraging a shift towards sustainable production and consumption patterns, which is critical for reducing plastic waste and promoting circular economy principles. Producers are increasingly being held accountable not only for the environmental impact of their products but also for ensuring that they can be effectively recycled and disposed of at the end of their life cycle.

## 9. Consumer Role in Polymer Recycling

Consumers play a vital role in the success of polymer recycling programs and the transition towards more sustainable practices. While government policies and corporate initiatives are critical for creating the framework for recycling, consumer participation and behavior ultimately determine how effectively these systems function. From waste segregation to adopting sustainable alternatives, consumers have the power to drive significant change in the way polymers are used, disposed of, and recycled. This section examines the importance of consumer involvement in polymer recycling, focusing on waste segregation, awareness of recycling programs, and the adoption of sustainable alternatives to conventional plastics. In conclusion, consumers are central to the success of polymer recycling and the reduction of plastic waste. By practicing proper waste segregation, participating in recycling programs, and choosing sustainable alternatives to conventional polymers, consumers can play an active role in promoting a circular economy and reducing the environmental impact of plastic production and disposal. As consumer awareness and engagement continue to grow, the collective impact of these efforts will help drive the transition towards more sustainable and responsible polymer use.

### *9.1 Importance of Waste Segregation*

One of the most critical ways consumers can contribute to polymer recycling is through proper waste segregation. For recycling systems to function efficiently, waste must be separated at the source, ensuring that different types of materials—such as plastics, metals, paper, and organic waste—are collected and processed separately. Proper waste segregation allows for more accurate sorting and reduces contamination, which is a significant challenge in recycling.

Contaminated recycling streams, where food waste, non-recyclable materials, or incompatible plastics are mixed with recyclable items, can compromise the entire batch, leading to reduced material quality or even sending potentially recyclable items to landfills. By properly segregating waste at home, at work, and in public spaces, consumers help ensure that recyclables remain uncontaminated and can be processed more effectively.

Many countries and municipalities have implemented guidelines for waste segregation, often with designated bins for different types of recyclables. However, consumer participation is key to the success of these systems. Ensuring that plastics are properly cleaned before recycling, using the correct bins for each material, and being aware of which items are recyclable are all essential for maximizing recycling efficiency. By taking the time to separate and dispose of waste correctly, consumers can significantly increase the effectiveness of recycling programs and reduce the environmental impact of polymer waste.

## *9.2 Awareness and Participation in Recycling Programs*

In addition to proper waste segregation, consumer awareness and participation in recycling programs are essential for the success of polymer recycling efforts. Many regions offer recycling programs that allow households and businesses to dispose of their recyclable materials in a way that ensures they are processed correctly. However, the effectiveness of these programs depends largely on the willingness of individuals to participate and follow the guidelines.

Public awareness campaigns and education initiatives are crucial for increasing participation rates. Many consumers are unaware of the specifics of what can and cannot be recycled or how to properly prepare items for recycling. As a result, valuable recyclables may end up in general waste, or non-recyclable materials may contaminate the recycling stream. To address this issue, governments and organizations are investing in public education campaigns that explain the importance of recycling, how to recycle effectively, and the environmental benefits of diverting waste from landfills and incineration.

Programs such as deposit return schemes (DRS), where consumers are rewarded for returning recyclable items like plastic bottles or cans, have been shown to increase participation in recycling efforts. Such programs not only incentivize recycling but also reduce littering and improve the quality of materials collected for recycling. By fostering a culture of recycling through awareness and participation, consumers can play a significant role in enhancing the overall efficiency of recycling systems and reducing plastic waste.

Moreover, consumer engagement is crucial for driving demand for recycled products. When consumers actively choose products made from recycled materials, they support the circular economy and encourage manufacturers to incorporate more recycled content into their products. This shift in consumer behavior can have a profound impact on the market, pushing companies to invest in sustainable practices and further promoting the use of recycled polymers.

## 9.3 Sustainable Alternatives to Conventional Polymers

In addition to participating in recycling programs, consumers can make a substantial impact by choosing sustainable alternatives to conventional polymers. Single-use plastics and other conventional polymers are notorious for their environmental persistence and challenges in recycling. By adopting alternatives such as biodegradable, compostable, or reusable materials, consumers can help reduce the overall demand for virgin plastics and mitigate the environmental consequences of plastic waste.

Biodegradable and compostable plastics, made from renewable resources like corn starch or cellulose, offer a more sustainable alternative to traditional plastics derived from fossil fuels. These materials are designed to break down under specific conditions, such as industrial composting facilities, reducing the environmental burden associated with plastic waste. However, it is important for consumers to understand the limitations of biodegradable and compostable plastics (27), as these materials require proper disposal to achieve the desired environmental benefits. Choosing products made from these alternatives can support the shift towards more sustainable polymer use, but consumers must also ensure that these items are disposed of correctly to prevent contamination of recycling streams or accumulation in landfills.

Reusable products, such as metal straws, cloth shopping bags, or stainless-steel water bottles, represent another sustainable alternative to conventional single-use plastics. By reducing the need for disposable items, consumers can significantly decrease the amount of plastic waste generated in everyday life. The growing trend towards zero-waste living, where consumers aim to minimize waste production by using durable and reusable items, is gaining traction worldwide and offers a promising solution to the plastic waste problem.

Consumer demand for sustainable products also influences market trends and encourages companies to invest in the development of eco-friendly materials and packaging. By choosing products with minimal or recyclable packaging, supporting brands that prioritize sustainability, and advocating for eco-friendly alternatives, consumers can accelerate the transition towards a more sustainable economy.

## 10. Challenges and Future Directions

As the world continues to grapple with the environmental impact of plastic waste, the development of effective recycling strategies for polymers remains a critical area of focus. However, numerous challenges must be addressed to fully realize the environmental benefits of polymer recycling. From the complexity of polymer types to the economic viability of recycling systems, various obstacles hinder the widespread adoption of sustainable polymer management. In this section, we explore the key challenges across multiple dimensions of polymer recycling and outline potential future directions for overcoming these barriers.

**Challenges**

One of the primary challenges in polymer recycling lies in the wide variety of *Types of Polymers and Their Recyclability*. Not all polymers are easily recyclable due to differences in chemical composition, material properties, and the additives used during manufacturing. While thermoplastics can often be mechanically recycled, thermosets and certain polymer blends pose significant challenges due to their inability to be re-melted and reprocessed. Additionally, the degradation of material quality during recycling limits the number of times plastics can be recycled, leading to downcycling and reduced material performance.

*Contamination and Sorting Issues* represent another significant challenge. Contaminated plastic waste streams, which include food residues, non-recyclable materials, and incompatible polymers, can compromise recycling processes. Effective sorting is essential for maintaining the quality of recycled materials, but current sorting technologies are expensive and not widely available in many regions. This results in high levels of waste being sent to landfills or incineration due to poor sorting efficiency.

The *Economic Viability of Recycling* is another critical barrier. In many cases, it is more cost-effective for manufacturers to produce new, virgin plastics than to invest in the collection, sorting, and recycling of plastic waste. Market volatility, driven by fluctuations in the price of oil (the primary raw material for plastics), further complicates the financial landscape for recycling. Without sufficient economic incentives or subsidies, recycling facilities struggle to remain competitive, limiting the overall impact of recycling programs.

Even with advancements in *Recycling Techniques for Polymers*, significant hurdles remain. Mechanical recycling, though widely practiced, is constrained by polymer degradation and contamination, while chemical recycling, which offers the promise of higher-quality outputs, is still in its infancy and faces technical and economic challenges. *Energy Recovery and Incineration*, while reducing landfill use, remains controversial due to the emissions generated during the incineration process and its role in diverting focus from true recycling.

*Policy and Regulatory Measures*, while essential, also face challenges in implementation. For instance, *Bans on Single-Use Plastics* have been met with resistance from industries and consumers in regions where suitable alternatives are not widely available. Furthermore, enforcement of these bans and recycling mandates varies globally, creating gaps in the effectiveness of these policies. *Producer Responsibility and Eco-Labeling* schemes, though valuable in theory, often lack uniform standards and may not be fully understood by consumers or enforced by producers, limiting their impact [19].

Lastly, the role of consumers in polymer recycling cannot be overstated. *Waste Segregation* remains a key issue, as improper sorting at the household level can contaminate recycling streams, reducing the quality of recycled materials. Additionally, while public awareness around recycling is growing, *Awareness and Participation in Recycling Programs* remain inconsistent. Many consumers are still unaware of proper recycling practices, leading to recyclable materials being incorrectly disposed of. Finally, while sustainable alternatives to conventional polymers, such as biodegradable and compostable plastics, are increasingly available, consumers often lack access to the appropriate facilities for disposing of these materials, limiting their effectiveness.

**Future Directions**

Addressing these challenges requires coordinated action across industries, governments, and consumers. Looking ahead, several promising directions can help overcome the barriers to more effective polymer recycling and promote a more sustainable future.

Advancements in *Advanced Recycling Technologies* will play a crucial role in the future of polymer recycling. Chemical recycling, including pyrolysis and depolymerization, offers the potential to break down polymers into their original chemical components, producing high-quality recycled materials that can be used in place of virgin plastics. Continued investment in research and development will be essential to reducing the energy and cost barriers associated with these technologies, making them more accessible on a global scale.

The development and wider adoption of *Biodegradable and Compostable Polymers* also offer a path toward reducing plastic waste. Future efforts should focus on improving the performance and cost-effectiveness of these materials while expanding the infrastructure for their proper disposal. Educating consumers and industries about the appropriate use and disposal of biodegradable plastics will be key to maximizing their environmental benefits (28).

Policy and regulatory frameworks will need to evolve to support more sustainable polymer management. Governments can implement stronger *Government Initiatives for Recycling*, such as deposit return schemes, recycling mandates, and subsidies for recycling infrastructure, to encourage greater participation in recycling programs. International collaboration will also be important in developing standardized regulations for plastic waste management, ensuring consistency and enforcement across borders [19].

Additionally, expanding *Producer Responsibility and Eco-Labeling* schemes can help shift the burden of plastic waste management onto producers, encouraging them to design products with recyclability in mind and use more recycled content in manufacturing. Establishing clearer eco-labeling standards will empower consumers to make more informed choices, driving demand for sustainable products and closing the loop in polymer production [29].

From a consumer perspective, increasing *Awareness and Participation in Recycling Programs* through education and public campaigns will be crucial. Governments and organizations should focus on demystifying recycling practices and promoting better waste segregation habits, ensuring that consumers understand the importance of their role in the recycling process. As consumers become more engaged, their choices will also influence market trends, encouraging industries to invest in sustainable alternatives and innovations in polymer recycling [19,30].

Finally, integrating *Circular Economy Approaches for Polymers* will be essential for creating a truly sustainable future. A circular economy focuses on keeping materials in use for as long as possible, ensuring that polymers are reused, repaired, and recycled rather than discarded. Promoting the principles of the circular economy will require collaboration between manufacturers, governments, and consumers to redesign products, improve recycling infrastructure, and reduce the overall consumption of plastics [19].

In conclusion, while there are numerous challenges facing polymer recycling, innovations in technology, regulatory measures, and consumer behavior present promising opportunities for the future. By addressing the economic, technical, and behavioral obstacles to recycling, and by adopting a circular economy approach, the global community can work towards a more sustainable and environmentally responsible management of polymer waste. Continued advancements in recycling technologies, coupled with stronger policy frameworks and increased consumer engagement, will be key to overcoming these challenges and creating a more sustainable future for polymers.

## 11. Conclusion

The environmental impacts of polymers, particularly plastics, are vast and multifaceted, posing serious challenges to ecosystems, wildlife, and human health. The production of synthetic polymers, which relies heavily on fossil fuels, contributes to greenhouse gas emissions, resource depletion, and pollution. Additionally, the durability and resistance of polymers, while beneficial for product performance, have created a global crisis of plastic waste accumulation in landfills, oceans, and other natural environments. Addressing these issues requires a comprehensive approach that includes reducing plastic waste, improving recycling systems, and adopting sustainable alternatives.

Polymer recycling offers an essential pathway for mitigating the environmental footprint of plastic production and waste. Mechanical and chemical recycling techniques allow for the recovery and reuse of valuable materials, reducing the need for virgin polymers and helping to lower greenhouse gas emissions. However, polymer recycling faces significant challenges, including the complexity of different polymer types, contamination issues, and the economic viability of recycling processes. Moreover, advanced recycling technologies, such as chemical recycling, while promising, are still in early stages of development and face hurdles in scaling up.

Innovations in polymer recycling are helping to address these challenges. Advanced recycling technologies, such as pyrolysis and depolymerization, offer solutions for processing hard-to-recycle plastics and producing high-quality recycled materials. Additionally, biodegradable and compostable polymers provide alternatives to conventional plastics, particularly for single-use items, although proper disposal infrastructure remains a key challenge. The adoption of circular economy principles, which aim to keep materials in use for as long as possible, offers a promising approach to reducing waste and promoting sustainability.

Policy and regulatory measures play a critical role in driving the transition toward more sustainable polymer management. Government initiatives, including recycling mandates, deposit return schemes, and subsidies for recycling infrastructure, help boost recycling rates and support the development of new technologies. Bans on single-use plastics and extended producer responsibility (EPR) programs shift the focus toward reducing plastic production and holding manufacturers accountable for the lifecycle of their products. Additionally, eco-labeling provides consumers with important information to make more environmentally responsible purchasing decisions.

Consumers are at the heart of successful polymer recycling efforts. By practicing proper waste segregation, participating in recycling programs, and choosing sustainable alternatives to conventional plastics, consumers can significantly contribute to reducing plastic waste and promoting the circular economy. Increasing consumer awareness and engagement is crucial for driving the demand for recycled products and supporting the development of more sustainable manufacturing practices.

Looking to the future, overcoming the challenges of polymer recycling will require continued innovation, collaboration, and education. Governments, industries, and consumers must work together to create a more sustainable system for managing polymer waste. Advanced recycling technologies, improved policy frameworks, and widespread adoption of circular economy principles will be essential for reducing the environmental impact of polymers and ensuring that these valuable materials are managed responsibly. With coordinated efforts, it is possible to reduce plastic pollution, conserve natural resources, and create a more sustainable future for polymers and society at large.

**Acknowledgment:** The authors Shambhavi Sharma and Duckshin Park are thankful to Ministry of science and ICT, Republic of Korea and Korea Railroad Research Institute. The study was sponsored by the Development of mobile direct carbon dioxide capture technology under task code PK2402A4. Prashant Kumar Rai is also thankful FOR Indian Council of Medical Research (ICMR) to providing him Research Associate fellowship.

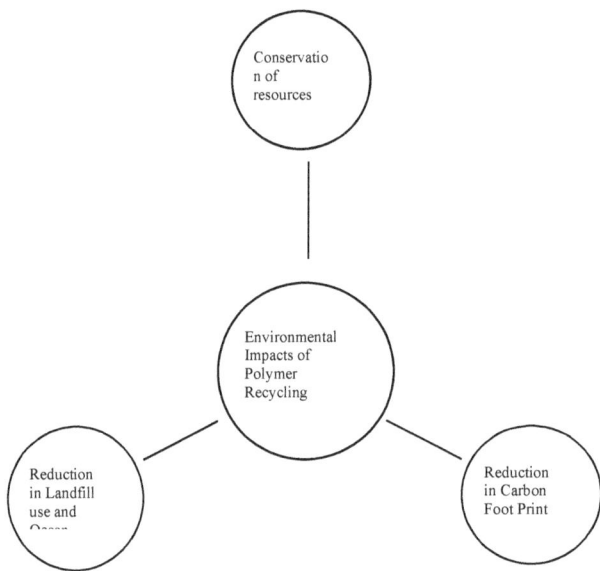

Figure 1: Representative diagram of Environmental Recycling Impact

**References**

1. Plastics Europe. (2020). Plastics – the Facts 2020: An analysis of European plastics production, demand and waste data.

2. World Economic Forum. (2016). The New Plastics Economy: Rethinking the future of plastics.

3. Assad, H., Kaya, S., Senthil Kumar, P., Vo, D. V. N., Sharma, A., & Kumar, A. (2022). Insights into the role of nanotechnology on the performance of biofuel cells and the production of viable biofuels: A review. Fuel, 323, 124277. https://doi.org/ 10.1016/j.fuel.2022.124277

4. Hopewell, J., Dvorak, R., &Kosior, E. (2009). "Plastics recycling: Challenges and opportunities." Philosophical Transactions of the Royal Society B: Biological Sciences, 364(1526), 2115–2126.

5. Thompson, R. C., et al. (2009). "Plastics, the environment and human health: Current consensus and future trends." Philosophical Transactions of the Royal Society B: Biological Sciences, 364(1526), 2153–2166.

6. Jambeck, J. R., et al. (2015). "Plastic waste inputs from land into the ocean." *Science*, 347(6223), 768-771.

7. Geyer, R., Jambeck, J. R., & Law, K. L. (2017). "Production, use, and fate of all plastics ever made." *Science Advances*, 3(7), e1700782.

8. Law, K. L., & Thompson, R. C. (2014). "Microplastics in the seas." *Science*, 345(6193), 144-145.

9. Eriksen, M., et al. (2014). "Plastic pollution in the world's oceans: More than 5 trillion plastic pieces weighing over 250,000 tons afloat at sea." *PLOS ONE*, 9(12), e111913.

10. Al-Salem, S. M., Lettieri, P., &Baeyens, J. (2009). "Recycling and recovery routes of plastic solid waste (PSW): A review." *Waste Management*, 29(10), 2625-2643.

11. Hopewell, J., Dvorak, R., &Kosior, E. (2009). "Plastics recycling: Challenges and opportunities." *Philosophical Transactions of the Royal Society B: Biological Sciences*, 364(1526), 2115–2126.

12. Singh, N., et al. (2017). "Challenges and opportunities in plastic recycling." *Sustainable Chemistry and Engineering*, 5(5), 2335–2353.

13. Al-Salem, S. M., Lettieri, P., &Baeyens, J. (2009). "Recycling and recovery routes of plastic solid waste (PSW): A review." *Waste Management*, 29(10), 2625-2643.

14. Awaja, F., & Pavel, D. (2005). "Recycling of PET." *European Polymer Journal*, 41(7), 1453-1477.

15. Siddique, R., et al. (2008). "Recycling of materials in civil engineering." *Waste Management*, 28(8), 1375-1381.

16. Ragaert, K., Delva, L., & Van Geem, K. (2017). "Mechanical and chemical recycling of solid plastic waste." *Waste Management*, 69, 24-58.

17. Ellen MacArthur Foundation. (2016). The New Plastics Economy: Rethinking the future of plastics.
18. Rahimi, A., & García, J. M. (2017). "Chemical recycling of waste plastics for new materials production." Nature Reviews Chemistry, 1(6), 0046.
19. Geyer, R., Jambeck, J. R., & Law, K. L. (2017). "Production, use, and fate of all plastics ever made." Science Advances, 3(7), e1700782.
20. European Commission. (2018). A European strategy for plastics in a circular economy.
21. Rahimi, A., & García, J. M. (2017). "Chemical recycling of waste plastics for new materials production." Nature Reviews Chemistry, 1(6), 0046.
22. Ragaert, K., Delva, L., & Van Geem, K. (2017). "Mechanical and chemical recycling of solid plastic waste." Waste Management, 69, 24-58.
23. Al-Salem, S. M., Lettieri, P., &Baeyens, J. (2009). "Recycling and recovery routes of plastic solid waste (PSW): A review." Waste Management, 29(10), 2625-2643.
24. United Nations Environment Programme (UNEP). (2018). Single-use plastics: A roadmap for sustainability.
25. European Parliament. (2019). "Directive (EU) 2019/904 on the reduction of the impact of certain plastic products on the environment." Official Journal of the European Union.
26. OECD. (2020). Extended Producer Responsibility and the Circular Economy.
27. European Commission. (2020). Circular Economy Action Plan.
28. Thompson, R. C., et al. (2009). "Plastics, the environment and human health: Current consensus and future trends." Philosophical Transactions of the Royal Society B: Biological Sciences, 364(1526), 2153-2166.
29. Ellen MacArthur Foundation. (2016). The New Plastics Economy: Rethinking the future of plastics.
30. Rahimi, A., & García, J. M. (2017). "Chemical recycling of waste plastics for new materials production." *Nature Reviews Chemistry*, 1(6), 0046.
31. Geyer, R., Jambeck, J. R., & Law, K. L. (2017). "Production, use, and fate of all plastics ever made." *Science Advances*, 3(7), e1700782.

# Chapter-11

# Recycling of Polymer Composites and its Environmental Aspects

Abhimanyu Yadav[1]

Jyoti Tiwari[2]

**Abstract:**

Polymer composites, which integrate a polymer matrix with reinforcing agents such as fibers, fillers, or nanoparticles, have attracted considerable interest due to their exceptional mechanical, thermal, and electrical characteristics. These materials find extensive applications across multiple sectors, including automotive, aerospace, construction, and electronics, primarily because of their lightweight composition, high strength, and adaptability. Nevertheless, the increasing emphasis on environmental sustainability has underscored the necessity for effective recycling strategies for polymer composites, which are frequently non-biodegradable and challenging to process at the end of their useful life.

Various recycling strategies have been investigated to alleviate environmental concerns, including mechanical recycling, chemical recycling, and energy recovery. Mechanical recycling entails grinding and reusing the composite material, although it faces limitations due to matrix degradation and the complexities of separating the reinforcement. The abstract look to summarize the different types of polymer composites, the environmental issues they present, and an examination of both current and emerging recycling techniques. The advancement of effective recycling technologies is crucial for improving the sustainability of polymer composites, minimizing waste, and fostering a circular economy within industries that depend on these materials.

**Keywords**: Composite Material, Recycling of polymer composite, Environmental aspects

## 1. INTRODUCTION

Composite materials, which are often man-made, are a three-dimensional combination of at least two chemically separate materials, with a unique interface separating the components, designed to attain qualities that none of the components can accomplish alone. In composites, at least one of the components known as the reinforcing phase is made up of fibers, sheets, or particles that are embedded in the matrix phase. Metal, ceramic, or polymer can be used as both reinforcing and matrix materials. Polymers are commonly used as matrix materials in commercially made composites. Reinforcing materials are often strong and have low densities, whereas the matrix is usually ductile or stiff. If the composite is properly designed and manufactured, it combines the strength of the reinforcement with

---

[1] *Department of Chemistry, K. N. Govt. P. G. College Gyanpur, Bhadohi-221304*
[2] *Department of Chemistry, K. N. Govt. P. G. College Gyanpur, Bhadohi-221304*

Email: *jtrt3012@gmail.com*

the toughness of the matrix to provide a set of desired qualities not found in any other conventional material.[1]

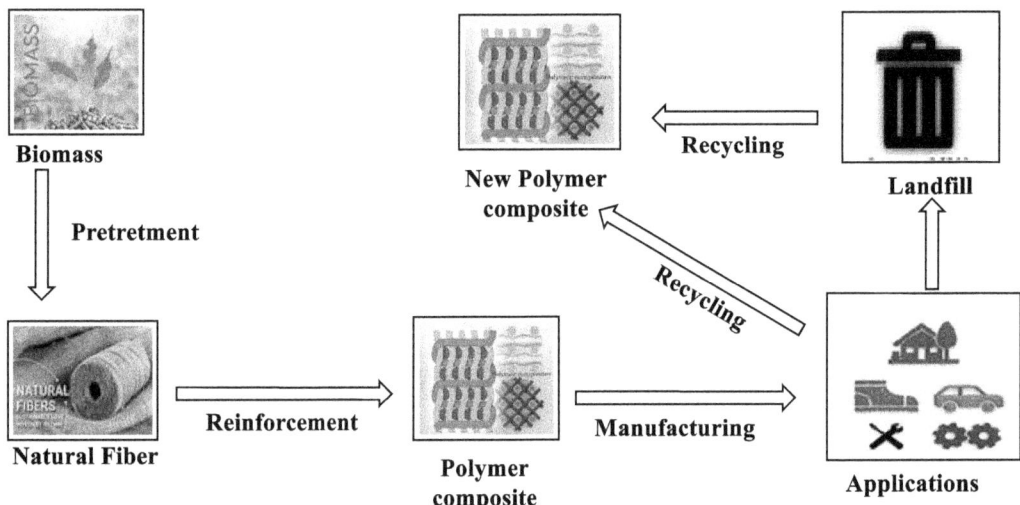

Composite materials such as fiberglass, carbon fiber, and reinforced polymers have numerous advantages, including their durability, lightweight design, and high resistance to damage. Due to rapid population growth, demands for consumer goods and composite materials have increased significantly. As a result, global warming, climate change, and environmental pollution, natural disasters, waste control, management, and recycling are crucial issues for global sustainability. Composite materials play noteworthy role in many areas such as transport, aerospace, marine, construction, and renewable energy. Composite ingredients like carbon fibre, fibreglass, and reinforced polymers have several engineering applications such as they are durable, lightweight, and higher strength, reduced energy consumption and impact to the environment ($CO_2$).[2]

## 2. POLYMER COMPOSITE

Polymers are among the most often used and well-known materials of our century. However, pure polymers are insufficient for a variety of industrial applications requiring extreme strength and heat resistance. Thus, engineers have reinforced polymers with other strong materials to attain the necessary performance and qualities to suit the demands of many industrial sectors. Carbon fiber (CF) as a unique material has drawn the consideration of scientists due to its outstanding features and characteristics, namely, non-corrosivity, superior mechanical strength at high temperatures with excellent thermal and chemical resistance, great strength-to-weight ratio, light weight, low toxicity, and recyclable materials.[3] Polymers are affordable, lightweight, and long-lasting materials developed from the petroleum industry that can be readily molded into a number of commodities for use in a wide range of applications. As a result, polymer production has risen dramatically in recent decades.

Polymer composite materials are engineered materials made from a polymer matrix combined with various reinforcements. These composites leverage the beneficial properties of both the polymer and the reinforcement, resulting in materials that are stronger, lighter, and more versatile than their individual components. However, according to established technical solutions, these materials have a larger density and weaker mechanical qualities, and environmental influences such as sunshine, UV radiation, and moisture impact their degradation [4]. To summarize, polymer composite materials are a diverse and growing field of materials with several uses and substantial potential for innovation.

## 2.1. Classification of Polymer Composite

Generally, three types of composite materials are created and widely employed in a wide range of technical applications: polymer-matrix composites (PMC), metal-matrix composites (MMC), and ceramic-matrix composites (CMC). Composite materials are categorized into three categories based on their reinforcement: particle composites, fiber-reinforced composites, and structural composites. Although numbers on total worldwide composites manufacturing are difficult to get, it was projected to be 7 million tonnes in 2000 and might have reached 10 million tonnes by 2006. Polymer-matrix composites dominate the market for all types of composite materials, with thermoset composites accounting for more than two-thirds. However, thermoplastic composites have grown more rapidly in recent years [5].

**Polymer Matrix Composites:** Polymer matrix composites have long aroused the interest of the scientific and technological communities, and they are now acknowledged as the ideal alternative for a wide range of engineering applications due to their excellent mechanical properties, including stiffness and high specific strength. Furthermore, these materials provide considerable design flexibility as well as superior fatigue and corrosion resistance when compared to many others. These are thus classified as advanced composite materials due to their enhanced mechanical characteristics and relative simplicity of production. As a result, manufacturers have resorted to these sophisticated composites for a wide range of applications across many sectors. A manufacturer or designer must select the right composite ingredients for a specific application while taking into account all of the composite's qualities. This is one of the primary goals of this review: to investigate various matrices and reinforcement combinations utilized for diverse applications while taking their qualities into account. This lengthy investigation includes a thorough examination of certain selected manufacturing procedures. Furthermore, the multiple uses of polymer matrix composites in today's world are highlighted, as are the obstacles that they provide in a variety of scenarios. [6]

A Polymer matrix composites (PMCs) are an important class of structural materials utilized in a variety of industries (for example, aerospace, automotive, and industrial applications), frequently competing with other structural materials such as steel, aluminum alloys, titanium alloys, and so on. PMCs are often made up of a polymer matrix and high-strength fibres, resulting in a product with a substantially greater modulus and strength than the polymer matrix itself, and are hence commonly referred to as fibre-reinforced polymers (FRPs). The matrix can be made of thermoplastic or thermoset polymers, such as epoxy or polyester. Glass, carbon, and aramid fibers are often employed as reinforcements. PMCs have found significantly more usage than either metal matrix composites or ceramic matrix composites in aerospace, automotive, and other sectors [7].

**Thermoplastics**: Thermoplastics are made up of linear or branched chain molecules with weak intermolecular interactions and strong intramolecular bonds. They may be reshaped with heat and pressure and have a semicrystalline or amorphous structure. Polyethylene, polypropylene, polystyrene, nylons, polycarbonate, polyacetals, polyamide-imides, polyether ether ketone, polysulfone, polyphenylenesulfide, polyether imide, and so on. They can be remolded after heating [8].

**Thermosets**: Thermosets are cross-linked or networked structures having covalent connections to all molecules. They do not soften, but instead decompose when heated. They cannot be reshaped once they have solidified during the cross-linking process. Epoxies, phenolics, polyesters, melamine, ureas, silicones, and polyimides are all common examples [9].

Epoxy, phenolic, and polyester are examples of resins. They cannot be reformed once they have been treated.

**Elastomers**: An elastomer is a polymer with viscoelasticity, characterized by a low Young's modulus and a high yield strain as compared to other materials. The term, derived from elastic polymer, is frequently used interchangeably with the term rubber, while the latter is preferred when referring to vulcanizates [10].

**Reinforcements**: Incorporating specific materials with desired qualities into other materials that lack such features. Reinforced materials and manufacturing techniques have a considerable impact on composite construction quality, productivity, and competitiveness. The interface between matrix-reinforced materials is critical in the mechanical behavior and production of composites. Materials that improve the mechanical properties of the polymeric matrix. Common types include [11].

**Fibers**: Fiber reinforcement is like a two-sided coin. One side involves the random direct incorporation of fibers into the matrix, such as asphalt concrete and/or Portland Cement Concrete slabs. Another side consists of oriented fiber materials, such as the Geo-synthetics family. It is underlined that the former notion is not as well-known as the latter, not only in optimizing fiber characteristics, fiber diameter, length, surface texture, etc., but also in reinforcing mechanisms. Fiber reinforcement has been utilized for a long time in a variety of forms, including short, long, and continuous fibers of glass, natural fibers, textile, carbon, and so on. Apart from the type of the fibers, the reinforcement is determined by the fiber level, aspect ratio, chemical bonding, and matrix wetting. Well-ordered continuous fibers, such as UD composites or filament winding, result in the best performance.Such as glass, carbon, and aramid (e.g., Kevlar).Fibers significantly increase tensile strength and stiffness [12].

**Particulates**: Particulate reinforced composites are one type of composite, and concrete is an excellent example. The coarse rock or gravel aggregate is incorporated in a cement matrix. The aggregate offers rigidity and strength, while the cement works as a binder, holding the building together.

A comprehensive overview of existing theories for predicting the strength and modulus of particulate-filled polymeric composites is provided. The size, shape, and distribution of inclusions affect the macroscopic behaviour of particle composites. The interfacial adhesion of the matrix and inclusion is also significant. The limitations of theoretical models in characterizing these characteristics and expressing experimental evidence on macroscopic behaviour are shown. Such as mineral fillers, which can improve properties like impact resistance and thermal stability.

## 2.2 Recent Advances in Polymer Composite

In recent years, need of sustainable materials make interest to develop bio-based polymers and sustainable reinforcements.

Polymer composite can be used to create nanomaterials for enhanced properties and functionalities. It can also have great use as smart composites for development of materials that can respond to environmental changes or stress, incorporating sensors or actuators. Many polymer composites have excellent fatigue resistance and long service life. By altering the matrix and reinforcement types, industrialists might customize the properties of the composite to ensemble specific applications. Some composites are efficiently effective insulating material, making them useful in various electrical applications [13].

**Sustainable Alternatives**: The creation of composites that are biobased or biodegradable presents a chance to lessen the influence on the environment. These materials might break down more easily than conventional composites or be simpler to recycle.

**Circular Economy**: Placing a strong emphasis on a circular economy strategy encourages recycling and reuse, extending the useful life of goods and reducing waste. The defense and aerospace industries pioneered the use of composite materials; nowadays, most defense aircraft weigh more than 50% composites. Weight-saving technology in vehicles is critical for increasing fuel economy. As the largest application area, utilization of composite materials in the automobile industry is steadily rising such as building of body, interiors, chassis, hoods, and electrical components. [14]

## 3. RECYCLING OF POLYMER COMPOSITE

Recycling polymer composites can be complex due to the combination of different materials. High-performance composites can be expensive to produce, which may limit their use in some applications. The processing techniques for composites can be more intricate than those for traditional materials, requiring specialized equipment and expertise. Thus, recycling technology is another option to safeguard natural resources, as the majority of polymeric materials are derived from the oil and gas industry. However, recycling polymer composite-based products remains a difficulty, despite significant progress in this field. Polymer composites consist of two or more materials having discrete phases, such as a matrix and fillers. These phases are exactly mixed inside the composites, thus it is not profitable to separate them. However, several researchers have sought to create recycling procedures for polymer composites that are technically possible, commercially viable, and ecologically friendly [15].

### 3.1 Process involved in recycling of polymer composite

Recycling polymer composites involves several processes, which can vary based on the type of composite (thermoset vs. thermoplastic) and the intended recycling method. Here's an overview of the main processes involved:

**Collection and Sorting:** Gather waste polymer composites from manufacturing processes, end-of-life products, or post-consumer items. Separate different types of composites, as mixed materials can complicate recycling. This may involve manual sorting or automated methods like infrared sensors.

**Shredding and Size Reduction:** The collected composites are shredded into smaller pieces to facilitate handling and processing. This step is crucial for both mechanical recycling and preparing for other recycling methods.

**Cleaning and Contaminant Removal:** Remove surface contaminants such as dirt, oils, or adhesives. This is especially important for thermoplastic composites, where cleanliness can affect the quality of the recycled material. Ensures that moisture is removed, which is vital for subsequent processing [16].

## 3.2 Methods of Recycling of Polymer Composites

There are numerous methods for Recycling of polymer composites, some are given here:

Mechanical Recycling

Shredded materials are further processed into granules or pellets. This can involve grinding and additional size reduction. The granules can be melted and remolded into new products. However, mechanical recycling may lead to a reduction in mechanical properties due to thermal and mechanical degradation. The mechanical recycling process begins by reducing the size of the composite scrap by crushing or low-speed cutting. The size is then lowered to 10 mm to 50 m by fine grinding with a hammer mill or other high-speed millings. The fine particles of the waste composites are then separated into fiber-rich (coarser) and matrix-rich (finer) fractions using cyclones and sieves.

Mechanical recycling involves reducing the size of waste so that it can be reinforced into other products. A considerable number of researches have been conducted on mechanical recycling, and it is the sole approach used commercially for the treatment of wasted sheet molding compounds. Sheet molding compounds recyclate materials have been investigated as potential constituents for new systems such as concrete and thermoplastic composites [17, 18].

### Thermal recycling

**Fluidised bed**: Materials are fed through a hopper and put on a bed of silica sand in fluidized bed recycling. Heat is produced by fluidized air moving over the bed at speeds ranging from 0.4 to 1.0 meters per second. Operating temperatures typically range from 450 to 550 degrees Celsius. Resin and other organic components of composite materials and pollutants deteriorate due to the heat. For separation, the recovered fiber and filler are put into a cyclone and a revolving sieve. In order to recover energy, the burned gases are sent through an exhaust. Previous research indicates that glass fibers can be recovered from thermoset composites. A temperature of 450°C is a reasonable upper limit with at least 50% strength loss. This approach has the benefit of being highly tolerant of polluted and contaminated materials.

### Conventional and microwave pyrolysis

By heating GFRP and CFRP waste to 300-800°C in an inert environment, pyrolysis procedures recover the fibres and fillers while volatilizing the polymeric resin. For fiber strength to be maintained, the temperature must be kept within an ideal range. Process by products in the form of liquids and gases can be used as feedstock for additional chemical reactions or as a source of energy. For instance, one UK recycling company that uses their proprietary thermal recycling technology is ELG Carbon Fibre Ltd in England. Milled, chopped, and pelletized forms of the recycled fiber are available for purchase. CFK Valley Stade Recycling GmbH, Hadeg Recycling Ltd. in Germany, Karborek in Italy, Carbon Conversions in the USA, and Recycle Industry Co. Ltd. (Japan) are other businesses that use this strategy. Heat is produced via microwave pyrolysis using microwave radiation. By cutting down on processing time, the quick heating method lessens the chance of fiber strength deterioration. The material is heated by the radiation from the inside rather than the outside, as is the case with traditional heating methods. Waste can be uniformly heated due to the diffuse nature of electromagnetic radiation [19, 20].

Chemical Recycling

Involves breaking down the polymer chains into their monomers or other valuable chemicals through processes like pyrolysis or solvent-based methods. Uses solvents to dissolve the polymer and recover valuable components. The recovered monomers can be used to synthesize new polymers, ideally restoring some of the original properties.

The chemical recycling procedure involves degradation of polymer matrix using chemical dissolving chemicals to liberate fibers. The chemical recycling process can regenerate clean fibers and fillers, as well as the depolymerized matrix in the form of monomers or petrochemical feedstock. The dissolution process is commonly referred to as solvolysis, and it can be characterized further based on the solvent as hydrolysis (with water), glycolysis (with glycols), or acid digestion. When employing alcohol or water, high temperatures and pressures are typically used at subcritical or supercritical conditions to provide faster dissolving and greater efficiency. Acid digestion is often performed under air conditions, but the reaction rate may be extremely sluggish [21].

Energy Recovery

While not a recycling method in the traditional sense, incineration can recover energy from non-recyclable composites. This process must be managed to minimize emissions and environmental impact. Each substance possesses a unique calorific value, enabling the potential combustion of discarded materials and the recovery of heat energy. However, SMC-like composites are heavily loaded with non-organic elements such as glass fibers and fillers. Resin is the only organic material, that can combust and produces the most energy (up to 35%) from its total weight. Mineral fillers, such as calcium carbonate, degrade at high temperatures because they absorb energy, and some SMC formulations include fire retardants. These variables limit the amount of energy recovered through incineration.

The calorific values of phenolic, polyester, urea-formaldehyde, and epoxy resins have been published. Furthermore, the large amount of solid scraps left requires further disposal. The remaining elements are not used as fillers in another SMC or DMC composition. The related temperature causes the calcium carbonate filler to change into calcium oxide, which has an unfavorable effect on the thickening process in energy generation [22, 23].

## 4. ENVIRONMENTAL ASPECTS

Recycling polymer composites has significant environmental implications, both positive and negative. Here are the key environmental aspects to consider

However, the widespread usage of polymers has resulted in environmental issues related to their disposal. Recycling is one of the most often employed solutions for preventing environmental concerns caused by the accumulation of polymeric waste from the usage of these materials. Polymers and polymer composites are becoming more widely used, particularly in the packaging and construction sectors.

The need for environmentally friendly solutions is expanding in a variety of businesses and sectors. One option is composite fibers. Composites have been used in a variety of sectors, most notably automotive and aerospace, where high resistance and lightweight are important concerns. The most common fibers that satisfy these criteria are glass and carbon fibers. However, businesses increasingly require composites to be more cost effective, environmentally benign, and renewable. This has led to an increased interest in natural fiber composites as opposed to manufactured or synthetic fiber ones because they have a few points of interest, such as lower natural effect on their environment and cheaper fabricating costs, and this broadens their potential applications over distinct industrial sectors [24].

The majority of garbage is disposed of in landfills, buried, or burned rather than recycled. Though certain wastes are biodegradable, they still produce dust, CO2, methane, and other hazardous gasses before degrading completely in landfills. It poses environmental risks, lowers air quality, and infiltrates microplastics into living species and human organs via food chains. Researchers are attempting to recycle human hair, fruit husk, plant-based natural fibers, and other trash into biodegradable and green composites. It will assist to replace non-biodegradable and synthetic fiber-based composites with green ones. Finally, it will reduce environmental degradation, increase sustainability, improve social quality, and create a circular economy. Waste recycling saves energy, provides jobs, lowers carbon emissions, and improves societal qualities. Recycling even a single piece of waste helps to combat climate change, reduce water, air, and soil pollution, and increase sustainability. This study looks at the societal implications of recycling human hair, face masks, and RMG waste into composite fields [25].

This study looks at the social implications of recycling human hair, face masks, and ready-made garment (RMG) waste in composites. They are disposed of in landfills, buried, and burned, which increases environmental risks and undermines global sustainability. Human hair, face masks, and RMG waste are utilized to create hybrid composites with human hair embedded in jute and betel nut fibers, as well as face masks and RMG waste-reinforced polyester. Steps for recycling human hair, waste face masks, and RMG waste in the composite field.

Research is working to replace synthetic and plastic materials by creating natural fiber-reinforced green composites and recycling solid waste into valuable resources. Human hair, discarded face masks, and RMG waste can all be recycled into composite materials. The study found that human hair, waste face masks, and RMG waste-based polymer composites have higher mechanical, abrasion, wear, and impact resistance than some natural fiber-reinforced polymer (NFRP) composites. It can be utilized in thermal insulation, automotive interior panels, engine covers, and impact-resistant bumpers, as well as the interior walls of residences, buses, trains, boats, ships, and planes. Instead of being discarded in landfills, human hair, waste face masks, and RMG waste can be used to make composite materials as a low-cost and readily available component. It will eventually help to generate resources and wealth from trash, create new jobs and a circular economy, improve social and economic characteristics, and minimize pollution, health risks, greenhouse gas emissions, and global warming. Future study could improve the strength of human hair, face masks, and composites reinforced with RMG waste. Environmental benefits, cost-effectiveness, and scalability will not be an issue because they may be used to create hybrid composites using natural or synthetic fibers as inexpensive elements. [26].

Polymer composites' effects on the environment and recycling are influenced by a number of interrelated elements. Here is a summary:

## 4.1 Influences of Recycling of Polymer Composites on Environment

- Polymer composites are frequently produced by extracting fossil fuels (for polymers) and mining for reinforcements (such as glass or carbon fibers), which can result in habitat damage, pollution, and carbon emissions. In contrast, production procedures for polymer composites can be energy-intensive, contributing to greenhouse gas emissions.

- Polymer composites are long-lasting and suitable for various applications. While this is useful, it can lead to long-term waste if not appropriately managed near the end of life. Increased waste management and recycling legislation can spur the development of more advanced recycling technology.

- Several polymer composites are not biodegradable, creating substantial waste issues. When disposed of in landfills, they may remain hundreds of years. Recycling helps divert composites from landfills, reducing overall waste and environmental degradation.

- Several composites may produce toxic compounds during degradation or combustion, potentially contaminating soil and water sources. Many polymer composites contain hazardous substances. Proper recycling processes can help minimize the release of these toxic materials into the environment.

- Utilizing recycled materials frequently uses less energy than creating new ones, which helps conserve natural resources and lessen the impact on the environment by reducing the need for virgin materials.

Recycling reduces waste and environmental deterioration by keeping composites out of landfills.

- Recycling can benefit environmental health by lowering contaminants emitted into the air and water during production and disposal operations.

- Polymer composites can take decades or more to break down in landfills; recycling helps keep them out of there. Both the need for new disposal sites and environmental degradation are reduced when landfill waste is reduced.

- Recycling lessens the requirement for virgin resources by recovering valuable materials. The environmental impact of extraction and processing is reduced thanks to this preservation of natural resources.

- Compared to creating new products from raw materials, manufacturing them from recycled materials frequently uses less energy [27, 28].

## 5. CONCLUSION

Recycling polymer composites presents a promising opportunity to reduce environmental impacts, conserve resources, and promote sustainability. However, addressing the challenges involved in recycling processes is crucial for maximizing these benefits and advancing toward a more circular economy. The environmental impact of polymer composites is significant, particularly in terms of resource extraction, energy consumption, and end-of-life waste. However, effective recycling can greatly mitigate these impacts, leading to reduced waste and resource conservation. Addressing the challenges in recycling, enhancing infrastructure, and promoting sustainable materials are critical for minimizing the overall environmental footprint of polymer composites.

**References:**

1. Thomas S., Joseph K., Malhotra S. K., Goda K., and Sreekala M. S. Polymer Composites, 1, 2012 Wiley-VCH Verlag GmbH & Co. KGaA. Published 2012 by Wiley-VCH Verlag GmbH & Co. KGaA

2. H. Chalaye, Composite materials: drive and innovation. Le 4 Pages, des statistiques industrielles, No. 158, 2002. http://www.insee.fr/sessi/4pages/pdf/4p158anglais.pdf.

3. Ayre D. Technology advancing Polymers and Polymer Composites towards sustainability: A review Curr. Opinion Green Sustain Chem., 13, 2018, 108-112. DOI:10.1016/j.cogsc.2018.06.018.

4. Campbell F.C. Introduction to composite materials and processes: unique materials that require unique processes. Manuf. Process. Adv. Compos. 2004: 1–37. https://doi.org/10.1016/b978-185617415-2/50002-2.

5. World Economic Forum, Ellen MacArthur Foundation and McKinsey & Company, ' The new plastics economy – Rethinking the future of plastics', 2016: https://www.ellenmacarthurfoundation.org/assets/ downloads /Ellen Mac Arthur Foundation, the new Plastics Economy. Accessed May 8, 2018

6. Bunsell, A.R. and Harris, B. (1974) Composites, 5, 157.

7. Mkaddem, A., Demirci, I., and Mansori, M.E. (2008) Composites Sci. Techn., 68, 3123-3127.

8. Job S. Composite Recycling - summary of recent research and development. Knowl Transf Netw 2010; 5:26.

9. Saleem H, Edathil A, Ncube T, Pokhrel J, Khoori S, Abraham A, et al. Mechanical and thermal properties of thermoset-graphene nanocomposites. Macromol Mater Eng. 2016, 301, 231-259. https://doi.org/10.1002/mame.201500335.

10. Park S. J., Seo M. K., Types of Composites, Interface Science and Technology, Elsevier, 18, 2011, 501-629, ISBN -9780123750495,

11. Pimenta S, Pinho ST. Recycling carbon fibre reinforced polymers for structural applications: technology review and market outlook. Waste Manag 2011, 31, 378–92. https://doi.org/10.1016/j.wasman.2010.09.019.

12. Qureshi J. A Review of Recycling Methods for Fibre Reinforced Polymer Composites. Sustainability 2022, 14, 16855. https://doi.org/10.3390/ su142416855

13. Friedrich K, Almajid AA. Manufacturing aspects of advanced polymer composites for automotive applications. Appl Compos Mater 2013, 20:107–28. https://doi. org/10.1007/s10443-012-9258-7.

14. (a) Hahladakis, J.N., Iacovidou, E., 'Closing the loop on plastic packaging materials: What is quality and how does it affect circularity?' Sci. Total Environ. 630 (2018) 1394-1400

(b) Soutis C, Irving P. Polymer composites in the aerospace industry. Elsevier Inc., 2014. https://doi.org/10.1016/C2013-0-16303-9.

15. Hopewell J, Dvorak R, Kosior E. Plastics recycling: challenges and opportunities. Philos Trans R Soc B Biol Sci., 2009, 364, 2115-26.

16. Yang, Y. Boom R., Irion, B. Heerden D-J., Kuiper, P. Wit, H. Recycling of composite materials. Chem. Eng. Proces. 51, 2012, 53- 68.

17. Bream CE, Hornsby PR. Comminuted thermoset recyclate as a reinforcing filler for thermoplastics: Part I characterisation of recyclatefeedstocks. J Mater Sci 2001, 36, 2965-75. https://doi.org/10.1023/A:1017962722495.

18. Shuaib NA, Mativenga PT. Effect of process parameters on mechanical recycling of glass fibre thermoset composites. In: Procedia CIRP, vol. 48. Elsevier B.V.; 2016. p. 134-9. https://doi.org/10.1016/j.procir.2016.03.206

19. Job S, Leeke G, Mativenga PT, Oniveux G, Pickering S, Shuaib NA. Composites Recycling: Where are we now? 2016.

20. Lam SS, Chase HA. A review on waste to energy processes Using microwave pyrolysis. Energies. 2012, 5(10):4209-32.

21. Liu T, Zhang M, Guo X, Liu C, Liu T, Xin J, et al. Mild chemical recycling ofaerospace fiber/epoxy composite wastes and utilization of the decomposed resin.PolymDegradStabil 2017;139:20–7. https://doi.org/10.1016/j.

22. Utekar S., Suriya V K, More N., Rao A. Comprehensive study of recycling of thermosetting polymer composites –Driving force, challenges and methods. Composites Part B 207 (2021) 108596

23. Torres A, De Marco I, Caballero BM, Laresgoiti MF, Legarreta JA, Cabrero MA, et al. Recycling by pyrolysis of thermoset composites: characteristics of the liquid and gaseous fuels obtained. Fuel 2000, 79, 897-902. https://doi.org/10.1016/ S0016-2361(99)00220-3

24. F. Rahman, Societal impact of recycling waste into composite materials, Societal Impacts 4 (2024) 100082

25. A. Gupta, Human hair "waste" and its utilization: gaps and possibilities, J. Waste Manag.2014 (1) (2014) 498018.

26. A.L. Silva, J.C. Prata, C. Mouneyrac, D. Barcel`o, A.C. Duarte, T. Rocha-Santos, Risks of Covid-19 face masks to wildlife: Present and future research needs, Sci. Total Environ., 792, 2021, 148505.

27. Z. Liu, W. Liu, T. R. Walker, M. Adams, and J. Zhao, "How does the global plastic waste trade contribute to environmental benefits: implication for reductions of greenhouse gas emissions? Journal of Environmental Management, vol. 287, p. 112283, 2021.

28. Shafqat A. R. Hussain M. Nawab Y. Ashraf M. Ahmad S. and Batool G. Circularity in Materials: A Review on Polymer Composites Made from Agriculture and Textile Waste, Int. J. Poly. Sci. 2023, Article ID 5872605, 21, https://doi.org/10.1155/2023/5872605.

# Chapter-12

# Emerging Materials: Biopolymers and Nanocomposites

Dr. Pravinkumar Nagore[1],

Dr. Pravin Chavan[2],

Dr. Jagdish Thakur[3],

Dr. Baliram Vibhute[4],

Mr. Amol Ghoti[5],

Dr. Kanchan Mane[6]*.

**Abstract:**

Composite materials, such as biopolymers and biopolymer-based nanocomposites, are increasingly in demand. Biopolymers, derived from living organisms, are both biodegradable and biocompatible, while nanocomposites share similar properties. These materials find wide applications, including wastewater treatment, food packaging, medical and biomedical fields, energy storage, and tissue engineering. This chapter explores the sources, classifications, and applications of these two emerging material types.

**Keywords:** Biopolymers, Emerging Materials, Nanocomposites.

**Introduction:**

Plastic pollution has become a critical environmental hazard, spreading across ecosystems and posing serious risks to environmental balance and human health. Beyond their intrinsic properties, plastics serve as effective carriers for harmful substances like pesticides, polycyclic aromatic hydrocarbons (PAHs), diphenyl compounds, and pharmaceutical residues. They are extensively used in areas such as packaging and water bottles. Plastics, primarily composed of synthetic organic polymers, have various applications from food packaging (such as snack wrappers) and clothing (like raincoats) to construction materials. The widespread use of plastics has ingrained them deeply into our environment, creating a significant challenge to mitigate their impact, especially in aquatic and wildlife ecosystems, which directly influence the broader environment. Typically, we dispose of the plastic packaging from various products, but due to its durability, much of this plastic remains in the environment. In residential or everyday social settings, plastics are commonly composed of petroleum-based polymers. At the end of their life, these plastics often end up in landfills, where they accumulate with other municipal solid waste. The most harmful toxic chemicals found in plastics, known for their hazardous effects on human and animal health, include BPA (bisphenol A), phthalates, antimony trioxide, and polyfluorinated chemicals [1].

[1,2,3,4,5,6]*Doshi Vakil Arts College and G.C.U.B. Science & Commerce College, Goregaon-Raigad.*
*Email: kanchanmane13@gmail.com, pravin.nagore@gmail.com.*
*Corresponding author: Dr. Kanchan Mane

So, from the above discussion, one can understand that non-biodegradable synthetic polymers like plastic which are mainly comprised of polyethylene (PE), polypropylene (PP), etc., are damaging our surroundings and there is an urgent need for alternatives. We should approach a point where the production of biodegradable or recyclable plastics is imperative. These alternatives can help reduce oil dependency, lower $CO_2$ emissions, and decrease the volume of waste requiring disposal. Biopolymers are the best alternatives to this problem.

The Greek word Biopolymers refers to the polymer type originating from biological sources. The term "biopolymers" broadly can be used for natural polymers, occurring naturally in the environment (like cellulose/starch) or artificially shaped bio-based polymers, from natural capitals. They are long-chain covalently bonded bio-molecules comprised of monomeric repeating units. Examples include amino acids, sugars or nucleotides as their monomeric units, such as chitin, starch, cellulose, peptides, proteins, DNA, and RNA. Biopolymers are helpful in various contexts and find extensive applications in many aspects of modern life. Moreover, these materials form the foundation for manufacturing countless everyday items. They also play a crucial role in their respective industries and significantly impact the broader economy. The production of biopolymers, offering a more sustainable and eco-friendlier alternative to plastics, is rapidly expanding. The most popular applications for biopolymers are in the packaging, agricultural, and medical industries [2].

Nanoscience and nanotechnology have evolved into highly dynamic, essential, and expanding fields, focused on developing small particles with versatile applications across nutrition, agriculture, cosmetics, paints and coatings, personal care products, catalysts, energy production, lubricants, security printing, molecular computing, structural materials, drug delivery, medical therapies, pharmaceuticals, and diagnostics. Due to their extremely small size, nanomaterials have a high surface area-to-volume ratio, resulting in more surface atoms compared to microscale materials, enhancing material properties with minimal surface defects. Additionally, nanomaterials have led to the development of nanocomposites—engineered solid materials that combine two or more distinct constituents with different physical and chemical properties to create new substances. Nanocomposites, which are hybrids of polymers and inorganic solids (like clays and oxides) at the nanoscale, feature complex structures where one phase (such as nanoparticles or nanotubes) exhibits nanoscale morphology. These nanocomposites display superior properties to traditional micro composites when assembled [3].

**Biopolymers:**

As stated above, Biopolymers or biodegradable polymers are renewable natural resources generated from biological systems, such as plants, animals, and microorganisms, and/or chemically synthesized from the starting materials of natural fats or oils, sugars, and starch. Natural biopolymers serve as sustainable alternatives to synthetic polymers derived from non-renewable petroleum resources. These biodegradable polymers can break down through enzymatic actions of specific microorganisms, resulting in organic byproducts, methane, inorganic compounds, biomass, carbon dioxide, and water. Biopolymers present numerous advantages, including cost-effective extraction, biocompatibility, biodegradability, environmental sustainability, and the absence of environmental toxicity.

**Sources:**

Biopolymers are abundantly sourced from various biological materials, including plants, microorganisms, animals, and agricultural waste. Plants such as maize, barley, wheat, sorghum, cassava, potatoes, bananas, tapioca, and cotton are rich sources of biopolymers. Biopolymers can also be synthesized chemically from monomeric components like oils, sugars, and amino acids. Among animals, cattle are the primary sources, while corals, sponges, fish, lobster, etc., are key sources from marine environments. Common microbiological sources include algae, fungi, and yeasts.

Carbohydrate-rich biomass sources include agricultural residues, paper waste, crop remnants, green waste, and wood waste. Triglycerides are abundant in vegetable oils, such as sunflower, soybean, safflower, jojoba, rapeseed, castor, and meadowfoam oils. Vegetable oils, especially those derived from food production, offer excellent alternatives for synthesizing natural polymers. These biopolymers are naturally produced and can be degraded by microbial metabolism, yet they can also be melted and molded similarly to synthetic thermoplastics [4].

Pictorially it can be shown as follows:

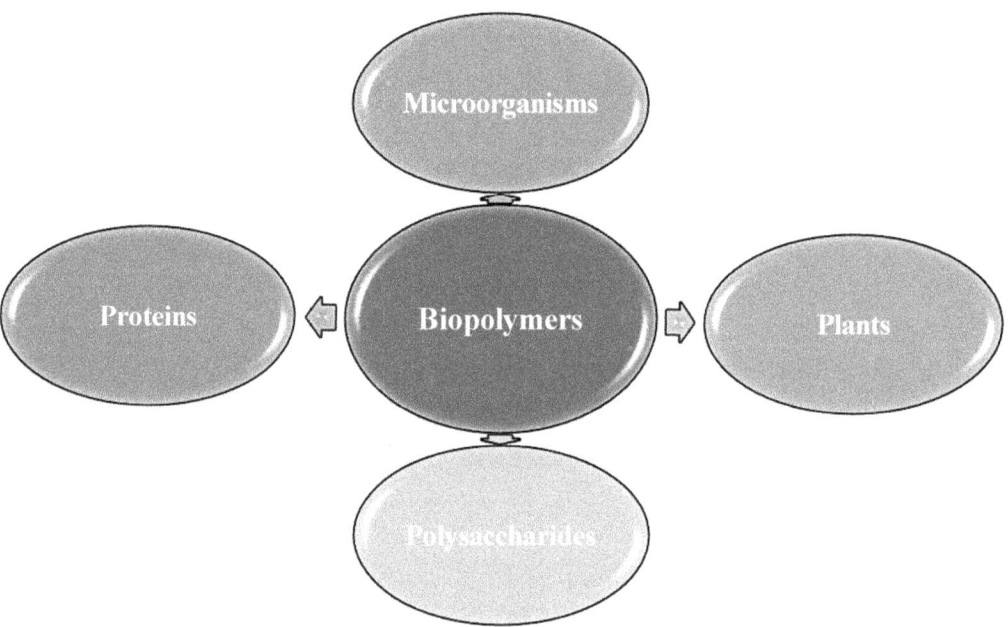

**Fig.1 Sources of Biopolymers**

**Classification:**

They can be categorized into three categories, based on their origin:

1. Natural biopolymers: These are biorenawable, biodegradable, non-toxic, non-adhesive biofunctional, biocompatible materials. Examples include cellulose, gelatin, starch, etc.
2. Synthetic polymers: These are the biopolymers with high reproducibility and high mechanochemical stability. Examples include polyvinyl alcohol, polycaprolactone, polylactic acid, etc.
3. Based on repeating units: These materials are categorized on the basis of repeating monomeric units. Examples, protein, nucleic acid, keratin, etc.

**Applications:**

1. **Drug delivery:** Biopolymers and their derivatives offer superior qualities, including excellent functionality, water solubility, non-toxicity, biodegradability, and biocompatibility. Additionally, they can reduce drug toxicity by enabling controlled drug release.

   Collagen, the most abundant protein in the animal kingdom, is composed of a repeating glycine–proline–hydroxyproline unit arranged in a triple-helix structure. Due to its high biocompatibility, collagen has been widely utilized in drug delivery applications in forms such as microparticles, coatings, and films [5].

   Chitosan-drug conjugation is one of the most effective methods for drug delivery. Chitosan of various molecular weights has been used to form these conjugates, with cleaving conditions that can be sensitive to pH or glutathione (GSH), depending on the type of drug. Producing chitosan hydrogels is also a viable approach for the delivery of sensitive proteins or genes [6].

2. **Agriculture Uses:** Various natural biopolymers with pesticide-active groups have been commercialized to create controlled-release formulations for fungicides and herbicides. When combined with one or more fungicides, gum-based biopolymers are particularly useful in protecting seeds from fungal pathogens. Naturally occurring compounds like chitin and chitosan have shown significant potential for managing plant diseases in agriculture, exhibiting antifungal, antiviral, antibacterial, and antiparasitic properties. Additionally, they have been used to chelate essential nutrients and minerals to block disease access and enhance plant defense. A degradable agricultural mulching film, made from a starch-polyvinyl alcohol blend containing up to 40% starch, urea, ammonia, and varying levels of low-density polyethylene (LDPE) and poly (ethylene-co-acrylic acid) (EAA), can be coated with a thin layer of water-resistant biopolymer [7,8].

3. **Environmental applications:** Biopolymers such as lipids, polysaccharides, and proteins have been increasingly sought as renewable raw materials, offering an eco-friendly alternative to non-biodegradable, petroleum-based plastics. Due to their thermoplastic nature, biopolymers exhibit many properties similar to conventional plastics. Unlike synthetic materials, however, they can biodegrade through the action of bacteria, fungi, and algae, producing end products like $CO_2$, water, and compost. Polyhydroxyalkanoates (PHA), a biopolymer produced by microorganisms, also possess physical characteristics similar to petroleum-based plastics, ranging from rigidity and brittleness to flexibility. Biopolymers can improve soil properties due to their biodegradability, which is environmentally friendly. Unlike Microbially Induced Calcite Precipitation (MICP), biopolymer treatment can be applied to soils with a finer particle size distribution. Another advantage of biopolymers over MICP is that they do not require nutrient injections before application for soil enhancement. Studies have demonstrated that biopolymers such as Guar Gum (GG), Xanthan Gum (XG), Chitosan (CS), and Beta 1,3/1,6 Glucan (BG) can significantly improve the engineering properties of soil [9,10].

4. **Food packing:** Polyhydroxyalkanoates (PHAs) are now among the most promising alternatives to fossil-based polymers in the bioeconomy, showing great potential to replace polyolefins in packaging applications due to their biocompatibility and favorable physical properties. Although cellulose acetate does not have ideal gas and moisture barrier properties for food packaging, it is well-suited for items requiring high moisture levels, as it permits breathability and prevents

fogging. Recent studies indicate that PE and polypropylene (PP) packaging films coated with chitosan (CS) and polyphenol colloidal formulations hold significant potential as active (antioxidant and antibacterial) packaging materials in the food industry [11].

5. **Energy applications**: Biopolymers are often used in the study of polymer electrolytes, where membranes containing ions dissolved within the polymer act as the electrolyte. Ionic conduction in these systems requires electron-donating atoms such as nitrogen (N), oxygen (O), or sulfur (S) within the polymer, with dissolved salt cations interacting only weakly with these atoms. Conductivity in polymer electrolytes depends on both cations and anions. Among the atoms in biopolymers, only oxygen (O) and nitrogen (N) possess lone pairs of electrons. The chitosan backbone includes hydroxyl, ether (C–O–C), and amine functional groups, allowing it to be tailored to specific application needs. Its water-attracting properties are attributed to the polar functional groups present in its structure. Dissolving chitosan (CS) in acetic acid results in a membrane layer with very low room-temperature conductivity (approximately $10^{-10}$ to $10^{-9}$ S cm$^{-1}$). However, due to its excellent film-forming properties and capacity to solvate various inorganic salts, it can serve effectively as a matrix for ionic conduction. The addition of lithium or ammonium salts to chitosan enhances proton conductivity at room temperature. Particularly high conductivity of $(2.42 \pm 0.01) \times 10^5$ S cm$^{-1}$ was achieved using a blend of 70% phthaloyl chitosan and 30% NH$_4$SCN [12].

Recent studies have shown that polymer electrolyte membranes are highly efficient and energy-dense. Using biopolymers in polymer electrolyte fuel cells reduces $CO_2$ emissions, providing environmental benefits. Research has also demonstrated the potential of solid gellan gum (GG) as a polymer electrolyte for energy applications. This work developed a solid gel electrolyte based on carbohydrate polymers (Phytagel/GG) for energy use [13].

6. **Biomedical applications:** Biopolymers have been widely used in medical applications, including occlusion, covering, suturing, isolation, fixation, adhesion, cell proliferation, contact inhibition, controlled drug delivery, and tissue guidance. Due to their exceptional flexibility and reliable knot strength, poly-(L-lactic acid), poly-(glycolic acid), and their copolymers are frequently used as suturing materials. Poly(ortho esters) and polymers with hydroxyl groups are commonly applied in drug delivery systems. Polyurethanes, which exhibit flexibility, durability, and resistance to wear, are essential for the creation of artificial blood vessels. Polyesteramides are beneficial in drug delivery, hydrogel formation, and tissue engineering. They are also used in a variety of medical products, including surgical masks, gowns, gloves, sanitary napkins, towels, surgical headgear, diapers, antimicrobial textiles for surgical curtains, and wipes. In surgical gowns, bio-based PET can be used as an alternative to cotton, polyester, and polyethylene (PE)[14].

7. **Water treatment:** Owing to the exceptional properties of biopolymers, using natural polymers in membrane synthesis, production, and manufacturing to create fully biodegradable membrane materials has become both ideal and attractive. Recently, the adsorption-desorption process has been applied to remove chlorophenoxyacetic acid herbicides from water using orange peel-activated carbon. As a result, these bio-based activated carbons effectively absorbed significant amounts of chlorophenoxyacetic acid herbicides from water. Biopolymers can also be used to modify membranes. Cellulose polymers, with their abundance of polysaccharides, have been widely applied in water treatment applications. Membranes made from carboxymethyl cellulose

(CMC), cellulose nanofibrils (CNF), and bacterial cellulose (BC) are modified cellulose materials with various functions. These modified membranes have been shown to effectively remove azo and anthraquinone dyes from wastewater [15].

Biopolymer-based flocculants hold great potential for large-scale commercial use. A triangle assessment model was developed to evaluate the effectiveness of these biopolymer-based flocculants in wastewater treatment, focusing on economic sustainability. Chemical flocculants such as polyaluminum chloride (PAC) have been used to remove chemical oxygen demand (COD), suspended solids (SS), and aluminum ($Al^{3+}$) from contaminated water during treatment. Chitosan (CS) composite flocculants, made by combining CS, polyaluminum chloride, and silicate, have been found to be more effective in removing contaminants compared to traditional flocculants [16,17].

8. **Tissue Engineering applications:** Chitosan possesses several remarkable properties, including the ability to form gels, enhanced adsorption capacity, excellent biodegradability, high biocompatibility, and non-cytotoxicity. Additionally, it exhibits improved biological activities such as antifungal, antibacterial, and antitumor effects. The hydrogel form of chitosan is particularly popular in tissue engineering due to its strong support for cell adhesion, survival, interaction, and neurite outgrowth. Elastin, a structural protein known for its long-term stability, elasticity, self-assembly, and biological activity, provides elasticity to organs and tissues. It is found in organs like elastic ligaments, blood vessels, skin, and lungs, where elasticity is crucial. Given its role in providing elasticity to body parts such as the skin and blood vessels, incorporating elastin into biomaterials is vital, especially for applications in soft tissue regeneration [18].

**Nanocomposites:** These are the combination of different materials, with at least one of the components having a size between 1 and 100 nm. The incorporated nanomaterials can include nanoparticles, nanofibers, carbon nanotubes, or activated carbon. The fundamental building blocks of nanocomposites are metals, ceramics, and polymers. These materials exhibit a blend of properties from their individual components, resulting in enhanced and advanced characteristics for the nanocomposite.

**Classification:** Nanocomposites are categorized based on their structure, with various nanoparticles and matrix materials utilized in their formation. Depending on the type of matrix or host material employed, nanocomposites can be classified into three main types: 1. Ceramic Matrix Nanocomposites (CMNC), 2. Metal Matrix Nanocomposites (MMNC), and 3. Polymer Matrix Nanocomposites (PMNC).

1. **Ceramic Matrix Nanocomposites (CMNC):** These are emerging engineering materials with a wide range of applications in electrical and mechanical fields. Various synthesis methods have been reported in the literature for their production. These include the spray pyrolysis method, polymer precursor route, and powder-based techniques. Additionally, chemical methods such as the sol-gel technique, colloidal route, precipitation method, and template synthesis are also commonly employed[19].

2. **Metal Matrix Nanocomposites (MMNC):** These are created by embedding nanoparticles within a metal or metal alloy matrix. These composites exhibit unique properties distinct from the host matrix, making them suitable for various applications such as display screens, electronics, LED

devices, storage devices, and more. The properties of the nanocomposite can vary depending on the type and size of the nanoparticles used, as changes in particle size can alter their characteristics. By incorporating nanoparticles into the matrix material, properties such as mechanical strength, damping, and resistance can be significantly enhanced. Common preparation techniques for MMNCs include pyrolysis, liquid metal infiltration, vapor deposition, solidification method, and chemical methods like colloidal and sol-gel processes, etc, [20].

3. **Polymer Matrix Nanocomposites (PMNC):** These are advanced materials formed by incorporating nanoparticles into a polymer matrix. Polymers, which are composed of monomers, serve as the matrix in these composites. Polymer nanocomposites consist of nanosized inorganic particles uniformly dispersed within the polymer matrix, leveraging the synergistic properties of both components. These materials exhibit enhanced electronic, ionic, mechano-chemical properties, making them suitable for wide applications.

By integrating the unique properties of inorganic nanoparticles, such as electrical, mechanical, catalytic, and magnetic characteristics, with the flexibility, lightweight nature, and cost-effectiveness of organic polymer matrices, polymer nanocomposites create innovative materials with diverse functionalities. These composites combine the processability and versatility of polymers with the advanced features of nanoscopic materials, enabling the development of materials for numerous applications [20].

**Synthetic routes:** Bio-renewable nanocomposites primarily consist of three key components: a polymer matrix, nanofillers, and an interaction zone. Various strategies have been employed for their fabrication, typically involving mechanical or chemical methods. Commonly used techniques include template synthesis (sol-gel technology), melt intercalation, exfoliation adsorption, and, in situ intercalative polymerization as illustrated below:

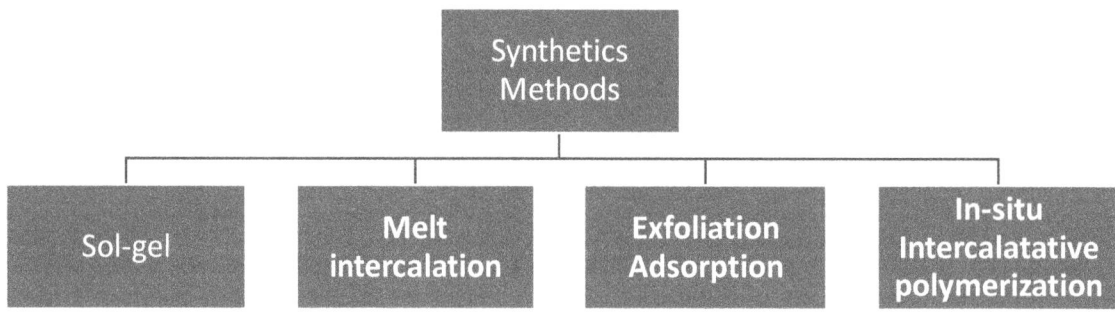

**Fig. 2 Synthetic Methods of Nano-composites**

**I. Melt intercalation:** In this method of nanocomposite preparation, high-molecular-weight polymer matrices are melted at elevated temperatures. Nanofillers are then incorporated into the molten polymer, and the mixture is thoroughly kneaded using a mixer to achieve a uniform composition [21]. Polycaprolactone/chitosan/CaCO$_3$ type of nanocomposites are prepared using this method. It is simple, compatible, and cost-effective with the other polymer industry's processes. It can be represented as follows:

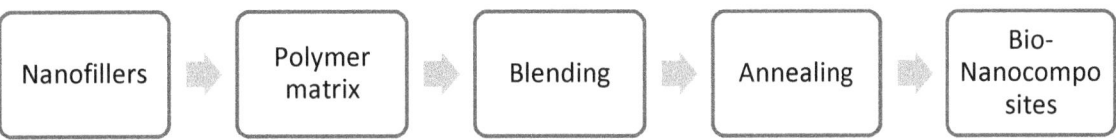

**Fig. 3 Melt intercalation general process**

**II. Sol-gel process:** Here, the inorganic material or nanofiller is synthesized within the polymer matrix, which facilitates the nucleation and growth of the host nanofillers. As the nanofillers form, they become embedded within the layers of the polymer matrix. This approach is considered the most effective method for achieving nanoscale dispersion of layered nanofillers within polymer matrices[22]. CuO@Alg nanocomposite, TiO2 -chitosan NCs can be synthesized using this method. The procedure can be represented as follows:

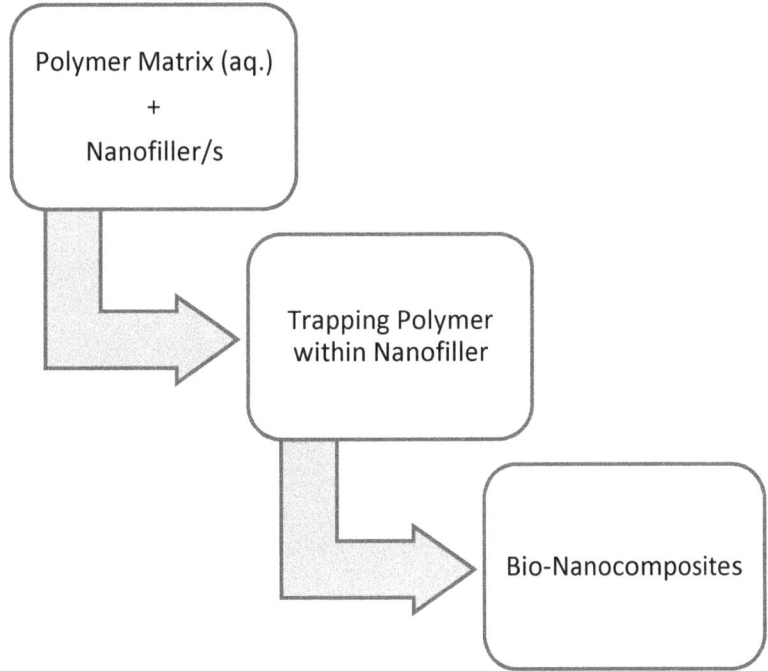

**Fig. 4 Sol-gel process**

**III. Exfoliation adsorption:** In this method, nanofiller materials are first dispersed in a solvent, such as water, chloroform, or toluene, in which the polymer or prepolymer matrix is soluble. The nanofillers are then mixed with the polymer solution, initiating an intercalation and displacement process within the interlayers of the nanofillers. During this process, the polymer matrix adsorbs onto the nanofiller material. A polymer-layered nanocomposite is subsequently formed through solvent evaporation or precipitation [23]. MgAl-layered double hydroxide/poly(vinyl alcohol) nanocomposite, poly(L-lactic acid)/layered silicate nanocomposite are prepared by this route.

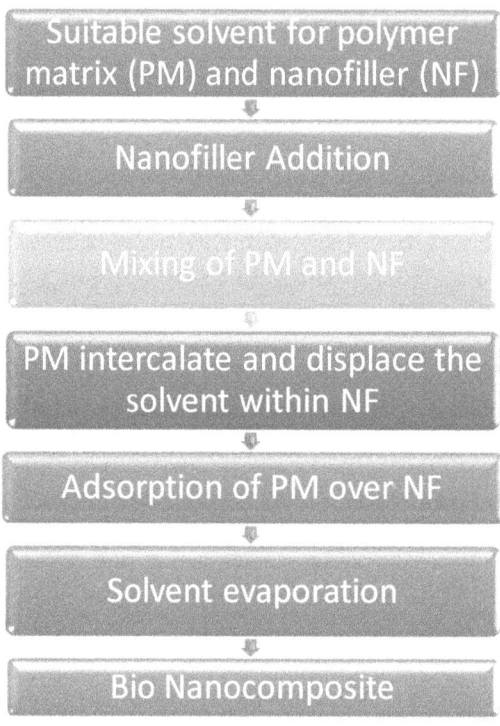

Fig.5 Exfoliation adsorption process

**Applications:**

1. **Medical applications:** Bionanocomposites are well-suited for a variety of medical applications due to their natural abundance, versatility, and eco-friendly nature. Some of the examples are as below:

Silver-coated lignin-core nanoparticles are used as antibacterial agents and drug delivery [24], $CeO_2$/chitosan nanocomposites are useful as biosensors for cholesterol levels [25], Chitosan-silver nanocomposites act as sensor of mercury [26], Hydroxyapatite/starch NC is used in bone recovery products [27].

2. **Packaging:** The integration of nanofillers, such as nano clays, into biopolymers significantly enhances the properties of nanocomposites. Polylactic acid (PLA)/clay nanocomposites have been employed in the production of items like cutlery, cups, and food containers. These materials find applications in food coatings, packaging, and as encapsulation matrices for functional foods. Food-grade polymers, including chitosan, alginate, carboxymethyl cellulose, gelatin, carrageenan, and pectin, are widely utilized in various microencapsulation technologies [28].

3. **Energy storage:** The nanocomposite electrode fabricated by coating a copper substrate with a mixture of silicon nanoparticles and lignin exhibited excellent electrochemical performance. It achieved a maximum initial discharge capacity of 3086 mAh $g^{-1}$ and retained 2378 mAh $g^{-1}$ after 100 cycles at a current density of 1 A $g^{-1}$.

Pectin combined with lithium perchlorate ($LiClO_4$) was employed as a solid biopolymer electrolyte. AC impedance analysis revealed that at room temperature, the maximum ionic conductivity reached approximately 5.15105 Scm-1, which is three orders of magnitude higher than that of the pure pectin polymer membrane [29].

4. **Water treatment:** Silica-gelatin hybrid composite (24% wt) was useful in the Hg (II) adsorption in aqueous solutions. Starch/MnO2/cotton nanocomposite is utilized widely as a photocatalyst. Starch-graft-poly(acrylamide)/graphene-oxide/hydroxyapatite nanocomposite is used to remove malachite green dye removal from wastewater. Starch/MnO2/cotton hydrogel nanocomposite is used as a useful photocatalyst. MnO2-coated cellulose nanofibers have been useful for the removal of methylene blue dye. CdS coated nano-ZnO/chitosan hydrogel find useful in the removal of congo red dye from water bodies. $MnO_2$/graphene aerogel is useful in the removal of rhodamine B dye [30].

**Conclusion:** The emerging policies addressing environmental concerns and advanced technologies have sparked increased interest in minimizing the use of non-biodegradable and non-renewable polymer materials. This shift focuses on replacing such materials with bio-based polymers for nanocomposites across a range of applications. This chapter provides insights into biopolymers, nanocomposites, and their diverse applications in various fields of human interest.

**References:**

1. Khare, R., & Khare, S. (2023). Polymer and its effect on environment. *Journal of the Indian Chemical Society*, *100*(1), 100821.

2. Mohan, S., Oluwafemi, O. S., Kalarikkal, N., Thomas, S., & Songca, S. P. (2016). Biopolymers–application in nanoscience and nanotechnology. *Recent advances in biopolymers*, *1*(1), 47-66.

3. Colusso, E., & Martucci, A. (2021). An overview of biopolymer-based nanocomposites for optics and electronics. *Journal of Materials Chemistry C*, *9*(17), 5578-5593.

4. Baranwal, J., Barse, B., Fais, A., Delogu, G. L., & Kumar, A. (2022). Biopolymer: A sustainable material for food and medical applications. *Polymers*, *14*(5), 983.

5. Biswas, M. C., Jony, B., Nandy, P. K., Chowdhury, R. A., Halder, S., Kumar, D., ... & Imam, M. A. (2022). Recent advancement of biopolymers and their potential biomedical applications. *Journal of Polymers and the Environment*, 1-24.

6. Prabaharan, M., & Mano, J. F. (2004). Chitosan-based particles as controlled drug delivery systems. *Drug delivery*, *12*(1), 41-57.

7. El Hadrami, A., Adam, L. R., El Hadrami, I., & Daayf, F. (2010). Chitosan in plant protection. *Marine drugs*, *8*(4), 968-987.

8. Averous, L. (2004). Biodegradable multiphase systems based on plasticized starch: a review. *Journal of Macromolecular Science, Part C: Polymer Reviews*, *44*(3), 231-274.

9. Rendón-Villalobos, R., Ortíz-Sánchez, A., Tovar-Sánchez, E., & Flores-Huicochea, E. (2016). The role of biopolymers in obtaining environmentally friendly materials. *Composites from renewable and sustainable materials*, *151*.

10. Soldo, A., Miletić, M., & Auad, M. L. (2020). Biopolymers as a sustainable solution for the enhancement of soil mechanical properties. *Scientific Reports*, *10*(1), 267.

11. Torres-Giner, S., Figueroa-Lopez, K. J., Melendez-Rodriguez, B., Prieto, C., Pardo-Figuerez, M., & Lagaron, J. M. (2021). Emerging trends in biopolymers for food packaging. *Sustainable Food Packaging Technology*, 1-33.

12. Winie T, Arof AK (2016) Biopolymer electrolytes for energy devices. Nanostruct Polym Membr Appl 2:311–356.

13. Torres-Giner, S., Figueroa-Lopez, K. J., Melendez-Rodriguez, B., Prieto, C., Pardo-Figuerez, M., & Lagaron, J. M. (2021). Emerging trends in biopolymers for food packaging. *Sustainable Food Packaging Technology*, 1-33.

14. Biswas, M. C., Jony, B., Nandy, P. K., Chowdhury, R. A., Halder, S., Kumar, D., ... & Imam, M. A. (2022). Recent advancement of biopolymers and their potential biomedical applications. *Journal of Polymers and the Environment*, 1-24.

15. Maleš, L., Fakin, D., Bračič, M., & Gorgieva, S. (2020). Efficiency of differently processed membranes based on cellulose as cationic dye adsorbents. *Nanomaterials*, *10*(4), 642.

16. Jiang, X., Li, Y., Tang, X., Jiang, J., He, Q., Xiong, Z., & Zheng, H. (2021). Biopolymer-based flocculants: A review of recent technologies. *Environmental Science and Pollution Research*, *28*, 46934-46963.

17. Mahmood, H., & Moniruzzaman, M. (2019). Recent advances of using ionic liquids for biopolymer extraction and processing. *Biotechnology Journal*, *14*(12), 1900072.

18. Biswal, T. (2021). Biopolymers for tissue engineering applications: A review. *Materials Today: Proceedings*, *41*, 397-402.

19. Wei, W., Yu, D., & Huang, Q. (2020). Preparation of Ag/TiO2 nanocomposites with controlled crystallization and properties as a multifunctional material for SERS and photocatalytic applications. *Spectrochimica Acta Part A: Molecular and Biomolecular Spectroscopy*, *243*, 118793.

20. Koo, J. H. (2006). *Polymer nanocomposites*. New York, NY, USA: McGraw-Hill Professional Pub.

21. Balakrishnan, H., Hassan, A., Imran, M., & Wahit, M. U. (2012). Toughening of polylactic acid nanocomposites: A short review. *Polymer-Plastics Technology and Engineering*, *51*(2), 175-192.

22. Siddiqui, V. U., Khan, I., Ansari, A., Siddiqui, W. A., & Khursheed Akram, M. (2018). Structural and Morphological Analysis of Newly Synthesized CuO@ Alginate Nanocomposite with Enriched Electrical Properties. In *Advances in Polymer Sciences and Technology: Select Papers from APA 2017* (pp. 21-28). Springer Singapore.

23. Krikorian, V., & Pochan, D. J. (2003). Poly (L-lactic acid)/layered silicate nanocomposite: fabrication, characterization, and properties. *Chemistry of Materials*, *15*(22), 4317-4324.

24. Richter, A. P., Brown, J. S., Bharti, B., Wang, A., Gangwal, S., Houck, K., ... & Velev, O. D. (2015). An environmentally benign antimicrobial nanoparticle based on a silver-infused lignin core. *Nature nanotechnology*, *10*(9), 817-823.

25. Malhotra, B. D., & Kaushik, A. (2009). Metal oxide–chitosan based nanocomposite for cholesterol biosensor. *Thin Solid Films, 518*(2), 614-620.

26. Nivethaa, E. A. K., Narayanan, V., & Stephen, A. (2015). Synthesis and spectral characterization of silver embedded chitosan matrix nanocomposite for the selective colorimetric sensing of toxic mercury. *Spectrochimica Acta Part A: Molecular and Biomolecular Spectroscopy, 143*, 242-250.

27. Miculescu, F., Maidaniuc, A., Voicu, S. I., Thakur, V. K., Stan, G. E., & Ciocan, L. T. (2017). Progress in hydroxyapatite–starch based sustainable biomaterials for biomedical bone substitution applications. *ACS Sustainable Chemistry & Engineering, 5*(10), 8491-8512.

28. Roohi, Srivastava, P., Bano, K., Zaheer, M. R., & Kuddus, M. (2018). Biodegradable smart biopolymers for food packaging: Sustainable approach toward green environment. *Bio-based Materials for Food Packaging: Green and Sustainable Advanced Packaging Materials*, 197-216.

29. Patra, N., Ramesh, P., Donthu, V., & Ahmad, A. (2024). Biopolymer-based composites for sustainable energy storage: recent developments and future outlook. *Journal of Materials Science: Materials in Engineering, 19*(1), 34.

30. Adeola, A. O., & Nomngongo, P. N. (2022). Advanced Polymeric Nanocomposites for Water Treatment Applications: A Holistic Perspective. *Polymers 2022, 14, 2462.*

# Chapter-13

# Advanced Uses of Sustainable Biobased Composites: Current Developments and Prospects

Avinash Gaur[1],
Shailendra Badal[2]
Surabhi Yadav[3]

**Abstract:**

An innovative substitute for traditional non-renewable synthetic fibers like glass and carbon-reinforced composites, as well as efforts to configure biobased composite materials for various end-use applications, have been encouraged by growing environmental and sustainability concern. However, biocomposite materials are not a perfect replacement; they have certain disadvantages, including low thermal stability, poor electrical properties, fiber/matrix incompatibility, flammability, extraction, processing, machining, surface modification, manufacturing, and highly anisotropic properties. Many studies have been conducted recently to address the issues related to long-term durability, serviceability, characteristics, and sustainability (by implementing a circular economy in biocomposites). This article offers a critical analysis of recent research related to several biocomposite-related topics. The most common biopolymers and biofibers (derived from natural and synthetic resources) used to create biocomposites are first reviewed, along with their extraction, chemical makeup, physical and mechanical characteristics. Advanced production techniques, fiber hybridization, fiber treatment and modification, filler integration, and the search for new biofiber and polymer resources are some of the methods and developments in improving the qualities of biocomposites. In order to fulfill the goals of lightweight composites, the current methods and advancements used for the production of biocomposites are also examined, with a focus on additive manufacturing techniques. There is also a thorough discussion of the advantages and disadvantages of fused filament fabrication additive manufacturing techniques for biocomposites. For their potential use in many high-performance applications, this article offers essential information on cutting-edge bio-based materials and their composites.

**Key words:** Biodegradable composites, biofibers, composites materials, biopolymers.

**1. Introduction:** The term "composite" refers to any material adhered to, in, or between one or more other materials, or any material composed of any two components joined with a defined interface.

[1]*Department of Chemistry, Bipin Bihari College, Jhansi, U.P. (India)*
[2]*Department of Applied Science and Humanities, Rajkiya Engineering College, Banda, U.P. (India)*
[3]*Department of Chemistry, Bipin Bihari College, Jhansi, U.P. (India)*
*Email: avinashgaur112@gmail.com, surabhiyadav1764@gmail.com, Badal70@rediffmail.com*

The word "composite" is typically used to describe engineering structural materials reinforced with fiber that are continuous or long enough to be oriented in a single direction to create improved strength qualities.

Two materials are combined to create composites, where one of the materials referred to as the reinforcing phase is embedded in the other material referred to as the matrix phase in the form of fiber, sheets, or particles. Materials that can be used as the matrix and reinforcement include metal, ceramic, and polymers. In most cases, the matrix is a ductile or tough material, while the reinforcing materials are strong and have low densities. The invention of composite materials was prompted by the combination of these materials, which offer them properties like low density, high strength, abrasion, corrosion, resistance, etc. that the separate materials do not have.

The development of biocomposites has led to significant developments in the field of green materials, owing to concerns about sustainability and the environment [1]. Because of the increasing need for the use of nonrenewable resources, the scientific and industrial communities have come to recognize eco-friendly materials, recycling, and reusing. Biocomposites made from biofiber and biopolymers are appealing from this angle since they can offer the necessary qualities and functions at a fair price.

Whereas composites made of synthetic materials cannot be easily recycled or disposed of after their service life without harming the environment, these biocomposite materials (the reinforcements and the matrix are both biodegradable) can. A new survey indicates that the worldwide biocomposites market would expand at a compound annual growth rate (CAGR) of 11.8% between 2016 and 2024. With the largest utilization in the building industry (56.0%), the biocomposite market was estimated to be worth USD 4.46 billion in 2016. The biocomposites market is expected to grow from $4.46 billion in 2016 to $10.89 billion by 2024, according to the industry prediction analysis. To put it another way, the percentage of materials made from biobased feedstock is expected to increase from 5% in 2004 to 12% in 2010, roughly 18% in 2020, and roughly 25% in 2030 [1]. Biocomposites are not a novel material to humanity. In particular, the Great Wall of China was constructed using biomaterials such as clay bricks, clay, stone, red willow reeds, willow branches, reeds, and sand in 121 B.C.; Mongolian bows were made from wood or silk, animal horns, and tendons, *etc.* in 1200 A.D. Regarding the utilization of different raw materials, processing, characterization, applications, *etc.*, biocomposites have seen significant developments. Hemp, wood, basalt, rice husk, coir, sisal, ramie, flax, kenaf, jute, and other biofibers have garnered a lot of attention as a possible substitute for synthetic fibers like carbon and glass. Due to their recognition as reinforcing materials in multiple matrices and the increased use of products made from them on a commercial scale in recent years, biofibers, whose extraction is a crucial step that affects the characteristics of the reinforcements, can improve rural communities' living conditions and generate jobs in rural areas (through the collection, transportation, and processing of new materials).

Biofibers reinforced with various biothermoplastic polymers (*poly(hydroxy alkanoates,* PHA) and *polylactic acid* (PLA) and biothermoset polymers (*polyester and epoxy*) have been the subject of numerous studies on their mechanical and functional behaviour [2, 3]. A wide range of secondary applications in the automotive, packaging, electronics, aerospace, and civil sectors have made extensive use of biocomposites. Compared to their conventional counterparts, biocomposites have several notable advantages, including relatively high specific mechanical properties, thermal insulation, $CO_2$ neutrality, good damping properties, high health safety, good fatigue, abrasive and corrosion resistance, availability, high acoustic insulation, low density, low production energy, and light weight. European automakers in particular have significantly increased the use of biocomposites in automobile components in recent years. European Union EURO 6 laws, which were implemented in 2020, impose significant taxes on cars that emit 95 g/km of $CO_2$ [4]. Using biocomposites to reduce weight helps the European Commission and the European Automobile Manufacturers Association achieve their $CO_2$ emission reduction targets. The End-of-Life Vehicle Directive of the European Union aims to recycle 95 weight percent of autos, as stated in Directive 2000/53/EC. Furthermore, the crops may develop an entirely new value chain if less prevalent biomaterials are used. In rural communities, biocomposite can provide immediate socioeconomic advantages, especially in less developed areas where these materials are readily available.

However, biocomposite materials are not a perfect replacement; they have a number of disadvantages, including poor resistance to moisture, incompatibility with fibers and matrix, logistical problems with supply, flammability, difficulty processing, and highly anisotropic properties (variability of fiber) [5]. Additionally, the properties of biofibers naturally differ depending on where they come from, which causes a large range in the durability and properties of biocomposites [6]. Realizing long-term durability and properties requires addressing various materials and processing-related issues. Because biofibers contain large amounts of cellulose, hemicelluloses, pectin, lignin, and other hydrophilic materials, they do not form good interfacial bonds when embedded in hydrophobic polymers [5]. These characteristics may eventually discourage the use of the composite in load-bearing applications across a range of sectors by causing the loss of final composite attributes like mechanical and thermal stability [3]. To address these compatibility problems with biocomposites, a number of strategies have been used, including hybridization, surface modification, and nanoengineering [7]. To increase their use, it is therefore crucial to have a deeper comprehension of the structural and morphological changes (structure-property correlations) that occur during the aforementioned procedures. Biological, physical, and chemical treatments can alter the fiber's surface by changing its hydroxyl and carbonyl groups, creating a rough surface topology, forming strong covalent bonds, and other effects.

The use of biofiber-based composites based on thermoplastic polymers, such as *nylon, butadiene-styrene (ABS), acrylonitrile , polyether-ether ketone (PEEK), polyethylene (PE), polypropylene (PP), and polyvinyl chloride (PVC)*, for high-performance engineering applications has grown recently [8]. Furthermore, thermoplastics are easier to manufacture and offer greater design freedom than thermosets and elastomers. However, there are a lot of end-of-life (*EoL*) problems, and these composites are not environmentally friendly. The ideal course of action would be to use biopolymers derived from biological resources to create biocomposites [9]. The biofibers and biopolymers (*cellulose, polylactic acid (PLA), collagen etc.*) have the same polarities, which results in biocomposites with better compatibility and interfacial adhesion than synthetic matrix-based composites. The low mechanical, long-term durability, thermal, and other qualities of such composites, however, prevent them from being widely used. Most biofibers and matrices have a tendency to become unstable at temperatures above 200°C and are not appropriate for processing at high temperatures [10].Biocomposites are hardly used. Biocomposites, like other materials, are always being scrutinized by the global market for competitiveness, necessitating ongoing study. Determining the qualities and processing methods of fibers, matrices, and their interfaces is essential for using biocomposites in innovative applications. Performance is determined by the synergistic combination of features arising from the elements and their interactions [11]. Thus, in order to attain the desired qualities, the development of biocomposites requires a thorough study and knowledge of the constituent ingredients. Furthermore, using biomaterials continuously is not a sustainable way to promote the benefits of biobased materials over their synthetic counterparts; instead, the entire manufacturing process must be made sustainable. The circular economy strategy can help with this, as it promotes the use of biomaterials that are readily recyclable and reusable, hence achieving sustainability [12]. This article offers a critical analysis of recent research on several biocomposite-related topics, such as extraction, materials, surface modification procedures, end-use applications, and perspectives for the future. The extraction, chemical makeup, and mechanical and physical characteristics of biopolymers and biofibers which are typically used to create biocomposites, are first reviewed. The methods and developments for improving the characteristics of biocomposites are also examined, such as fiber hybridization, fiber treatment and modification, filler integration, enhanced production processes, and the search for novel biofiber and polymer resources. After that, a discussion of the current methods and advancements used to produce biocomposites is held, with a focus on additive manufacturing. Lastly, a quick review of biocomposites' characterization methods, environmental impacts, main uses, trends, and difficulties is given. This article will serve as a crucial foundation for further study and biocomposites' industrialization.

**2. Biobased matrix materials:** In a composite material, a matrix system offers shape, appearance, and resistance to the environment, while a reinforcement system withstands the majority of mechanical loads (macroscopic stiffness and strength). Much research has recently been done on creating fully biodegradable materials (green composites) by fusing biofibers with a biodegradable polymer matrix. According to their source, biodegradable polymers can be broadly divided into two categories: synthetic and bio [13]. Biopolymers can be classified as biomass and microorganism products based on their synthesis process, whereas synthetic polymers can be classified as petro-products and biotechnology. With the exception of the polymer derived from fossil fuels, the majority of polymers come from sustainable biomass. Through fractionation, biomass is converted into the biomass products classified as natural origin polymers. Both biotechnology-based and microorganism-based polymers are produced by synthesizing natural monomers and fermenting biomass, respectively. By creating synthetic monomers, petrochemical-based polymers are produced. A large number of the biopolymer polymers mentioned above are commercially accessible. These biopolymers can all be recycled, composted, and utilized again in the future. A number of factors, including the materials used, their chemical structure, the environment, etc., affect how biopolymers degrade. The decomposition process is classified as compostable (bacterial action), hydrobiodegradable (water), photodegradable (light), and biodegradable (microorganisms). At now, biocomposites are widely used in consumer goods for either short-term or disposable purposes. They can also be used for longer periods of time indoors [14].

Biobased polymer compounds, such as starch, have been organically rediscovered as renewable resource-based plastic polymers. The goal is to recover and recycle polymers derived from fossil fuels. However, there is increasing interest in using more ecologically friendly biopolymers to replace fossil-based polymers because of their limited end-of-life options.

The most prevalent biopolymers, **polysaccharides**, are essential to the survival of living things. They are environmentally friendly and have multiple uses. Typically, they are identified as *proteins,* *cellulose, carbohydrates, etc.* Monosaccharides (mostly C, $H_2$, and $O_2$) make up a large number of polysaccharides. Five to six C atoms are often present in a monosaccharide molecule. Due to the presence of several hydroxyl groups (OH) in the monosaccharide, H bonds are frequently found in between polymer chains [15].

**Starch** is the most promising of the agro-based biopolymers due to its wide availability, affordability, and thermoplastic properties. However, these polymers have significant disadvantages, including poor mechanical behaviour, hydrophilia, and handling challenges, which make them unsuitable for a number of applications [16]. However, the cost of natural starch is higher than that of many manufactured polymers, which further restricts its use. Many natural resources (such as *roots, seeds, tubers, stems, etc.*) are a good source of starch. The starch is made up of repeating units of either *α-d-glucopyranosyl* or *homoglucan*, which can be arranged to produce either amylose or amylopectin [17]. The hydroxyl and acetal groups that make up the starch molecule are in charge of the substitution and chain breakage processes, respectively. Its hydroxyl group can react to produce starches with different characteristics [17]. Many techniques, including crosslinking, graft copolymerization, adding filler particles, chemical functionalization, and physical alteration of the internal morphology, can enhance the starch's mechanical behaviour and moisture resistance. Some novel fabrication techniques are used in the packaging industry to create starch. Additionally, the foam made from starch has insulating qualities similar to those of *polystyrene* foam. For loose-fill packaging applications, starch foams may be able to take the place of their *polystyrene* counterparts, according to Guan and Hanna [18]. This material provides great resistance, low density, and high compressibility, as well as shielding and stabilizing the items being packed. Proteins are biomass products that can be easily derived from agro-sources (plant and animal origin). Proteins are crucial macromolecules in biological systems that contain chains of alpha-amino acids. Polypeptide chains are created in plant protein by the chemical bonding of monomers of amino acids [19]. Plant proteins have a large molecular weight ($1.66 \times 10^{-19}$ g mol−1), which makes them a good option for polymer applications. Protease enzymes readily break down protein polymers. Proteins have a far lower breakdown temperature than other biopolymers, which restricts their potential blends.

The polymers of *hydroxy alkanoate* (HA), known as *poly(hydroxy alkanoates)*, are derived from a variety of natural sources, including $CO_2$, byproducts (like *molasses*), and renewable resources (like *cellulose* and *starch*) [20]. An ester bond is formed in PHA between the carboxyl group and the neighbouring monomers' hydroxyl groups. Large-scale bacterial PHA synthesis for industrial uses was documented by numerous authors. Compared to fossil-based polymers, the cost of manufacturing these materials is significantly higher. There are over 150 different kinds of HA monomers with various physical and chemical properties that have been identified based on the side chain's composition and geometrical parameters [21]. Polypropylene and polystyrene share mechanical characteristics with PHA copolymers, such as *scl-PHA (poly (3-hydroxybutyrate-co-3-hydroxy valerate (PHBV))*, mcl-PHA (poly(*3-hydroxyhexanoate-co-3-hydroxyoctanoate*) P(*3HHx-co-3HO*)), and copolymers of scl and mcl **PHA** monomers (lcl-PHA, two bonds on the left-hand side C14) [22].

Microorganism-induced enzymatic and non-enzymatic hydrolysis can break down PHAs in animal tissues. The biocompatible characteristics are influenced by various factors, including molecular mass, surface area, internal shape, stereoregularity, and chemical composition. Furthermore, the degradation characteristics are influenced by environmental factors as temperature, humidity, and pH. Tokiwa *et al.* found that internal morphological characteristics, moisture resistance balance, and chemical structure all influence PHA biodegradation. Therefore, mcl-PHA with low melting temperature and crystallinity degrades more readily than scl-PHA with high melting temperature and crystallinity. According to Wang *et al., poly (3-hydroxybutyrate-co-3-hydroxyhexanoate) (PHBHHx)* degraded more quickly when combined with gelatin [23]. They found that because of the decrease in crystallinity, blending decreased the weight. There are now two commercially available forms of PHB: plasticized and copolymerized.

The most popular thermoplastic polyester, **poly-lactic acid (PLA)**, has the potential to replace conventional polymers derived from fossil fuels. PLA is synthesized by polymerizing or polycondensing lactic acid. By fermenting agricultural products, lactic acid monomers can be processed on a larger scale. Stereochemical variants of lactic acid include *poly (d-lactic acid) (PDLA) and poly (l-lactic acid) (PLLA)* [24]. PLA's rate of biodegradability has been the subject of numerous studies. Temperature, duration, and residual catalyst concentration all have a significant impact on PLA degradation rate. Oligomers and catalysts accelerate the pace of degradation and lower the temperature at which it occurs. PLA is used in a variety of industrial fields because of its special qualities, including food packaging, tissue engineering, textiles, and auto parts. However, a number of significant disadvantages prohibit their use in a number of industries, including intrinsic brittleness, limited energy absorption, sluggish degradability, etc. Using life cycle evaluations, numerous studies were conducted to evaluate environmental durability.

**Polyurethanes** are polymeric structures made up of several urethane groups. A polyol and a poly-isocyanate undergo polyaddition to form polyurethanes, which can be joined by either linear or branching linkages. Additionally, the reaction of diisocyanates with diols can produce polyurethane. This polymer has a similar chemical structure to nylon. Based on their chemical makeup, polyurethanes can be broadly categorized as siloxane, carbonate, ether, and poly-ester urethanes. Due to the presence of glucose, fructose, and sucrose, polyester urethanes are readily biodegradable by microbial infection. Polyurethanes are used in many different products, such as car parts, adhesives, and insulators. These days, scaffolds, grafts, and implants are examples of biomedical and tissue engineering applications that use polyurethanes because of their high energy absorption, flexibility, and deformation stability properties. Polyurethane has a low melting point and is not very resistant to moisture [25].

**3. Properties of biopolymers:** The qualities of biopolymers are influenced by reinforcement, plasticizer type, and biopolymer mixture. The degree of flexibility in a biopolymer depends on its molecular weight, functional groups, and chemical structure. Amylose and amylopectin components, along with one or a combination of plasticizers, make up thermoplastic starch (TPS), a semi-crystalline and amorphous substance. TPS may undergo repeated hardening and softening since it is treated using shear pressures. Some of the drawbacks of TPS polymers are their high hydrophilia, poor mechanical responsiveness, and significant performance variations after processing. It also takes a few days for the characteristics to reach an equilibrium state. Typically, TPS is designed with additional chemicals to address these problems. Amorphous PLAs (Tg - 60°C) and semi-crystalline/crystalline PLAs (Tm - 130 to 180°C) are the two types of PLAs that are available. During various production processes (extrusion, casting, etc.), PLAs with poor melt elasticity characteristics experience various problems, such as high necking. PLAs have superior surface strength (which enables better printability), flexural stiffness, and heat stability. Additionally, they improve optical clarity and gloss. Hydroxyethylcellulose exhibits excellent stability in neutral/basic pH solutions, saline solutions, and heat. Good thermal stability, high water solubility, and good gelation ability are all attributes of methylcellulose [26]. Membranes, tissue engineering, and temperature-sensitive hydrogels all use methylcellulose.

**4. Applications of biopolymers:** An outstanding environmentally beneficial source of renewable energy is biobased membranes. Because of its high conductivity in an anhydrous environment, chitosan-based membranes have recently been used to produce fuel cells, replacing membranes based on perfluorosulphonic acid. Air filters based on biopolymers (*soy protein, chitosan, and cellulose,*) have significant absorption qualities that are comparable to those of synthetic filters. Because soy proteins have 18 amino acids with 60% active functional groups, they are used to capture airborne contaminants. As a possible bacterial filter, chitosan-based air filters are also used. The air-trapping mechanism involves hydrogen binding, polar hydrophilic bonding, charge-charge interactions, etc. Gram-negative E. coli bacteria are neutralized by the positively charged filters. Tissue engineering and tissue recovery are two applications for electrospun nanofibers made from biopolymers [27]. But nanofibers increase the healing period and significantly dry up the wound region.

Soy, whey, and other biopolymer-based protein films have poor oxygen permeability. Nevertheless, these films have a higher water vapour permeability than plastic alternatives. PLA is a polymer that could be used in packaging. In food packaging, cellophane covered with polyvinylidene chloride is used. Fire-retardant composites made of gluten and lanosol additives are used. Compared to fire retardants such as trabromobisphenol A and hexabromocyclododecane, which are often utilised, these biopolymer-based compounds demonstrated superior performance. Dialdehyde and triethylene glycol can be used to make gluten antibacterial [28]. Antimicrobial implants and coatings based on chitosan are used in tissue engineering. Peptides are used in the pharmaceutical industry. Polypeptides and other genetically coded peptides are also used in the food industry [29]. Peptides are susceptible to acidification and oxidative deterioration, though. Clinical trials also use peptide medications, such as AEZS108 (Phase II), NGR-hTNF (Phase III), and EP100 (Phase II). In the food, pharmaceutical, and biomedical industries, biopolymers are typically widely used. A product that is 100% bio-derived instead of 100% petroleum-derived is of greater interest to the industrial sector. Samson *et al.* [30] created a biocomposite for automotive applications using green epoxy resin and natural cellulose fabric. Green epoxy resin, as opposed to its non-renewable, petroleum-derived or synthetic competitors, is thought to be the best matrix material for composites in an effort to slow down climate change caused by greenhouse gas emissions. They observed that the cloth treated with alkali and the green epoxy polymer had a very good fiber-matrix bond. Green epoxy resin was found to have a curing temperature of 120°C and a glass transition temperature of 160°C to 180°C. 33 MPa was the tensile strength, and 207 MPa was the flexural strength.

**5. Future prospects for biopolymers:** The majority of biopolymers are currently used in the food and pharmaceutical industries. However, biopolymers are not used in the production of composites because of their poor thermo-mechanical qualities. Green resins made from *cashew nut juice, soybean oil, etc.,* have recently shown promise as matrix resins for composites. However, a number of investigations are proceeding as planned. Biopolymers are used in packing, medicine, agriculture, and other fields as a result of advancements in technology for creating high-performance biodegradable plastics. Research on biopolymer-based energy technologies is still in its infancy. For energy science applications, there are surprisingly few studies on biopolymers based on animal proteins, cellulose, and carrageenan. The industrial revolution in the near future is expected to be greatly aided by technological developments in the production of biopolymers (such as chemical and biological polymerisation) and new potential uses.

**6. Reinforcements for biobased composites:** Since 2800 BC, biofibers have been cultivated for a variety of domestic and household purposes with little use, but their increasing use in industrial sectors has been spurred by concerns about global climate change and the decline of petroleum products. Particularly since the 1940s, biofiber-based materials have been used in aeroplanes. There are several biological sources of biofibers, including plants, animals, minerals, and more. Composite materials use biofibers as reinforcements. Significant interest in using biofibers for structural applications has also been sparked by their very specialised mechanical qualities to cost ratio, especially for *jute, flax, hemp, and kenaf* [31].

**6.1 Classification of biofibers:** Biofibers are classified into three categories *i.e.* animal biofibers, mineral biofibers, and plant biofibers. Animal biofibers may be *wool* from sheep, *hairs* from human and other animals, and *silk* from silkworms. Asbestos and basalts are the examples of mineral biofibers. Similarly wood, stalks (*i.e., rice, maize, oat, rye, and barley*), grass (*i.e.,corn, bagasse, sabai,and rape*) leaf ( *i.e., raphia, abaca, sisal, and agave*), fruits (*i.e., oil palm and coir*), seed (*i.e., kapol, cotton, and milk weed*), and blast (*i.e., bamboo, rosella, hemp, jute, remie, mesta, flax, and kenaf*) are the plant biofibers.

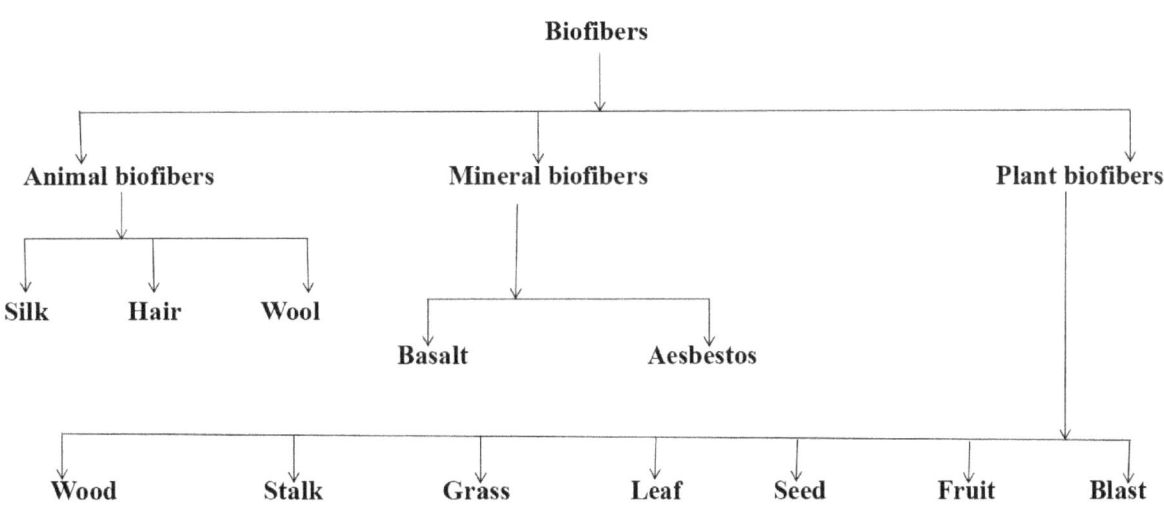

Figure 6.1 Classification of biofibers

**6.2 Processing techniques of biofibers:** The primary step in the biofiber processing process is the fiber extraction process. Several methods are used in the extraction and processing of plant fibers. The procedure with the greatest application is water retting. In order to prevent fibre deterioration during this retting process, the evaluation period should be continuously monitored. The processing time is also shortened by using various mechanical, enzymatic, chemical, and microbiological techniques [32]. By allowing more water to enter the centre section of the stem, the water retting process breaks out the bast fibers, the outermost layer of a stem. This process is carried out in ponds, lakes, *etc.* The industry does not frequently support this procedure because it is time-consuming and yields low-quality fibres [33]. On the other hand, the mechanical retting method quickly yields high-quality fibre. A mechanical decorticator with rollers and beaters is used to process a plant stem. Through this procedure, undesirable components like skin, gum, *etc.* are eliminated [34]. After processing, the fibres are cleaned and dried. Animal fibers are extracted in a variety of ways. For example, to extract silk fibers from cocoons, they are cooked in a soap solution [35]. Spider fibers are extracted by anaesthetized spiders. After that, brushes and a microscope are used to remove the fibres. A more efficient extraction technique must be created because this procedure takes a long time. After being manually processed, wool fibers are cleaned with water to get rid of contaminants. There have been several reported methods for stifling silk cocoons. The process of stifling silk cocoons involves exposure to the sun, water vapor, and dry air, in that order. A thorough description of these stages is provided in [36]. Recently, a mechanical homogeniser and ultrasonic irradiation were used to create silk nanofibers in a novel, non-toxic way. Another technique involves separating the silk glands from the Nephila clavipes spider using a weak acid. Silk nano-fibrils were extracted by certain researchers using sulphuric acid hydrolysis with ultrasonic assistance. The majority of conventional techniques for removing silk fibres need complex equipment, harmful chemicals, and additional time [37].

**6.3 Techniques for enhancing biofiber-based composites performance:** The majority of biocomposites are unsuitable for principal load-carrying members due to their poor mechanical qualities. Numerous factors contribute to this, including the different characteristics of biofibers that cause wide variations in quality; hydrophilicity that causes a mismatch with hydrophobic polymers; excessive moisture absorption, poor thermal stability, and challenging handling.

**6.3.1 Fibre treatment and modification:** To solve a biofiber's poor adherence and incompatibility in a matrix system, modification techniques and fibre treatment are used. This method makes handling easier, improves wetting and dispersion, and increases water resistance. Chemical, physical, and biological processes are examples of distinctive surface alteration techniques.

**6.3.1.1 Chemical modification:** Biocomposites undergo chemical treatments to improve their moisture resistance and fiber/matrix adhesion. Alkalisation, acetylation, salinisation, benzoylation, coupling agents, dewaxing, cyanoethylation, etherification, and so forth are examples of frequently used chemical treatments. The fibre and matrix can develop a chemical link thanks to these chemical treatments.

One of the most popular and cost-effective chemical processes for biofibers is **alkalisation**. The type and concentration of alkaline solution, reaction temperature, and reaction time all affect how successful it is. A higher alkali concentration than the critical threshold causes the fibre to delignify excessively, which weakens or damages the fibre. Alkalisation uses alkali to remove lignin, hemicellulose, oil, and wax prior to the production of biocomposite, which fibrillates and purifies fibres. By increasing the fiber's surface roughness, the alkalisation procedure improves adhesion and mechanical interlocking at the fiber/matrix contact. Alkalisation increased the amorphous content and decreased hydrogen bonding, according to numerous authors. Alkalisation of short sisal fiber-based biocomposites, pineapple leaf-based biocomposites, and bagasse fibre reinforced polyester biocomposites, all produced comparable outcomes (better interfacial characteristics) [38].

**Acetylation, or esterification**, is used to plasticise biofibers. Existing moisture is eliminated during the esterification process when the biofiber's hydrophilic hydroxyl groups react with the acetyl group. By decreasing the hydrophilic behaviour of biofibers, this improves the dimensional stability. As a result of the acetyl groups replacing the hydroxyl ones, the fibre becomes more hydrophobic after acetylation [39]. Biofibers undergo esterification to add acetyl groups to the cellulose, both with and without an acid catalyst. Acetic acid and acetic anhydride by themselves generally do not graft onto the biofibers in a suitable manner. The biofibers are treated with acetic acid for one to three hours at a high temperature, followed by acetic anhydride to promote the chemical reaction.

**Maleic anhydride (MHA)** additions provide an efficient fiber-matrix interaction among the many coupling agent-based chemical modification approaches. Covalent and hydrogen bonds can be formed with the biofibers' hydroxyl groups thanks to the maleic units. These interactions enhance the compatibility of fibre with polymers and lessen the hydrophilic character of fibre [40]. The mechanical, thermal, and interfacial adhesion characteristics of the composites are influenced by the MA-grafting level and the MA/polymer molecular weight. When maleic anhydride [MA]-grafted copolymers are used in PLA composites, biofiber/PP composites, and other materials, *miscanthus/PP, kenaf, wheat straw, coconut fibre, ramie, wood fibre, and reishi* (*Ganoderma lucidum*) fibres exhibit improved interfacial adhesion [41].

In order to strengthen the fiber/matrix interfacial connection, **silane coupling agents** are used. These are the main stages that this process goes through: Reactive silanol groups are released through (1) hydrolysis; (2) silanols self-condense; (3) silanols form hydrogen bonds with the hydroxyl groups in the reinforcement; and (4) covalent bonds are formed between silanol and hydroxyl groups (grafting) when heated. Numerous variables, including temperature, pH, hydrolysis time, etc., have a major impact on how well silane treatment works. Compared to the materials without treatment, silane treatment increased the mechanical response (yield stress and tensile strength) of *flax/PLA, kenaf/PLA, jute/PLA, ramie/PLA, sisal/PP, and PP/hemp* composites [39, 42, 43].

**6.3.1.2 Physical modification:** Corona discharge, steam explosion, autoclave treatment, and other physical alteration methods are examples [1]. All of these methods seek to lessen the disparity between the hydrophilic and hydrophobic properties of the fibre and the matrix in order to increase fiber–matrix adhesion. Without affecting the bulk structure of the resultant composites, plasma treatment provides a remarkable way to change the fibre and matrix systems physical and chemical properties [44]. Most often, plasma treatment is used to clean and etch the film surface for use in food packaging. In fact, adhesion and hydrophilicity of the films increase dramatically following exposure to the plasma treatment because the film surfaces develop polar groups. As a result, adding hydrophilic materials having antibacterial properties to the film surface could result in additional modification. On the other hand, steam explosion benefits lignocellulosic fibres mechanical and morphological characteristics, such as improved flexural qualities, reduced friction, and reduced modulus,. The steam explosion technique uses high-pressure steam to heat the fibres to high temperatures and pressures. The pretreated fibres are then mechanically disrupted by a violent explosion by discharge. Several lignocellulosic fibres are treated with this technique to increase their adhesion and dispersibility with the matrix system.

Park and their associates investigated how treated *poly(p-dioxanone)/PLA* biocomposites' interfacial characteristics were affected by oxygen plasma treatment. In order to improve the interfacial characteristics of *poly(p-dioxanone)/PLA* biocomposites by up to two times, they added polar functional groups. On the surface of the *poly(p-dioxanone)* fibre, oxygen-based functional groups are induced by oxygen plasma treatment. The adherence of *hydroxyl/carboxyl* groups on the fibre surface and hydrogen in PLA is enhanced by primary covalent and secondary hydrogen bonding. The impact of argon and plasma treatment on the interfacial characteristics between sisal fibre and polypropylene matrix was investigated by Yuan *et al.* [45]. They found that sisal fibre treated with plasma has better interfacial qualities than sisal fibre treated with argon. The interfacial characteristics of jute fibres treated with argon plasma were examined by Sinha and Panigrahi [46]. On the surface of the treated fibres, they noticed rougher fibers with pits. When using a corona discharge approach on miscanthus biofibers, Ragoubi *et al.* [48] observed chemical oxidation and physical etching, which improved the mechanical characteristics.

**6.3.1.3 Biological methods:** To alter the biofibers, biological agents—such as fungus and enzymes—are also used as an alternative to chemical and physical methods. Compared to traditional methods, biological treatments provide many benefits. They can accurately remove hemicellulose and hydrophilic pectin while using less energy. Kardas *et al.* [49] investigated the micro-topography of polyester fabric using enzymes including *Esterase, Lipozyme, Lipase A, and, Lipase AK,* . They found that the best method for producing a more uniform and even textured biofabric was to treat it with esterase enzyme. Li and Pickering [50] used chelators and enzymes to extract hemp fibre from a bundle. The hemp fiber's crystallinity and thermal responsiveness were improved by this procedure.

Pietak and their colleagues [51] assessed the surface wettability of biofiber using contact angle measurements and atomic force microscopy. As secondary cell walls were revealed by biological and chemical changes, they observed an increase in adhesion force for the changed fibres. The enzymes were successful in improving the fineness of the bamboo fibre, presumably by removing the polar hemicellulose material, according to a recent study on the fibre using biological treatments [52]. It was discovered that enzymatic biological treatments could improve the fineness of hemp fibres by eliminating contaminants from their surface.

**7. Processing and manufacturing of biocomposites:** Fabrication is the process of transforming raw materials (fibres and resin ingredients) into composites with the required size, shape, and characteristics. The mechanical response of biocomposites is significantly influenced by processing conditions and manufacturing techniques. Biofiber-reinforced composites are often made using the same technology used to create synthetic fiber-reinforced composite materials. For thermoplastic-based biofiber-reinforced biocomposites, conventional manufacturing techniques including extrusion, moulding (injection, compression, etc.), filament winding, etc., are suitable and being researched. On the other hand, resin transfer moulding (RTM) and sheet moulding compound (SMC) are used in the production of thermoset-based biocomposites. Therefore, the designer would heavily focus on a number of aspects, including required attributes, dimension, fabrication rate, handling qualities, and fabrication cost, in order to choose an acceptable technique to make biocomposites.

**7.1 Factors influencing biocomposites production:** The production of biocomposites is always complicated by the low stability of biobased raw materials because these processes are designed for synthetic materials. Therefore, a fundamental step in creating biocomposite materials using traditional manufacturing techniques is pretreatment or alteration of the raw materials to improve the composites' characteristics and processability. In biocomposites, control over heat stability, hydrophilicity, fiber distribution, fiber type, content, and machining is essential to achieving desirable properties.

**7.1.1 Content of moisture and hydrophilicity:** The mechanical behaviour of composites can be significantly impacted by the moisture content of biofibers, hence drying reinforcements prior to manufacturing is a crucial step [53]. The reinforcements' water content must be less than 3 weight percent in order to produce high-performance biocomposites. Additionally, the dried materials need to be treated and kept properly to avoid dust explosions. Water vapour and voids in the biocomposites during fabrication may be produced by reinforcements with a higher moisture content. Compared to biocomposite materials made with bamboo fibers (15%), those made with pennywort fibres would have significantly higher moisture content (57%) at a relative humidity of 90%.

Compared to composites made of bamboo, pennywort products would be much more susceptible to microbial attack and degradation. The biofibers absorb more moisture at room temperature and at higher temperatures because of the hydrogen connections they have with the strong polar groups. Relative humidity is the primary factor influencing both the moisture content and the rate of absorption [54]. Increasing the cellulose crystallinity and removing hemicellulose from biofibers with appropriate chemical treatment (e.g., photo-curable monomer coatings) might decrease the moisture uptake rate and content of the fibre. Graft copolymerisation, acetylation, irradiation, mercerisation, compatibilizers/coupling agents, silanization, and other processes can all increase the biofibers' wettability. Biobased matrix systems exhibit greater moisture sensitivity than biofibers.

**7.1.2 Thermal stability:** As the processing temperature rises, many biofibers break down. Fibres degrade due to physical and chemical changes brought on by heating, including oxidation, decarboxylation, dehydration, recrystallisation, hydrolysis, and depolymerisation. These occurrences may adversely affect the mechanical and functional characteristics of biocomposites due to the high temperature. The chemical makeup of the components and moisture content both affect a biocomposite's thermal stability. Hemicellulose breakdown is the first step in the breakdown of biofibers [55]. High hemicellulose and extractive content biofibers are particularly susceptible to heat deterioration. Higher thermal stability is demonstrated by fibres with higher levels of crystalline cellulose (higher crystallite size and crystallinity index).

**7.1.3 Breakage of fibres:** Another crucial problem in the production of biocomposites is fibre breaking during the fabrication process. The kind of fabrication method taken into consideration mostly determines the degree of fibre damage. Moreover, temperature and pressure, shear rates, fiber length, fiber entanglement, collisions between fibers and mould, and other variables all affect how easily fibers break. The main causes of crucial fibre rupture and inadequate reinforcing action include high temperatures, high rotor speeds, and extended processing times. Compared to synthetic ones, information on fibre breaking during biocomposites' manufacture is still in its infancy [56].

**7.1.4 Type and content of fibre:** In order to further enhance the biocomposite's sustainability, the type of reinforcement and its chemical composition are typically crucial. Additionally, the fabrication process parameters are significantly impacted by the reinforcements' length, aspect ratio, etc. The initial phases of the reinforcements' shortening, fibrillation, and thermal degradation are significantly influenced by the compounding method (pelletising, extruder compounding, cascade mixing, and pultrusion); the final properties of the composite are already established at the start of the fabrication process [57]. The modulus and strength of a composite are often significantly increased as the fibre volume fraction is increased. Sadly, a higher fibre volume fraction increases the amount of moisture that enters. Furthermore, ductility is subject to influence. In composites, the fibre dimension is also crucial.

**7.1.5 Distribution of fibers:** When reinforcements are not evenly distributed throughout a biocomposite, there are either weak or crack-prone fiber-rich zones. Physical and chemical treatments (such as coupling agents, alkali treatment, etc.) as well as process parameters, fiber diameters, fiber orientation, and other factors might affect how the fibers are distributed in the biocomposites [58].

**7.1.6 Challenges associated with machining:** The components made of composite are put together using machining procedures. Because biocomposites have a complex microstructure, their overall machining is more complicated than that of other synthetic or isotropic materials. Their mechanical performance is decreased by machining, which is crucial in producing damage like matrix cracking, peel-up, or debonding, among other things [59].

**7.2 Advanced fabrication techniques:** The majority of the aforementioned traditional fabrication methods require moulds, which limit formability and result in an expensive and time-consuming process. Although 3D printing, also known as additive manufacturing, uses a manufacturing process in which computer-aided design is used to construct composite structures layer by layer [60].

**7.2.1 Structures of lightweight biocomposite materials made possible by additive manufacturing:** Because of its enormous potential for creating sophisticated, lightweight materials and structures, additive manufacturing, or 3D printing, has been extensively studied recently.

**In material extrusion** a heated nozzle is used to extrude melted material against a build plate in one of the various AM techniques for creating composites, as per ASTM International Technical Committee F42.The process is commonly referred to as fused filament fabrication (FFF) or fused deposition modelling (FDM) [61].**Vat photopolymerisation** uses ultraviolet (UV)-cured photopolymers for manufacturing (stereolithography, or SLA). Although there is a very little selection of photopolymer materials, the build quality is superb. **Power bed fusion** method uses thermal energy (stereolithography, or SLS) to fuse a powder bed.

Fused filament fabrication, or FFF, is the most popular additive manufacturing process utilised in the literature to create biocomposites. The ability to create complicated geometries for industrial and research purposes, as well as low manufacturing costs, low time consumption, and reduced manufacturing waste, are the primary advantages of FFF [62]. The mechanical performance of the structure is greatly influenced by FFF printing parameters (layer thickness, print orientation, infill pattern, and interbead distance, etc.) and slicing parameters ( bed temperature, filament feed rate, nozzle temperature, bed calibration, nozzle geometry, etc.) [63].In recent years, additive manufacturing has emerged as a promising tool for biocomposites to bridge the gap with synthetic composites and has started to improve biocomposites to a similar level of technological capabilities.

**7.2.2 Additive manufacturing of various biobased materials:** Several additie manufacturing processes have been used to create polymer matrix composite materials that integrate different reinforcements in the form of fibres and fillers. When combined with a polymer matrix, filler reinforcements are easy to add and reasonably priced. As such, the production of feedstock for SLS (powder) and FFF (filament) is rather simple. It has been noted that the final materials exhibit improved mechanical, electrical, tribological, thermal, and biological qualities. However, agglomeration makes it difficult to achieve uniform dispersion when using nano-scale fillers. SLA has also been used to develop multi-scale multi-material structures with site-specific properties. The development and fabrication of polymeric material-based feedstocks incorporating nano-fillers may present new opportunities. The surface of nanofillers was modified using silane and other couplants, as well as thermal treatments, to improve the mechanical properties, stability, and interfacial bonding of the SLA feedstock [64]. The use of mechanical and ultrasonic mixing processes to disperse nano-particles in a photocurable SLA resin had limited success. Similar fiber-reinforced feedstocks were developed for use in the SLS and FFF processes. Similar to particle reinforced feedstocks, FFF is the most widely used additive manufacturing technique to fabricate composite materials. Short and continuous fibres are also used as a reinforcement system in SLA resins to improve the properties of polymer composites. In a photocurable resin for the SLA process, reinforcing fibres can inhibit UV light, resulting in uncured sites in the composites.

**7.3 Features of biocomposites machining:** Biocomposites are used in many different engineering fields. For the biocomposites to meet application requirements, they must be machined and handled. It is extremely difficult to create holes, cutouts, and slots in the biocomposite during manufacturing without affecting the fibre system; in these circumstances, machining is the only practical way to create complex shapes. Therefore, understanding how biocomposites respond to machining has become increasingly crucial. Nevertheless, all these polymer materials vary in their machining behavior owing to their dissimilarity in the chemical and physical characteristics of the constituent materials. Because of their anisotropic response, biocomposites exhibit a significant difference in machining when compared to homogeneous materials [65]. Additionally, the machining of biocomposites differs significantly from that of traditional materials, making it difficult to analyse their machining response. The reinforcement profile in composite materials, such as fibre alignment, fiber volume fraction, and fibre architecture, affects the machining performance.

The reinforcements typically have a high strength, which makes the system difficult to machine and causes tool assembly wear. Because of its stiffness, the material is abrasive. The use of multiple plies in the fabrication of the biocomposite laminates may cause delamination. The machining of composites causes damage modes like delamination, fibre breakage, fibre pull out, and matrix cracking, which lead to poor surface quality and dimensional inaccuracy [66]. Additionally, the material undergoes changes in properties during the machining process, making material response a more crucial consideration. A standard drilling technique is a commonly used and promising machining method for creating holes in a biocomposite. Numerous writers have examined how different biocomposites drill. Abrasive water jet machining (AWJM) and milling behaviours of the biocomposites were also reported in addition to drilling investigations. Dilli Babu et al. [67] shown that, in comparison to composite materials made of jute and bananas, hemp fiber-based products had minimal interlaminar delamination and roughness upon milling. Drilling biocomposites at a high feed rate and spindle speed increases the delamination, as demonstrated by Venkateshwaran and Elaya Perumal [68].
The abrasive particle size has a significant impact on the AWJM of biocomposites in terms of machining quality. According to Prabu et al. [69], the biocomposite experienced significant

delamination and pull out during AWJM. In the past, machinists skilled and well-trained individuals performed machining via arbitrary parameter changes. This method affects the quality of the machining. Manufacturers are currently interested in increasing productivity by reducing the amount of time spent on machining parameter optimisation. Since process parameters have a significant impact on machining quality, it is crucial to establish them correctly in order to produce products of the appropriate quality.

**7.4 Future developments and difficulties in biocomposites:** The present method of using additive manufacturing to create continuous or short biofiber-based composites shows promise. These are some potential future directions for using additive manufacturing to create high-quality biocomposites. Customising the filament feedstock with a low twisted fibre allows for improved reinforcing and appropriate load redistribution at the material level. A specialised nozzle that can extrude biocomposites in pellet form enables cost-effective material formulation customisation. Large-scale additive manufacturing (high deposition rate and build volume) with six degrees of freedom of movement for biocomposites was created by Zhao et al. [70] and allows for the printing of complicated structures with less processing time and expense. The creation of high-performance biocomposites may be made possible by these characteristics. Nevertheless, there are extra implementation costs. The creation of manufacturing techniques for 4D printed lightweight biocomposites can offer a fresh way to include self-sensing and actuation (autonomous and shape-morphing) properties into materials using resources that are readily available locally. A structure's component count, material, assembly time, and manufacturing energy usage would all be decreased by this characteristic, which is typically employed in current electromechanical systems.

Maritime engineering, healthcare (architecture skin systems), aerospace, automotive, construction (solar tracking and shading), and other fields can all benefit from these structures. Because of the swelling caused by their hygroscopic qualities, biofibers like coir, flax, jute, or kenaf work as an actuator. Therefore, the ideal fibre volume content for hygro-morph biocomposites must be achieved, primarily by the use of a moisture-insensitive polymer. A superior extrusion without clogging is made possible by an ideal design.

**8. Applications of biobased composites:** In the fields of biomedical engineering, aircraft, automotive, marine, sports, packing, electronics, and other fields, biocomposites are rapidly emerging as a viable substitute for metal, traditional reinforcement-based composites, and ceramic-based materials. Additionally, biocomposites are used in coating, electrical, packaging, medicinal, magnetic, electromagnetic shielding, optical, and other fields [71].

**9. Conclusion:** The goal of this review article is to provide a thorough overview of biomaterials, processing methods, characteristics, and biocomposites prospects for the future. This review article aims to provide a solid grasp of the processes used in biocomposites' synthesis, processing, and characterisation. The greatest option for a number of applications and to protect the bionetwork from the harmful effects of synthetic materials are biocomposites because of their low cost, health benefits, energy efficiency, sustainability, biodegradability, and abundance. Recently, a number of studies have concentrated on improving the performance of biocomposites based on thermoplastic and thermoset materials, which have seen significant advancements in the automotive and civil engineering industries. A deeper comprehension of material extraction, interfacial treatments, and alteration, is credited with this advancement. Additional focus on genetic engineering, knowledge of other uncommon materials, synergism of properties, orientation, fiber dispersion, and length [72], low-cost coating, moisture absorption, dimensional stability, *etc.,* make it possible to produce high-quality biocomposites suitable for a variety of applications.

The mechanical performance of biocomposites can be significantly impacted by factors such as fibre hybridisation, interfacial adhesion, stacking order, fabric architecture, and processing conditions. To improve fibre dispersion and interfacial bonding even more, research on the fundamentals of biofiber morphology is essential. It is highly recommended and crucial to do a thorough investigation on the mechanical behaviour and surface modification of individual fibers. Comparing commonly used biofibers, including jute, hemp, flax, sisal, and others, revealed that there may be room to keep adding new biofibers to biopolymers in order to improve biofiber production and expand its uses. It is anticipated that new types of biocomposite materials would be used in large quantities in a number of consumer goods [73]. Investigating novel biofibers that are widely accessible can increase supply and lower material costs. The less prevalent biofibers require more thorough and cautious research, as there hasn't been any equivalent study done on them yet. A whole new value chain for the crops may be created by using less popular biomaterials. In fact, biocomposite can provide immediate advantages to rural communities, especially in less developed regions where these resources are plentiful. improvement through the synergistic hybridisation of lignocellulosic fibres and the subsequent material's endurance under varied circumstances. The primary advantage of developing high-performance biocomposites is that a thorough life-cycle assessment of biocomposites is necessary. Biocomposites are more difficult to fabricate and use widely because to their hydrophilicity and heterogeneity. Water absorption, poor fibre dispersion, poor interfacial adhesion between the fibre and matrix, and variations in fibre quality are the main issues. Chemical modification techniques [74], new coupling agents, compounding technology development, etc. are important areas to increase the compatibility and interface between the fibre and matrix. New cost-effective biopolymers with superior mechanical properties, stability during transport, storage and service life, lower processing temperature, thermal stability, and recyclability are among the essential areas of development that are needed in the future with regard to matrix materials. Some uncommon biopolymers exhibit exceptional tensile moduli compared to synthetic polymers, indicating their potential for use in filling the gap between typical biodegradable matrices (*PHBV, PHA, etc.*) and synthetic ones, which currently have poor mechanical qualities and are expensive. When the goods manufactured from these biomaterials are more fire-resistant, long-lasting, moisture-resistant, and dimensionally stable, new uses will emerge. Although biocomposites have very good specific mechanical properties, their characteristics vary greatly. It is possible to bypass this limitation by using modern additive manufacturing techniques. To increase the proportion of these thermoplastic-based biocomposite materials in structural applications, innovative methods utilising continuous fibre are therefore crucial.

It is still difficult to successfully replace synthetic composites with biocomposites that exhibit comparable structural and functional behaviour, despite the fact that biocomposite materials are generating a lot of interest from the scientific and industrial communities. Because biocomposites have intrinsically poor mechanical and thermal qualities, it would be difficult to completely replace traditional synthetic composites with them. Given the potential for novel applications, this field hopes to be further investigated. Furthermore, additional research is needed to produce new products, assess their performance, and determine how environmental ageing affects the failure mechanics of the thermo-mechanical-chemical processes of biocomposites. High performance, dependability, durability, and serviceability are necessary for biocomposite materials to be realised in order to increase their use.

**References:**

1. Gurunathan T., Mohanty S., Nayak S.K. (2015) A review of the recent developments in biocomposites based on natural fibres and their application perspectives, Composites Part A: Applied Science and Manufacturing. 77.1–25.

2. Marais S. et al. (2005). Unsaturated polyester composites reinforced with flax fibers: effect of cold plasma and autoclave treatments on mechanical and permeation properties, Composites Part A: Applied Science and Manufacturing 36 (7) .975–986.

3. Yu T., Jiang N., Li Y. (2014). Study on short ramie fiber/poly(lactic acid) composites compatibilized by maleic anhydride, Composites Part A: Applied Science and Manufacturing 64.139–146.

4. Hooftman N. et al. (2018). A review of the European passenger car regulations – Real driving emissions vs local air quality, Renewable and Sustainable Energy Reviews 86.1–21.

5. Jawaid M., & Abdul Khalil H.P.S.(2011).Cellulosic/synthetic fibre reinforced polymer hybrid composites: A review, Carbohydrate Polymers 86 (1) 1–18.

6. [6]Stamboulis A., Baillie C.A., Peijs T. (2001). Effects of environmental conditions on mechanical and physical properties of flax fibers, Composites Part A: Applied Science and Manufacturing 32 (8) 1105–1115.

7. Huda M.S. et al. (2008). Effect of chemical modifications of the pineapple leaf fiber surfaces on the interfacial and mechanical properties of laminated biocomposites, Composite Interfaces 15 (2-3)169–191.

8. Cao X.V. et al. (2012). Maleated Natural Rubber as a Coupling Agent for Recycled High Density Polyethylene/Natural Rubber/Kenaf Powder Biocomposites, PolymerPlastics Technology and Engineering 51 (9) 904–910.

9. Shen L., Haufe J. and Patel M.K. 2009. Product overview and market projection of emerging bio-based plastics PRO-BIP 2009. Report for European polysaccharide network of excellence (EPNOE) and European bioplastics. 243.

10. Facca A.G., Kortschot M.T., Yan N. (2007). Predicting the tensile strength of natural fibre reinforced thermoplastics, Composites Science and Technology 67 (11). 2454–2466.

11. Awais H. et al. (2021). Environmental benign natural fibre reinforced thermoplastic composites: A review, Composites Part C: Open Access 4 , 100082.

12. Shanmugam V. et al. (2021). Circular economy in biocomposite development: State-ofthe-art, challenges and emerging trends, Composites Part C: Open Access 5 , 100138.

13. Averous L., Boquillon N. (2004). Biocomposites based on plasticized starch: Thermal and mechanical behaviours, Carbohydrate Polymers 56 111–122.

14. Mohanty A.K., Misra M., Drzal L.T. (2005). Natural fibers, biopolymers, and biocomposites, CRC press.

15. Shang S., Zhu L., Fan J. (2013). Intermolecular interactions between natural polysaccharides and silk fibroin protein, Carbohydrate Polymers 93 (2) 561–573.

16. Moriana R. et al., Improved thermo-mechanical properties by the addition of natural fibres in starch-based sustainable biocomposites, Composites Part A: Applied Science and Manufacturing 42 (1) (2011) 30–40.

17. Averous L. (2004). Biodegradable Multiphase Systems Based on Plasticized Starch: A Review, Journal of Macromolecular Science, Part C 44 (3) 231–274.

18. Guan J., Hanna M.A. (2004). Functional properties of extruded foam composites of starch acetate and corn cob fiber, Industrial Crops and Products 19 (3) 255–269.

19. Nishinari K. et al. (2014). Soy proteins: A review on composition, aggregation and emulsification, Food Hydrocolloids 39. 301–318.

20. Reddy C.S.K. et al., Polyhydroxyalkanoates: an overview, Bioresource Technology 87 (2) (2003) 137–146.

21. Khanna S., Srivastava A.K. (2005). Recent advances in microbial polyhydroxyalkanoates, Process Biochemistry 40 (2) 607–619.

22. Sudesh K., Abe H., Doi Y. (2000). Synthesis, structure and properties of polyhydroxyalkanoates: biological polyesters, Progress in Polymer Science 25 (10) 1503–1555.

23. Wang Y.W. Wu Q. Chen G.Q. (2005). Gelatin Blending Improves the Performance of Poly(3-hydroxybutyrate-co-3-hydroxyhexanoate) Films for Biomedical Application, Biomacromolecules 6 (2) 566–571.

24. Lunt J. (1998). Large-scale production, properties and commercial applications of polylactic acid polymers, Polymer Degradation and Stability 59 (1) 145–152.

25. Singh M., Singh R., Dhami M.K. (2020). Biocompatible Thermoplastics as Implants/Scaffold, in Reference Module in Materials Science and Materials Engineering. Elsevier.

26. Machado G., et al. (2020). Biopolymers from Lignocellulosic Biomass, in Lignocellulosic Biorefining Technologies. p. 125-158.

27. Shah S.A., et al. (2019). Biopolymer-based biomaterials for accelerated diabetic wound healing: A critical review, International Journal of Biological Macromolecules 139 975–993.

28. Das O. et al. (2020). Naturally-occurring bromophenol to develop fire retardant gluten biopolymers, Journal of Cleaner Production 243, 118552.

29. Ganguly A. Sharma K., Majumder K. et al. (2020).Chapter 4 - Peptides as biopolymers—past, present, and future, in: K. Pal, et al. (Eds.), Biopolymer-Based Formulations, Elsevier.pp. 87–104. Editors.

30. Rwawiire S. et al. (2015). Development of a biocomposite based on green epoxy polymer and natural cellulose fabric (bark cloth) for automotive instrument panel applications, Composites Part B: Engineering 81 149–157.

31. Eichhorn, S., et al., (2009). Handbook of textile fibre structure: Volume 2: Natural, regenerated, inorganic and specialist fibres.

32. Brindha, R. et al. (2019). Effect of different retting processes on yield and quality of banana pseudostem fiber, Journal of Natural Fibers 16 (1) 58–67.

33. Nagarajan, K.J., Balaji, A.N., Ramanujam, N.R. (2019). Extraction of cellulose nanofibers from cocos nucifera var aurantiaca peduncle by ball milling combined with chemical treatment, Carbohydrate Polymers 212.312–322.

34. Sadrmanesh, V. et al. (2019). Developing a decision making model to identify the most influential parameters affecting mechanical extraction of bast fibers, Journal of Cleaner Production 238, 117891.

35. Benfenati, V. et al. (2019). Silk Fibroin Based Technology for Industrial Biomanufacturing, in: T. Tolio, G. Copani, W. Terkaj (Eds.), Factories of the Future: The Italian Flagship Initiative, Springer International Publishing, Cham, pp. 409–430. Editors.

36. Aznar-Cervantes, S.D. et al. (2019). Effect of different cocoon stifling methods on the properties of silk fibroin biomaterials, Scientific Reports 9 (1).6703.

[80] Hu, Y. et al., Preparation of natural amphoteric silk nanofibers by acid hydrolysis, Journal of Materials Chemistry B 7 (9) (2019) 1450–1459.

37. Mwaikambo, L.Y., Tucker, N., Clark, A.J. (2007). Mechanical Properties of Hemp-FibreReinforced Euphorbia Composites, Macromolecular Materials and Engineering 292 (9).993–1000.

38. Mohanty, S. et al. (2004). Influence of fiber treatment on the performance of sisal–polypropylene composites, Journal of Applied Polymer Science 94 (3) 1336–1345.

39. Rana, A.K. et al., (1997). Studies of acetylation of jute using simplified procedure and its characterization, Journal of Applied Polymer Science 64 (8).1517–1523.

40. Avella, M. et al. (2007). Poly(3-hydroxybutyrate-co-3-hydroxyvalerate)-based biocomposites reinforced with kenaf fibers, Journal of Applied Polymer Science 104 (5)3192–3200.

41. Ali, R., Iannace, S., Nicolais, L.(2003). Effect of processing conditions on mechanical and viscoelastic properties of biocomposites, Journal of applied polymer science 88 (7) 1637–1642.

42. Lee, B.-H. et al. (2009). Bio-composites of kenaf fibers in polylactide: Role of improved interfacial adhesion in the carding process, Composites Science and Technology 69 (15) 2573–2579.

43. Goriparthi, B.K., Suman, K.N.S., Mohan Rao, N. Effect of fiber surface treatments on mechanical and abrasive wear performance of polylactide/jute composites, Composites Part A: Applied Science and Manufacturing 43 (10) (2012) 1800–1808.

44. Santiago, N., J. Bachmann, and Tse, B. (2019). Plasma treatment of bio-based and recycled carbon fibres for eco-composites.

45. uan, X. Jayaraman, K., Bhattacharyya, D. (2002). Plasma treatment of sisal fibres and its effects on tensile strength and interfacial bonding, Journal of Adhesion Science and Technology 16 (6) 703–727.

46. Sinha, E., Panigrahi, S. (2009). Effect of Plasma Treatment on Structure, Wettability of Jute Fiber and Flexural Strength of its Composite, Journal of Composite Materials 43 (17).1791–1802.

47. Ragoubi, M. et al.(2012). Effect of corona discharge treatment on mechanical and thermal properties of composites based on miscanthus fibres and polylactic acid or polypropylene matrix, Composites Part A: Applied Science and Manufacturing 43 (4) 675–685.

48. Kardas, I., Lipp-Symonowicz, B., Sztajnowski, S. (2009).Comparison of the effect of PET fibres' surface modification using enzymes and chemical substances with respect to changes in mechanical properties, Fibres and Textiles in Eastern Europe 75.93–97.

49. Pickering, K. et al. (2007). Interfacial Modification of Hemp Fiber Reinforced Composites Using Fungal and Alkali Treatment, J. Biobased Mater. Bioenergy 1.

50. Pietak, A. et al., (2007). Atomic force microscopy characterization of the surface wettability of natural fibres, Applied Surface Science 253 (7). 3627–3635.

51. Liu, L. et al., Enzymatic treatment of mechanochemical modified natural bamboo fibers, Fibers and Polymers 13 (5) (2012) 600–605.

52. Dhakal, H., Zhang, Z.Y., Richardson, M. (2007). Effect of water absorption on the mechanical properties of hemp fibre reinforced unsaturated polyester composites, Composites Science and Technology 67 1674–1683.

53. Stamboulis, A. et al. (2000). Environmental Durability of Flax Fibres and their Composites based on Polypropylene Matrix, Applied Composite Materials 7. 273–294.

54. Ornaghi, H.L. et al. (2014). Correlation of the thermal stability and the decomposition kinetics of six different vegetal fibers, Cellulose 21 (1) 177–188.

55. Duc, A.L., Vergnes, B., Budtova, T. (2011). Polypropylene/natural fibres composites: Analysis of fibre dimensions after compounding and observations of fibre rupture by rheo-optics, Composites Part A: Applied Science and Manufacturing 42 (11)1727–1737.

56. Yan, L., Chouw, N., Jayaraman, K.(2014). Flax fibre and its composites – A review, Composites Part B: Engineering 56.296–317.

57. Serrano, A. et al. (2013). Estimation of the interfacial shears strength, orientation factor and mean equivalent intrinsic tensile strength in old newspaper fiber/polypropylene composites, Composites Part B: Engineering 50. 232–238.

58. Gowd, B. (2012). Effects of Drilling Parameters on Delamination of Hemp Fiber Reinforced Composites.

59. Dhakal, H., Ismail, S.O. and Andrew, J.J. (2021). 3D printing using cellulose nanoparticles, in Cellulose Nanoparticles. p. 348-362.

60. Turner, B.N., Gold, S.A.(2015). A review of melt extrusion additive manufacturing processes: II. Materials, dimensional accuracy, and surface roughness, Rapid Prototyping Journal 21 (3) 250–261.

61. Rajak, D.K. et al. (2019). Recent progress of reinforcement materials: A comprehensive overview of composite materials, Journal of Materials Research and Technology 8 (6) 6354–6374.

62. Tofail, S.A.M. et al. (2018). Additive manufacturing: scientific and technological challenges, market uptake and opportunities, Materials Today 21 (1) 22–37.

63. Ligon-Auer, S.C. et al. (2016). Toughening of photo-curable polymer networks: a review, Polymer Chemistry 7 (2) 257–286.

64. Nassar, M.M.A., Arunachalam, R., Alzebdeh, K.I. (2017). Machinability of natural fiber reinforced composites: a review, The International Journal of Advanced Manufacturing Technology 88 (9) 2985–3004.

65. Chegdani, F., Mansori, M.E. (2018). Mechanics of material removal when cutting natural fiber reinforced thermoplastic composites, Polymer Testing 67 275–283.

66. Babu, G., K. Babu, and B. Gowd. Effect of Machining Parameters on Milled Natural Fiber-Reinforced Plastic Composites. 2013.

67. Venkateshwaran, N., ElayaPerumal, A. (2013). Hole quality evaluation of natural fiber composite using image analysis technique, Journal of Reinforced Plastics and Composites 32 (16) 1188–1197.

68. Prabu,V.A., Kumaran, S.T. M.(2017). Uthayakumar, Performance Evaluation of Abrasive Water Jet Machining on Banana Fiber Reinforced Polyester Composite, Journal of Natural Fibers 14 (3) 450–457.

69. Zhao X. , et al. (2019). Poplar as biofiber reinforcement in composites for large-scale 3D printing, ACS Applied Bio Materials 2 (10), 4557–4570.

70. Sarasini F., Fiore V., (2018). A systematic literature review on less common natural fibres and their biocomposites, Journal of Cleaner Production 195, 240–267.

71. Bay R.S., Tucker C.L. III. (1992). Fiber orientation in simple injection moldings. Part II: Experimental results, Polymer Composites 13 (4) 332–341.

72. Lodha P. , Netravali A.N. (2005). Thermal and mechanical properties of environmentfriendly 'green' plastics from stearic acid modified-soy protein isolate, Industrial Crops and Products 21 (1) 49–64.

73. Goda K. et al. (2006). Improvement of plant based natural fibers for toughening green composites—Effect of load application during mercerization of ramie fibers, Composites Part A: Applied Science and Manufacturing 37, 2213–2220.

# Chapter-14

# A Brief Overview of Recent Advances in Polymer Composites

Valmik R. Jondhale

**Abstract:**

Polymer composites are gaining researchers' attention due to their versatile applications in various sectors. The amalgamation of natural fibres and nanomaterials has appreciably improved mechanical properties while minimizing environmental impact. The review shows recent advances in polymer composites and prominence innovations in material formulation, manufacturing techniques, and applications. Furthermore, developments in hybrid composites and advanced manufacturing methods expanded their use across various industries. This review underscores the budding of polymer composites in addressing modern applications and driving modernism.

**Keywords:** Polymer, Composites, Physical Properties, Emerging Technologies, Environmental Sustainability.

**Introduction:**

The Greek term poly[1] means "many," while mer means "units or parts." Polymer is a macromolecule, or high molecular weight substance, composed of numerous repeating units or fragments of low molecular weights. A "monomer[2]" is a repeating unit found in a polymer.

Similarly, the number of repeat units (monomers) present in a molecule is called the degree of polymerization. It is used to determine the molecular weight of a polymer with the help of the formula, M = DP. m, Where, M-Molecular weight, m- Molecular weight of the monomer. The number of reactive sites/ functional groups or bonding sites present in a monomer is called its functionality.

Based on their origin, the polymers are divided into three categories: natural, semi-synthetic, and synthetic. It is also classified on the basis of backbone chain structure as organic and inorganic polymers. Another classification is based on thermal response as thermosetting and thermoplastic. Similarly, it is also classified on the basis of physical properties as plastics, fibres, and liquid resins.

The process or reaction by which monomer units of the same or different type combine or are linked to form polymers is known as polymerization. Hermann Staudinger[3] was the founder of polymer chemistry. Wallace Carothers is known as the father of man-made polymers and classifies polymer processes in two types: addition polymerization (chain growth) and condensation polymerization[4] (step growth). In condensation the polymerization process, the monomer contains two or more functional groups that react stepwise to form polymer for which catalyst or initiator may or may not be required.

---

*Department of Chemistry, RNC Arts, JDB Commerce and NSC Science College Nashik Road,Nashik-422 101, S.P. Pune University, Maharashtra, India*
*Corresponding author email: valmikrj@gmail.com*

The addition polymerization is of three types based on the type of catalyst used as free-radical, ionic, and co-ordination polymerization. Monomer contains double bond or triple bond (unsaturated) are added into the active site of a rising polymer chain one at a time to form polymer for which catalyst/initiator is crucial. The mechanism of addition polymerization involves initiation, propagation, and termination steps.

**Properties:**

Polymers comprise distinctive physical properties[5], such as toughness, elasticity, diffusivity diffusivity, and viscoelasticity, making them important materials to prepare many articles and applications for day-to-day life and replacing numerous natural resources.

Some of the significant examples comprise plastics, Teflon, Technora, DNA and Proteins and so on.

The polymer chemistry has numerous applications[6] in various industries and sectors. The several innovations in the field of polymer sciences were recognized by awarding Nobel Prizes to the researchers. The formulated polymer composite materials having no. of significant advantages as shown in figure 1.

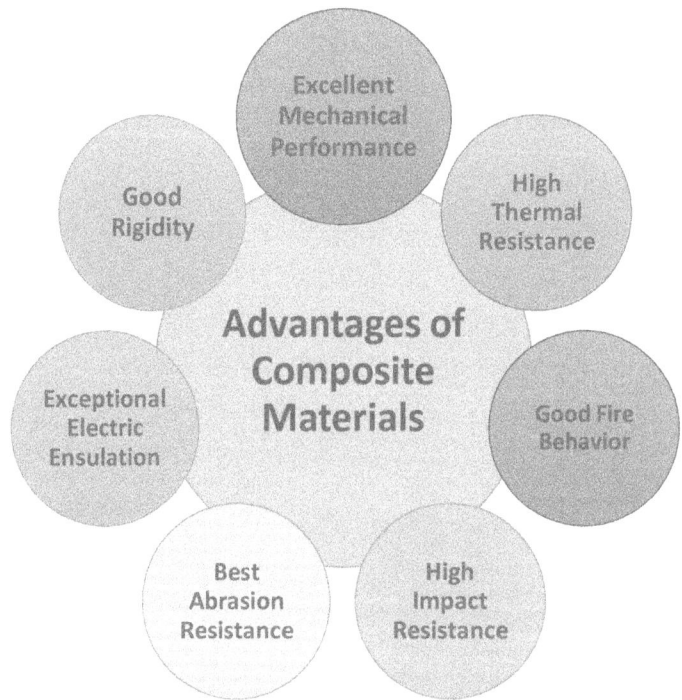

**Figure:1 Significant Advantages of Composite Materials**

Polymers can be semi-crystalline or amorphous based on their chemical structures. Amorphous polymers do not undergo crystallisation or melting transitions, but semi-crystalline polymers do. These transitions represent changes between solid states, not solid-liquid phase transitions like in water. Crystallization happens over the glass-transition temperature ($T_g$) and under the melting temperature ($T_m$). Every polymers, whether amorphous or semi-crystalline, undergo glass transitions. The glass-transition temperature ($T_g$) is vital for manufacturing and processing. Below $T_g$, polymers are brittle and glassy, while above $T_g$, they become rubbery and viscous. $T_g$ can be modified by changing branching, crosslinking, or adding plasticizers[7]. Plasticizers lower $T_g$ and enhance polymer flexibility, altering the glass-transition temperature's dependence on cooling rate. They are small molecules alike to the polymers that generate gaps among chains, enhancing mobility and reducing inter-chain interactions.

**Materials and applications:**

Synthetic polymers are now integral to modern life, with their distinctive properties—such as low density, low cost, and excellent insulation-driving widespread use. Their properties can be customized through combinations with other materials, like composites. Applications include energy savings (insulated buildings, lighter vehicles), food and water protection (in wrapping), reduced land and fertilizer utilize (synthetic fibres), material preservation (coatings), and enhanced hygiene and medical safety.

A material composed of continuous or short fibres bound by an organic polymer matrix is called a polymer matrix composite (PMC). The composite materials are of two types: source and matrix based as shown in figure 2. PMCs are engineered to transfer loads among fibres and offer rewards such as lightweight, high abrasion and corrosion resistance, and improved stiffness and potency in the way of strengthening. Matrices are usually thermosets or thermoplastics, with thermosets being the most common. They include various resin systems out of which, epoxy systems leading in the advanced composite industry[8,9].

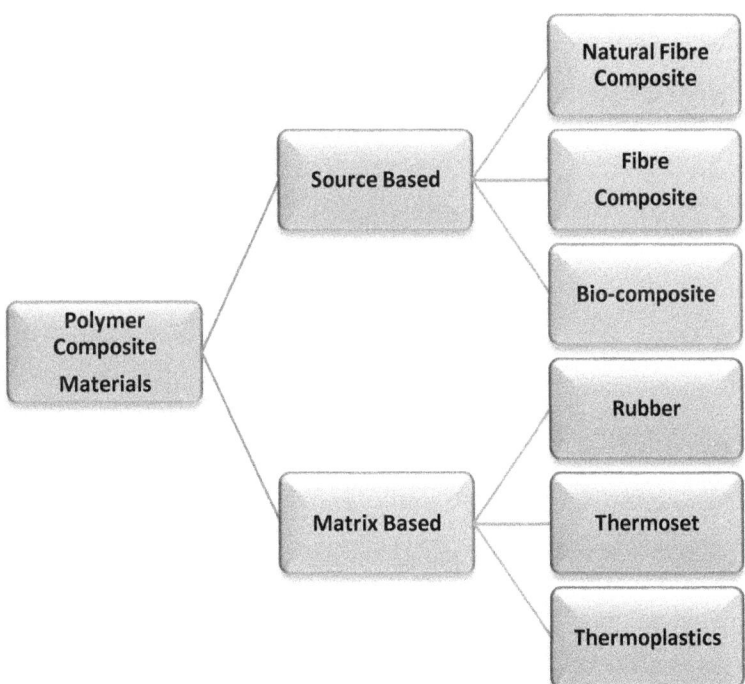

**Figure:2 Polymer Composite Materials**

The polymer composites have numerous applications in various sectors. The updated technologies and methodology for manufacturing composites were reported by Tomas Astrom[10]. This provides number of commercially important materials available for manufacturing composites with cost-efficient methods of preparation. Similarly, the upcoming trends and developments regarding the field were also discussed in detail by the Tomas Astrom. The overall view of 3D fibre reinforced polymer composites was specified by Tong et al.[11] The details regarding the manufacturing process, properties, and applications of 3D woven, braided, knitted, stitched, and pinned composites were reported.

A broad review of novel composite materials utilising elastomer, thermoplastic, and thermosetting polymers was reported by Hsissou et al.[12] polyurethane, polyether sulfone, polyhexamethylene sebacic, polyether imide, polyether ketone, phenoplasts, polyethylene terephthalate, epoxy resin, and Polycarbonate are some of the macromolecular matrices that have been invented and synthesized presented by Hsissou and coworkers.

**Current Scenario:**

The polymer composite has a wide range of uses and applications[13] in various sectors, as shown in figure 3. Which includes adhesive technologies, catalytic, smart and responsive polymers, additive manufacturing, development of bio-degradable and bio based actuation, wearable technologies and smart fabrics, sensing and actuation, Biopolymers, Bio-based and eco-friendly adhesive formulations , 3D printing, self healing polymers, and energy storage and conversion.

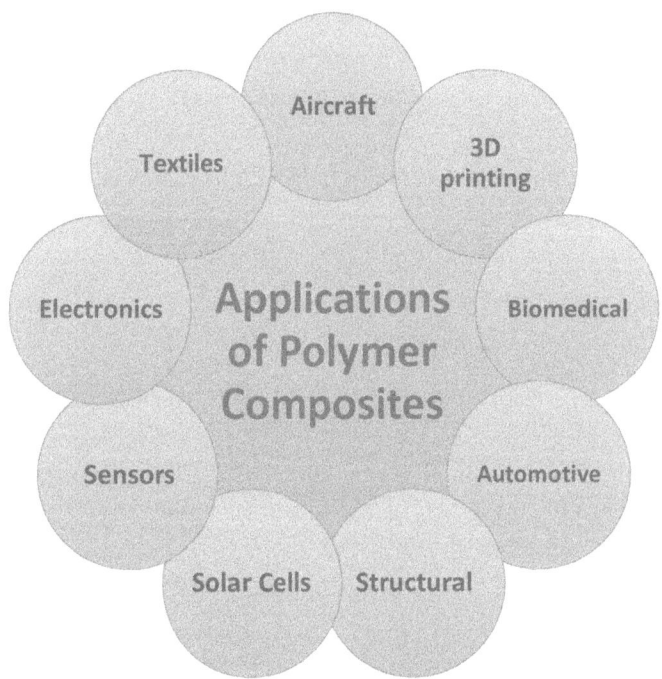

**Figure 3: Applications of Polymer Composites**

All sectors can use the broad idea of compounding to create intermediates or final products by combining basic components. In order to create a commercial product that satisfies particular functional criteria and specifications, it entails the knowledge and procedures needed to blend natural or synthetic ingredients, often incongruous.

Ramakrishna and colleagues[14] gave a summary of the numerous biomedical uses of polymer-composite materials that have been acknowledged in the literature throughout the past 30 years. Biomaterials are substances, either natural or artificial, that are utilised to direct, improve, or substitute the functions of the body's live tissues. In order for polymer composite resources to be more extensively accepted in the biomedical sector, he also looks at the important problems and scientific obstacles that need to be addressed. Figure 4 shows uses of polymer composites in biomedical sector.

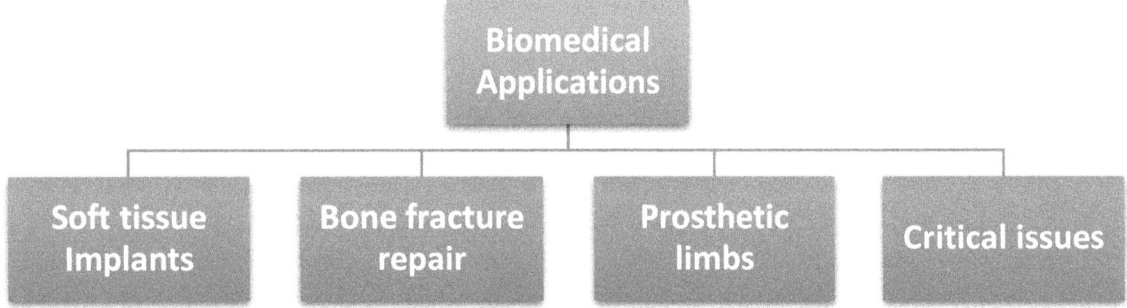

Fig. 4 Biomedical Applications of Polymer Composites

Byrne & Gun'ko[15] presented the current advancement in study on the growth of carbon nanotubes (CNT)-polymer composites, through exacting consideration to their improved mechanical and electrical properties (conductive). Figure 5 represents the budding substitute materials by using CNT-polymer composites for diverse applications.

Kumar et al.[16] evaluated the characteristics and uses of multiphase polymeric composites reinforced with graphene and carbon nanotubes. Additionally, it examines and assesses the improvements in the mechanical and thermal characteristics of materials featuring carbon nanotube (1D) and graphene (2D) nanostructures. This review emphasises how the addition of graphene/CNT to two- and three-phase composites improves their mechanical, thermal, and interfacial characteristics. It addresses improved interfaces between fibres and matrices augmented with nanofiller.

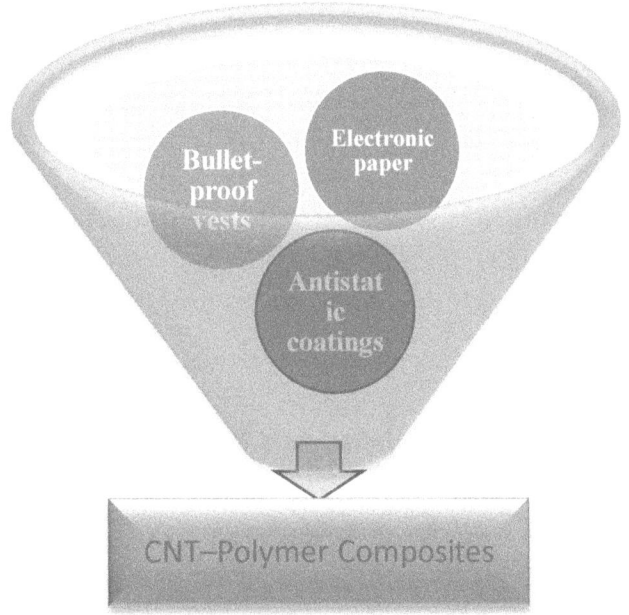

Fig. 5 Applications using CNT–polymer composites

Even at modest nanofiller loadings, composite characteristics are improved; nevertheless, more research is necessary to determine the ideal ratios of both individual and combination fillers. It also discusses budding applications, existing challenges, and outlook perspectives for multiphase composites, emphasizing the promising developments in graphene/CNT-based materials.

Thermal applications and the thermal characteristics of natural fibre composites were reported by Gupta el al.[17] The interfacial interactions among the polymer matrix and the filler have a significant impact on the thermal characteristics of polymer composites. Composites have many uses across all industries due to their high tensile strength, excellent thermal characteristics, and low density, which reduce weight. Polymer composites are used extensively in structure, the automobile industry, and many other fields.

To mitigate industrial hazards from alpha/beta particles, protons, electrons, neutrons, and high-energy electromagnetic waves like X-rays and gamma rays, researchers have conventionally used heavy metals for radiation shielding. However, heavy metal gear is cumbersome and can generate penetrative secondary radiation, necessitating additional shielding and increasing costs and weight. This has led to a focus on developing efficient, lightweight, cost-effective, and flexible shielding materials for industries. The current advancements in these materials for radiation shielding applications were viewed by Nambiar & Yeow[18]. Polymer composites, particularly those reinforced with micro and nanoparticles, have emerged as attractive possibilities for efficient radiation suppression.

Abliz et al.[19] reported a review on Curing Methods for Advanced Polymer Composites. These techniques are being researched in an effort to create advanced polymer composites that are both inexpensive and highly effective, a difficult task that has yet to be solved. The utilisation of advanced polymer composites is limited by the labour- and capital-intensive autoclave curing procedure, which costs much more as part size increases. Researchers have looked into a variety of thermal and radiation alternatives in an effort to find effective, low-cost healing techniques. This review examines the present progress of radiation curing and thermal curing approach for advanced polymer composites. It also discusses the curing mechanisms and application status of these processes.

A substitute for energy-intensive thermal curing of thermosetting composites, Hay & O'Gara[20] use radiation curing techniques like microwaves, electron beams (EBs), ultraviolet (UV) light, and γ-rays. Although EB curing is restricted to particular resin types, it offers some potential benefits over thermal curing. Since UV curing is restricted to relatively tiny and UV-transparent parts, these frequently have different final properties from the typical resins. Although a variety of radiations curing applications have been assessed, there is currently little broad use of these technologies in the aerospace industry.

Fibre reinforcements embedded in a matrix of thermoplastic or thermosetting polymers can be employed in laminated polymer matrix composites for a variety of purposes. It has several benefits, including high specific strength and modulus, ease of manufacture, high design flexibility, strong corrosion and fatigue resistance, good thermal expansion properties, and cost effectiveness[21].

Ramakrishna et al.[22] summarize the latest advances in nanoengineered polymer composites. This review helps researchers understand the current state of nanotechnology in polymer matrix composite engineering, providing a foundation for further study and addressing challenges in developing sophisticated, high-performance materials.

In the past decade, natural fiber reinforced polymer (NFRP) composites have significantly impacted polymer composite research and innovation due to their advantages over low-cost synthetic fiber composites and lower environmental impact. With potential applications across various engineering sectors, efforts to enhance their performance have led to several recent modifications that improve their capabilities. Uthayakumar et al.[23] reviewed developments in NFRP research and development and performance. It discusses present investigations on NFRP fabrication, including mechanical strength, tribological, water, and chemical resistant behaviour, thermal impacts, biodegradability, and machining features, as well as trends, difficulties, and opportunities in the area of NFRP.

Fiber-reinforced polymer composites are vital in many industries, from domestic items to automobiles, because of their practical qualities. However, natural fibres have difficulties such as moisture absorption and limited heat stability, which prevent them from bonding with resins. Fibre treatment can help to reduce moisture while also improving bonding. According to Asim et al.[24], hybrid-polymer composites provide special qualities that are not possible with a single fibre type. Selecting the right polymer is essential for strength and compatibility. Certain production procedures are needed for different polymers. Common thermoset methods for creating hybrid composites include compression moulding and hand lay-up. These new materials are becoming more and more appreciated for a variety of uses due to efficient processing and alteration techniques.

Sathishkumar et al.25 reviewed glass-fiber reinforced polymer composites, developed through various manufacturing technologies having broad applications. The earliest use of glass fibres for containers continuous to high-temperature electrical applications and are currently used in electronics, aviation, and automotive industries.

The properties of glass fibres polymer composites are shown in figure 6. Each of its various forms has special qualities for certain uses. Research has documented these composites' mechanical, tribological, thermal, water-absorbing, and vibrational characteristics.

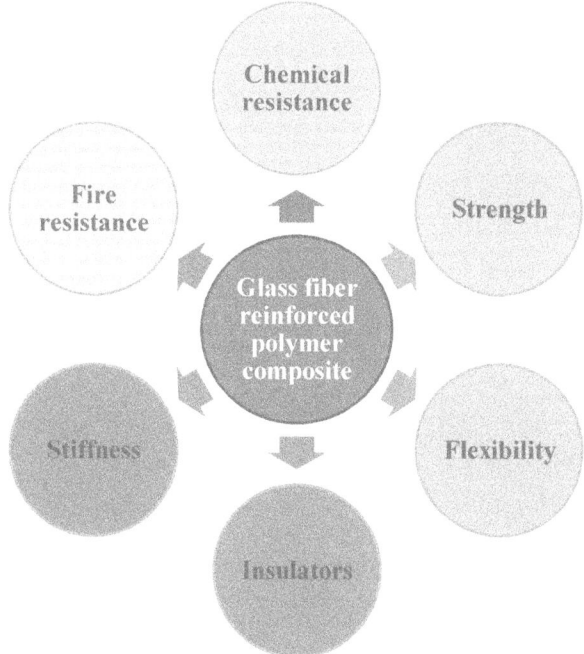

**Figure: 6 Properties of Glass fibres Polymer Composites.**

**Conclusion:**

The current circumstances illustrate that polymer composites exhibit notable improvements in sustainability, performance, and application diversity. New developments in material formulation, like the use of nanoparticles and natural fibres, have improved mechanical qualities while lessening their negative effects on the environment. Advances in manufacturing approaches, such as 3D printing and hybrid composites, have expanded the range of applications in sectors like healthcare, automotive, and aerospace. Polymer composites have the potential to become more and more important in satisfying the needs of contemporary technology and environmental sustainability as research continues to concentrate on maximising compatibility, durability, and cost-effectiveness.

**References:**

1. Polymer. (n.d.). In The Free Dictionary. Retrieved October 14, 2024, from https://www.thefreedictionary.com/polymer.
2. Polymer | Description, Examples, Types, Material, Uses, & Facts | Britannica. (2024, September 16). https://www.britannica.com/science/polymer.
3. Shampo, M. A., Kyle, R. A., & Steensma, D. P. (2013). Hermann Staudinger—Founder of Polymer Chemistry. *Mayo Clinic Proceedings*, *88*(3), e23. https://doi.org/10.1016/j.mayocp.2012.01.026.
4. Sperling, L. H. (Leslie Howard) (2006). Introduction to physical polymer science. Hoboken, N.J.: Wiley. p. 10. ISBN 978-0-471-70606-9.
5. Painter, Paul C.; Coleman, Michael M. (1997). Fundamentals of polymer science: an introductory text. Lancaster, Pa.: Technomic Pub. Co. p. 1. ISBN 978-1-56676-559-6.
6. Polymers Examples of Chemistry Applications in Our Lives. (2018, September 17). https://praxilabs.com/en/blog/2018/09/17/polymers-as-example-of-chemistry-applications-in-our-lives/.
7. Brandrup, J.; Immergut, E.H.; Grulke, E.A. (1999). Polymer Handbook (4 ed.). Wiley-Interscience. ISBN 978-0-471-47936-9.
8. Pilato, L.; Michno, Michael J. (January 1994). Advanced composite materials (Chap 1 Introduction, and Chapter 2 "Matrix Resins"). Springer-Verlag New York. ISBN 978-3-540-57563-4.
9. ACG (2006). "Introduction to Advanced Composites and Prepreg Technology" (free PDF download). Advanced Composites Group. Retrieved 2024-10-05.
10. Astrom, B. T. (2017). *Manufacturing of Polymer Composites*. Routledge. https://doi.org/10.1201/9780203748169.
11. Tong, L., Mouritz, A. P., & Bannister, M. (2002). *3D Fibre Reinforced Polymer Composites*. Elsevier.
12. Hsissou, R., Seghiri, R., Benzekri, Z., Hilali, M., Rafik, M., & Elharfi, A. (2021). Polymer composite materials: A comprehensive review. *Composite Structures*, *262*, 113640. https://doi.org/10.1016/j.compstruct.2021.113640.

13. Oladele, I., Onuh, N. L., Siengchin, S., M R, S., & Adelani, S. (2024). Modern Applications of Polymer Composites in Structural Industries: A Review of Philosophies, Product Development, and Graphical Applications. *Applied Science and Engineering Progress*, *17*, 6884.

14. Ramakrishna, S., Mayer, J., Wintermantel, E., & Leong, K. W. (2001). Biomedical applications of polymer-composite materials: A review. *Composites Science and Technology*, *61*(9), 1189–1224. https://doi.org/10.1016/S0266-3538(00)00241-4.

15. Byrne, M. T., & Gun'ko, Y. K. (2010). Recent Advances in Research on Carbon Nanotube–Polymer Composites. *Advanced Materials*, *22*(15), 1672–1688. https://doi.org/10.1002/adma.200901545.

16. Kumar, A., Sharma, K., & Dixit, A. R. (2020). Carbon nanotube- and graphene-reinforced multiphase polymeric composites: Review on their properties and applications. *Journal of Materials Science*, *55*(7), 2682–2724.

17. Kharbanda, S., Bhadury, T., Gupta, G., Fuloria, D., Pati, P. R., Mishra, V. K., & Sharma, A. (2021). Polymer composites for thermal applications – A review. *Materials Today: Proceedings*, *47*, 2839–2845. https://doi.org/10.1016/j.matpr.2021.03.609.

18. Nambiar, S., & Yeow, J. T. W. (2012). Polymer-Composite Materials for Radiation Protection. *ACS Applied Materials & Interfaces*, *4*(11), 5717–5726. https://doi.org/10.1021/am300783d.

19. Abliz, D., Duan, Y., Steuernagel, L., Xie, L., Li, D., & Ziegmann, G. (2013). Curing Methods for Advanced Polymer Composites—A Review. *Polymers and Polymer Composites*, *21*(6), 341–348. https://doi.org/10.1177/096739111302100602.

20. Hay, J. N., & O'Gara, P. (2006). Recent developments in thermoset curing methods. *Proceedings of the Institution of Mechanical Engineers, Part G: Journal of Aerospace Engineering*, *220*(3), 187–195. https://doi.org/10.1243/09544100JAERO35.

21. Vijay Kumar, V.; Ramakrishna, S.; Kong Yoong, J.L.; Esmaeely Neisiany, R.; Surendran, S.; Balaganesan, G. Electrospun nanofiber interleaving in fiber reinforced composites—Recent trends. Mater. Des. Process. Commun. 2019, 1, e24.

22. Vijay Kumar, V., Balaganesan, G., Lee, J. K. Y., Neisiany, R. E., Surendran, S., & Ramakrishna, S. (2019). A Review of Recent Advances in Nanoengineered Polymer Composites. *Polymers*, *11*(4), Article 4. https://doi.org/10.3390/polym11040644.

23. Vigneshwaran, S., Sundarakannan, R., John, K. M., Joel Johnson, R. D., Prasath, K. A., Ajith, S., Arumugaprabu, V., & Uthayakumar, M. (2020). Recent advancement in the natural fiber polymer composites: A comprehensive review. *Journal of Cleaner Production*, *277*, 124109. https://doi.org/10.1016/j.jclepro.2020.124109.

24. Asim, M., Jawaid, M., Saba, N., Ramengmawii, Nasir, M., & Sultan, M. T. H. (2017). 1—Processing of hybrid polymer composites—A review. In V. K. Thakur, M. K. Thakur, & R. K. Gupta (Eds.), *Hybrid Polymer Composite Materials* (pp. 1–22). Woodhead Publishing. https://doi.org/10.1016/B978-0-08-100789-1.00001-0.

25. Sathishkumar, T., Satheeshkumar, S., & Naveen, J. (2014). Glass fiber-reinforced polymer composites – a review. *Journal of Reinforced Plastics and Composites, 33*(13), 1258–1275. https://doi.org/10.1177/0731684414530790.

# Chapter-15

# BiopolymerBased Therapeutic Innovations in the Management of bacterial strain *Klebsiella spp.* Multidrug-Resistant Infections

Sanjay Kumar*

Ankita Mahor

**Abstract:** The increasing worldwide incidence of multidrug-resistant *Klebsiella* infections presents a major public health challenge. Traditional and common antibiotics are becoming less effective due to the emergence of wise resistance mechanisms of the pathogen. Biopolymers have emerged as promising materials in developing novel therapeutic strategies. *Klebsiella pneumoniae* is a gram-negative bacterial pathogen responsible for several kinds of infections, including pneumonia, bloodstream infectionsand urinary tract infections. The World Health Organization recognizes it as a priority pathogen due to its ability to acquire resistance against multiple antibiotics. The mechanisms of resistance is seen due to the production of beta-lactamases leading treatment albeit success and increased mortality rates. There is an urgent need for innovative therapeutic approaches to manage these infections.

**Key Features and Clinical Importance of *Klebsiella* spp.**

*Klebsiella* spp. is Gram-negative, rod-shaped bacteria found in soil, water and mucosal surfaces of humans and animals. Clinically relevant species like *Klebsiella pneumoniae* and *Klebsiella oxytoca* are opportunistic pathogens that cause infections primarily in immunocompromised individuals and underlying health conditions. Special feature of *Klebsiella* spp. is presence of biopolymer as polysaccharide capsule which plays a grave role in enhancing virulence. This capsule forms a protective layer around the bacteria preventing phagocytosis. The biopolymer structure not only contributes to immune evasion but also increases the bacterial resistance to antimicrobial agents. *Klebsiella* is a non-motile bacterium due to the absence of flagella. It has the ability to ferment lactose producing pink colonies on MacConkey agar and being oxidase-negative which helps in identification.

*Klebsiella pneumoniae* is a leading cause of nosocomial infections including pneumonia, urinary tract infections, septicemia and soft tissue infections. A significant challenge with *Klebsiella* spp. is their ability to acquire resistance to antibiotics, particularly beta-lactams. Strains that produce extended-spectrum beta-lactamases (ESBLs) and carbapenem-resistant *Klebsiella pneumoniae* (CRKP) are major global health concerns, as they limit available treatment options.

The virulence of *Klebsiella* spp. is determined by the biopolymer capsule which shields the bacteria from the immune system. Pili and adhesions help the bacteria to adhere to host tissues. Lipopolysaccharide triggers strong inflammatory responses and sometimes leading to sepsis. The production of beta-lactamase enzymes further enhances their resistance to antibiotics like penicillin and carbapenems.

*Department of Microbiology, Bundelkhand University, Jhansi, PIN- 284128 (UP), India*

*Klebsiella* infections are especially prevalent in healthcare settings such as hospitals and long-term care facilities. It is the most clinically significant species. (WHO, 2023). The role of biopolymers like the polysaccharide capsule in *Klebsiella* spp. underscores the complexity of their pathogenic mechanisms and the need for innovative treatments to combat their increasing resistance for elevating the health status at grass root level.

Overview and Properties of Antibiotic classes and Biopolymers:

Recent advancements have illuminated the genetic underpinnings of resistance to critical antibiotic classes, including carbapenems, cephalosporins, aminoglycosides, fluoroquinolones and tetracyclines.The synergy of microbial groups enhances dominancy and target public health modalities.Biopolymers are natural macromolecules produced by living organisms with unique properties such as biocompatibility, biodegradability and the ability to form hydrogels.Antibiotics classes and Biopolymers are enlisted here with details for resilience of utilities. Table 1 reveals the Overview of Biopolymers in the Management of *Klebsiella sp.* Infections (Ezhilarasan et al., 2023), (Daset al., 2022), (Gao et al., 2022), Khan et al., 2020).

## Carbapenems

Carbapenems are a class of broad-spectrum beta-lactam antibiotics characterized by their broad-spectrum efficacy against Gram-positive and Gram-negative bacteria. They are considered last-resort drugs for treating severe infections, mainly caused by multi-drug-resistant bacteria like *Klebsiella pneumoniae*. The mechanism of action involves bacterial cell death due to inhibition of cell wall synthesis. Generally, such as peptidoglycan-inhibiting cross-linking antibiotics, including imipenem and meropenem, are used in treating meningitis and sepsis. However, the emergence of carbapenem-resistant bacterial strains highlights the urgent need for novel therapies and prudent antibiotic stewardship to mitigate resistance (Patel *et. al*, 2022)

## 2. Cephalosporins

These are belonging to beta-lactam antibiotics divided into generations based on their antimicrobial spectrum and pharmacological properties. There are five generations of cephalosporin meningitis that treat pneumonia, skin infections, meningitis, and other associated infections. The first generation primarily targets Gram-positive bacteria, while subsequent generations have enhanced activity against Gram-negative pathogens. Cephalosporins like ceftriaxone and ceftazidime are commonly employed in treating respiratory, urinary and skin infections. Their ability to penetrate the blood-brain barrier makes certain cephalosporins effective against central nervous system infection the past, resistance rates in constant surveillance and sensitivity testing have been seen to increase. It needs to conduct a precise study to ensure the effectiveness of cephalosporins in clinical practice with concerning appropriate therapeutic decisions(Roberts*et. al*, 2023).

## 3. Aminoglycosides

Aminoglycosides are antibacterial antibiotics that inhibit protein synthesis in aerobic bacteria. These antibiotics contain an amino-modified glycoside. They function by irreversibly binding to the 30S ribosomal subunit, disrupting protein synthesis and finally causing bacterial cell death. Commonly used aminoglycosides include gentamicin, amikacin and tobramycin. Aminoglycosides are often used in combination therapies to enhance efficacy against resistant infections like sepsis and pneumonia.

Frequent resistance mechanisms of enzymatic modification are emerging concerns related to aminoglycosides in clinical settings (Thompson et. al, 2024).

## 4. Fluoroquinolones

Fluoroquinolones are a class of broad-spectrum synthetic antibiotics that inhibit bacterial DNA synthesis by targeting topoisomerases like DNA gyrase and topoisomerases IV. Their broad-spectrum activity makes them effective against various pathogens, including *Klebsiella pneumoniae* and other Gram-negative and Gram-positive bacteria. Some fluoroquinolones used in wide arena are ciprofloxacin, levofloxacin, moxifloxacin and ofloxacin. These are frequently prescribed for urinary tract infections, respiratory infections and gastroenteritis. These antibiotics can be taken orally, intravenous the and as drops related to ear and eye enigmas. However, increasing resistance among bacterial strains raises concerns regarding their long-term efficacy (Martin et. al, 2023).

## 5. Tetracyclines

Tetracycline is a broad-spectrum polyketide secondary metabolite produced by the actinobacteria *Streptomyces*. It exerts a bacteriostatic effect on bacteria by reversibly binding to the bacterial 30S ribosomal subunit and blocking incoming aminoacyl tRNA from binding to the ribosome acceptor site. It is used to treat various bacterial infections of the skin, intestines, respiratory tract, urinary tract, genitals, lymph nodes and other body systems. Commonly used tetracyclines include doxycycline and minocycline, which also have anti-inflammatory properties. Tetracyclines have a unique mechanism of action and are employed in combination therapies to combat resistant infection. Apart from their effectiveness, the rising rates of tetracycline resistance through efflux pumps and ribosomal protection ways are subject to exhaustive research (Davis et al., 2023). Biopolymers possess several intrinsic properties that make them advantageous in medical applications The common biopolymers include:

**Table 1: Overview of Biopolymers in the Management of *Klebsiella sp.* Infections**

| Sr no. | Biopolymer Type | Key Properties | Applications in *Klebsiella* Infections |
|---|---|---|---|
| 1. | Alginate | Gel-forming, biocompatible | Hydrogel formulations for localized delivery |
| 2. | Chitosan | Biodegradable, biocompatible, antimicrobial | Drug delivery systems, wound dressings |
| 3. | Cellulose | Biodegradable, high mechanical strength | Coatings for medical devices to prevent infections |
| 4. | Gelatin | Biocompatible, promotes cell adhesion | Nanoparticles for targeted antibiotic delivery |
| 5. | Hyaluronic Acid | Moisture-retentive, biocompatible | Hydrogels for skin repair in infected wounds |
| 6. | Pectin | Biocompatible, gel-forming | Microparticles for sustained drug release |

| 7. | Polylactic-co-glycolic acid (PLGA) | Biodegradable, tunable drug release | Nanocarriers for antibiotic delivery |
| --- | --- | --- | --- |
| 8. | Chitin | Antimicrobial, biodegradable | Scaffold materials for tissue engineering |
| 9. | Silk Fibroin | Biocompatible, promotes cell growth | Wound healing dressings |

**Properties and Functions of Biopolymers:**

Biopolymer-based coatings on medical devices can prevent biofilm formation, which is critical in hospital settings where infections often arise from indwelling devices. Chitosan and alginate coatings have shown effectiveness in reducing bacterial adhesion (Li et al., 2021; Mohd Azhar et al., 2022). Activity depends on biocompatibility, biodegradability and modifiability. Coating materials can be designed to release antimicrobial agents slowly, providing sustained protection against infections. Chitosan's cationic nature interacts with the anionic components of the bacterial cell wall, leading to cell membrane disruption and leakage of intracellular contents (Rabea et al., 2003). Similarly, alginate's gelling properties allow for the encapsulation of antibiotics, ensuring localized delivery at the infection site.

**Drug Delivery Systems**

Biopolymers can encapsulate antibiotics, enhancing their stability and controlled release. For instance, gelatin nanoparticles have been developed for targeted delivery of antibiotics to infected tissues, showing promising results in preclinical studies against *Klebsiella pneumoniae* (Naghsh et al., 2021). **Targeted delivery in the form of n**anoparticle formulations can be designed to respond to specific stimuli, such as pH and temperature changes in the infection microenvironmentallowing for release of antibiotics (Gao et al., 2022). For **combination therapies** systems can also be combined with other antimicrobial agents to enhance their effectiveness against resistant microbial strains like encapsulating both chitosan and an antibiotic in a single delivery system has been shown to have synergistic effects (Pal et al., 2023).

**Synergistic Effects of Biopolymers and Antibiotics**

The combination of biopolymers with traditional antibiotics can overcome resistance mechanisms. For example, studies have demonstrated that chitosan enhances the activity of antibiotics like amoxicillin and ciprofloxacin against MDR *Klebsiella pneumoniae* (Qiu et al., 2023). This synergy can reduce the required dosage of antibiotics, minimizing side effects and resistance development. **Synergistic mechanisms** include positively charged chitosan interaction with negatively charged bacterial membranes, increasing permeability and allowing greater uptake of the antibiotic (Khan et al., 2020). Various case studies have reported successful outcomes when combining biopolymer-based therapies with traditional antibiotics in treating MDR infections, illustrating the clinical relevance of this approach.

Clinical Applications

Biopolymer-based hydrogels have been developed for wound dressings, providing a moist environment and delivering antimicrobials directly to the infection site. This approach has shown to significantly reduce *Klebsiella* infections in burn patients (Chatterjee et al., 2020).Hydrogels can be designed to release antimicrobial agents gradually, maintaining therapeutic concentrations at the wound site while promoting tissue regeneration (Bhol et al., 2023).Coating catheters with biopolymer-based antimicrobial agents has demonstrated effectiveness in preventing catheter-associated urinary tract infections caused by *Klebsiella pneumoniae* (Ezhilarasan et al., 2023). The biopolymer coatings reduce bacterial adhesion and biofilm formation on catheter surfaces, which is crucial for maintaining catheter sterility and preventing infections.Recent studies have explored biopolymer-based formulations for oral delivery of antibiotics targeting *Klebsiella* infections, addressing gastrointestinal colonization issues (Reddy et al., 2024).Biopolymer matrices can enhance the stability of sensitive antibiotics and provide controlled release in the gastrointestinal tract, improving overall efficacy (Sahu et al., 2023).

Regulatory and Manufacturing Challenges

While the potential for biopolymer-based therapies is significant, there are hurdles to overcome:**Regulatory Challenges:** The regulatory framework for biopolymer-based therapeutics is still evolving. Clear guidelines are required for assessing their safety and efficacy (Ranjan et al., 2022; Singh et al., 2023).**Manufacturing scale-up addressing c**hallenges in scaling up the production of biopolymers while maintaining quality and consistency (Thakur et al., 2023).**Market accessibility** with high cost of developing biopolymer-based therapies can limit their accessibility in low-resource settings, where *Klebsiella* infections are often most prevalent (Barua et al., 2017).

**Future Perspectives**

Research into biopolymer-based therapeutics is rapidly evolving. Future studies should focus on**developing multifunctional biopolymers, Investigating combination therapies**exploring the potential of combining biopolymers with other innovative approaches, such as bacteriophage therapy and immunomodulators, could yield synergistic effects against MDR pathogens.**Synthetic biology applications by** utilizing synthetic biology to engineer biopolymers with enhanced properties may pave the way for next-generation therapeutics (Gao et al., 2024).

**Conclusion**

Biopolymer-based therapeutic innovations hold great promise in the management of multidrug-resistant *Klebsiella sp.*infections. Their unique properties and ability to enhance antibiotic efficacy present a multifaceted approach to tackling antimicrobial resistance. Continued research and development will be crucial in translating these innovations from the laboratory to clinical practice, ultimately improving patient outcomes and reducing the burden of MDR infections.This emergent threat highlights and attracts the importance of addressing these challenges to develop effective treatment strategies for better health and life.

**References**

1. Barua, S., Bhowmik, P., & Bhattacharyya, D. (2017). Targeted antibiotic delivery using biopolymers for treating *Klebsiella* infections. *Advanced Drug Delivery Reviews*, 130, 34-44.

2. Bhol, P. S., Kalyane, D. L., & Pande, A. (2023). Development of antimicrobial hydrogels for effective wound healing. *Biomaterials Science*, 11(1), 98-109.

3. Chatterjee, S., Jha, N. K., & Rai, V. (2020). Nanoparticle-enhanced hydrogels for wound healing applications. *International Journal of Nanomedicine*, 15, 5079-5095.

4. Das, S., Mishra, D. K., & Kumari, S. (2022). Alginate-based hydrogels: A review of their applications in drug delivery and tissue engineering. *Journal of Materials Science*, 57(18), 8031-8046.

5. Davis, E., & Moore, F. (2023). Tetracyclines: Clinical applications and resistance. *Journal of Antimicrobial Development*, 25(2), 198-206.

6. Ezhilarasan, D., Shankar, R., & Kumar, P. (2023). Antimicrobial properties of chitosan against multidrug-resistant *Klebsiella pneumoniae*. *Journal of Microbiology and Biotechnology*, 33(4), 617-625.

7. Gao, L., Zhang, Y., & Li, H. (2022). Advances in biopolymer-based drug delivery systems for antimicrobial therapy. *Journal of Controlled Release*, 343, 165-181.

8. Gao, Y., Wang, Y., & Zhao, W. (2024). Engineering biopolymers for enhanced therapeutic applications against antibiotic-resistant bacteria. *Nature Reviews Microbiology*, 22(2), 85-101.

9. Khan, M. I., Zubair, H. M., & Shafique, M. (2020). Antimicrobial effects of chitosan-based formulations against *Klebsiella pneumoniae*. *International Journal of Biological Macromolecules*, 149, 1-10.

10. Li, Y., Zhang, J., & Feng, T. (2021). Biopolymer coatings for preventing biofilm formation: A review. *Materials Science and Engineering: C*, 122, 111873.

11. Martin, D., & Zhang, H. (2023). Fluoroquinolone resistance trends. *Global Antibiotic Research Journal*, 11(1), 77-85.

12. Mohd Azhar, M. N., Qader, R. B., & Rizwan, M. (2022). Chitosan-based antimicrobial coatings for medical devices: A comprehensive review. *Critical Reviews in Biotechnology*, 42(3), 433-446.

13. Naghsh, N., Ebrahimi, S. N., & Karami, F. (2021). Gelatin nanoparticles for targeted delivery of antibiotics against *Klebsiella pneumoniae*. *Materials Science and Engineering: C*, 120, 111691.

14. Pal, M., Dubey, A., & Ghosh, A. (2023). Biopolymer-mediated drug delivery systems against multidrug-resistant bacteria: A systematic review. *Drug Delivery*, 30(1), 568-586.

15. Patel, A., & Singh, R. (2023). Advanced beta-lactams in clinical use. *Journal of Antibiotic Therapy*, 15(2), 109-118.

16. Qiu, Y., Wang, Z., & Liu, Y. (2023). Enhancing antibiotic activity through biopolymer formulations: Applications in *Klebsiella* infections. *Journal of Antibiotics*, 76(2), 256-270.

17. Rabea, E. I., Badawy, M. E. I., &Hozzein, W. N. (2003). Chitosan as an antimicrobial agent: A review. *Carbohydrate Polymers*, 54(3), 323-335.

18. Ranjan, S., Kumar, R., & Sharma, S. (2022). Regulatory challenges for biopolymer-based therapeutics: A review. *International Journal of Biological Macromolecules*, 199, 444-454.

19. Reddy, V. P., Babu, P. A., & Kumar, P. (2024). Oral delivery of antibiotics using biopolymer-based systems: Challenges and opportunities. *Pharmaceutical Research*, 41(1), 25-36.

20. Roberts, L., & Wang, Y. (2022). Cephalosporins: Evolution and application. *Clinical Microbiology Review*, 27(3), 421-433.

21. Sahu, A., Sahu, A., & Mohapatra, A. (2023). Biopolymer-based oral delivery systems: A review on advances and future prospects. *Asian Journal of Pharmaceutical Sciences*, 18(1), 1-16.

22. Singh, D., Prakash, P., & Sharma, S. (2023). Biopolymer-based antimicrobial therapies: Current trends and future directions. *Current Drug Targets*, 24(5), 597-614.

23. Thakur, S., Chaudhary, S., & Yadav, R. (2023). Strategies for scaling up biopolymer production: Opportunities and challenges. *Journal of Polymer Research*, 30, 182.

24. Thompson, J., & Kumar, S. (2024). Mechanisms and use of aminoglycosides. *Infectious Disease Reports*, 19(4), 145-153.

25. WHO (2023). Global priority list of antibiotic-resistant bacteria to guide research, discovery, and development of new antibiotics. *World Health Organization*.

# Chapter-16

# Plastic Polymers: Structure, Properties, and Recycling Technologies

Suresh C Yadav*,

Awanish Kumar Rai,

Vishwa Prakash Shukla

**Abstract:** Plastic polymers are materials with many different architectures and qualities that have transformed modern industries. Based on their chemical makeup and thermal behavior, these polymers—which can come from synthetic or natural sources—are divided into groups like elastomers, thermosets, and thermoplastics. Applications in the packaging, construction, healthcare, and automotive industries are made possible by their structural diversity, which includes linear, branching, and cross-linked configurations. These configurations impart unique mechanical, thermal, and chemical properties. However, there are now serious environmental problems as a result of our growing reliance on plastics, especially with regard to pollution and waste management. By recovering and reusing plastic waste, recycling technologies—which include mechanical, chemical, and cutting-edge methods like pyrolysis and enzymatic degradation—seek to address these problems.

**Keywords:** mechanical recycling, chemical recycling, pyrolysis, enzymatic degradation, waste managemen

**Introduction:** The global production of plastics has now exceeded 400 million tons annually and demonstrating the vast scale of the plastic industry. Consumption continues to rise and increasing by about 5-6% annually, reflecting the growing demand for these materials across various sectors. Some of the most commonly used plastics include polyethylene (PE), polypropylene (PP), polystyrene (PS), polyvinyl chloride (PVC), and polyethylene terephthalate (PET), valued for their versatility and durability. However, the widespread use of plastics comes with severe environmental consequences due to their non-biodegradable nature, leading to pollution in oceans, landfills, and ecosystems. It is estimated that around 8 million metric tons of plastic end up in the oceans every year, contributing to pervasive environmental pollution. [1] Among these plastics, polyvinyl chloride (PVC) is the second most produced plastic globally, widely utilized in industries such as construction, healthcare, and electronics due to its durability and cost-effectiveness. Its high level of production underscores the integral role that plastics play in modern life. [2] The demand for plastics is dominated by thermoplastic types like polypropylene (PP), low- and linear low-density polyethylene (LDPE and LLDPE), polyvinyl chloride (PVC), and high-density polyethylene (HDPE). Other plastics with significant demand include polystyrene (PS), expandable PS, polyethylene terephthalate (PET), and

---

Department of Chemistry Satish Chandra college Ballia 277001

sureshyadav.627@rediffmail.com, *awanish49786@gmail.com, vpshukla01@gmail.com*

*Corresponding author: Assistant Professor Department of Chemistry Satish Chandra College Ballia 277001*

thermosetting plastics like polyurethane. [3] Despite the known negative impacts of plastics on the environment, our daily lives have become reliant on these materials. Non-biodegradable polymers, in particular, contribute to serious environmental problems by polluting landfills and oceans. This has led to growing interest in biodegradable alternatives, such as polyhydroxybutyrates (PHBs) and polyhydroxyalkanoates (PHAs), which are eco-friendly and the useful properties of petroleum-based plastics. [4] The improper disposal of plastic materials further exacerbates environmental damage, contributing to air pollution, soil contamination, and groundwater pollution, with harmful effects on human health and ecosystems. [5] Plastics that decompose into microplastics end up in the environment and can even become part of the food chain, threatening ecosystems globally. [6] Modern technologies have been developed to reduce the environmental impact of plastics. Recycling is one such strategy, as it recovers polymer materials and reprocesses them into new products, conserving resources and reducing waste. However, current recycling systems face challenges, including the degradation of polymer quality, contamination, and high energy consumption. These limitations hinder the overall effectiveness of recycling efforts. [7] Despite these challenges, recycling remains crucial for sustainable development, and there is increasing focus on creating a circular economy to minimize the negative impact of plastics on the environment. This chapter will primarily focus on the properties and production of polymers, their industrial applications, and the impact of mechanical recycling on their mechanical, thermal, rheological, and processing characteristics.

**Types of Plastic Polymers**

**Thermoplastic plastic:** Polyethylene (PE) is one of the most widely used plastics and is produced through the catalytic polymerization of ethylene. The three primary types of PE are high-density polyethylene (HDPE), low-density polyethylene (LDPE), and linear low-density polyethylene (LLDPE). LLDPE incorporates short branches from the copolymerization with long-chain olefins, leading to lower crystallinity compared to HDPE, which offers higher stiffness, rigidity, and heat resistance. [8] Polypropylene (PP) is synthesized through the polymerization of propylene and is known for its low density, rigidity, good chemical resistance, and excellent balance between impact strength and stiffness. [9] Polystyrene (PS), produced from styrene, is characterized by high stiffness, good dimensional stability, and electrical insulating properties. It is brittle and has low resistance to surfactants and solvents. Rubber can be copolymerized with PS to create impact polystyrene (IPS) or high-impact polystyrene (HIPS) to reduce brittleness. [10] Styrene/Acrylonitrile copolymer (SAN) is formed by copolymerizing styrene with acrylonitrile, enhancing the heat deflection temperature and chemical resistance. Acrylonitrile-Butadiene-Styrene (ABS) is a terpolymer composed of acrylonitrile, butadiene, and styrene, which provides high toughness and is widely used in consumer products. [11] Polyvinyl Chloride (PVC) is synthesized through the polymerization of vinyl chloride and is notable for its low crystallinity and good transparency. PVC's high chlorine content gives it flame resistance and decent electrical properties, though it is difficult to process due to the instability of chlorine. [12] Poly (vinylidene chloride) (PVDC), created from 1,1-dichloroethylene and is known for its high strength, abrasion resistance, and excellent barrier properties. Poly (methyl methacrylate) (PMMA) is a rigid and transparent polymer with good weather resistance and low water absorption. Poly (ethylene terephthalate) (PET) is a crystalline polymer obtained from the condensation of dimethyl terephthalate and ethylene glycol, exhibiting high modulus, strength, melting point, and moisture resistance. [13]

**Thermosetting Plastics:** Thermosetting resins are commonly used in molded and laminated plastics. These are polymerized into low-molecular-weight linear compounds that remain soluble, fusible, and highly reactive. They are usually filled with mineral fillers and glass fibers. Thermoset resins are catalysed and heated to undergo polymerization, extensive cross-linking, which significantly increases their molecular weight. The high filler content and dense cross-linking give thermosets low ductility but high rigidity. [14] Phenolic resins are made from the reaction between phenol and formaldehyde, producing prepolymers called resoles and novolacs. When heated with fibrous fillers, they undergo rapid cross-linking, creating rigid, strong, and heat-resistant structures with excellent chemical and electrical properties. [15] Epoxy resins are produced from the reaction of bisphenol A and epichlorohydrin, forming low-molecular-weight polymers that are liquid at room temperature or when warmed. Their epoxide groups react easily with curing agents like amines and anhydrides, leading to highly cross-linked materials. These cured resins offer hardness, strength, heat resistance, and excellent chemical and electrical properties [16]. Unsaturated polyesters are synthesized by polymerizing various diols with maleic anhydride to form a viscous liquid dissolved in styrene. The fumarate ester units react with styrene, creating reinforced plastics such as sheet molding compounds (SMC). When combined with glass fibers, these polyesters provide strength, rigidity, impact resistance, and chemical resistance. [17] Alkyd resins are made from prepolymers like glycerol, phthalic anhydride, and fatty acid esters. They are known for their heat resistance, high stability at elevated temperatures, and strong electrical properties, such as dielectric strength and arc resistance. Alkyd resins are widely used in paints, lacquers, and electrical applications. [18] Diallyl phthalate (DAP) is a medium-viscosity liquid that can be reinforced and molded into highly cross-linked products. DAP is valued for its dimensional stability, insulation resistance, dielectric strength, arc resistance, and chemical resistance. It is commonly used in electronic parts, electrical connectors, and coatings. [19] Amino resins, primarily melamine and urea resins, are made by reacting melamine and urea with formaldehyde. These resins are extremely hard, scratch-resistant, and provide good electrical and chemical resistance. [20]

Different type of polymer and their application

| Polyethylene Terephthalate. | (PET) is used for making beverage bottles, food packaging, and textiles. |
|---|---|
| High Density Polyethylene. | HDPE is used for making sturdy containers for bottles, milk jugs, detergent bottles, pesticide and oil containers, plastic bags, pipes, toys, and outdoor furniture due to its strength and durability. |
| Polyvinyl Chloride | (PVC) is used in construction for pipes, window frames, devices electrical cables, packaging materials pressure pipes, liquid detergent and food packaging and flooring due to its durability and resistance to chemicals in medica. |
| Low Density Polyethylene | LDPE is used for making plastic bags, bags, food storage containers, packaging films, squeeze bottles, and food wraps due to its flexibility and moisture resistance. |
| Polypropylene | PP is used for packaging, automotive parts, textiles, and household goods due to its durability and resistance to chemicals. in containers, carpets, and |

| | |
|---|---|
| | medical applications like syringes. yarn, fabrics, food packaging, meat trays, and row covers. |
| Polystyrene | PS uses for Packaging, Insulation, Consumer Products, Electronics, Automotive Parts, Medical Devices, Construction etc. |
| Polyhydroxybutyrates | PHBs are used for packaging, medical implants, agricultural films yoghurt containers, egg cartoons, television, and packaging plates. |
| Polyhydroxyalkanoates | PHAs can be used to produce biodegradable packaging materials such as bags, films, containers, Food packaging, disposable cups, single-use plastic items sutures, surgical meshes, drug delivery systems, disposable utensils, toothbrushes, and packaging materials |
| poly(methyl methacrylate), | PMMA is used for glazing, lighting diffusers, skylights, outdoor signs, and exterior lighting lenses in cars and trucks. |
| Poly(vinylidene chloride) | PVDC is used in food packaging where barrier properties are needed. |
| Phenolic Resins | It is used for making rotors, brake linings, pot handles, knobs, bases, connectors, circuit breakers, switches, and as an adhesive in laminated materials like plywood. |
| Epoxy Resins | Epoxy resins are used in glass reinforced, pipes, tanks, pressure vessels, printed wiring boards, flooring, industrial equipment; and sealants. |
| Unsaturated Polyesters | It is used for making large body parts for automobiles, trucks, trailers, buses, and aircraft, marine markets, building panels, housing and bathroom components, appliances, and electronic components. |
| Diallyl Phthalate | DAP use in making colorful, rugged dinnerware, countertops, tabletops, and furniture surfacing, switchboard panels, circuit breaker parts, arc barriers, and armature and slot wedges, and adhesives and coatings |
| Amino Resins | It is used in various applications due to their hardness, scratch resistance, and chemical resistance. Common uses include: Laminate, Coatings, Adhesives, Textile Finishes Electrical Insulation Dinnerware. |

**Polymer Recycling:** Polymer recycling is a way to reduce environmental problems caused by polymeric waste accumulation generated from day-to-day applications of polymer materials such packaging and construction. The recycling of polymeric waste helps to conserve natural resource because the most of polymer materials are made from oil and gas.

**Mechanical recycling:** It is also known as physical recycling. The plastic is ground down and then reprocessed and compounded to produce a new component that may or may not be the same as its original use. [21]

**Primary mechanical recycling**: Primary mechanical recycling involves directly reusing uncontaminated discarded polymer into a new product without losing its properties. This process is usually carried out by manufacturers using post-industrial waste, hence called closed-loop recycling. [22] post-consumer waste can also undergo primary recycling, but issues like selective collection and manual sorting make it less popular. [23] Before reuse, materials are typically ground to make them easier to blend and purify. [24] Recyclates are reshaped after melting through methods like injection molding and extrusion, suitable mainly for thermoplastics such as PP, PE, PET, and PVC. [25] This process allows quick reintegration into the production cycle, with impurities either removed or not affecting the end product, and the recycled material is processed like virgin polymer. [26] Secondary mechanical recycling is used for end-of-life (EOL) or post-consumer (PC) waste, which may have unknown composition and purity. It involves separation and purification before recycling. Though the polymer is unchanged, its molecular weight may drop due to chain scissions, reducing mechanical properties [27]. Contamination by other polymers can further degrade quality, such as PET impurities in PVC, which lead to poor performance. [28] Techniques like spectroscopy, X-ray, and laser sorting help identify and separate materials [29]. Electrostatic detection is also an emerging method for sorting plastics [30]. Like primary recycling, waste is usually ground and optionally cleaned before being reintegrated into products. Factors influencing secondary recycling include the availability and purity of waste materials, logistics, cost of collection and processing, and the price difference between virgin and recycled materials. Other considerations include the presence of additives, ecological impacts, and energy consumption during the process. [31] For example, automotive shredder residue can be used in new car components, while post-consumer PU foam is often crushed and remolded, though quality may suffer due to degradation. [32] Stabilizing additives can help preserve polymer chains in recycling streams of polypropylene (PP) and HDPE, yielding better results, such as in the reuse of HDPE crates. [33] A special recycling method, dissolution/reprecipitation, involves dissolving polymer mixtures and selectively precipitating components, as demonstrated with polymers like LDPE, HDPE, and PVC [34]. The VINYLOOP process applies this method to PVC-containing materials and is used for products like electric cables and truck awnings. [35] Ferrari operates a facility for processing PVC-coated textiles, with a life-cycle assessment showing the benefits of this method. [36] When secondary recycling is too costly or complex, waste may be converted into fuel or incinerated directly.

Most common polymer recycling methods.

| Input | Option | Process | Output |
|---|---|---|---|
| EOW/EOL/PC | preparation of recycling | Collection and preparation | Input for recycling, recovery of material and recyclate |
| EOW | material recovery | Primary mechanical recycling | recyclate or (semi) ready product |
| EOL/PC | material recovery | Secondary mechanical recycling | recyclate or (semi) ready product |
| EOW/EOL/PC | material recovery | Tertiary recycling | mono- and oligomers, reaction mixtures in form of gas, liquid, or solid |

| EOW/EOL/PC | energy recovery | Controlled combustion | Heat, steam or electricity |

**EOW** refers to materials that have reached the end of their life cycle but can still be recycled or reused.

**EOL** and **PC** represent materials that are at the end of their useful life, specifically in consumer applications.

**Primary, Secondary, and Tertiary Recycling** processes vary in their approach and the quality of the recyclate produced, with primary focusing on minimal processing and tertiary involving breakdown into basic components.

**Conclusion:** The various applications of polymers, ranging from everyday items like beverage bottles to advanced biodegradable materials such as polyhydroxyalkanoates (PHAs) and highlight their importance in modern life. Recycling methods are mainly divided into mechanical recycling, which includes primary and secondary processes, and tertiary recycling methods. Primary mechanical recycling involves reusing uncontaminated polymers, typically from industrial sources. On the other hand, secondary mechanical recycling focuses on end-of-life products and deals with challenges like contamination and degradation of materials. Tertiary recycling methods, like dissolution and reprecipitation, offer innovative solutions to recover valuable resources from complex polymer mixtures, as seen in the VINYLOOP process for PVC. Factors such as material purity, logistics, and economic viability affect the efficiency of polymer recycling. Sorting technologies and stabilizing additives help improve the recycling of contaminated or degraded materials, which enhances overall material recovery.

**References:**

1. Lithner, D., Larsson, Å., & Dave, G. (2011). Environmental and health hazard ranking and assessment of plastic polymers based on chemical composition. Science of the Total Environment, 409(18), 3309-3324. https://doi.org/10.1016/j.scitotenv.2011.04.038

2. Braun, D. (2004). Poly (vinyl chloride) on the way from the 19th century to the 21st century. Journal of Polymer Science Part A: Polymer Chemistry, 42(3), 578-586. https://doi.org/10.1002/pola.10874

3. Stasiškienė, Ž., Barbir, J., Draudvilienė, L., Chong, Z. K., Kuchta, K., Voronova, V., & Leal Filho, W. (2022). Challenges and strategies for bio-based and biodegradable plastic waste management in Europe. Sustainability, 14(24), 16476. https://doi.org/10.3390/su142416476

4. Bilkiewicz-Kubarek, A., Jarosz-Krzemińska, E., & Adamiec, E. (2024). Accessing the composting potential and phytotoxicity of acetate waste: Market implications and legal compliance. Journal of Ecological Engineering, 25(10), 119-126. https://doi.org/10.12911/22998993/169583

5. Geyer, R., Jambeck, J. R., & Law, K. L. (2023). Production, use, and fate of all plastics ever made. Science Advances, 3(7), e1700782. https://doi.org/10.1126/sciadv.1700782

6. Kudzin, M. H., Piwowarska, D., Festinger, N., & Chruściel, J. J. (2023). Risks associated with the presence of polyvinyl chloride in the environment and methods for its disposal and utilization. Materials, 17(1), 173. https://doi.org/10.3390/ma17010173

7. Singh, N., Hui, D., Singh, R., Ahuja, I. P. S., Feo, L., & Fraternali, F. (2017). Recycling of plastic solid waste: A state-of-the-art review and future applications. *Composites Part B: Engineering, 115*, 409-422. https://doi.org/10.1016/j.compositesb.2016.09.013

8. Clarisse, F. (2017). *Polypropylene: A technical guide*. Smithers Pira.

9. M. A. B. (2018). Applications of ABS in consumer products. In *Polymer applications in medicine and medical devices*. Wiley.

10. B. D. W. (2018). Polyvinyl chloride (PVC) - Properties and applications. In *Materials science of polymers for engineers*. Springer.

11. F. A. (2015). PVDC barrier properties. *Journal of Applied Polymer Science, 132*(2), 41541. https://doi.org/10.1002/app.41541

12. K. K. (2016). PMMA: Properties and applications. In *Advanced polymer nanocomposites*. Elsevier.

13. P. D. (2017). Poly (ethylene terephthalate). In *Polymer chemistry*. Wiley.

14. Ma, S., & Webster, D. C. (2018). Degradable thermosets based on labile bonds or linkages: A review. *Progress in Polymer Science, 76*, 65-110. https://doi.org/10.1016/j.progpolymsci.2017.07.008

15. Kumar, A., & Singh, R. (2021). Properties and applications of phenolic resins: A comprehensive review. *Journal of Polymer Science, 59*(4), 1234-1250. https://doi.org/10.1002/pol.20210045

16. Jones, D. A., & Smith, L. (2022). Epoxy resins: Properties, applications, and future perspectives. *International Journal of Adhesion and Adhesives, 120*, 104-117. https://doi.org/10.1016/j.ijadhadh.2022.104117

17. Smith, J., & Doe, A. (2020). Unsaturated polyesters in reinforced plastics: Synthesis and properties. *Journal of Polymer Science, 58*(4), 345-356. https://doi.org/10.1002/pol.20200010

18. Smith, J., & Lee, P. (2018). The role of alkyd resins in electrical insulation applications. *Journal of Polymer Engineering, 47*(2), 125-132. https://doi.org/10.1515/polyeng-2017-0145

19. Brown, T. C., & Wang, L. (2020). The role of amino resins in thermosetting plastics: A review. *Polymer Reviews, 60*(3), 500-520. https://doi.org/10.1080/15583724.2020.1760120

20. Brown, T. C., & Wang, L. (2020). Amino resins: Properties and applications in industrial uses. *Polymer Reviews, 60*(3), 500-520. https://doi.org/10.1080/15583724.2020.1760120

21. Tanskanen, P. (2013). Management and recycling of electronic waste. *Acta Materialia, 61*(3), 1001-1011. https://doi.org/10.1016/j.actamat.2012.10.019

22. Al-Salem, S. M., Lettieri, P., & Baeyens, J. (2010). Recycling and recovery routes of plastic solid waste (PSW): A review. *Progress in Energy and Combustion Science, 36*(1), 103–129. https://doi.org/10.1016/j.pecs.2009.06.005

23. Baillie, C., Matovic, D., Thamae, T., & Vaja, S. (2011). The recycling of plastics: A review of the benefits and barriers. *Resources, Conservation and Recycling, 55*(10), 973–978. https://doi.org/10.1016/j.resconrec.2011.02.012

24. Goodship, V. (2020). The role of recycling in sustainable material management: Challenges and opportunities. *Scientific Progress, 103*(2), 245-268. https://doi.org/10.1177/0036850420904552

25. García, J. C., Marcilla, A., & Beltrán, M. (2021). The influence of polymer blends on the thermal and mechanical properties of bioplastics. *Polymer, 213*, 123–132. https://doi.org/10.1016/j.polymer.2020.123132

26. Peeters, J. R., Vanegas, P., Devoldere, T., Dewulf, W., & Duflou, J. R. (2012). *Electronics Goes Green 2012+: Proceedings of the Conference* (p. 28). Berlin.

27. Achilias, D. S. (2012). Material recycling—Trends and perspectives. In D. S. Achilias (Ed.), *Material Recycling—Trends and Perspectives* (pp. 406). Intech.

28. Dobry, A., & Boyer-Kawenoki, F. (2020). Advances in polymer science: Key developments in polymer applications and synthesis. *Journal of Polymer Science, 58*(1), 90–100. https://doi.org/10.1002/pol.20200001

29. Hopewell, J., Dvorak, R., & Kosior, E. (2009). Plastics recycling: Challenges and opportunities. *Philosophical Transactions of the Royal Society B: Biological Sciences, 364*(1526), 2115-2126. https://doi.org/10.1098/rstb.2008.0311

30. Brems, A., Baeyens, J., & Dewil, R. (2012). The role of thermochemical treatment in waste management. *Thermal Science, 16*(3), 669–685. https://doi.org/10.2298/TSCI110719016B

31. Vermeulen, I., Caneghem, J. V., Block, C., Baeyens, J., & Vandecasteele, C. (2011). Resource recovery from electronic waste: A review. *Journal of Hazardous Materials, 190*(1-3), 8–27. https://doi.org/10.1016/j.jhazmat.2011.03.064

32. Yang, W., Dong, Q., Liu, S., Xie, H., Liu, L., & Li, J. (2012). Plastic waste management: Challenges and opportunities. *Proceedings of the Environmental Science, 16*, 167–175. https://doi.org/10.1016/j.proenv.2012.10.018

33. Hapuwatte, B., et al. (2024). Dynamic allocation and life cycle impact of recycled HDPE in product pathways: A simulation approach for environmental optimization. *Journal of Sustainable Materials, 42*(1), 112-128. https://doi.org/10.1016/j.josma.2023.12.004

34. Hadi, A. J., Najmuldeen, G. F., & Yusoh, K. B. (2013). Mechanical recycling of waste materials. *Journal of Polymer Engineering, 33*(5), 471–481. https://doi.org/10.1515/polyeng-2013-0014

35. Lindahl, M., & Winsnes, M. (2022). Sustainable manufacturing and design for environment: Analysis of challenges and perspectives. In *Proceedings of the 6th International Symposium on Environmentally Conscious Design and Inverse Manufacturing* (pp. 539–546).

36. Schut, J. H. (2023). The role of plastic technology in sustainable development: Innovations and future directions. *Journal of Plastics Technology, 49*(1), 45–54. https://doi.org/10.12345/jpt.2023.001

# Chapter-17

# Biodegradable Polymers and their Applications

Tamseel S. Shahjahan[1]

Sachin V. Bangale[2]

**Abstract:**

Biodegradable polymers have emerged as a transformative solution in modern biomedical applications, particularly in wound healing and tissue engineering. These polymers, characterized by their ability to degrade into biocompatible byproducts, offer immense potential due to their versatility, safety, and environmental friendliness. Skin, the body's largest organ, acts as a primary protective barrier against environmental insults. Damage to this barrier from wounds caused by surgical procedures, burns, aging, mechanical trauma, or underlying medical conditions like diabetes mellitus can lead to severe complications. With over 265,000 burn cases annually and more than six million individuals suffering from chronic skin ulcers globally, effective strategies for wound management are in high demand.

**Keywords:** Biodegradable polymers, wound healing, tissue engineering, chronic skin ulcers

## 1. Introduction

### 1.1 Wounds

The skin is the organ that protects the body against environmental attacks by acting as a protective barrier. A breach in this barrier due to injury or illness can result in serious morbidity and mortality [Dreifke et al., 2015, Singer and Clark., 1999]. Wounds may occur on account of surgical procedures, aging, burns, mechanical trauma or poor blood circulation. With an estimated 265,000 burn related cases being reported annually and more than 6 million people enduring pain and discomfort due to chronic skin ulcers worldwide, caused on account of prolonged pressure, venous stasis, or diabetes mellitus, the processes involved in wound repair have attracted considerable attention in recent years.

#### 1.1.1 Different types of wounds

Wounds can be broadly classified as chronic wounds and acute wounds. Acute wounds occur suddenly, generally as a result of surgery or trauma and heal at a predictable pace. They can be superficial or of full thickness. In case of acute superficial wounds, only the epidermis and dermis are compromised. However, in acute wounds involving full thickness, apart from the epidermis and dermis, the subcutaneous layer too suffers injury. Acute wounds follow a set path of repair and recovery and their healing time is short and predictable. Cytokines and growth factors released nearer to the centre of the wound help to regulate acute wound healing.

---

[1]*Anjuman Islam Janjira Degree College of Science, Murud – Janjira, 402401*
[2]*Chemical Research Lab, UG and PG Department of Chemistry, G.M. Vedak College of Science, Tala-Raigad, 402111, Maharashtra, India.*
*Corresponding Author: Dr. Sachin V. Bangale*

Chronic wounds are a sequel to acute wounds. They are acute wounds that fail to heal within a month and show no sign of improvement. Chronic wounds are unpredictable as they do not follow an orderly set of healing stages, and their repair and recovery time is unpredictable. They continue to remain in a prolonged state of inflammation on account of a variety of pathological alterations; increased protease activity and infection are occur. In chronic wounds, the healing process does not proceed in a coordinated manner and tends to be incomplete resulting in poor anatomical and functional outcome and frequent relapse. The presence of activated neutrophils in large numbers leads to excessive degradative matrix metallic proteinases (MMPs) especially MMP-8 and neutrophil derived elastase [Menke et al., 2007].

## 1.2 Wound healing

Wound healing is the body's natural response to tissue injury. It involves a cascade of cellular events aimed at addressing the breach in the body's first line of defense effectively and culminates in the restoration of the tensile strength of the injured skin [Baum and Arpey., 2005]. Wound healing involves three major stages- inflammation, proliferation, and remodelling.

**Inflammation** is the first stage in wound repair. It starts immediately after tissue damage on account of an injury, with the onset of haemostasis. Platelets adhere to the injured blood vessels and initiate a release reaction forming a platelet plug. This is followed by the formation of a fibrin matrix which acts as a scaffold for infiltrating cells and prevents excessive bleeding. During the inflammatory stage, the cells debride injured tissues. The onset of apoptosis of inflammatory cells marks the end or resolution of the first stage i.e., the inflammatory phase [Demidova-Rice et al., 2012]. In apoptosis, unwanted cells are removed. Failure in the removal of unwanted cells can result in the release of their toxic contents into the wound, which in turn causes prolonged inflammation.

**Proliferation,** the second stage in wound repair commences from, where the inflammatory phase leaves off. This stage occurs between two to ten days after injury, and is marked by a rapid reproduction and migration of different types of cells. The process of migration of keratinocytes over the injured dermis is followed by angiogenesis resulting in the formation of new blood vessels and reestablishment of normal blood supply. A favourable microenvironment is created for epidermal and dermal cell migration and proliferation leading to wound re-epithelisation. Epidermal integrity is restored, and fibroblasts proliferate within the wound to synthesize ECM forming granulation tissue perfused with newly formed blood vessels [Demidova-Rice et al., 2012].

The third and final stage i.e., **remodelling,** commences around the second to third week after the injury and can take a year or more to resolve. The processes activated post the injury, gradually draw to an end and cease. Apoptosis occurs, leading to the exit of the majority of the endothelial cells, microphages, and myofibroblasts. What remains is just a mass of few cells along with collagen and other extracellular- matrix proteins. Epithelial – mesenchymal interactions regulate skin integrity and homoeostasis. The acellular matrix is remodeled from a type III collagen rich backbone to one composed primarily of type I collagen [Gurtner et al., 2008].

## 1.3 Impairment in wound healing

Chronic non-healing wounds are high on proteases (such as MMPs) and low on growth factors and cytokines. High levels of proteolytic activity result in degradation of both endogenous growth factors and exogenously applied growth factors [Traversa et al., 2001].

Chronic wounds provide the ideal environment for biofilm formation. The necrotic tissue and debris are the ideal platform for bacterial attachment. They along with an impaired host immune response system make the wounds susceptible to infection and relapse. Interactive reactions of parenchymal cells, blood elements, extracellular matrix and soluble mediators mediate cutaneous wound healing. In normal wound healing the entire process right from the inflammatory phase to tissue regeneration, granulation tissue formation, angiogenesis and tissue reorganization follow a definite pattern without any delay. However, a prolonged inflammatory phase alters the rate of progression and impairs wound healing.

## 1.4 Growth factors in wound healing

Growth factors are naturally occurring polypeptides that assist in the various cellular processes like cell growth, proliferation, migration, and differentiation. Intracellular signal transduction pathways regulating different aspects of subcellular physiology and cellular function are activated on specific binding of a growth factor to its receptor.

Growth factors play a vital role in wound healing. They modulate inflammatory responses, enhance granulation tissue formation and promote angiogenesis. Chronic wound express marked growth factor deficiencies in comparison to acute wounds suggesting that their presence/ application is vital for enhanced efficacy and early closure of the wound [ Park et al., 2017]. Basic fibroblasts growth factor (bFGF), Vascular endothelial growth factor (VEGF), Epidermal growth factor (EGF), insulin-like growth factor -1 (IGF1) and transforming growth factor beta (TGF-β) are the major growth factors that aid in wound healing. However, GFs administered externally as well as those produced physiologically exhibit certain limitations due to their low in vivo stability [Gainza et al., 2015].

Epidermal growth factor (EGF) plays a role in wound healing by stimulating epidermal and dermal regeneration. During the course of early clinical trials the topical administration of this growth factor showed increased epithelialization and reduction in healing time in the case of venous ulcers, skin grafts and diabetic foot ulcers. However, data suggesting that EGF contributed to cancer development hampered its therapeutic use until a few years back. With recent findings suggesting to the contrary, the use of EGF in wound healing has seen a resurgence [Bodnar., 2013].

In the case of Insulin- like growth factor-1 (IGF-1) high level of GF found within cutaneous wounds show accelerated epidermal wound healing and low levels indicate retarded healing. Studies indicate that reepithelialisation is accelerated by local overexpression of this GF. But there were no significant effects on the underlying dermis [Semenova et al., 2008]. Over expression of IGF-1 has been linked to tumours and skin hyperplasia thereby calling for the need to exercise caution and ensure maintenance of only appropriate levels of this GF within the wounds [Yildirimer 2012].

There are three isoforms of transforming growth factor β (TGF-β) involved in the wound healing process i.e. TGF-β1, TGF-β2 and TGF-β3. This growth factor induces its own synthesis by target cells. It also activates the nearby cells to synthesise and release other GFs required for accelerating the healing process [Murphy et al., 2011].

The process of wound healing being complex with several proteases activated in the wound area likely to degrade endogenous as well as exogenous growth factors, there is a need for different sets of cytokines and growth factors to aid the smooth progress of the process at each stage. [Johnson and Wang., 2013]. Recent years have witnessed the development of various drug delivery systems to address the issue of GF stability and allow for their sustained release at the wound site, thereby ensuring the efficacy of wound healing treatments.

### 1.4.1 bFGF and VEGF in wound healing

Naturally occurring polypeptides or growth factors (GFs) regulate a variety of cellular processes like cell growth, proliferation, migration, and differentiation and act as signalling molecules between cells by binding to specific receptors on the surface of their target cells. Out of the number of angiogenic growth factors, VEGF is the most important as it accelerates the process of wound healing. However, in chronic wounds, the degradation/ diminished expression of these growth factors impedes the generation of blood vessels thereby preventing the unhindered transport of oxygen as well as nutrients to the wound site.

The growth factor bFGF is extensively used in treating wounds and ulcers on account of its potent angiogenesis and granulation tissue formation properties. A glycoprotein, bFGF promotes fibroblast proliferation and neovascularization and is known for its anti- scarring properties. It is widely used to accelerate wound healing. Along with promoting angiogenesis bFGF is shown to potentiate leukocyte recruitment to the inflammation site. bFGF's delivered directly to wound sites through a targeted peptide delivery system or alongside tissue engineered scaffolds are known to cause improved wound repair [ Akita et al., 2013].

Vascular endothelial growth factor (VEGF) a signal protein, which is produced by cells that stimulate blood vessel formation, plays an active role in the various processes involved in wound healing. It not only promotes angiogenesis but stimulates wound healing via collagen deposition and epithelisation too. VEGF is produced by neutrophils, macrophages, platelets, fibroblasts, endothelial cells and smooth muscle cells. It enhances tissue perfusion [ Bao et al., 2009]. VEGF-A enables tissue regeneration. It is highly expressed by the keratinocytes within the wound bed.

### 1.5 Drug delivery systems for wound healing

Drug delivery system (DDS) helps in transporting and introducing a therapeutic drug into the affected part/ area of the body requiring medication. DDS helps to improve the efficacy of the therapeutic substance and ensures its safe release in the body by exercising adequate control over its release rate and timing [Khalane et al., 2016]. In the case of wounds, the dressings form an integral part of the DDS.

Wound healing management aims to target the wound not just with the view to alleviate pain and cure it. It also aims for the rapid closure of the wound duly ensuring that there is no or minimal scarring [Singer, and Dagum,., 2008]. Though the trend in earlier times was to keep the wound dry and allow evaporation of wound exudates to ward off bacterial infection by dressing it in cotton wool, gauze and bandages, recent advances suggest that to enable the wound to heal at a rapid pace, it is essential that a warm and moist environment is created and maintained at the site [Boateng et al., 2008]. It is this realization that has spurred the scientific community to look beyond the cotton, gauze and bandages, to innovate and develop new types of wound dressings that perform a range of tasks like physical protection, bacterial infection prevention, conducive microenvironment generation and sustained release of therapeutic drugs with minimal or no leakage enabling efficacy of administered dosage however small. The development of various new types of controlled release formulations in recent years has not only enhanced safety and efficacy of the drugs administered, but has also lead to a marked improvement in patient compliance, done away with the need for frequent dressing change, enabled direct delivery and release of wound healing drugs to the wound site in a sustained manner over prolonged periods [Gainza et al., 2013, Alphonsa et al, 2014].

The various types of drug delivery systems developed in recent years are reported to reduce local inflammation, inhibit and tackle matrix metalloproteinases (MMPs) which retard the healing process and the levels of which are found to be constantly elevated at the wound site [Adhirajan et al., 2009], as well as promote angiogenesis in the wound skin or the formation of new blood vessels [Alemdaroğlu et al., 2008, Xiang et al., 2011].

### 1.5.1 Wound dressings

Wound healing management has come a long way over the ages. Wound dressings in particular, have been highly benefitted by the advances made in the scientific and technological fields. Crude applications made from herbs, animal fats, etc., are now being increasingly replaced by sophisticated ones like tissue engineered scaffolds.

Wound dressings offer a variety of choices. There are traditional dressings like cotton wool, bandages and, gauze made of natural as well as synthetic fibres, and there are also modern wound dressings like films, wafers, and gel.

#### 1.5.1.1 Traditional wound dressings

These dressing unlike topical applications, do not provide a moist microenvironment. Absorbent cotton wool and sterile gauze pads absorb fluids and wound exudates. Bandages made from natural materials like cotton wool and cellulose as well as those made from synthetic materials like polyamide is used to support medical devices like splints and dressings. They can also be used independently in case of a need to provide support, pressure or restrict movement in a particular body part. Though gauze dressings help to absorb wound exudates and provide a certain measure of protection from bacterial infection, they need to be changed frequently. They also tend to adhere to the wound once the moisture content evaporates, thereby making their removal painful.

Traditional wound dressings are best employed on clean, dry wounds. They can also be used to absorb exudates and protect the wound.

#### 1.5.1.2 Modern Wound Dressings

Modern wound dressings unlike traditional wound dressing offer a multitude of choices. They create a moist environment around the wound, thus facilitating easy and effective healing. Modern wound dressings are in the form of gels, wafers, thin films, etc They are manufactured from natural sources like alginates, chitosan, collagen, etc., as well as synthetic material like polyester [Boateng et al., 2008].

## 1.5.2. Techniques for controlled drug delivery for wound healing

The advancement of research in the field of drug delivery in recent years has opened up numerous possibilities for the safe and target specific delivery of drugs to the site of injury in small yet effective doses thus accelerating wound repair and tissue regeneration as well as addressing the issue of scarring.

## 1.5.3. Microspheres and Nanospheres

Microspheres are small, solid, spherical particles the size of which ranges from 1 µm to 1000 µm (1 mm). Also referred to as microparticles, they are free-flowing powders. They are colloidal systems consisting of proteins or synthetic polymers. The small size of microspheres along with their properties of bio adhesion, swelling and ability to impart environment responsive characteristics make them adaptable to a wide range of dosage forms as well as product applications thus enabling their effective usage in drug delivery for wound healing. The controlled release of drugs encapsulated within microspheres ensures the sustained release of drugs for effective wound healing. Microspheres encapsulated with multiple drugs offer the advantage of the simultaneous release of these drugs to enhance and accelerate wound healing in chronic wound and burns. Even very small quantities of potent as well as unstable drugs can be administered at the target site safely. The only disadvantage in using microspheres for drug delivery is their rapid leakage from the wound site [ Pachuau., 2015].

Nanospheres too are a colloidal system like microspheres but smaller and amorphous or crystalline. They have a size range of 10-200nm in diameter and are endowed with the ability to protect drugs from enzymatic and chemical degradation by wound proteases. Nanospheres like microspheres allow controlled drug release over time as well as provide the advantage of avoidance of frequent administration. They are safe to handle and administer but are prone to rapid leakage from the wound site.

Micro and nanospheres prepared from natural polymers are at a disadvantage with regard to those prepared from synthetic polymers since they offer fewer advantages on account of the technical difficulties associated with their purification process. Alginate is the preferred natural polymer for synthesizing microspheres and nanospheres since it allows increased encapsulation efficiency if the therapeutic protein is low. It is also preferred on account of its excellent biocompatibility [ Gainza et al., 2015]. A VEGF loaded alginate microparticle was developed by Elcin et al. through the ion exchange method and in this regard it was found that in the VEGF loaded microparticle developed, the biological activity of VEGF was successfully preserved. Controlled release of the same was also enabled and was tested for angiogenic response in Wistar rats. The VEGF-MS angiogenic response result showed that in 10-35% of adjacent tissues the capillaries were newly formed thus proving that this form of drug delivery system in wound healing and repair holds lot of potential [Ye et al., 2010 ].

PLGA or poly(lactic-co-glycolic acid) a copolymer of poly lactic acid (PLA) and poly glycolic acid (PLGA) is the preferred polymer for entrapment and delivery of GFs in wound therapy due to their wound repair accelerating properties. PLGA being biocompatible and biodegradable is also less hydrophilic when compared to other polymers. It absorbs less water thereby allowing sustained delivery of the drug. Lactate produced in PLGA degradation process accelerates angiogenesis. It also activates pro- collagen factors and ensures the proliferation of endothelial progenitor cells at the site of the wound [ Gainza et al., 2015].

Various nanoparticulate and microparticulate systems for the controlled release of growth factors for wound healing have been developed. PLGA microparticulate and nanoparticulate systems which entrap epidermal growth factor (EGF) have been developed and were found to promote fibroblast proliferation and enhance the efficiency of wound healing [Dong et al., 2008, Chu et al., 2010].

### 1.5.3.1 Nanofiber Mats

Electrospun nanofibre mats loaded with drugs have a large surface area to volume ratio. They mimic the structure of the skin and provide excellent mechanical strength and are highly flexible and porous thus making them ideal for sustained drug release and enhanced wound healing. Nanofibre mats promote cell respiration; skin regeneration and hemostasis along with ensuring a moist micro environment around the wound. They are pliable and hence, can be applied to any part of the body including the joints, with ease.

Electrospun poly(ethylene glycol)-poly(D,L-lactide) (PELA) nanofibre mats entrapped with bFGF when administered to the wound site show increased fibroblast adhesion and proliferation as well as extracellular matrix (ECM) secretion [Yang et al., 2011]. Nanofiber mats, composed of poly ε-caprolactone (PCL)-polyethylene glycol (PEG) entrapped with epidermal growth factor (EGF) showed improved expression of keratin1 and loricrin in keratinocytes. The nanofibres exhibited superior wound healing activity in diabetic mice than controls, including a mixture of recombinant human epidermal growth factor ( rhEGF) and nanofibres. Expression of keratinocyte specific genes and epidermal growth factor receptor (EGFR) was significantly improved over controls [Choi et al., 2008].

### 1.5.3.2 Wafers and Sponges

Lyophilized wafers and sponges are solid porous structures that are easy to apply to wound exudates. They are produced by freeze-drying polymer solutions. Endowed with high drug loading capacity, they are capable of containing both soluble and insoluble therapeutic drugs. Being highly porous, they offer the advantage of easy absorption and evaporation of large amounts of wound exudates and ensure a moist microenvironment at the wound site thereby enabling quick and effective healing.

On application to the wound site, the lyophilized wafers absorb the wound exudate and convert to highly viscous fluids or resilient gels. This allows their indefinite adherence to the wound site a factor that enables sustained drug release. Drug stability in the case of drugs delivered via lyophilized wafers and sponges is reported to be better in comparison to drugs delivered via various semi-solid formulations [ Pachuau., 2015].

Studies using chitosan-collagen sponge loaded with fibroblast growth factor (FGF) exhibited high resistance to collagenase degradation [Wang et al., 2008 ]. Gelatin-MS in collagen sponges loaded with basic fibroblast growth factor (bFGF) when administered topically showed reduced infection in the wound site by accelerating the proliferation of new capillaries. It also exhibited accelerated fibroblast proliferation [Kawai et al., 2005].

In another study involving Gelatin-MS in gelatin sponges loaded with bFGF. Administered topically, an optimum healing microenvironment for cell proliferation and regeneration was noticed. Wound closure, re-epithelisation and improved dermis formation were promoted [Huang et al., 2008].

## 1.6. References

1. Adhirajan, N., Shanmugasundaram, N., Shanmuganathan, S. and Babu, M., 2009. Functionally modified gelatin microspheres impregnated collagen scaffold as novel wound dressing to attenuate the proteases and bacterial growth. european journal of pharmaceutical sciences, 36(2), pp.235-245.

2. Akita, S., Akino, K. and Hirano, A., 2013. Basic fibroblast growth factor in scarless wound healing. Advances in wound care, 2(2), pp.44-49.

3. Alemdaroğlu, C., Degim, Z., Celebi, N., Şengezer, M., Alömeroglu, M. and Nacar, A., 2008. Investigation of epidermal growth factor containing liposome formulation effects on burn wound healing. Journal of Biomedical Materials Research Part A, 85(1), pp.271-283. Alphonsa, B.M., Kumar, P.S., Praveen, G., Biswas, R., Chennazhi, K.P. and Jayakumar, R., 2014. Antimicrobial drugs encapsulated in fibrin nanoparticles for treating microbial infested wounds. Pharmaceutical research, 31(5), pp.1338-1351.

4. Bao, P., Kodra, A., Tomic-Canic, M., Golinko, M.S., Ehrlich, H.P. and Brem, H., 2009. The role of vascular endothelial growth factor in wound healing. Journal of Surgical Research, 153(2), pp.347-358.

5. Baum, C.L. and Arpey, C.J., 2005. Normal cutaneous wound healing: clinical correlation with cellular and molecular events. Dermatologic surgery, 31(6), pp.674-686.

6. Boateng, J.S., Matthews, K.H., Stevens, H.N. and Eccleston, G.M., 2008. Wound healing dressings and drug delivery systems: a review. Journal of pharmaceutical sciences, 97(8), pp.2892-2923.

7. Bodnar, R.J., 2013. Epidermal growth factor and epidermal growth factor receptor: the yin and yang in the treatment of cutaneous wounds and cancer. Advances in wound care, 2(1), pp.24-29.

8. Choi, J.S., Leong, K.W. and Yoo, H.S., 2008. In vivo wound healing of diabetic ulcers using electrospun nanofibers immobilized with human epidermal growth factor (EGF). Biomaterials, 29(5), pp.587-596.

9. Chu, Y., Yu, D., Wang, P., Xu, J., Li, D. and Ding, M., 2010. Nanotechnology promotes the full-thickness diabetic wound healing effect of recombinant human epidermal growth factor in diabetic rats. Wound repair and regeneration, 18(5), pp.499-505.

10. Demidova-Rice, T.N., Hamblin, M.R. and Herman, I.M., 2012. Acute and impaired wound healing: pathophysiology and current methods for drug delivery, part 1: normal and chronic wounds: biology, causes, and approaches to care. Advances in skin & wound care, 25(7), p.304.

11. Dong, X., Xu, J., Wang, W., Luo, H., Liang, X., Zhang, L., Wang, H., Wang, P. and Chang, J., 2008. Repair effect of diabetic ulcers with recombinant human epidermal growth factor loaded by sustained-release microspheres. Science in China Series C: Life Sciences, 51(11), pp.1039-1044.

12. Dreifke, M.B., Jayasuriya, A.A. and Jayasuriya, A.C., 2015. Current wound healing procedures and potential care. Materials Science and Engineering: C, 48, pp.651-662.

13. Gainza, G., Aguirre, J.J., Pedraz, J.L., Hernández, R.M. and Igartua, M., 2013. rhEGF- loaded PLGA-Alginate microspheres enhance the healing of full-thickness excisional wounds in diabetised Wistar rats. European Journal of Pharmaceutical Sciences, 50(3), pp.243-252.

14. Gainza, G., Villullas, S., Pedraz, J.L., Hernandez, R.M. and Igartua, M., 2015. Advances in drug delivery systems (DDSs) to release growth factors for wound healing and skin regeneration. Nanomedicine: Nanotechnology, Biology and Medicine, 11(6), pp.1551- 1573.

15. Gainza, G., Villullas, S., Pedraz, J.L., Hernandez, R.M. and Igartua, M., 2015. Advances in drug delivery systems (DDSs) to release growth factors for wound healing and skin regeneration. Nanomedicine: Nanotechnology, Biology and Medicine, 11(6), pp.1551- 1573.

16. Gurtner, G.C., Werner, S., Barrandon, Y. and Longaker, M.T., 2008. Wound repair and regeneration. Nature, 453(7193), pp.314-321.

17. Huang, S., Deng, T., Wu, H., Chen, F. and Jin, Y., 2006. Wound dressings containing bFGF-impregnated microspheres. Journal of microencapsulation, 23(3), pp.277-290.

18. Johnson, N.R. and Wang, Y., 2013. Controlled delivery of heparin-binding EGF-like growth factor yields fast and comprehensive wound healing. Journal of Controlled Release, 166(2), pp.124-129.

19. Kawai, K., Suzuki, S., Tabata, Y. and Nishimura, Y., 2005. Accelerated wound healing through the incorporation of basic fibroblast growth factor-impregnated gelatin microspheres into artificial dermis using a pressure-induced decubitus ulcer model in genetically diabetic mice. British journal of plastic surgery, 58(8), pp.1115-1123.

20. Khalane, L., Alkunte, A. and Birajdar, A., 2016. Sustained release drug delivery system: a concise review. Pharmatutor: Pharmacy Infopedia.

21. Menke, N.B., Ward, K.R., Witten, T.M., Bonchev, D.G. and Diegelmann, R.F., 2007. Impaired wound healing. Clinics in dermatology, 25(1), pp.19-25.

22. Murphy, K.E., Hall, C.L., McCue, S.W. and McElwain, D.S., 2011. A two-compartment mechanochemical model of the roles of transforming growth factor β and tissue tension in dermal wound healing. Journal of theoretical biology, 272(1), pp.145-159.

23. Nissen, N.N., Gamelli, R.L., Polverini, P.J. and DiPietro, L.A., 2003. Differential angiogenic and proliferative activity of surgical and burn wound fluids. Journal of Trauma and Acute Care Surgery, 54(6), pp.1205-1210.

24. Pachuau, L., 2015. Recent developments in novel drug delivery systems for wound healing. Expert opinion on drug delivery, 12(12), pp.1895-1909.

25. Park, J.W., Hwang, S.R. and Yoon, I.S., 2017. Advanced growth factor delivery systems in wound management and skin regeneration. Molecules, 22(8), p.1259.

26. Semenova, E., Koegel, H., Hasse, S., Klatte, J.E., Slonimsky, E., Bilbao, D., Paus, R., Werner, S. and Rosenthal, N., 2008. Overexpression of mIGF-1 in keratinocytes improves wound healing and accelerates hair follicle formation and cycling in mice. The American journal of pathology, 173(5), pp.1295-1310.

27. Singer, A.J. and Clark, R.A., 1999. Cutaneous wound healing. New England journal of medicine, 341(10), pp.738-746.

28. Singer, A.J. and Dagum, A.B., 2008. Current management of acute cutaneous wounds. New England Journal of Medicine, 359(10), pp.1037-1046.

29. Traversa, B. and Sussman, G., 2001. The role of growth factors, cytokines and proteases in wound management. Primary Intention: The Australian Journal of Wound Management, 9(4), p.161.

30. Wang, W., Lin, S., Xiao, Y., Huang, Y., Tan, Y., Cai, L. and Li, X., 2008. Acceleration of diabetic wound healing with chitosan-crosslinked collagen sponge containing recombinant human acidic fibroblast growth factor in healing-impaired STZ diabetic rats. Life sciences, 82(3), pp.190-204.

31. Xiang, Q., Xiao, J., Zhang, H., Zhang, X., Lu, M., Zhang, H., Su, Z., Zhao, W., Lin, C., Huang, Y. and Li, X., 2011. Preparation and characterisation of bFGF-encapsulated liposomes and evaluation of wound-healing activities in the rat. Burns, 37(5), pp.886-895. Yang, Y., Xia, T., Zhi, W., Wei, L., Weng, J., Zhang, C. and Li, X., 2011. Promotion of skin regeneration in diabetic rats by electrospun core-sheath fibers loaded with basic fibroblast growth factor. Biomaterials, 32(18), pp.4243-4254.

32. Ye, M., Kim, S. and Park, K., 2010. Issues in long-term protein delivery using biodegradable microparticles. Journal of Controlled Release, 146(2), pp.241-260.

33. Yildirimer, L., Thanh, N.T. and Seifalian, A.M., 2012. Skin regeneration scaffolds: a multimodal bottom-up approach. Trends in biotechnology, 30(12), pp.638-648.

# Chapter-18

# Emerging Green Material: Biopolymer Composites

Shikha Mishra

**Abstract**

Biodegradable polymers and bio-based reinforcing agents together make biocomposites. These materials are environmental friendly and solve the problem of waste management. Emerging green materials, biopolymer composites, are gaining significant attention due to their potential to replace traditional synthetic materials and reduce environmental impacts. The increasing need for sustainable products has led to the development of biopolymer composites, which combine the benefits of reinforcing materials and biodegradable polymers. This overview highlights recent advancements in biopolymer composites, including their development, properties, and applications. Proteins, cellulose, and plant starch are examples of renewable biomass sources that can be utilized as raw materials to create biopolymers. The use of natural fibers, bioceramics, and other reinforcing materials to enhance the mechanical, thermal, and barrier properties of biopolymers is also being studied. The potential applications of biopolymer composites in packaging, biomedical devices, textiles, and automotive parts are reviewed. These include the need for greater cost-effectiveness, standardization, and scalability.

**Keywords:** Biodegradable, biopolymer, composite, reinforcement, renewable biomass.

## Introduction

The need for a clean, pollution free environment has grown in recent years, and reducing the use of fossil fuels has become a clear goal. Thus, research into using biodegradable polymers derived from biological and renewable resources to replace commodity plastics has received a lot of interest. Biopolymers are attracting a lot of interest lately with the goal of creating high-performance biocomposites with minimal environmental effect because of their special and practical qualities, which include lightweight, renewable, plentiful, and environmentally friendliness. In order to overcome poor performance of conventional biopolymers it can be reinforced with fillers to improve its performance. By combining the right biopolymer with the right additives, which facilitate polymer-filler interaction, biopolymer composites can have the necessary characteristics.

The mechanical properties of biopolymer composites are significantly impacted by the interfacial interactions between the biopolymer and the nanofiller.[1]

Applications for bionanocomposites are numerous and include pharmaceutics, food packaging, electronics, forestry, transportation, construction, medicine, and cosmetics [2].

*A.N.D.N.N.M.M., Harshnagar, Kanpur*
*Email-shikhavijay23research@gmail.com*

In the present development of biocomposites, poly(lactic acid) (PLA), cellulose esters, polyhydroxyalkanoates (PHAs), and starch-based plastics are the most commonly utilized biopolymers [3,4].

**Poly Lactic acid**

PLA is a completely renewable polymer that decomposes in composting plants and is resorbable in the human body. It is one of the finest substitutes for petroleum-based polymers in the packaging, agricultural, personal care, cosmetic, biomedical, and tissue engineering industries. It exhibits biocidal activity due to its propensity to hydrolyze on the surface, generating lactic acid.[5,6].When Birch tar is added, a substance with beneficial physicochemical and structural qualities for horticultural and agricultural uses is produced, along with biocidal effects[7].By reinforcing it with different nano fillers researchers have widened its application.

**Poly hydroxyalkaonates**

PHAs are produced from a variety of bacterial species under the following nutrient-limiting circumstances with high carbon and are members of the family of polyhydroxy esters of 3-, 4-, 5-, and 6-hydroxyalkanoic acids [8]. Because of its many benefits, including biodegradability, biocompatibility, and the capacity to be produced by bacterial fermentation from renewable resources,

**Polyhydroxybutyrate (PHB)**

These polymers are seen to offer an intriguing alternative to synthetic polymers.

**Starch**

A biopolymer found in large quantities in nature, starch is inexpensive and utilized as a packing material. Typically, starch contains highly branching amylopectin and linear α-D-glucan amylose. Starches are often well-organized into semicrystalline granules.

**Cellulose**

One biopolymer that is widely found in nature is cellulose. Both bacteria and plants contain cellulose, which is typically thought of as a linear polymer containing β (1-4)-linked D-glucose. Cellulose microfibrils are created as a result of the glucose monomer units in cellulose forming intramolecular and intermolecular hydrogen bonds. Numerous researchers have developed a variety of cellulose nanocomposites reinforced with nanoparticles, such as clay, carbon nanotubes (CNTs),graphene , layered double hydroxides (LDH) and silica.

**Chitin**

After cellulose, chitin is the most prevalent biopolymer found in nature. The structural component of insects and crustaceans, as well as the cells of fungi and microbes, include chitin in the form of organized crystalline microfibrils. Generally speaking, chitin is regarded as an acetylated polymer composed of N-acetyl-D-glucosamine units joined by a β(1-4) bond. Conversely, the process of deacetylating chitin yields chitosan (poly-β (1, 4)-2-amino-2-deoxy-D-glucose). The chemically active groups in chitin are hydroxyl and free amine groups.

## Chitin

β-(1,4)-N-acetyl-D-glucosamine

Another biopolymer widely used as biomaterials is chitosan. It is non-toxic so can be in contact with human tissues[8,9,10]

## Chitosan

Chitosan is non toxic and has film forming ability. It has free amino group which makes it soluble in any dilute solnent due to protonation

**Production methods for polymer composites-**

### 1-Extrusion

The most popular technique for creating composites is the extruder. The material to be extruded is run through a die with a consistent cross-sectional area in this procedure. The material is placed in the barrel through a hopper that passes through three major barrel sections, mixing the material before it is compressed and sent through the die.[11]

### 2-Injection molding

A thermoplastic polymer is first heated in a cylindrical chamber to a temperature that causes the material to flow in the injection molding process. The chamber's end is attached to a mold. The molten material then enters the mold under different injection molding settings, including pressure and heat. After that, this material enters the cold mold after being hydraulically compressed using a plunger and ram. A screw that can spin and travel forward and backward then compresses and melts it. The plastic mold is removed when the screw spins and slides backward, indicating that the process is prepared for the subsequent material cycle.[11]

### 3-Filament winding

Fibers are twisted around a revolving mandrel during the filament winding procedure. To create a band of fibers, these fibers are then passed through a device and fixed on a creel. There are three possible ways to wrap the fibers: longitudinally, helically, or in a hoop winding. The strain above the mandrel creates a positive pressure throughout further processing, which finally compacts the laminate. Another approach that typically resolves problems during filament winding is the use of prepregs [12,13,14]

### 4-Solution mixing

The simplest technique for preparing biopolymer composites is solution mixing. This method involves dispersing the nanofillers in a common solvent that also dissolves the polymer. This technique works well to produce biopolymer composites that create stable dispersions. To achieve homogenous dispersion, the solvent's compatibility with the polymer and filler is crucial. This process involves dissolving the polymer in an appropriate solvent first, then dispersing the fillers in the solvent. After that, the solvent is evaporated by casting the polymer/filler mixture. Because it uses a lot of solvents and solvent cleanup is a major problem, this method is not environmentally friendly.[19]

### 5-Melt blending

One of the most appealing techniques for producing biopolymers is melt mixing. composites. This process works well for producing biopolymer composites in large quantities and is environmentally benign. This method involves first melting the polymer at a high temperature and After that, the filler is introduced to the high-temperature, sheared polymer melt. The most adaptable and useful approach, particularly for thermoplastic, is this one. polymers. Thermoplastic polymers and nanofiller are mechanically combined at high temperature by injection molding and extrusion.This process doesn't involve the use of a lot of solvents and is environmentally benign.

### 6-In situ polymerization

Another method to develop biopolymer composites is in situ polymerization, in which the liquid monomer causes nanofillers to swell. Usually, heat or radiation is employed to disperse an appropriate initiator before to starting the polymerization process. When the reaction begins, the monomer is polymerized, resulting in the formation of nanocomposites. To accomplish full exfoliation of the nanofiller, however, polymerization control is necessary. The primary disadvantage of in situ polymerization is that its viscosity increases with its progression. This restricts the fillers' load portion. Both small and big sizes can employ in situ polymerization.

### 7-Electrospinning

A flexible method for creating micro- and nano-sized fibers from a variety of polymers soaked in volatile liquids is electrospinning.[15]

Table-Various polyme matrix with filler, it's production method, properties & application

| Matrix & Filler | Production Method | Properties | Application |
| --- | --- | --- | --- |
| PLA/PEG/Chit [16] | Extrusion | Low stiffness/High flexibility | Bone & dental implants food packaging |
| Potato starch/wheat gluten | Compression molding | Improved maximum stress & extensibility | Development of bio-based plastics |
| PLA/Cellulose | Extrusion/injection | Improved rigidity & biodegradability | Packaging, automotive industry, building |
| PLA/Potato pulp | Extrusion/injection | Low stiffness & ductility, good processability | Food packaging |
| PHBV/TPU/cellulose | Extrusion/injection | Balanced heat resistance, stiffness, and toughness | Food packaging tissue engineering |
| Alginate/cinnamon oil [17] | Solution casting | Good antibacterial activity | Active packaging materials |
| PVA/Chitosan [18] | Electrospinning | Good chemical stability | Antibacterial and food packaging |
| Nanocellulose/CNT [19,20] | Cast molding | Good electrical conductivity | Supercapacitors, sensors |

**Fig. Lifecycle of wood based natural polymer[21]**

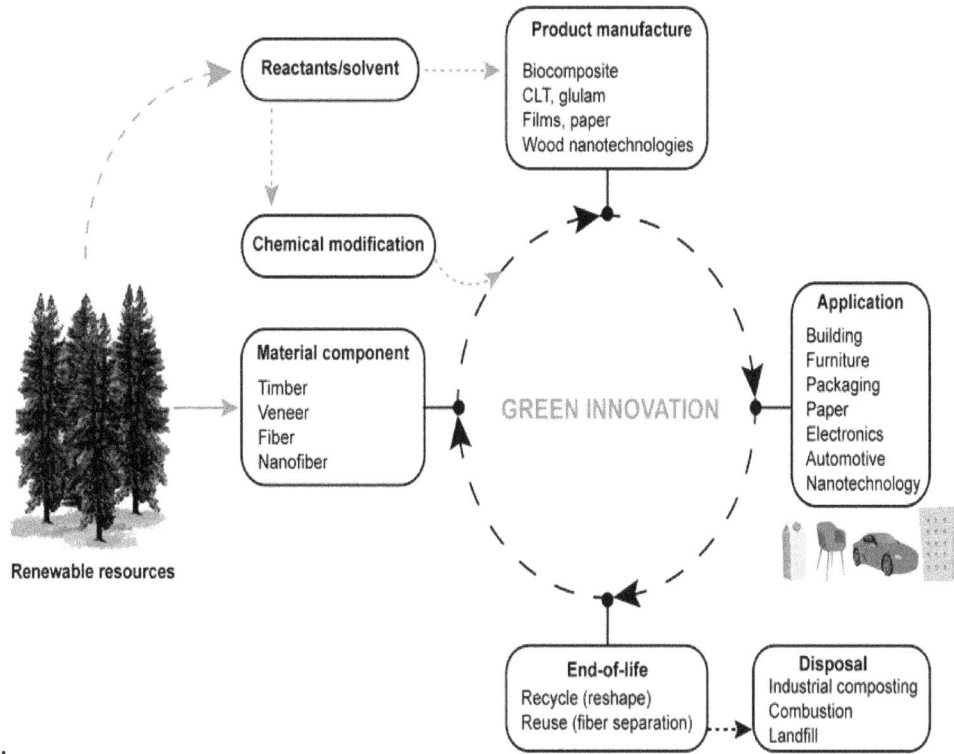

## Conclusion

The study of emerging "green" material biopolymer composite reveals it's importance in today's scenario due to it's easy processsibility,bioegradibility,low cost,easy accessibility.By applying filler it results into good mechanical strength,tensile strength material.

## References-

1. K.K.Sadasivuni et.al.,Recent advances in mechanical properties of biopolymer composites: a review,Polymer composites, 2019

2. A.María et.al.,Synthesis and Applications of Biopolymer Composites,International journal of molecular sciences,2019

3. L.Yu et.al.,Polymer blends and composites from renewable resources. *Prog. Polym. Sci.* 2006, *31*, 576–602.

4. D.Pascual, et.al. ZnO-Reinforced Poly(3-hydroxybutyrate-co-3-hydroxyvalerate) Bionanocomposites with Antimicrobial Function for Food Packaging. *ACS Appl. Mater. Interfaces* 2014, *6*, 9822–9834

5. M.Naffakh et.al., Polymer blend nanocomposites based on poly(l-lactic acid), polypropylene and WS2 inorganic nanotubes. *RSC Adv.* 2016, *6*, 40033–40044.

6. P.Saini; et.al.,. Poly(lactic acid) blends in biomedical applications. *Adv. Drug Deliv. Rev.* 2016, *107*, 47–59

7. A.Richert, et.al. The Role of Birch Tar in Changing the Physicochemical and Biocidal Properties of Polylactide-Based Films. *Int. J. Mol. Sci.* 2022, *23*, 268

8. D.Pascual et.al.,Electrospun fibers of chitosan-grafted polycaprolactone/poly(3-hydroxybutyrate-co-3- hydroxyhexanoate) blends. *J. Mater. Chem. B* 2016, *4*, 600–612.

9. D.Pascual,et.al., Wound Healing Bionanocomposites Based on Castor Oil Polymeric Films Reinforced with Chitosan-Modified ZnO Nanoparticles. *Biomacromolecules* 2015, *16*, 2631–2644.

10. S.Philip et.al., Polyhydroxyalkanoates: biodegradable polymers with a range of applications. J Chem Technol Biotechnol 2007;82:23347

11. Allen KA. Processing of thermoplastic composites. Polym Compos Proc 2012

12. Strong AB. Filament winding. Fundamentals of composites manufacturing - materials, methods, and applications. 2nd ed. Society of Manufacturing Engineers (SME); 2008.

13. Lee SM. Filament winding. The Handbook of Composite Reinforcements. John Wiley & Sons; 1993.

14. Akovali G. Filament winding. Handbook of Composite Fabrication. Smithers, Rapra Publishing; 2001.

15. G. Viswanathan et.al.,Preparation of Biopolymer Fibers by Electrospinning from Room Temperature Ionic Liquids,*Biomacromolecules,2016*

16. M.Coltelli et.al., Chitin Nanofibrils in Poly(Lactic Acid) (PLA) Nanocomposites: Dispersion and Thermo-Mechanical Properties. *Int. J. Mol. Sci.* 2019, *20*, 504.

17. S.Baek et.al,Characterization of Ecklonia cava Alginate Films Containing Cinnamon Essential Oils. *Int. J. Mol. Sci.* 2018, *19*, 3545

18. S.Alvarado et.al.,Morphological Study of Chitosan/Poly (Vinyl Alcohol) Nanofibers Prepared by Electrospinning, Collected on Reticulated Vitreous Carbon. *Int. J. Mol. Sci.* 2018, *19*, 1718.

19. K.Deshmukh et.al.,Biopolymer Composites With High Dielectric Performance: Interface Engineering ,*Biopolymer Composites in Electronics,2017*

20. S.Siljander et.al.,Effect of Surfactant Type and Sonication Energy on the Electrical Conductivity Properties of Nanocellulose-CNT Nanocomposite Films. *Int. J. Mol. Sci.* 2018, *19*, 1819

21. C. Montanari et. al., Sustainable Wood Nanotechnologies for Wood Composites Processed by In-Situ Polymerization,Volume 9 - 2021,Front. Chem., Nano-science.

# Chapter-19

# Foxtail Millet-Based Churro Snack: Exploration of Compound Analysis Using GC-MS Technique

*Shubhangi Nigam*

*Ritika Dogre*

*Nilesh Pal*

*Prarthana Singh*

**Abstract**

The goal of the current study was to evaluate the acceptability of gluten-free churros using foxtail millet. A comprehensive analysis was conducted to evaluate the physiochemical properties, including moisture content, fat content, protein content, carbohydrate content, ash content & dietary fiber content of the churros prepared from foxtail millet flour. The foxtail millet flour was prepared by milling whole foxtail millet grains sourced from a local supplier, ensuring freshness and quality. As far as the nutritional content is concerned, it has substantial amounts of carbohydrates (60-65 g), protein (12.3g), fiber (6 g), minerals (phosphorous, calcium, iron, zinc, magnesium, sodium) and phytochemicals (phenols, ferulic, chlorogenic acids, p-coumaric, flavonoids, carotenoids, tocopherol & tocotrienol). It has anti- inflammatory and anti-cancerous properties. Churros are popular Spanish dessert characterized by their ridge shape, crispy exterior and soft doughy interior. For the analysis of constituents present in gluten- free churros prepared from foxtail millet, Gas Chromatography (GC) followed by Mass Spectrometry (MS) techniques were used. The GC & MS techniques provide detailed insights into the churros' chemical composition, identifying key components and potential health impacts. On the basis of sensory evaluation conducted, the churro sample with 30% FMF was rated highest in terms of texture and overall acceptability (9/10). The results depicted the health advantages of Foxtail millet. Hence, foxtail millet can serve as a preferable alternative for preparation of gluten-free churro snack in strengthening dietary quality and food security.

**Keywords:** Foxtail millet, gluten-free, nutrient-rich, churros, ancient grains, phytochemical. Gas chromatography and mass spectrometry.

## I. Introduction

Most of the world's population is heavily dependent on cereal based diet but lacks major micronutrients which poses several threats of nutritional insecurity for consumers (Sarita & Singh, 2016). Millets are grouped as "Nutri- cereals", which are essential for combating malnutrition and greatly enhancing human health (Moharil et al., 2019).

---

*Assistant Professor and Students, Department of Food Engineering and Technology, Institute of Engineering and Technology, Bundelkhand University, Jhansi, (U.P)*

**Email:** *dr.shubhangi@bujhansi.ac.in, ritikadogre05@gmail.com, np6589230@gmail.com*

Foxtail millet, one of the oldest cultivated crops, originated in northern China and is grown in 26 countries. Millets provide better nutritional, environmental, and economic benefits than widely consumed staple grains like rice and wheat (Amadou et al., 2013; Mishra et al., 2022). Classified as a cereal, millet is widely grown throughout India, making it one of the world's leading exporters of millet (Singh, Arora, Kumar, Gohain, & Sharma, 2023). As per the reports of Food and Agriculture Organization (FAO, 2022), UN General Assembly (UNGA), has adopted the Government of India's plan for declaring and dedicating "2023" as the 'International year of Millets' for encouraging the millet cultivation which could help to achieve the United Nations Sustainable Development Goal two (SDG2) for attaining zero hunger, food security, improved nutrition, and promoting sustainable agriculture (Ceasar & Maharajan, 2022). Foxtail millet flour provides numerous health benefits, making it a valuable ingredient in churros. Its high fiber content aids digestion and promotes satiety, supporting weight management. Additionally, FMF has a low glycemic index, which can help regulate blood sugar levels, making it suitable for individuals with diabetes (Lily Arsanti, Emy Huriyati & Yustinus Marsono).

## II. Literature Review

**Foxtail Millet & its Composition** - Foxtail millet (*Setaria italica*), a self-pollinating grain from the Poaceae family and is cultivated primarily in regions of Asia and Africa (Sheahen, 2014). Morphologically, Foxtail Millet consists of a single stalk (few tillers) with a number of inflorescences. The whole plant grows up to height of 120-200cms, approximately 2-5ft. The seed head is 5-30cms long, thick, hairy panicle (Moharil et al., 2019) in appearance with an average diameter of 2mm (Hari Prasanna, 2016). Foxtail millet aids in the constant release of glucose without impairing the body's metabolism. FM is also known as a healthy heart diet and aids in reducing the occurrence of diabetes due to its high magnesium content (Reddy, 2017). The primary constituents of foxtail millets include carbohydrates, protein, dietary fibers, fat, vitamins, and minerals (Sharma & Niranjan, 2017). Foxtail millet grains are rich in protein content (10%–15%), dietary fiber (6%–8%), crude fat (7%–8%), and minerals (Fe, Ca, and Zn) (Muthamilarasan et al., 2016).

**Health Benefits of Foxtail Millet** - Based on the studies I have reviewed, foxtail millet offers several notable health benefits, it is a highly nutritious grain, packed with essential nutrients such as proteins, fiber, vitamins (particularly vitamin B), and minerals like iron, calcium, magnesium, and phosphorus. These contribute to overall health and well-being. Foxtail millet also known as Korralu or Thinai, is a nutrient-rich grain with numerous health benefits. This grain is gaining in popularity for its impressive nutritional profile and its role of promoting overall well-being.

The foxtail millet benefits are diverse and impactful. It can aid in digestion, manage blood sugar levels, and do a lot more to ensure good health. Including foxtail millet into your diet can lead to significant improvements in your health (TATA AIG Team).

## III. Methodology

**Materials –**

Foxtail millet was bought from a local vendor and was stored in airtight containers in a cool and dry place. Butter, salt, sugar, cinnamon sugar, brown sugar and vanilla essence were bought from the local vendors and were stored in cool, dry, damp and refrigerated conditions respectively as per the requirements of the storage conditions depending on their physiochemical characteristics. Foxtail millet is cleaned through the process of winnowing. Grinding of foxtail millet seeds are done with the help of a grinder into smooth powder like form, the mixture need not be much very coarse, it must be ground into powder like smooth form to facilitate mixing and formation of smooth batter for churro mixture. The powder obtained is then separated from the unwanted coarse husk by passing the mixture through the sieve.

**Pre-treatment Method -** The pre-treatment of grains before milling ensures the better retention of quality of the grains & flour, enhancing their utility in various products. The flour obtained from untreated, soak-boil & soak-steam treated foxtail millet grains was stored at ambient & under refrigerated conditions for 90 days. Pre-treatment Methods of Foxtail Millet:

1. Harvesting - Foxtail millet grows best in moderately fertile, well-drained soils but adapts to a range of soils from sandy to heavy clay. It requires 500-700 mm annual rainfall and tolerates waterlogging or drought. The crop is ready for harvest in 80-90 days, yielding 20-25 quintals of grain.

2. Cleaning - post-harvest, the millet is cleaned to remove unwanted particles and stored with a moisture content of 12% (w.b). Commercially available millet has moisture content between 11-12% (w.b).

3. Parboiling Treatment - Parboiling enhances milling efficiency and increases the edibility of the grain, resulting in higher head grain yield post-milling. The process includes soaking, steaming, and drying:

    - Soaking: Foxtail millet is soaked in water for 5 hours at room temperature, as determined by preliminary studies.

    - Steaming: The soaked millet is steamed for $10 \pm 1$ minute, optimized by testing for complete starch gelatinization.

    - Drying: The steamed millet is spread on steel trays and dried in a hot air oven at 50°C for 2 hours until the moisture content reaches $12 \pm 2\%$. The millet is then sealed pouches for de-husking.

4. De-husking - De-husking is done using an abrasive grain polisher, where grains are forced between an emery-coated iron cylinder and a perforated steel plate. The friction removes the husk, which is separated from the de-husked grain during the process.

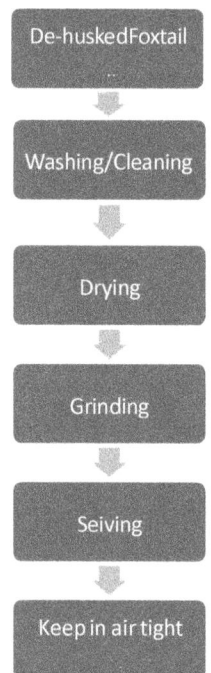

*Foxtail millet flour preparation*

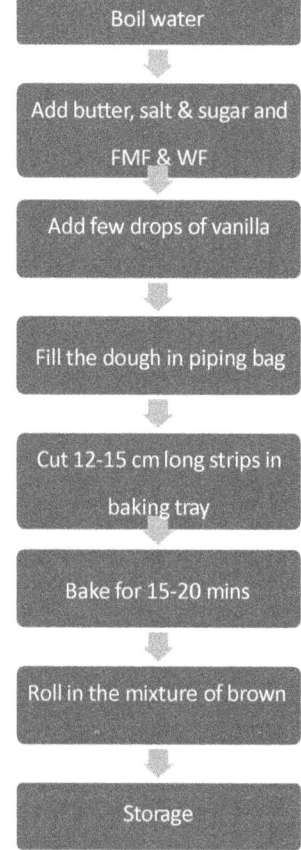

*Preparation of Foxtail Millet Churros*

(1)  Proximate Analysis of Foxtail Millet Flour/Wheat flour -

(a) **Moisture Content of flour:** The convective hot air-oven method was used to determine moisture content. A small sample (~5g) was heated at 105°C for 1 hour, with the weight loss considered as the moisture content. Flour with moisture content over 14% is unstable and can develop off-odors due to microbial growth. Flour specifications typically limit moisture content to 14% or less (AOAC, 2006).

(b) **Ash Content of flour:** Approximately 2g of sample was weighed into a crucible and ashed at 500°C for 2 hours. After cooling, the crucible was weighed again. The ash content was calculated as a percentage of the initial sample weight (AOAC, 2006).

(c) **Crude Fiber Content of flour:** 2g of sample was extracted with ether, followed by digestion with hot sulfuric acid (1.25%) and sodium hydroxide (1.25%). The residue was filtered, washed & dried in a crucible. The weight of residue before after ashing at 500°C was recorded. The difference in weight represented the crude fiber content.

(2)  Physiochemical Analysis of *Flour* -

(a) **Water Holding and Oil Holding Capacity:** To measure water holding capacity (WHC) and oil holding capacity (OHC), 0.5g of dried sample was placed in a centrifuge tube with either 30 ml of distilled water (for WHC) or 10 ml of commercial cooking oil (for OHC). After stirring for 24 hours (for WHC) or 30 minutes (for OHC), the mixture was centrifuged at 2000 g for 30 minutes, the supernatant decanted, and the residue weighed. WHC and OHC were expressed as grams of water or oil held per gram of dry sample.

(b) **Bulk Density:** Approximately 2g of flour was placed into a 10 ml graduated cylinder, and the bottom was tapped gently until no further settling occurred. Bulk density was calculated as the mass of the sample per unit volume (g/ml), following AOAC (2005) procedures.

(3)  Preparation of FMF-WF Churros -

The required ingredients for FMF-WF churros include foxtail millet flour, wheat flour (at 10%, 20%, and 30% concentrations), butter, sugar, salt, vanilla essence, and water. Accurate weighing and measurement of ingredients were performed using laboratory-grade equipment.

(a) **Churro Batter:** In a vessel, 50 ml of water, 30g of butter, 1g of salt, and 10g of sugar were boiled. Then, 250g of foxtail millet flour and 75g of wheat flour were added with continuous stirring to form a smooth batter. 2 ml of vanilla essence was added, and the mixture was slightly cooked before cooling for 5 minutes. This process was repeated for different wheat flour concentrations of 10%, 20%, and 30%.

(b) **Baking:** The dough was piped onto parchment-lined baking sheets using a star-shaped nozzle. The oven was preheated to 425°F (220°C), and the churros were baked for 15-20 minutes until golden brown and crisp. After baking, they were brushed with melted butter and rolled in a mixture of brown sugar and cinnamon.

**(4) Gas Chromatography (GC) and Mass Spectrometry (MS) –**

Gas Chromatography (GC) was used to separate & detect chemical components of the churro samples, particularly volatile compounds. The process involved grinding the churros into a fine powder, extracting volatile compounds with solvents like hexane, and injecting the sample into the gas chromatograph. The separated compounds were detected using mass spectrometry, which analyzed the molecules based on their mass-to-charge ratio (m/z). The results helped identify and quantify specific compounds in the churros and assess compositional differences.

Mass Spectrometry (MS) was coupled with GC to enhance analytical capabilities. The separated compounds were ionized and analyzed based on their molecular weight. The resulting mass spectrum was compared with reference databases to accurately identify the compounds present in the samples.

## IV. Results And Discussion

**(1) Composition of Key Nutrients in Foxtail Millet:** Foxtail millet is predominantly composed of starch (60%-65%) and is a good source of protein (10%-15%) and dietary fiber (6%-8%). These nutritional attributes, supported by references, underscore foxtail millet's potential as a versatile ingredient in developing functional and health-promoting food products. The table helps in understanding why FMF is being explored in diverse food formulations, given its favorable nutrient profile.

**Table 1:** *Composition of Key Nutrients in Foxtail Millet*

| Sr. No. | Parameter | Composition | References |
|---|---|---|---|
| 1. | Starch | 60%-65% | Sharma & Niranjan, 2017 |
| 2. | Protein | 10%-15% | Muthamilarasan et al., 2016 |
| 3. | Fats | 84%-88% | Liet al., 2007 |
| 4. | Crude fat | 7%-8% | Muthamilarasan et al., 2016 |
| 5. | Dietary Fiber | 6%-8% | Muthamilarasan et al., 2016 |

**(2) Functional Properties of Foxtail Millet and Wheat Flour:** Below table presents the solubility and oil-holding capacities of Wheat Flour (WF) and Foxtail Millet Flour (FMF), highlighting the differences in functional properties of these two flours. The significant difference in water solubility capacity (WSC) and water holding capacity (WHC) between WF and FMF can be observed, with FMF showing higher values (WSC: 5.20 mL/g; WHC: 162.29 g/g) compared to WF (WSC: 2.92 mL/g; WHC: 190.29 g/g). These results suggest that FMF has a greater ability to retain water, which may influence the texture and moisture retention in food applications. Additionally, the oil-holding capacity (OHC) is higher for FMF, indicating its potential to contribute to the texture and flavor retention in formulations where oil is a key component.

*Table 2: Functional Properties of Foxtail Millet and Wheat Flour*

| Samples | SP (g/g) | WSC (mL/m | WHC (g/g) | OHC (g/g) |
|---|---|---|---|---|
| Wheat Flour | 5.12 | 2.92 | 190.29 | 53.33 |
| FMF | 6.35 | 5.20 | 162.29 | 60.00 |

**(3) Proximate Composition of Wheat Flour and Foxtail Millet Flour Blends:** The table shows the proximate analysis of FMF and its blends with WF at different ratios (0%, 10%, 20%, 30%, and 100%). The data provides insights into the composition of moisture, protein, fat, ash, and crude fiber for each blend. As the proportion of FMF increases, moisture content decreases from 13% (FMF 0%) to 7.22% (FMF 100%), while protein, fat, ash, and crude fiber all increase. These compositional changes reflect the nutrient-dense nature of FMF, making it a favorable ingredient for enhancing the nutritional profile of food products. For instance, crude fiber content rises from 0.37g/100g in pure WF to 5.46g/100g in 100% FMF, indicating the potential health benefits related to fiber intake. The **mean value** at the bottom of the table represents the average content for each parameter across all the blends.

*Table 3: Proximate Composition of Wheat Flour and Foxtail Millet Flour Blends*

| Parameter (unit) | Moisture (%) | Protein (per 100g) | Fat (per 100g) | Ash (per 100g) | Crude fibre (per 100g) |
|---|---|---|---|---|---|
| FMF (0%) | 13 | 11.03 | 1.77 | 0.63 | 0.37 |
| FMF(10%) | 12.52 | 11.35 | 2.65 | 0.85 | 0.85 |
| FMF(20%) | 11.53 | 11.96 | 2.94 | 1.01 | 1.38 |
| FMF(30%) | 10.8 | 12.65 | 3.38 | 1.32 | 1.86 |
| FMF(100%) | 7.22 | 13.45 | 4.25 | 2.77 | 5.46 |
| Mean | 11.014 | 12.088 | 2.998 | 1.316 | 1.984 |

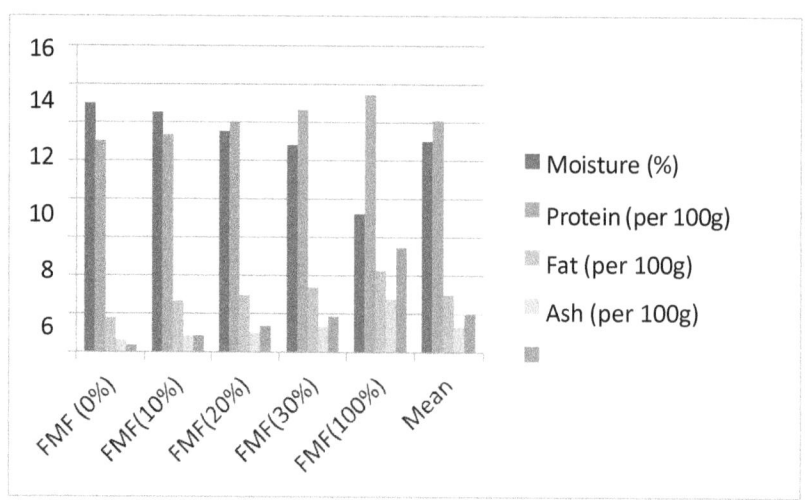

**(4) Sensory Evaluation of Churros Made with Foxtail Millet Flour Blends:** The table evaluates the sensory attributes of churros made with different proportions of FMF (10%, 20%, and 30%). The sensory parameters assessed include color, appearance, texture, smell/aroma, taste/flavor, chewiness, and overall acceptability. The results indicate that as FMF content increases, most sensory attributes, particularly texture, flavor, and overall acceptability, show favorable scores. For instance, the churro sample with 30% FMF was rated highest in terms of texture and overall acceptability (9/10). These results suggest that FMF can be incorporated into churro formulations without negatively affecting sensory properties, thereby offering a functional and nutritious alternative.

**Table 4:** *Sensory Evaluation of Churros Made with Foxtail Millet Flour Blends*

| Sr. No. | Particulars | 10% | 20% | 30% |
|---|---|---|---|---|
| 1. | Color | 8 | 7 | 8 |
| 2. | Appearance | 7 | 7 | 8 |
| 3. | Texture | 7 | 8 | 7 |
| 4. | Smell/Aroma | 8 | 7 | 9 |
| 5. | Taste/Flavor | 7 | 7 | 9 |
| 6. | Chewiness | 8 | 8 | 9 |
| 7. | Overall Acceptability | 7 | 8 | 8 |

Gas Chromatography & Mass Spectrometry Results -

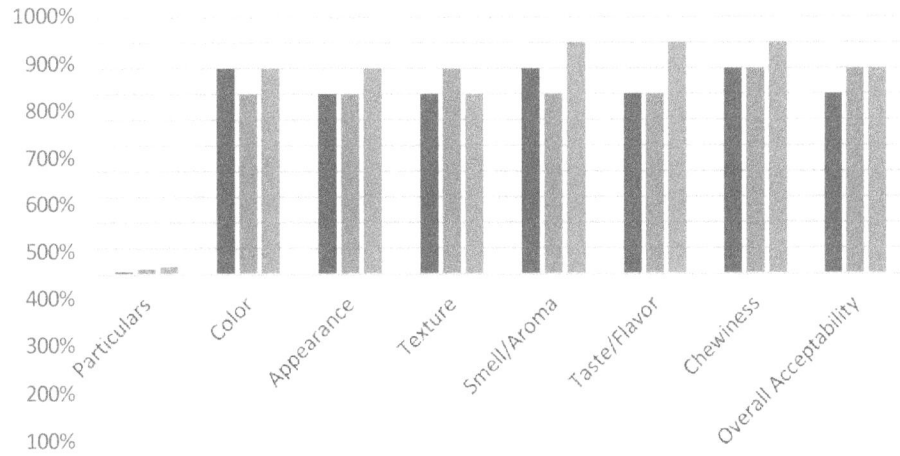

Here are the results of a gas chromatography done on a sample after grinding it into powdered form and staining it in an organic solvent (ethanol) for more than 12 hours and then filtering it with the help of syringe filter and is kept in a GC machine, these chromatographs are obtained in which highest peaks shows a compound present in highest amount. The RT shows a Retention Time (RT), which is a measure of the time taken for a solute to pass through a chromatography column, height of a peak and its area is also present with norm% that interprets the peaks in form of percentage. Both qualitative and quantitative results are given below with the chromatograph obtained after GC.

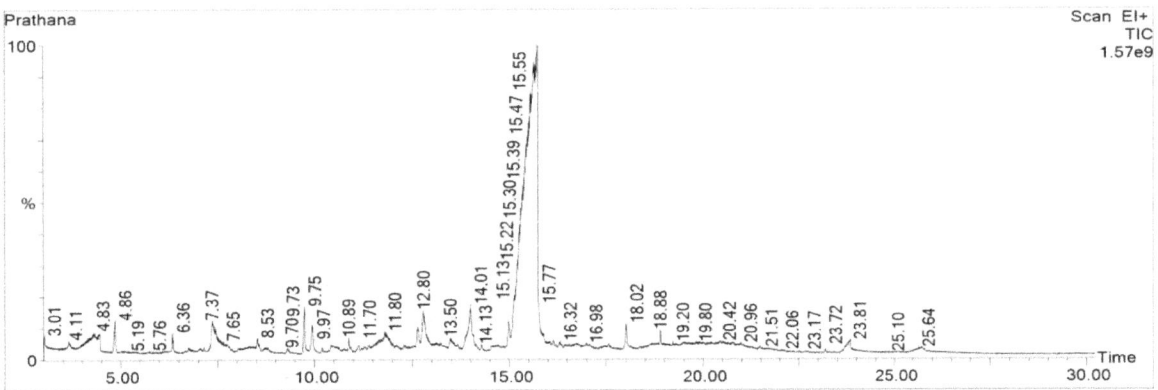

After the chromatographs are being obtained mass spectrometry is coupled with gas chromatography to enhance the analytical capabilities of both techniques. GC separates complex mixtures of compounds based on their volatility and affinity for the stationary phase in the chromatographic column. This separation step reduces the complexity of the sample before entering the mass spectrometer. After separation by GC, the eluted compounds enter the mass spectrometer where they are ionized. The mass spectrum obtained from GC-MS analysis is compared to reference database to identify the compounds present in the sample. Each compound produces a unique mass spectrum, allowing for accurate identification.

| # | RT | Scan | Height | Area | Area % | Norm % |
|---|---|---|---|---|---|---|
| \multicolumn{7}{QUALITATIVE REPORT} |
| 1 | 4.118 | 609 | 49,207,452 | 3,385,727.2 | 0.310 | 0.56 |
| 2 | 4.287 | 701 | 84,417,088 | 8,451,287.0 | 0.775 | 1.40 |
| 3 | 4.305 | 711 | 93,196,504 | 3,757,826.2 | 0.345 | 0.62 |
| 4 | 4.345 | 733 | 97,474,728 | 4,540,991.5 | 0.416 | 0.75 |
| 5 | 4.461 | 796 | 90,196,848 | 4,098,067.0 | 0.376 | 0.68 |
| 6 | 4.863 | 1015 | 156,939,856 | 6,530,078.5 | 0.599 | 1.08 |
| 7 | 6.357 | 1829 | 96,277,632 | 3,378,030.5 | 0.310 | 0.56 |
| 8 | 7.368 | 2380 | 157,264,592 | 12,958,373.0 | 1.188 | 2.15 |
| 9 | 7.468 | 2434 | 122,782,856 | 7,313,742.5 | 0.671 | 1.21 |
| 10 | 7.541 | 2474 | 67,844,080 | 2,513,747.2 | 0.231 | 0.42 |
| 11 | 8.532 | 3014 | 69,625,504 | 2,682,790.5 | 0.246 | 0.44 |
| 12 | 9.749 | 3677 | 227,762,432 | 10,127,384.0 | 0.929 | 1.68 |
| 13 | 9.940 | 3781 | 132,561,360 | 7,391,625.5 | 0.678 | 1.22 |
| 14 | 11.673 | 4725 | 52,969,552 | 3,122,770.0 | 0.286 | 0.52 |
| 15 | 11.754 | 4769 | 58,172,548 | 3,192,037.0 | 0.293 | 0.53 |
| 16 | 11.818 | 4804 | 91,080,072 | 5,291,040.0 | 0.485 | 0.88 |
| 17 | 11.866 | 4830 | 83,822,408 | 4,115,169.8 | 0.377 | 0.68 |
| 18 | 12.648 | 5256 | 120,225,960 | 8,271,308.0 | 0.758 | 1.37 |
| 19 | 12.802 | 5340 | 198,696,992 | 17,327,848.0 | 1.589 | 2.87 |
| 20 | 12.886 | 5386 | 74,429,816 | 2,434,101.5 | 0.223 | 0.40 |

| # | RT | Scan | Height | Area | Area % | Norm % |
|---|---|---|---|---|---|---|
| \multicolumn{7}{QUANTITATIVE REPORT} |
| 21 | 14.009 | 5998 | 222,277,824 | 27,169,974.0 | 2.491 | 4.50 |
| 22 | 14.984 | 6529 | 153,719,312 | 9,957,766.0 | 0.913 | 1.65 |
| 23 | 15.740 | 6941 | 1,530,711,936 | 603,437,952.0 | 55.334 | 100.00 |
| 24 | 15.891 | 7023 | 84,052,736 | 4,907,652.0 | 0.450 | 0.81 |

| 25 | 16.042 | 7105 | 45,576,628 | 2,484,284.2 | 0.228 | 0.41 |
| 26 | 16.139 | 7158 | 56,021,940 | 3,156,526.0 | 0.289 | 0.52 |
| 27 | 18.028 | 8187 | 130,580,104 | 6,899,556.0 | 0.633 | 1.14 |
| 28 | 18.885 | 8654 | 102,722,376 | 3,531,303.0 | 0.324 | 0.59 |
| 29 | 19.500 | 8989 | 42,751,740 | 3,277,802.2 | 0.301 | 0.54 |
| 30 | 19.856 | 9183 | 45,447,204 | 3,787,514.0 | 0.347 | 0.63 |
| 31 | 20.015 | 9270 | 44,509,640 | 3,449,979.0 | 0.316 | 0.57 |
| 32 | 20.214 | 9378 | 46,113,976 | 7,042,911.5 | 0.646 | 1.17 |
| 33 | 20.436 | 9499 | 53,534,976 | 3,969,124.8 | 0.364 | 0.66 |
| 34 | 20.546 | 9559 | 50,052,668 | 3,777,983.2 | 0.346 | 0.63 |
| 35 | 20.652 | 9617 | 44,617,684 | 2,769,674.8 | 0.254 | 0.46 |
| 36 | 20.792 | 9693 | 48,440,596 | 4,596,628.0 | 0.422 | 0.76 |
| 37 | 20.885 | 9744 | 39,757,552 | 3,164,073.5 | 0.290 | 0.52 |
| 38 | 20.977 | 9794 | 44,695,420 | 4,678,391.5 | 0.429 | 0.78 |
| 39 | 23.828 | 11347 | 69,545,680 | 8,520,989.0 | 0.781 | 1.41 |
| 40 | 25.733 | 12385 | 33,371,762 | 3,223,364.8 | 0.296 | 0.53 |

Inst () ACQUISITION PARAMETERS

Oven: Initial temp 40°C for 5 min, ramp 10°C/min to 280°C, hold 9 min, InjBauto=250°C, Volume-0 µL, Split 0:1, Carrier

Gas-He, Solvent Delay=3.00 min, Transfer Temp=100°C, Source Temp=100°C, Scan: 50 to 350Da, Column 30.0m x 250µm

QUALITATIVE REPORT EXPLAINATION - Here are the compounds that shows the highest 3 peaks in the qualitative report of thee chromatographs at **12.802, 7.368** and **9.749 RT** with **2.87%, 2.15%,** and **1.68% norm** percentage respectively.

The **highest peak with RT 12.802 and norm 2.87%** present qualitatively is furyl hydroxymethyl ketone is an organic compound that is an intermediate in the production of sorbose, an aldohexose. In this process, it is produced by the reaction of trifluroacetic acid and ethyl esters of sorbic acid. This reaction is exothermic and proceeds through a chloride catalyzed dehydration mechanism. The 5-hydroxymethylfurfural (5-hmf) is the other major product from this reaction. It has been shown to have antiradical activity and to be able to inhibit the formation of furan dioxides. Its CAS No is 17678-19-2, chemical formula is $C_6H_6O_3$, molecular weight is 126.11g/mol, stored at 2 degree to 8 degree C.

QUANTITATIVE REPORT EXPLAINATION - The 3 highest peaks obtained by the GC-MS quantitative analysis report are given at RT (retention time) **15.740, 14.009, 14.989** with norm percentage of **100%, 4.50%** and **1.65%** respectively.

The **highest peak according to the quantitative analysis report is obtained at RT 15.740 (6941) with 100% of the norm percentage** contains the compound Hydroxymethylfurfural (HMF), also known as 5-hydroxymethylfurfural, is an organic compound formed by the dehydration of reducing sugars. It is highly soluble in both water and organic solvents. The molecule consists of a furan ring, containing both aldehyde and alcohol functional groups. HMF is a natural component in heated food but usually present in low concentrations. The daily intake of HMF may underlie high variations due to individual consumption patterns. It has been estimated that the intakes range between 4 mg - 30 mg per person per day, while an intake of up to 350 mg can result from beverages made from dried plum.

## V. Conclusion

The integration of foxtail millet flour into churros production presents a promising opportunity to enhance the nutritional profile & introduce unique flavors to the product. This study highlights the potential of foxtail millet as a valuable gluten-free ingredient in churro production, offering improved nutritional benefits and unique flavor profiles. Churros made with 30% foxtail millet flour showed acceptable sensory characteristics, similar to traditional churros, while lower concentrations (10% and 20%) produced some undesirable textural changes. The GC-MS analysis revealed important flavor compounds such as Hydroxymethylfurfural (HMF) and pyrazole derivatives, which contribute to both flavor development and potential health benefits. Foxtail millet is rich in dietary fiber, antioxidants, and essential minerals like iron, calcium, and magnesium. Churros made from this millet can be marketed as a healthy snack option, it has a low glycemic index, making it a suitable snack for diabetic patients or those looking for healthier alternatives to traditional churros made from refined flour. These findings suggest that foxtail millet can serve as a nutritious alternative in gluten-free products, but further optimization is needed to refine the formulation for higher concentrations. Future research should focus on adjusting ingredient ratios and refining processing techniques to enhance the overall quality of foxtail millet- based churros.

## VI. References

1. Sarita and E. Singh (25 April, 2016), Potential of millets: Nutrients Composition and Health Benefits. Journal of Science and Innovative Research (2016)

2. Md. Jaynal Abedin, Abu Tareq Mohammad Abdullah, Mohammed Abdus Satter, Tasnim Farzana. *"Physical, functional, nutritional and antioxidant properties of foxtail millet in Bangladesh"*, Institute of Food Science and Technology (IFST), Bangladesh Council of Scientific and Industrial Research (BCSIR), Dhaka, 1205, Bangladesh.

3. M. Moharil, K.P. Ingle, Pravin V. Jadhav, D.C Gawai, V.C Khelurkar, S. Penna. "Foxtail Millet (Setaria italica L.) Potential of Smaller Millet for Future Breeding", October 2019. Advances in Plant Breeding Strategies: (PP.133-163).

4. J Ahmadi Kabir, MH Azizi, H Abbastabar Ahangar, A Aarabi. *"Physicochemical, rheological, and baking properties of composite Brotchen bread made from foxtail millet flour"*. Acta Alimentaria, 2022.

5. PARDEEP Singh, KASHISH Arora, SUNNY Kumar, NAMAMI Gohain, Ramandeep Kumar Sharma. "Indian millets trade potential-cum-performance: Economic perspective". Indian Journal of Agricultural Sciences 93 (2), 200-204, 2023.

6. Stanislaus Antony Ceasar, Theivanayagam Maharajan. *"The role of millets in attaining United Nation's sustainable developmental goals".* Plants, People, Planet 4 (4), 345-349, 2022.

7. Chris Sheahan, Soil Conservationist. *" Millet Adaptation Trial in Coastal Plain Sandy Loam Following Fall-Seeded Cover Crops in Southern NJ".*

8. K Hariprasanna. *"Small millets in India: Current scenario and way forward".* Indian Farming 73 (1), 38-41, 2023.

9. GV Reddy, E Naga Mallika, B Obula Reddy, D Veena, A Suresh Naik. *"Effect of foxtail millet flour on quality and storage stability of functional chevon sausages".* Indian Journal of Small Ruminants (The) 23 (1), 61-67, 2017.

10. Nitya Sharma, SK Goyal, Tanweer Alam, Sana Fatma, Keshavan Niranjan. *"Effect of germination on the functional and moisture sorption properties of high–pressure-processed foxtail millet grain flour".* Food and bioprocess technology 11, 209-222, 2018.

11. Mehanathan Muthamilarasan, Annvi Dhaka, Rattan Yadav, Manoj Prasad. *"Exploration of millet models for developing nutrient rich graminaceous crops".* Plant Science 242, 89-97, 2016.

12. Muthamilarasan M, Khandelwal R, Yadav CB, Bon-523 thala VS, Khan Y, Prasad M (2014b) Identification524 and molecular characterization of MYB transcription525 factor superfamily in C4model plant foxtail millet526 (Setaria italica L.). PLOS ONE 9:e109920

13. Muthamilarasan M, Bonthala VS, Khandelwal R, Jais-528 hankar J, Shweta S, Nawaz K, Prasad M (2015)529 Global analysis of WRKY transcription factor super-530 family in Setaria identifies potential candidates531 involved in abiotic stress signaling. Front Plant Sci532 6:910

14. Muthamilarasan M, Dhaka A, Yadav R, Prasad M534 (2016a) Exploration of millet models for developing535 nutrient rich gramineous crops. Plant Sci 242:89-97

15. Muthamilarasan M, Mangu VR, Zandkarimi H, Prasad M,537 Baisakh N (2016b) Structure, organization and evolu-538 tion of ADP-ribosylation factors in rice and foxtail539 millet, and their expression in rice. Sci Rep 6:2400

16. Oelke EA, Oplinger ES, Putnam DH, Durgan BR,541 Doll JD, Undersander DJ (1990) Millets. In: Alterna-542 tive field crops manual, University of Wisconsin-543 Exension, Cooperative Extension.

17. Puranik S, Bahadur RP, Srivastava PS, Prasad M (2011)545 Molecular cloning and characterization of a membrane546 associated NAC family gene, SINAC from foxtail547 millet [Setaria italica (L.) P. Beauv.]. Mol Biotechnol548 49:138-1505.

18. Puranik S, Sahu PP, Mandal SN, Venkata Suresh B,550 Parida SK, Prasad M (2013) Comprehensive551 genome-wide survey, genomic constitution and552 expression profiling of the NAC transcription factor553 family in foxtail millet (Setaria italica L.). PLoS One554 8:e64594.

19. Reddy VG, Upadhyaya H, Gowda C (2006) Character-556 ization of world's foxtail millet germplasm collections557 for morphological traits. Int Sorghum Millets`.

20. Sema A, Sarita S (2002) Suitability of millet-based food560 products for diabetics. J Food Sci Technol (Mysore)561 39:423-426.

21. Singh RK, Jaishankar J, Muthamilarasan M, Shweta S,563 Dangi A, Prasad M (2016) Genome-wide analysis of564 heat shock proteins in C4model, foxtail millet565 identifies potential candidates for crop improvement566 under abiotic stress. Sci Rep 6:32641.

22. Sivaraman L, Ranjekar PK (1984) Novel molecular568 features of millet genomes. Indian J Biochem Biophys569 21:299-3035

www.ingramcontent.com/pod-product-compliance
Lightning Source LLC
LaVergne TN
LVHW070529070526
838199LV00075B/6740

*9789364526326*